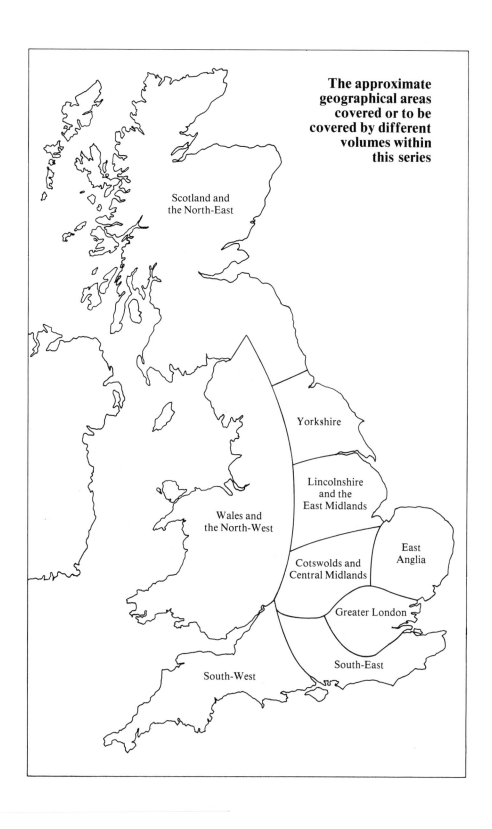

**The approximate
geographical areas
covered or to be
covered by different
volumes within
this series**

Scotland and
the North-East

Yorkshire

Lincolnshire
and the
East Midlands

Wales and
the North-West

East
Anglia

Cotswolds and
Central Midlands

Greater London

South-East

South-West

ACTION STATIONS

4. Military airfields of Yorkshire

Bruce Barrymore Halpenny

PSL Patrick Stephens, Cambridge

First published March 1982
Reprinted July 1982

British Library Cataloguing in Publication Data

Halpenny, Bruce Barrymore
 Military airfields of Yorkshire.—
 (Action stations; 4)
 1. Great Britain. *Royal Air Force*
 2. Air bases—England—Yorkshire
 I. Title
 358.4'17'094281   DA89.5

 ISBN 0-85059-532-0

Photoset in 9pt and 10 on 11pt English Times by
Manuset Limited, Baldock, Herts. Printed in Great Britain
on 100 gsm Fineblade coated cartridge and bound by
The Garden City Press, Letchworth, Herts,
for the publishers, Patrick Stephens Limited, Bar Hill,
Cambridge, CB3 8EL, England.

18992

Contents

Introduction

This fourth volume in Patrick Stephens' *Action Station* series covers Yorkshire and the north-east of England. To keep in some sort of order I have listed at the end of the airfields, Allerton Park Castle, Heslington Hall and Fylingdales in order to make it a comprehensive volume for, although not airfields, they each had an important part to play which, in the case of the latter, is still very much so today.

Not shown on the airfields map are certain glider sites which had little or no RAF involvement. These are: Neasham, just a few miles east of Scotch Corner on the main A1 road; Carlton Moor, situated on the northern end of the Cleveland Hills between the A172 and B1257 roads to the south of Carlton village; and Sutton Bank on the edge of the Hambleton Hills. The others which are not covered but need a mention are the helicopter station on the beach front at Hartlepool and No 1104 Marine Craft Unit which formed in 1946 and had been operating out of Bridlington until it closed down on December 31 1980. The closure ended 51 years of RAF service for although 1104 MCU was formed post-war, marine craft had been operating out of Bridlington since May 1929 providing range safety and armoured target boats for the Skipsea Range.

A mention must also be made of Filey Sands for it was here that Robert Blackburn had a three-roomed bungalow and a hangar which was on top of the cliffs. A wide concrete slipway ran from it down to the sands and a winch was used to haul up a machine after a flight. In the latter part of 1910 he brought the Blackburn Monoplane here. After 18 months the Blackburn School was transferred from Filey to Hendon where Harold Blackburn (now Wing Commander) was in charge. These were very early days and such men as Norman Blackburn were the ones who started it all in Yorkshire. Another company which deserves mention is Slingsby, of glider fame.

On the 1935 Aeronautical Map, RAF Edition (war), there were only 14

Opposite *Bombing up 'Z'-Zombie of 408 Squadron at Linton-on-Ouse in April 1944. This view shows the bomb-aimer's position and window, a large perspex dome with a flat clear view panel let into the lower half with a glycol spray pipe let into the upper rim for anti-icing use. The bomb-sight was positioned above this and immediately behind it was an upholstered body rest for the bomb-aimer, who would kneel behind it on the upholstered cover of the escape hatch. The switch and pre-selector panel was at the side of the compartment to the right, with the bomb-tit in its housing. To the left was the camera control and behind it the F24 camera with its 5-in focal lens projecting through the floor, which can be clearly seen in the photograph.*

airfields listed for the area covered by this volume. They were Brough, Catfoss, Catterick, Church Fenton, Dishforth, Driffield, East Heslerton, Hull, Leconfield, Linton-on-Ouse, Thornaby, West Hartlepool, Yeadon and York. From this list, Yeadon was the main one and it was classed as a land aerodrome with Air Light. But it was never developed into an operational airfield and the shadow factory decided its role. One mystery is East Heslerton which cannot be traced and appears in name only.

From that early beginning Bomber Command began to expand and Britain was to be turned into the densest air base the world has ever known. A large part of the big bomber attacks came from the little Yorkshire villages and they are now part of history. But names, like tunes, are traditional triggers of the memory—Burn, Lissett, Church Fenton, Croft, Middleton St George—the list is long for they are names of airfields in use during the Second World War. Add to them tunes such as 'White Christmas' by Bing Crosby, the Glen Miller music, Tommy Dorsey, Vera Lynn and 'Room 504' and one must think of those wartime days. As the years pass by the memory becomes selective and only the more memorable moments stand out. Our memories have tended to congregate in attic trunks and the annual ritual of Remembrance Day on which the deeds we remember become increasingly dim. Our songs have rung throughout Europe for almost seven decades yet we are taught less and less in school about the whys and wherefores of what we called our grandest hours. Therefore, it has been my pleasure to record those airfields, and those who served on them. I have kept to the same format as in my Lincolnshire book, *Action Stations 2*, and having explained that in that introduction I will not do so again here. One can read about the training units such as were based at Riccall and Topcliffe where accidents were almost daily. Few people have any idea of today's costs of today's accidents. A World War 2 Spitfire cost about £5,000; the price of the Tornado is some £3,000,000. As in my other book I tried to make the book come alive with first-hand narratives, to mention where possible names and places and to follow crews and squadrons as they are posted from station to station, particularly the fighter squadrons, so that the reader might understand the hectic life and strain under which they operated. It was Bomber Command's policy not to leave any empty beds and to have them filled straight away by new crews: this can be seen in the case of Sergeant Charles Whitmore when he and his crew arrived at Leeming. One can also see an example of squadrons forming like at Leconfield. The bomber crews worked as a team and the bomb-aimer always called out 'left' and 'right' whilst the gunners always called 'port' and 'starboard'.

Many did survive the war and, like Harry Drummond, worked their way through the ranks as their odds of survival grew shorter. Harry Drummond arrived at Leconfield on November 3 1939 as an AC2. By 1941, he was a Sergeant Pilot at Dishforth and Middleton St George with 76 and 78 Squadrons. His tour of ops completed, he was posted to Driffield as Sergeant Pilot instructor and then Pilot Officer instructor on No 2 BAT Flight which was then starting to form. He was then posted to Marston Moor as Pilot Officer instructor on Halifaxes and, still in the same role, moved to 102 Squadron at Topcliffe, Dalton and Pocklington. Late 1942 saw him posted to Rufforth as Flight Lieutenant commanding 158 Conversion Flight. From November 1 1942 to November 9 1944, originally as Flight Commander and finally as Wing Commander, he was CO 1658 HCU and Deputy Station Commander at Riccall.

Then he was posted to Marston Moor as Wing Commander OC 1652 HCU and Deputy Station Commander. After the war his subsequent service was at North Luffenham before being posted overseas to HQ, Mediterranean Allied Air Forces, Caserta, Italy, before he was released from active service and transferred to Reserves in October 1945. He today lives at Barkingside, Essex and is an active member of the St John Ambulance Air Wing.

In 1940 who would have thought that, within six months, Denmark, Holland, Norway, Belgium and France would have fallen under the 'jackboot'? On August 1 1940 the Royal Air Force had only 2,913 front line aircraft and we needed all the help we could get from our Colonial cousins.

In December 1939, the Canadian Cabinet signed an agreement with Great Britain, Australia and New Zealand to train aircrew. Despite only having 3,100 airmen of all ranks, 270 largely obsolete aircraft and 19 war-worthy Hurricane fighters, Canada committed itself to operate the Empire Air Training Scheme and over the next five years turned out 131,553 pilots, navigators and air gunners on a hundred airfields hacked out of the bush and prairie land from Nova Scotia to Vancouver Island.

The Canadians were soon aboard troop ships bound for England and one of the first to arrive was Edward Curotte from New Brunswick. It was not quite home-from-home and his first introduction to the field kitchen arrangement he will never forget. 'It was the most distasteful messing ever encountered in my Service life. One could taste sand and grit in all the greens served which, to top it all, were boiled to a 'glop' soup in a large open kettle from which the contents were ladled by an enormous cook who refused to wear anything but a singlet. The weather was warm and at each bend of his bountiful body sweat droplets would fall in the soup making ringlets on the greasy surface. Finally this reached all proportion of decency and I therefore contacted our medical officer, one Dr Rankin, who applied his authority. Conditions improved, but not totally.'

The Canadians arrived with a fair amount of funds for many had sold cars or such before proceeding overseas. Not all sections were helpful but William C. Heine was not one to sit back. The RAF performed as the armed forces always do, irrationally. They were prepared to send several thousand aircrew trainees, all British, to training stations in Canada, and to send a score of Canadians, most of whom hadn't seen home for some time, to Rhodesia. William Heine recalls: 'I telephoned RCAF headquarters in London and protested mightily on behalf of other Canadians and myself. A week later I was called up in front of an irate RAF Wing Commander who wanted to know who was running the depot, but who also had the compassion to listen to the story of a delegation of Canadians, for whom I was the spokesman. As a result we were all sent to Canada (in my case to EFTS and SFTS stations within an hour or two of my home)'.

During the Second World War the whole of the Vale of York became one huge landing strip with airfields every few miles. To look at the map on page 125 for Linton-on-Ouse will give some idea of the circuit overlap and if you picture 30+ aircraft taking off from each airfield one can then see just how crowded the skies were. The Vale of York was often referred to as the 'chamber pot' of England. Fate decreed this was to be the home of No 4 Group and No 6 Group, Royal Canadian Air Force, who had the most northerly stations and, in 1943, Yorkshire provided all the airfields for those two bomber groups. The exit point for Group was Flamborough Head and for Command it was Beachy Head in Sussex.

The British and American bomber groups were stationed in Lincolnshire and East Anglia (see Vols 1 and 2) where the weather was better and there were fewer obstacles to fear when flying blind at low altitude. The atmospheric conditions were much more against the Yorkshire-based squadrons.

The wartime skies were filled with perils such as the world had never known. However, it did not stop the bomber crews who faced nightly journeys of six, seven, eight or more hours across the hostile skies crammed inside a metal-ribbed skeleton framework. Unrelenting storms and ice tried to pluck the aircraft from the sky, many times achieving success. Death winged along every minute of the journey—death that came in a sudden hail of gunfire or from a single flak shell. Such were the daily hazards of the aircrew members of Bomber Command, each one a volunteer who flew from these airfields. 55,573 aircrew, 1,363 male ground staff and 91 WAAFs died while serving with Bomber Command.

Canada—the name worn proudly on the shoulder flash by so many brave young men—soon became accepted in Yorkshire. A Portuguese explorer named Cortereal sailed up the St Lawrence in his search for a route to India. Not finding this his men cried aloud 'Canada', which meant 'nothing here'. The Indians heard this so often they cried out 'Canada' to all newcomers in the hope it would make them depart as quickly as the Portuguese had done. The name 'Canada' stuck to the country as it has done to the people of Yorkshire and Lincolnshire.

Yorkshire became the home of the Canadians and Betty's cafe in York became a favourite rendezvous. Cakes were sold at the corner entrance and in the panelled Oak Room is the original mirror inscribed with the autographs of hundreds of aircrew.

The Canadians returned home but, for ever in their hearts and minds would be a little piece of old Blighty. Memories of the war and the comedy shows like ITMA, which starred Tommy Handley, Colonel Chinstrap of 'I don't mind if I do', Mrs Mopp, whose favourite saying was 'can I dq you now, sir?', and many, many more. Each station had a favoured public house which became a way of life during those wartime years. It was here with a little civilian company they could 'flush away' their operational fears.

Bomber Command played a major role but, during the Battle of Britain, it gained small public recognition for the part it played in the bombing of the barges. On July 4 1940 the Air Ministry gave Bomber Command orders to attack enemy ports and shipping. By September the concentration of barges in the Channel ports looked very threatening and from September 5 Bomber Command gave these targets top priority. Operation 'Sea Lion' was imminent and, on September 7, the British Government issued a warning that an invasion might take place within the next few days. That night Bomber Command attacked the barges and military dumps in the Channel ports and the raids were highly successful. On September 11, Hitler postponed the date of 'Sea Lion' to September 24. Bomber Command took advantage of the delay and on September 13 mounted another large raid on the barges. The bombing was successful and in Ostend port alone no less than 80 huge barges were sunk. The Germans lost 84 barges in Dunkirk on September 17 and by the 19th had lost almost 200. Bomber Command's successes must, therefore, take a fair share of the credit for Hitler's September 17 decision to postpone Operation 'Sea Lion' indefinitely. For many historians the climax of the Battle of Britain came on September 15 when the battle raged from dawn to dusk.

For those who so successfully bombed the Channel ports in 1940 some recognition should have been made, and a distinctive clasp should have been awarded, like the one awarded to the Fighter Command personnel. Bomber Command had destroyed a large part of the shipping and equipment on which the invasion depended and, on October 13, Hitler postponed the operation until the spring of 1941—but in fact the plan was dead.

It was strange how the awards were given out. In the RAF the awards of the DFM to NCOs (and, exceptionally, airmen) were far fewer than the DFC to officers. Possibly snobbery in high places—it cannot be ruled out. The crews, whatever the rank, worked as a team and the pilot, regardless of rank, was always Captain of the aircraft.

Many DFCs were well and truly earned but some seemed to get them automatically on completing a tour or getting half-way through one. A DFM on the other hand was generally awarded after some 'shaky do' in which the NCO had acted with distinction.

For the bomber crews Bomber Command demanded a certain number of points (124 in 1944—144 in 1945). Each mission was worth three points if the target were west of 6° longitude and four points if it were to the east of this longitude. On each mission the RAF lost on average five per cent. But in practice the law of averages did not apply because some crews went missing on their first few missions, some the first trip.

There is no parallel in warfare to the courage of those aircrew as they carried the war into the heart of Nazi Germany. Within hours the crews were transferred from peaceful Yorkshire to the hostile skies above Germany and German occupied countries. The German pilots had but one order—bring them down before they reach Germany. The steady beat of mass bombers flew through walls of flak. It was a time of death and injury for all too many. But, it was a time when a band of brothers-in-arms stood between freedom and Nazism and gained immortality. As Shakespeare wrote in *King Henry V*, 'That island of England breeds very valiant creatures; their mastiffs are of unmatchable courage'. In the Battle of Britain Nelson's expectation that 'every man will do his duty' was amply fulfilled by those who served on all the airfields.

It is all a little ironic that no wartime airfield should have been preserved as a memorial and I have made my views very clear in my earlier book. It is a wilful obliteration of history and today from the decaying remains of a once-busy airfield only the Ghost Squadrons are airborne on a summer's evening. It was the spirit in these airfields and aircraft that fought to keep the world free. So, spare a moment for the past, that part of it which belongs to the Royal Air Force, and the airfields. It was from these Yorkshire airfields that the aircrew took off nightly to sow devastation across the Nazi homeland. On a summer's evening—stand for a moment and look into the Yorkshire sky—in the comparative quietness you might catch an echo of the throbbing, threatening, doom-laden pregnant bombers as they struggle to gain height.

Bruce Barrymore Halpenny
Grantham June 1981

Acknowledgements

At the time this is written over four decades have passed since the start of World War 2 and the trail is growing cold in search of survivors.

As with my previous work the bulk of the information came from records and from the log books, letters, etc, of the participants. In all, over 1,000 people have contributed to my two books in this series. They gave freely of their time in interviews and for various reasons not every personal story or experience could be included. All material used is genuine and every statement or quote in both this and my other book is reinforced by documentary or photographic evidence or by the corroboration of others who witnessed the event described. All crashes mentioned in my books are backed-up with the engine numbers and retained in my files. For reasons of historical truth, hearsay, or third party accounts, were not included and I hope the many contributors will understand. Among the many contributors who must be singled out for special thanks are:

Barry Abraham, Stockport, Cheshire for his help with photographs and other material; *Airforce* magazine, Ottawa, Canada; The Earl of Ancaster, KCVO, of Grimsthorpe Castle, Bourne, Lincolnshire; Airfield Research Group.

Bill Baguley of Woodthorpe, Nottingham, for ready assistance to help with outside photography and with research material; Lord Balfour for his help with World War 1 data, and for his two photographs of that period; Doug Bancroft (ex-158 Squadron) of Modbury, South Australia, for his help with material and photographs and his most welcome visit over Easter 1981; Mr E. Barker of British Aerospace, Kingston-Brough Division, for his help with Brough and Holme-on-Spalding Moor; Dave Benfield for his ready assistance to help with research data and photographs; Ken Border of Swindon, Wiltshire, for his help with airfield data and hangar photographs and material; my dear friend Mrs Lillian Briggs of Leeds for her wartime material which included private letters from her husband who was killed in action; The British Library, London; J.M. Bruce/ G.S. Leslie collection of photographs for Marske, Catterick and Redcar.

Councillor K.A. Cairns, Guildhall, Kingston upon Hull; Canadian Forces Photo Unit, Ottawa, Canada; Canadian War Museum, Ottawa, Canada; Richard (ex-427 Squadron, RCAF) and Isobel Crossey, Ontario, Canada, for photographs and book; Edward H. Curotte, ARW (ex-6106 RCAF), Campbellton, Canada. From one of his weekly letters: 'P.S.—Do not let the cold stop you from travelling to London... solution... take your secretary with you. Eisenhower took his ATS driver for the same reason. What is good or should I say what *was* good enough for Ike surely should be good for Bruce Halpenny'.

Roy Day of Herts for photographs; Walter Dinsdale, MP (Brandon), House of Commons, Ottawa, Canada; Mr Ray Dixon; Directorate of History, National Defence HQ, Ottawa, Canada; Wing Commander H.H. Drummond, AFC, DFM, Essex, for his help with wartime data and photographs.

Stephen Elliott, for his assistance with present-day photography; Squadron Leader D.A. Exley, CRO, RAF Finningley, Doncaster, for his help with airfield data and photographs.

Captain A.J. Faith, RHA, of Alanbrooke Barracks, Topcliffe; Mike Fazackerley, Dan-Air Services Ltd, Tees-side Airport, Darlington, for present day photography; Michael Fisher of Bradford for his help with outside photography and present day material of the airfields; Neville Franklin for aircraft identification and photographic help; Mr Les Fuller, Retford, Nottinghamshire, for ready assistance with wartime information and photographs; R.D. Frey.

Allan R. George, Ministry of Defence, Whitehall, London; Peter Green of Irby, South Humberside, for Lightning photograph; Mr Norman Gundill, Managing Director and Secretary, Pontefract Park Race Co Ltd.

Mrs Kath Hal! (Auntie Kath) of Market Rasen, Lincolnshire, for the wartime riddle that I have never forgotten and even today, it brings a smile to my lips when I hear or read about that certain fighter. The riddle: 'If a shoulder strap of a lady's bra should break, what aircraft would it be?' Answer: One Mustang (one must hang); Gordon Halpenny, who worked on airfield camouflage before joining the Army and taking part in the D-Day landings, for his incomplete section on airfield camouflage; Ex-Sergeant Harold Hamnett of Riondel, BC, Canada, for his excellent wartime photographs of Skipton-on-Swale; Mr Hardy and Mr Gregory (Nottingham) for their valued help and understanding in the production of this book; William C. Heine, Editor of The London Free Press, London, Ontario, Canada, for his wartime experiences; Mr Joe Hitchman of Sheffield for 158 Squadron material; Squadron Leader L. Hook, RAF Linton-on-Ouse, York; Rodney Houldsworth for printing some of the many photographs and assisting with the outside photography work on many occasions; F.E. Hurrell, Editor of the *Darlington & Stockton Times*.

Mr Ken Irlam, North Vancouver, BC, Canada.

Trevor Jones, Darlington, for his photographic material; Richard Joseph (ex-424 Squadron), Thousand Oaks, California, for his wartime data, which was most helpful. He says: 'I wish, truly, I had more to tell but the fear and the turbulent bowels of those moments served to block out much of the local atmosphere'.

Honourable J. Gilles Lamontagne (ex-425 Squadron, RCAF), Minister of National Defence, Ottawa, Canada, for his wartime data and photographs; The Chief Librarian, *Yorkshire Post*

Newspapers Ltd, Leeds, who put at my disposal their library and assisted me in every way possible during my research; The Director of Library Services, Central Library, Leeds; Peter Liddle's 1914-1918 Personal Experience Archives, presently housed within Sunderland Polytechnic, which covered Marske; Geoff Lenthall of Grimsby for his photographs and post-war material; Squadron Leader T. Lockwood, RAF Church Fenton; Pat and Jim Lowne, Grimsby, for letting me involve them with my research and putting up with my family and I for many weekends.

Major G.E. MacManus, CO, Canadian Forces Photographic Unit, Ottawa; Sean Manning of Grantham for his interest in my work and his help with research material; Mr F. Manders, Central Library, Newcastle upon Tyne; John and Cyril Middleton of Lincoln for the reproduction of the many photographs; Wing Commander D. Milne, RAF Leeming, for his help with present-day data and photographs.

A.C. Newton, Managing Director, High Gosforth Park Co Ltd, Newcastle upon Tyne, for his help in trying to trace the involvement of Ripon in World War 1.

Bjorn Olsen, Ski, Norway, for the photograph of Halifax *W1048* during recovery.

Reg Payne; Mr Ray Peden, Vernon, BC, Canada, for his help with material and photographs; Hans Plantz—for his time taken over all the German and Polish translations for both of my books; Lieutenant Colonel A.G. Price (Retd) regarding material for Driffield and Leconfield; Air Commodore H.A. Probert, MBE, MA, RAF (Rtd), Head of Air Historical Branch, MoD, London; Hank Pudlowski (ex-433 Squadron, RCAF), Alberta, Canada.

RAF Museum at Hendon; Nick Roberts for his help with the maps and crash information; Mr R.G. Roberts, Director Libraries and Amenities, Humberside County Council, Hull; Squadron Leader I.A. Rodgers, RAF Fylingdales, North Yorkshire, for his help with photographs and material.

Ulrich Schmitt from Ludwigshafen, Germany, a town razed to the ground; during my many visits I have never ceased to be amazed at what they have achieved since the war as today on the old site stands a new city. Schmitt bears no malice and during one of my visits he proposed a toast to the Queen. With his accent, schnapps, wine and brandy it came out as 'God shave the Queen'. That might have passed but then someone hicked 'hear hear'; Mr G.P. Seller, Airport Director, Leeds Bradford Airport, Yeadon, Leeds; P. Sotheran for Bleriot photograph at Redcar; Mrs Anne South, Chalfont St Giles, Bucks, for the wartime photographs and material; Doctor Charles Spalding for making it possible to keep going and survive the English weather; *The Sporting Life*, London; Bud Stevenson, Ontario, Canada, for his World War 1 data and photographs of the log-pages.

Tees-side Airport Committee, (Miss J. Hanson), Darlington, for the post-war photographs; Julian C. Temple; J.A. Todd; Mr Frank Twitchett of Leeds for his material and photograph of No 145 Squadron.

Squadron Leader R.J. Wallis, RAF Catterick; Mr Maurice Wedgewood, Deputy Editor of *The Northern Echo*, Darlington; John White, Montague, Canada, for his wartime material; Charles Whitmore (ex-429 Squadron, RCAF) of Hantsport, Nova Scotia, Canada, for his great help with research material and photographs; Mr M.F. Wood, Director of C.H. Wood (BFD) Ltd, for photographs of Yeadon.

York Race Committee, The Racecourse, York.

Again, a special thank-you to my valued friend and assistant, Margaret Morris of Lincoln, who at various times worked as my secretary and spent many hours of typing and re-typing.

I must again thank my wife, who, when I was most seriously ill, organised my research and kept order in the camp and, with the light at the end of the tunnel, spent hours proof-reading. Thanks also to my son Baron who tried to help in his way and who had to do without me for long periods.

My very special thanks for all those who loaned me material and photographs, with apologies to any who I might have forgotten.

The author would be interested to receive any new facts, photographs or other material for incorporation in future publications.

Glossary

AAC Army Air Corps.
AACU Anti-Aircraft Co-operation Unit.
AAF Auxiliary Air Force.
AAP Aircraft Acceptance Park.
AC Aircraftsman.
AEF Air Experience Flight.
AFC Air Force Cross.
AFEE Airborne Forces Experimental Establishment.
AFS Advanced Flying School.
AFTS Advanced Flying Training School.
ANS Air Navigation School.
AOP Air Observation Post.
ASR Air-Sea Rescue.
ATA Air Transport Auxiliary.

Base Home aerodrome.
BATF Blind (or Beam) Approach Training Flight.
BCBS Bomber Command Bombing School.
BCIS Bomber Command Instructors' School.
BCDU Bomber Command Development Unit.
BDTF Bomber Defence Training Flight.
Bf Bayerische Flugzeugwerke (Messerschmitt).
BMEWS Ballistic Missile Early Warning System.

CFS Central Flying School.
CGM Conspicuous Gallantry Medal.
CGS Central Gunnery School.
Chastise Code name for the attack on the Ruhr dams by No 617 Squadron on May 16/17 1943.
C & M Care and Maintenance.
CO Commanding Officer.
Course (T) True compass course of aircraft with no magnetic variation and deviation correction made.

'Cookie' Name given to a 4,000 lb high-capacity bomb.
Cpl Corporal.
'Crossbow', operation The campaign against V-weapons.
CU Conversion Unit.

D-Day June 6 1944—Allied armies began landing in Normandy with support from both Tactical and Strategic Air Forces (operation 'Overlord').
DFC Distinguished Flying Cross.
DFM Distinguished Flying Medal.
'Dodge', operation Ferrying home troops from Italy. Many 8th Army Desert Rats, etc, by air.
Drift Leeway made by the aircraft in flight caused by wind, measured in degrees.
DSO Distinguished Service Order.

E/A Enemy aircraft.
EFTS Elementary Flying Training School.
ELG Emergency Landing Ground.
ENSA Entertainments National Service Association.
ETA Estimated Time of Arrival.
'Exodus', operation Repatriation by air of British ex-PoWs from the continent.

FAA Fleet Air Arm.
FAF French Air Force.
FIDO Fog Investigation and Dispersal Operation.
FIS Flying Instructors School.
Flimsy List of aerodromes in War Theatre area. Names, positions, signal letters, secret code radio call signs which were changed every 24 hours. Printed on rice paper. The navigator had to destroy by eating when the

aircraft was abandoned over enemy territory.

F/Lt Flight Lieutenant.

F/O Flying Officer.

FS Fighter School.

F/Sgt Flight Sergeant.

FTC Flying Training Command.

FTR Failed To Return.

FTS Flying Training School.

Fw Focke-Wulf Flugzeugbau.

'Gardening' Code name for sea mine-laying by aircraft.

GCA Ground Control Approach.

GCI Ground Controlled Interception.

Gee Medium-range radio aid to navigation and target identification with ground transmitters and airborne receiver.

Group Pool Squadron Training unit.

GS Glider School.

GSU Group Standardisation Unit.

HCU Heavy Conversion Unit.

HGCU Heavy Glider Conversion Unit.

HGMU Heavy Glider Maintenance Unit.

H2S Airborne radar aid to navigation and target identification.

HTCU Heavy Transport Conversion Unit.

Hun German.

ICBM Inter-Continental Ballistic Missile.

IFF Identification Friend or Foe.

Intruder operations Offensive night operation to a fixed point or specified target.

IRBM Intermediate Range Ballistic Missile.

ITS Initial Training School.

Ju Junkers Flugzeug and Motorenwerke AG.

LAC Leading AirCraftsman.

LFS Lancaster Finishing School.

'Manna', operation Dropping of food to the starving Dutch people.

MAP Ministry of Aircraft Production.

MATS Military Air Transport Service.

MCA Ministry of Civil Aviation.

MCU Marine Craft Unit.

MDAP Mutual Defence Aid Programme.

Me Messerschmitt AG.

Met Weather report—Meteorological conditions.

METS Multi-Engined Training Squadron.

'Millennium', operation Code name for the first 1,000-bomber raid on Cologne, May 30/31 1942.

MoD Ministry of Defence.

MT Motor Transport *or* Mechanical Transport.

MU Maintenance Unit.

MUG Mid-Upper Gunner.

NAAFI Navy, Army and Air Force Institutes.

NCO Non-Commissioned Officer.

NF Night fighter.

'Nickel' Leaflets, usually propaganda.

'Noball' Code name for a V1/V2 site.

NUAS Northumberland Universities Air Squadron.

Oboe Ground-controlled target-marking and blind-bombing device utilising radio beams.

OCTU Officer Cadet Training Unit.

OCU Operational Conversion Unit. These are training units that provide conversion for pilots transferring from one type of aircraft to another.

Ops Operations.

OTU Operational Training Unit.

(P)AFU (Pilot) Advanced Flying Unit.

PFF PathFinder Force—aircraft formation which locates and marks bomb target.

PFS Primary Flying Squadron.

PoW Prisoner of War.

'Pundit' Name for aerodrome identity letters, flashing lights on ground in Morse Code.

RAAF Royal Australian Air Force.

RAFVR Royal Air Force Volunteer Reserve.

RATF Radio Aids Training Flight.

RAuxAF Royal Auxiliary Air Force.

RCAF Royal Canadian Air Force.

RFC Royal Flying Corps.

Required Track True compass course of route of aircraft on a Mercator Chart.

Rhubarbs Low-level attacks by pairs of aircraft on road and rail traffic under low cloud conditions.

RLG Relief Landing Ground.

RNAS Royal Naval Air Service.

RNEFTS Royal Navy Elementary Flying Training School.

RNZAF Royal New Zealand Air Force.

RS Reserve Squadron.

R/T Radio-Telephone.

SAC Senior AirCraftsman. *Also* Strategic Air Command.
SAR Search And Rescue.
SBC Small Bomb Container.
Scramble Immediate take-off on operations.
Scrubbed Mission cancelled.
SFTS Service Flying Training School.
SHQ Station Headquarters.
SNCO Senior Non-Commissioned Officer.
SOC Struck Off Charge.
SOE Special Operations Executive.
S/Ldr Squadron Leader.

TAF Tactical Air Force.
TDS Training Depot Station.
TI Target Indicator.
'Totalize', operation The Canadian Army offensive at Falaise, August 1944.

TS Training Squadron.
TTF Target Towing Flight.

VE-Day May 8 1945, Victory in Europe.
VJ-Day August 15 1945, Victory over Japan.

WAAF/WRAF Womens Auxiliary/ Royal Air Force.
W/Cdr Wing Commander.
Window Metallised strips dropped from aircraft to simulate aircraft echoes to disrupt enemy radar systems.
WO1 Warrant Officer, 1st Class: Air Force rank.
W/T Wireless-Telegraph.

YUAS Yorkshire Universities Air Squadron.

Short glossary of Royal Air Force slang

In both the First and Second World Wars the language became adventurous and slang was the easiest or laziest way to bring out the richness. Some of the words go back to the days of the Royal Flying Corps, for example, a Flight Sergeant becomes Chiefy, this dating back to the days of the Naval Air Service when a man discharging duties to those of a Flight Sergeant held the rank of Chief Petty Officer. By abbreviation a Wing Commander becomes Wingco, and a Group Captain becomes Groupy.

Many types of aircraft have either a nickname or a slang name: for instance a Spitfire was a Spit and a Hurricane a Hurry. A Lysander was a Lizzie, a Miles Magister, Maggie and an Anson, Annie; often called Limping Annie from the uneveness of its engine-note.

From aircraft we pass to the Service Police who came in for many unprintable slang words: on some stations they were known as Snoops or Snoopers but throughout they became best known as Snowdrops from the white top worn on their hats.

The following list is by no means stabilised for there are marked variances between bomber and fighter pilots.

Adj, the The Adjutant. (Adopted from the Army from the abbreviation Adj).
Ammo Ammunition.
Apron A hangar's tarmac surround.

Bale out To make a parachute landing.

Beat up To attack either in play or for real a given target.
Belly Lower fuselage of an aircraft.
Belly-landing A landing made with wheels up.
Blackouts or twilights WAAF issue knickers or pantees (blackouts winter weight; twilights summer weight and lighter coloured).
Blood wagon or meat wagon Ambulance.
Bought it To be killed or to be shot down.
Brassed off or Browned off Fed up, in low spirits.
Bumf Leaflets dropped from the aircraft or official correspondence, from bum-fodder (toilet paper).

Char Tea.
Chiefy Flight Sergeant.
Civvy street Civilian life.
Clobber To destroy.
Collect a gong To be awarded a decoration.
Circuits and bumps Those circuits and landings which are practised by aspirant pilots.
Clueless Without knowledge, ignorant.
Cooler A guard or detention room.

Do a bunk To leave without permission.
Drill, the right The correct method.
Drink, in the To crash in the sea.

Eggs, lay To lay mines in enemy waters.
Erk, an AirCraftsman or AirCraftswoman in the RAF.

Fan The propeller.

Fizzer To be put on a charge.

Flak Anti-aircraft fire.

Flap Panic; disturbance.

Flight Flight Sergeant.

Flight Louie Flight Lieutenant.

Flip A short flight in an aircraft.

Freeman, Hardy and Willis or Pip, Squeak and Wilfred The 1914-15 Star, the Overseas Service and the Victory medals of the First World War or the three respective ribbons worn on the tunic's left breast. The former phrase came from a well-known shoe chain and the latter from a comic-strip. If the first medal (the 1914-15) be missing the other two are known as Mutt and Jeff—from two cartoon characters.

Gen Information of any kind.

George The automatic pilot.

Glamour boys Fighter pilots.

Gremlin A mischievous sprite of the RAF held responsible for all mishaps.

Halibag Halifax aircraft.

Hedge-hopping Flying just above the ground.

Hurri Hurricane.

Kipper Kite Aircraft protecting fishing fleets in the North Sea.

Kite Aeroplane.

Limping Annie An Anson aircraft.

Lizzie A Lysander aircraft.

Mae West Life-saving waistcoat, inflated if wearer falls into the sea, a name derived from the bust of the actress.

Mickey Mouse Bomb-dropping mechanism of some types of bomber aircraft.

Office Cockpit of aircraft, also name of rear-gunner's position of the Lancaster/Halifax.

On your knees Too tired to stand.

Operational Anything that works.

Pack up To cease to function.

Pancake To crash-land an aeroplane with wheels up.

Peel off, to To break formation.

Piece of cake Easy.

Play pussy, to Hide in the clouds.

Plonk Recruit.

Pull your finger out To get on with it.

Prang To crash.

Pulpit Cockpit of aircraft.

Queen Bee Senior Administrative WAAF officer on a station.

Queen Mary A very long, low-slung articulated vehicle designed for the transportation of airframes.

Rang the bell Got good results.

Rookie A recruit.

Ropey Uncomplimentary adjective, eg, ropey landing.

Scrambled eggs The gold braid on the cap of a Group Captain or higher-ranking officer.

Scotch mist Implies that one is suffering from bad eyesight.

Scrounge To obtain illicitly or by audacious opportunism.

Scrub To call off, to cancel.

Second Dickey Second Pilot.

Shaky do Dangerous operation.

Shooting a line Exaggerated talk.

Snowdrop RAF policeman.

Spun in Any bad mistake.

Sprog Brand new uniform—newly commissioned officer.

Square-bashing Drill on the square or parade ground.

Stooge Stand-in.

Stooging about Patrolling an area.

Tail-end Charlie Rear-gunner in a bomber or the pilot of rear aircraft in a formation.

Tapes Non-Commissioned Officer's stripes.

Tear a strip off Reprove severely.

Tiddly Intoxicated.

Tiggerty-boo In correct order.

Tin fish A torpedo.

Topside In the air.

Touch bottom Crash.

Train, driving the Leading more than one squadron into battle.

U/S Unserviceable.

WAAF A member of the Women's Auxiliary Air Force.

Weave, to Evasive action by aircraft.

What's cooking? What's happening?

Wimpey A Wellington bomber.

Wingco Wing Commander (also *Winco*).

Wizard First class, highest praise.

Write-off A crashed aircraft beyond repair.

Hangar types found in Yorkshire

Prior to the First World War most British military aviation activity was concentrated in Southern England, much of it in the Salisbury Plain area where several of the earliest aerodromes were laid out, but by the end of that conflict landing grounds and aerodromes had been established in most parts of the United Kingdom where the terrain was suitable.

In Yorkshire some fields and racecourses were requisitioned for use as landing grounds both by Home Defence Squadrons and by Coastal Patrol Flights, but these sites were rarely provided with permanent buildings and they quickly reverted to their original use when the war finished, leaving very few traces. Several aerodromes were constructed in the district to house Training Depot Stations or Aircraft Acceptance Parks and these usually had more substantial accommodation, including permanent hangars, some of which have survived to the present time. One of the earliest, and best preserved, hangars in Yorkshire is a large wooden RFC 1915 Pattern, the only one left on the former Tadcaster aerodrome which closed in 1919 shortly after 38 Training Depot Station disbanded. More common is the RFC 1917 Pattern, often called the Belfast hangar, which has brick walls with a curved roof supported by intricate

Yeadon, early 1930s. An excellent photograph of the early hangars, then referred to as aeroplane sheds. The large one on the right is a Bessoneau hangar. This was a canvas type and was erected in large numbers during World War 1. The aeroplanes are DH 60 Moths.

Above *'B1' hangar at Dalton (photographed September 1980).* **Below** *Royal Flying Corps 1915 hangar at Tadcaster (photographed June 1980).* **Bottom** *The elegant 'C' hangar with the distinctive squared-off ends: Linton-on-Ouse 1980.*

wooden Belfast trusses; several of these are still standing at Sherburn in Elmet and at the former aerodrome at Marske.

The years immediately following the Great War saw very little new building on the few aerodromes which remained in service, but in 1924 a new type was designed as a general purpose aeroplane shed to replace old wartime buildings or to supplement them. This was the 'A' type which was steel-framed with brick walls and a ridged roof covered with toughened asbestos sheeting; clear width was 120 ft and each end was covered by four metal sliding doors. Although quite a number of this type were built during the late 1920s and early '30s, very few of them were in Yorkshire; however, in 1980 there was still one in fair condition on the edge of the former airfield at Catfoss.

The early 1930s saw the emergence of a complete range of standard buldings for the large number of new and enlarged airfields envisaged under the RAF Expansion Plans. The airfields themselves followed standard layouts as far as local conditions permitted, using standard buildings permutated according to the intended duty of the airfield. By this time the 'A'-type hangar had been improved into the 'C' type Gabled as the general purpose aeroplane shed and this was further developed into the 'C' type Hipped, a well-designed steel-framed, brick-walled building with six sliding metal doors covering the 150 ft clear width at each end. Four or five of the 300 ft-long version of the 'C' type Hipped were constructed on the airfields built during the mid-1930s for Bomber Command, the four usually being in an arc on the edge of the landing ground with the fifth, where present, behind the arc. A shorter, seven-bay version of the 'C' Type was built in much smaller numbers, usually on airfields intended for Fighter Command; often only two were constructed with sufficient space between them to allow a third to be added later if necessary, and perusal of the plans shows that the layout was usually arranged to enable these hangars to be extended to the standard length at a later date if required. Groups of the 300 ft-long 'C' hangars survive at several airfields in the area such as Linton-on-Ouse, Dishforth and Driffield, while Church Fenton has a pair of the seven-bay variety; it is most unusual to find both versions on the same airfield but Catterick is an exception, the hangar adjacent to the A1 road being the standard length and the next one being only seven bays long.

A shortage of resources in the late 1930s, particularly time and many conventional building materials, brought the first signs of austerity to the permanent airfields then in the course of being built. The permutation of standard designs was still used but some of the buildings were simplified; in particular the elegant 'C' was replaced by the 'C1' of the same size and using a basically similar frame. However, much of the external cladding was toughened asbestos and the distinctive 'squared-off' ends of the 'C' were missing. Numbers of these hangars were built in Yorkshire including five at Leeming which are still used to house the training aircraft that use this airfield.

By 1939 it was still RAF policy to group together all the buildings on new airfields then being constructed, and to provide each major airfield with permanent hangars. The need to get these new airfields into service quickly created a need for a simpler type of hangar than the 'C' family, a type that could be built more easily and rapidly. The result was the 'J' type and the very similar 'K', both of which were steel-framed with a curved roof, the entire structure covered by metal sheeting. Considerable numbers of these types appeared in 1940 and 1941 and examples may still be seen at the former bomber airfields of

Pocklington, Middleton St George and Holme-on-Spalding Moor (see aerial photograph on page 92).

Even these types proved too complex to provide for the large number of airfields planned for construction in 1942-43 so another design of main hangar was adopted as a replacement, the 'B1' type which originated about 1942. This was a steel-framed hangar with a steeply pitched roof, all covered with corrugated iron sheets. Not as large as the 'J' Type, it nevertheless could accommodate any of the aircraft in RAF service at that time and one was erected on many of the bomber airfields brought into service in the mid-war years, usually plus two or three other hangars for squadron or flight servicing. Several 'B1' hangars may still be found on the edges of former airfields in the area, one in particular at Dalton being in very good condition having received some new cladding in the late 1970s.

Several types of temporary hangars had been in small scale production before the outbreak of World War 2, the 'Callender' and 'Bellman' being perhaps the best known, and these had been erected on several non-operational airfields. When war became inevitable there was a great demand for simple hangars and in 1940 the Tees-side Bridge and Engineering Company designed and put into production the first models of their 'Transportable Hangar' or 'T' type. The early examples of this pattern were erected on the technical sites of major airfields to supplement the main hangarage and were of the original 'T2' type, steel-framed with a medium-pitched roof, the entire structure covered by cranked metal sheets. By 1942 the 'T2' (Home) 3653/42 had emerged as the main hangar of the 'T' family. It was mass-produced and erected on almost every airfield of any importance constructed between then and the end of the war. This was metal-framed with commercial sheeting cladding and had a clear width of 113 ft 6 in; it was produced in 10 ft 5 in-long bays, the most common version having 23 bays to give an overall length of 239 ft 7 in. Having learnt the lesson of dispersal and, given the changing face of air-war and the need for the

View inside 'J' hangar at Tees-side (ex-Middleton St George).

'C1' hangars at Leeming. These replaced the 'C' and the squared-off ends are missing. The control tower is on the left and the tall brick building on the right is the water tower.

heavy four-engined bombers only to be inside the hangar for a major service, most of the late-pattern 'T2's were erected on sites around the airfield perimeters instead of being grouped together on a technical site. Because of the relative ease with which these hangars could be dismantled many were removed at the end of the war and rebuilt elsewhere, sometimes on other airfields where additional hangarage was required and sometimes on sites far removed from the nearest airfield, perhaps as warehouses. Many 'T2' hangars still survive on their original bases, two at Breighton being in good condition in 1980 when they were in use by a local contractor for storage.

Finally, no brief note on British military hangars would be complete without mention of the 'Blister' series of hangars. These originated about 1941 and were simple curved shelters with no separate side walls and no end doors, although many were fitted with canvas curtains which gave some protection from the weather. The earliest were Miskins timber type but the vast majority were steel-framed with corrugated iron covering like the Dorman Longs Blister which appeared in 1942. Few still survive after almost four decades and most of the survivors have been removed to farmyards where they are enjoying a new lease of life as barns and the like.

The military airfields of Yorkshire

1	Acaster Malbis	47	Linton-on-Ouse
2	Appleton Wiske	48	Lissett
3	Atwick	49	Lowthorpe
4	Barlow	50	Marske
5	Bellasize	51	Marston Moor (Tockwith)
6	Beverley	52	Melbourne
7	Binsoe	53	Menthorpe Gate
8	Brancroft	54	Middleton
9	Breighton	55	Middleton St George (Goosepool)
10	Brough	56	Murton
11	Burn	57	Netherthorpe
12	Carlton	58	Owthorne
13	Carnaby (Bridlington)	59	Plainville
14	Catfoss	60	Pocklington (Barmby)
15	Catterick	61	Pontefract
16	Church Fenton	62	Redcar
17	Copmanthorpe	63	Riccall
18	Cottam	64	Ripon
19	Croft (Neasham)	65	Rufforth
20	Cullingworth (Manywells Height)	66	Sandtoft
21	Dalton	67	Scalby Mills
22	Dishforth (Ripon)	68	Scorton
23	Doncaster	69	Seacroft
24	Driffield (Eastburn)	70	Seaton Carew
25	Dunkeswick	71	Sherburn in Elmet
26	East Moor	72	Shipton
27	Ecclesfield	73	Skipton-on-Swale
28	Elvington	74	Snaith (Pollington)
29	Farsley	75	South Cave
30	Finningley	76	South Otterington
31	Firbeck	77	Tadcaster (Bramham Moor)
32	Full Sutton	78	Thirsk
33	Gilling	79	Tholthorpe
34	Helperby (Brafferton)	80	Thornaby
35	Holme-on-Spalding-Moor (Spaldington)	81	Thorne
		82	Topcliffe
36	Hornsea Mere	83	West Ayton
37	Howden	84	West Hartlepool (Greatham)
38	Huggate Wold	85	Wombleton (Welburn Hall)
39	Hull (Hedon)	86	Wombwell (Broomhill)
40	Hutton Cranswick	87	Yeadon (Leeds/Bradford)
41	Kettleness	88	York (Clifton, Rawcliffe)
42	Kirkleatham		
43	Knavesmire		Group HQs
44	Leconfield	89	Allerton Park Castle
45	Leeming	90	Heslington Hall
46	Lindholme (Hatfield Woodhouse)		

Early Warning Station
91   Fylingdales

20

BRADFORD

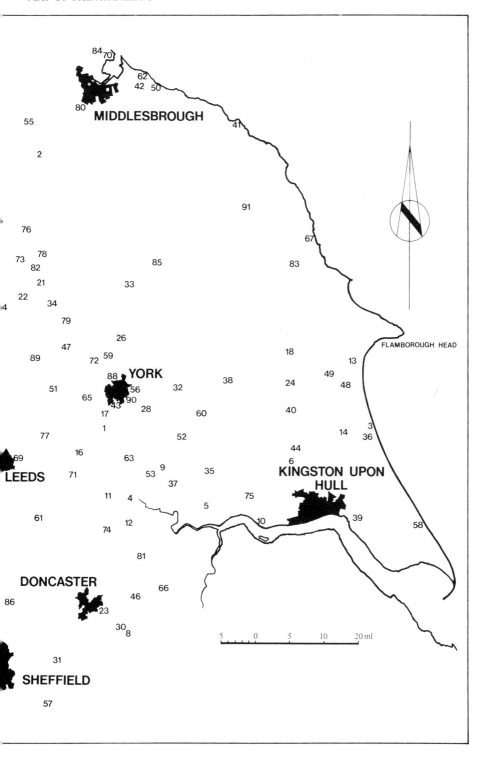

84 70

62
42 50

80 **MIDDLESBROUGH**

55

2

41

91

76

67

73 78
82
21
22 34
79

85

83

FLAMBOROUGH HEAD

26
47 59
89 72
88 **YORK**
51 56
65 90
43
17 28
1

18
13
49
24 48
32 38
60 40

77
16
69 63
LEEDS 71 53 9 35
37

14 3
36

52

44
6
KINGSTON UPON
HULL

11 4
5
61 12
74
75
10
39
58

81

DONCASTER
86
23
30
8

66
46

5 0 5 10 20 ml

31
SHEFFIELD

57

The airfields

Acaster Malbis, Yorkshire

105/SE577430. S of York, to W of the B1222 road

This site was not far from the First World War airfield of Copmanthorpe, but it was a thousand times worse than even that site which was considered unsuitable for development.

Construction work started during the latter part of 1941 and it was laid out as a grass airfield, intended to be used by fighters. The airfield was situated a few miles south of the city of York between the villages of Acaster Selby and Acaster Malbis, the latter giving it its name. The airfield was close to the west bank of the River Ouse and its position was soon to be proved as completely unsuitable due to the frequent mists which were caused by the river.

However, despite its unsuitability the airfield opened in January 1942, in No 12 Group, Fighter Command, RAF, as a satellite for Church Fenton. The first and, as it turned out, the only fighter squadron to be based at Acaster Malbis was No 601. This unit arrived from Duxford on January 6, with the new American Bell Airacobra fighters which proved unsuitable as an operational aircraft.

Major technical problems and bad weather were the cause of many crashes. On February 12 1942 one crashed through the ice on the flooded banks of the River Ouse and the pilot was drowned. With the unsatisfactory state of both airfield and aircraft, the unit's stay was very brief and on March 25 1942, No 601 moved to Digby after having re-equipped with Spitfires.

Being unsuitable as a fighter station the airfield was transferred to No 21 Group, Flying Training Command, on April 7 1942, and the Oxfords of 'W' and 'X' Flights of No 15 (Pilot) Advanced Flying Unit took up residence. But this did not solve the problem and this unit also lost aircraft due to misty conditions along the River Ouse. Having been found unsuitable for training aircraft also, No 15(P) AFU moved out on January 25 1943 and the airfield closed.

The obvious signs were ignored for, despite being rejected by both Fighter and Flying Training Commands because of its stupid location near to a river, the site was then developed into a heavy bomber station. The whole area was nothing but drains and dikes yet construction work started and Acaster Malbis was rebuilt to the standard pattern with three concrete runways, the main one being 5,940 ft long

Control tower type 343/43 at Acaster Malbis (photographed May 1970).

and the two intersecting ones each 4,020 ft. The runways were encircled by a perimeter off which were 18 'spectacle' hardstandings. It was also complete with two 'T2' hangars and hutted accommodation for the personnel dispersed around the surrounding area. The bomb dump was sited in Stub Wood to the east of the airfield.

Acaster Malbis re-opened in 1943, in No 4 Group, Bomber Command, but it did not receive any operational units. It would have been suicidal if it had done. Then, on November 1 1944, the airfield was transferred to No 7 (Training) Group, Bomber Command, but again it did not house any operational units. Acaster Malbis was a 'white elephant' and the only use to which it was put was to provide circuit training facilities for the aircraft of nearby Heavy Conversion Units.

No 4 Aircrew School, a non-flying unit, moved in for a short time in late 1944 and from about the same time the site gained another resident—91 Maintenance Unit—which used the airfield and the surrounding woodlands for the storage of bombs.

Acaster Malbis, where heads should have been rolled—planners', not aircrews'—finally closed on February 28 1946, after a useless life. The country road across the site is again re-opened and divides the airfield. The control tower and one 'T2' hangar are still intact and the latter is used by a haulage firm. The Nissen huts of the sick quarter site are also intact. The communal site to the north-west is used as a pig farm and a short length of the main runway was retained and is used occasionally by a light aircraft.

Appleton Wiske, Yorkshire
93/NZ402064. SE of Darlington

Situated south of the B1264 road, just north-east of the village of Appleton Wiske after which it was named, this was another of the many First World War sites. It was classed as a 2nd Class Landing Ground with an area of only 38 acres. At the time the site was listed as heavy loam and clay soil being surrounded by agricultural fields with many trees. This ground was used by 76 Squadron while on Home Defence Duties. It was quickly abandoned after the First World War and there is no trace of it today. Appleton Wiske was a very primitive site

but it was surveyed as a possible World War 2 airfield although found unsuitable and abandoned.

Atwick, Yorkshire
107/TA188513. N of Hornsea

Situated on the sparsely populated Yorkshire coast just to the north of the village of Atwick, this is another First World War site with very little history. Its location was three miles from Hornsea Railway Station and it was listed as a 2nd Class Landing Ground. It covered an area of 50 acres in open surroundings, half a mile from the sea. The site was another used as a landing ground by 76 Squadron, Royal Flying Corps. There is no record of any regular use at Atwick until May 1918 when it was then occupied by 504 Flight of 251 Squadron, Royal Naval Air Service, which operated with DH 6s on anti-U-boat patrols. The landing ground closed immediately after the war and there is no trace of it today.

Barlow, Yorkshire
105/SE655285. S of Selby between the A1041 road and the River Ouse

In 1917, this airfield with an area of 880 acres was leased to Armstrong Whitworth for the construction of airships and a large airship shed and other buildings were erected. The *R.25* was completed in 1917 and the following year the *R.29*. By the time the *R.33*, which incorporated data from the German *LZ65* (force-landed in England in 1916), was completed, the war was over and with it the military life of Barlow. The *R.33* was eventually scrapped and the forward control car is now in the RAF Museum at Hendon. With the end of the airship era Barlow was, once again, just another village. Today, the site is an RAOC depot and a large airship shed, 700 ft by 150 ft by 100 ft, can still be seen in the depot grounds.

Barmby (Pocklington), Yorkshire
See Pocklington

Bellasize, Yorkshire
106/SE830275. E of Howden to S of the A63 road

Bellasize opened in April 1916 and was used by 33 Squadron, Royal Flying Corps, with their BE2c aircraft from April to October 1916. The site was also used during the autumn of that year by the Avro 504s of 76 Squadron, Royal Flying Corps. Sited between the A63 and the River Ouse, the airfield was subject to flooding and saw little use during the First World War. It was listed as a 1st Class Landing Ground and covered an area of 33 acres.

During the Second World War the airfield was again brought into use as a relief landing ground for No 4 Elementary Flying Training School at Brough from November 1939 until July 1945, when the airfield officially closed. It had a single grass runway of approximately 2,000 ft.

Beverley, Yorkshire

106/TA020400. N of Kingston upon Hull

Situated on the west side of Beverley to the north of the A1079 road, the airfield was established on the present-day racecourse. The hangars and all other buildings were established in the south-west corner of the site with easy access from the main road. Like many other racecourses in the First World War it was pressed into immediate use and from March to October 1916, both the Head-quarters and 'C' Flight of No 33 Squadron were based here with their BE2c and 2d aircraft. Their main task was the patrolling of the Humber ports.

That same year also saw No 6 Reserve Squadron, Royal Flying Corps, with Curtiss JN3s and 4s operating from Beverley. Also, on March 1 1916, No 47 Squadron, Royal Flying Corps, was formed at Beverley and flew alongside 33 Squadron on Home Defence duties before

going to Macedonia the following September.

In April 1917, No 90 TS arrived from Doncaster and in November of that year 80 Squadron arrived with Sopwith F1 Camels, but this unit remained only a few weeks and moved out on January 27 1918. Flying ceased after the war but part of the site remained with the RAF and during the 1930s a radio section operated from here and the Royal Air Force's first radio telephone sets were tested through Beverley in 1938.

During the Second World War the site was used by the Army and today it is once again used for the Sport of Kings.

Binsoe, Yorkshire

99/SE255800. NW of Ripon

This World War 1 landing ground was situated north-west of Binsoe between the B6267 and A6108 roads. It was a large grass field of 35 acres which gave an area 380 × 400 yards and it was listed as a 3rd Class Landing Ground. It was used in this capacity by No 76 Squadron with their Avro 504s from 1916 to 1918. There were no permanent buildings and very little use was made of the site. It reverted to its former use immediately after the Armistice in 1918.

Brafferton (Helperby), Yorkshire

See Helperby

Bramham Moor (Tadcaster), Yorkshire

See Tadcaster

An Armstrong Whitworth FK3 which crashed at Beverley.

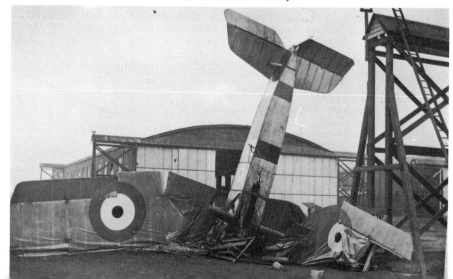

Brancroft, Yorkshire

111/SK665973. SE of Doncaster

Brancroft Farm was just a convenient field that was retained by the farmer and used as a landing ground for 'A' Flight, No 33 Squadron, Royal Flying Corps, on Home Defence duties. During 1918 the unit operated from here very briefly with a few Avro 504 fighters. Its role was the air defence of Leeds and Sheffield which were munitions-producing areas. The site was never developed but during the Expansion of the RAF in the mid-1930s, land a mile or so to the north of the World War 1 landing ground was developed into a bomber station which became RAF Finningley.

Breighton, Yorkshire

106/SE720350. N of Howden on W side of the B1228 road

Breighton was one of south Yorkshire's bomber stations on which construction work started in 1941. It was situated on the south side of the A163 road close to the village of Bubwith which was in the north-west corner. The B1228 road formed the eastern boundary and in the south-west corner nestled the little village of Breighton which gave its name to the airfield. This site was probably influenced by its close proximity to two World War 1 sites: Menthorpe Gate a mile or so to the west and Howden about two miles to the south-east.

It was a standard bomber station with three paved runways, but these were very unusual in so far as they had a common intersection. The runways were encircled by a perimeter track around which were a number of 'frying pan' type dispersals. The technical site in the north-west corner was provided with two hangars and there was a further 'T2' on the southern boundary. All three runways were subsequently lengthened to Class A standards by extensions on their eastern ends, the main runway being on an east-west axis and stretching almost to the B1228 road. The perimeter track was also extended and further hardstandings were added.

Breighton opened in January 1942 in No 1 Group, Bomber Command, as a satellite for Holme-on-Spalding Moor. The first to take up residence was 460 Squadron, RAAF, which arrived that same month from Molesworth, Huntingdonshire. This unit, code letters 'UV' but later changed to 'AR', was equipped with Wellington Mk IVs. Although classed as an RAAF squadron, there were only 38 Australians among the aircrews.

After a short working-up period the squadron began operations on March 12/13 when five of its aircraft were despatched to bomb Emden. Not a successful start, however, for only one believed it bombed Emden, the others did not know where they had bombed, and one failed to return.

On September 15 1942, the resident unit was withdrawn for re-arming with four-engined bombers. The squadron now had on strength 66 Australian aircrew members which was 50 per cent of requirements.

Preliminary training was already under-

Breighton Halifax B II, EY-E of No 78 Squadron. Note rectangular fins, circa 1943. These were introduced in 1943 to cure the rudder stalling experienced under certain conditions with the original triangular fin.

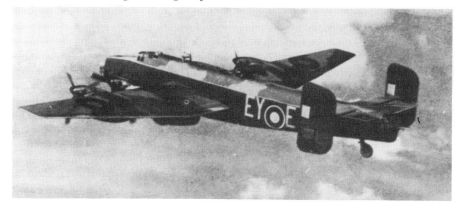

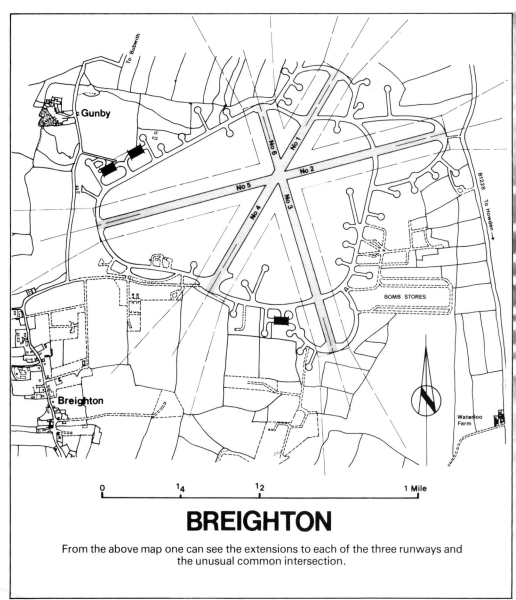

BREIGHTON

From the above map one can see the extensions to each of the three runways and the unusual common intersection.

way for 460 Squadron Conversion Flight had been formed during August with Halifax aircraft and had moved immediately to Holme-on-Spalding Moor so that operations could continue from Breighton, but these became less and less because lost aircraft were not replaced. The Wellington was being phased out of Bomber Command operations and when only five remained with 460 Squadron they were transferred to No 142 Squadron at Waltham which still operated with Wellingtons.

On September 1, Wing Commander K.W. Kaufman, DFC, took over command of 460 Squadron and on the 26th of the month the Conversion Flight returned and replaced its Halifaxes with four Lancasters and four Manchesters. Three fatal crashes during air-firing and bombing tests marred the period of conversion but nevertheless by the end of

October the squadron had reached a high degree of proficiency with the new aircraft and was now ready for operations with its new Lancasters.

On October 7, No 460 Conversion Flight merged with 103 Conversion Flight from Elsham Wolds into No 1656 Heavy Conversion Unit, code letters 'BL' and 'EK', which was officially formed here on the 10th of the month under Wing Commander Hubbard. On the 26th of the month it moved to Lindholme.

No 460 Squadron had only just returned to operations when, on November 23 1942, Kaufman was forced through illness to hand over his command to Wing Commander J.F. Dilworth, DFC, who remained at the head until the following February. On the 16th of the month Wing Commander C.E. Martin took over 460 Squadron. He was the first Empire Air Training Scheme graduate to command a heavy-bomber squadron.

On May 14 1943, the resident squadron moved to Binbrook in Lincolnshire. The move took place by air and there was no interruption in operations.

In June 1943, Breighton was transferred to No 4 Group, Bomber Command, and on 16th of the month No 78 Squadron arrived from Linton-on-Ouse. This was a Halifax squadron and Breighton was to remain its base for the remainder of the war.

No 78 Squadron took part in the many major raids including the epic raid on the Peenemünde experimental rocket base on August 17/18 1943 when 23 of its bombers bombed from 7,000 ft. It also took part in attacking the invasion targets which included the marshalling yards at Le Mans, Lille, Juvisy and Trappes. The squadron also attacked the coastal gun battery at Mont Fleury on the night of June 5/6 1944 in direct support of the Allied landings.

Mont Fleury was one of 4 Group's targets and a force of 124 bombers was despatched with 522 tons of bombs. The casemates at Mont Fleury were believed to hold Russian 122 mm guns but in fact only one gun was installed. German security was certainly very good. Along with other squadrons, No 78 bombed at just after 04.30 hours on June 6, but it was a waste of time for the gun was only slightly damaged and during the assault it fired until captured by ground forces. After the Normandy invasion the Breighton bombers continued to give support with

attacks on German troops in the Caen and Falaise areas.

The New Year brought bad weather conditions and during January 1945 the squadron was only able to make nine operations. During the spring they bombed targets in support of the Allied thrust into Germany. By April a few Halifax B VIs became available, but in no great numbers and the last operational mission of the war was on April 25 1945, when 20 Halifaxes bombed gun batteries on the island of Wangerooge.

The squadron's war effort comprised 6,017 bombing sorties and 320 minelaying sorties with a loss of 182 aircraft. It dropped approximately 17,000 tons of bombs and destroyed 31 enemy aircraft.

On May 7 1945, along with the rest of 4 Group squadrons, it transferred to Transport Command and operated Halifax Mk VIs in the transport role until converting to Dakotas in July 1945. No 78 Squadron moved to Egypt in September 1945 and the following year the station was abandoned by the RAF.

Today, the control tower has been demolished and many of the buildings have long since disappeared. However, the dispersed sites to the south-east are still intact. No 2 runway has been built on and an industrial site occupies the one-time technical area. One 'T2' hangar is intact and used for storage of wood by timber importers. The butts and water tower are still there as a reminder of those wartime days and the east-west runway is used by crop-spraying light aircraft.

Bridlington (Carnaby), Yorkshire
See Carnaby

Broomhill (Wombwell), Yorkshire
See Wombwell

Brough, Yorkshire
106/SE945256. W of Kingston upon Hull on S side of the A63 road

Brough has a long military connection going back to Roman times, so it was not surprising that it should be selected for an airfield. Brough was listed on the 1935 war map as a land and water aerodrome. Situated on the north bank of the River Humber a few miles west of Hull, it also has a long association with flying going back to the First World War. It was here that the Blackburn Aircraft Company

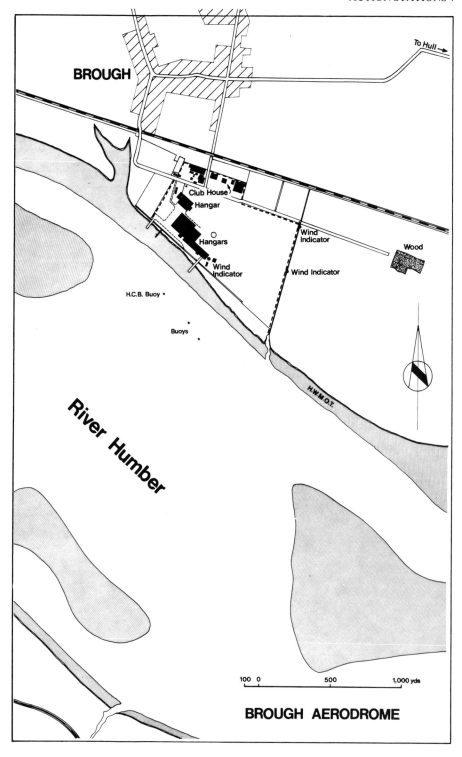

BROUGH

To Hull →

Club House
Hangar
Hangars
Wind Indicator
Wind Indicator
Wind Indicator
Wood
H.C.B. Buoy
Buoys
H.W.M.O.T.
River Humber

100 0   500   1,000 yds

BROUGH AERODROME

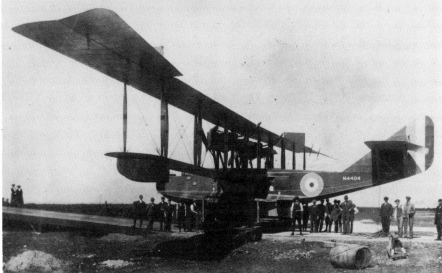

Top *A winter scene at Brough and a Blackburn Kangaroo rides out a snow storm. The Kangaroo's active service was chiefly given as the equipment of an anti-submarine squadron at Seaton Carew near the mouth of the River Tees.* **Above** *Phoenix-built flying boat, Felixstowe F3 N4404 at Brough.*

established a factory. Mark Swann, a friend of Blackburn's, had been sent to look for a suitable site to test seaplanes and flying-boats for Blackburn and, en route to the coast, he chanced upon Brough in the East Riding of Yorkshire, and there found all the space needed for an aerodrome. At the time Blackburn thought the site offered excellent facilities but it did not come up to expectations due in part to tidal conditions, and also to sea mist.

However, an experimental steel hangar and a slipway were built on the west side of the landing area. This work was completed in time for the erection and flight trials of the second GP seaplane in late 1916. As a seaplane the GP did not go into large production but a landplane version, which became known as the

Kangaroo, was produced in considerable numbers. However, soon after the GP trials the Government commandeered both hangar and slipway for the remainder of the war. Further buildings were then erected including two corrugated iron hangars. Brough then became No 2 (Northern) Marine Acceptance Depot and handled most of the Royal Naval Air Service float seaplanes until the end of the Great War.

With the Armistice in November 1918 orders for military aircraft came to a sudden end and many firms were put out of business. Blackburn was determined to weather the post-war slump and began to operate several converted ex-RAF Kangaroos which would carry passengers and freight to the Continent. Due to the slump this scheme was not a success and, in 1924, the company began training officers of the RAF Reserve. A flying school was formed in January 1924 with Captain Norman Blackburn as manager. It was equipped with Kangaroos, Avro 548as, Dart seaplanes and Blackburn Bluebirds. It soon became one of the established RAF Reserve schools where pilots received their annual refresher courses.

1924 proved a busy year. In the summer the ungainly Cubaroo took to the air from Brough. With a wingspan of 88 ft this single-engined biplane was probably the largest in existence anywhere in the world. It had been built to meet an Air Ministry specification for a long-distance coastal defence aircraft that could carry a bomb load of 1½ tons. The tail was a biplane formation and the main undercarriage had four wheels. 1924 also saw two prototypes of the parasol-winged three-seat Airedale take shape. This was a deck-landing reconnaissance aircraft with an ingenious method of wing folding, whereby the wings hinged to bring the leading edges uppermost and the span parallel to the fuselage. It must have been a sad sight for Blackburn when, after all design problems had been overcome and the preliminary test flights completed, they watched a Service pilot who had called to collect the aircraft for trials at Martlesham Heath, crash the first prototype at Brough.

With the Reserve School in full operation, work began at Brough in the late 1920s on the Nile flying-boat design for the service via the Nile and the African lakes. A company called Cobham-Blackburn Air Lines Ltd had been formed but Imperial Airways inaugurated a landplane service on this route and the Cobham-Blackburn company disbanded.

In 1925 Blackburn finally decided to close down the Olympia works in Leeds (which later re-opened in the mid-1930s). The company had started there in 1914

and during the war years was able to use the neighbouring Roundhay Park as an airfield. After the war flying had ceased and it had reverted to its former status as a public open space. The transfer from Leeds to Brough was a slow process and was not completed until 1932.

Brough continued to play an important role and aircraft were produced for both the Fleet Air Arm and the RAF. Late in 1930 work started at Brough on the construction of the twin-engined Segrave high-performance four-seat cabin monoplane. 1931 had produced the Blackburn B-2 trainer and over 40 of these side-by-side two-seater biplanes were built. Many of them were used for RAF Reserve training and continued in service right up to the early part of World War 2.

The B-5 was produced as the standard FAA torpedo bomber and many were supplied to the Royal New Zealand Air Force. The B-6 torpedo-spotter-reconnaissance aircraft was an improvement for it had a watertight fuselage which was an asset if ever the aircraft force-landed in the sea. This first flew in 1933 and was in reality the proto-type of the Shark. With the Shark the wings could be folded with the bombs in place, which greatly eased the work of the armourers on board a carrier. In addition to being built at Brough for the FAA, the Portuguese Navy and the Royal Canadian Air Force, the Shark was produced in Canada at the Boeing Aircraft factory at Vancouver. Whereas the Brough-built Sharks had Armstrong Siddeley Tiger engines, the Canadian-built ones had the Bristol Pegasus.

In July 1934 a most unusual-looking aircraft began taxying trials at Brough. This was the four-gun F3 fighter biplane in which the pilot had an excellent view due to its low-set wings. Unfortunately it was plagued by cooling problems and, when structural weaknesses appeared, Blackburn could not meet the agreed delivery date. Consequently, it never flew.

Opposite page, top to bottom *Fairey Barracuda, which looked a very 'bitty' aircraft especially with the undercarriage down. Here it is seen in flight which improved its lines. It provided all the prime needs for its role as a torpedo-carrier, good view, low landing speed and high degree of manoeuvrability. The engine in the Barracuda was a 1,200 hp Rolls-Royce Merlin 30; Blackburn Beverley C1 XH123. One of nine production aircraft; Brough 1939—Blackburn Roc L3084 with engine test bed. Very similar to the Skua, the Blackburn Roc was a Fleet Air Arm carrier-based fighter with four machine-guns carried in a power-operated turret, mounted at the rear of the cockpit. The Roc was first flown in 1938 and it was used extensively in the earlier years of the war in North Sea and Mediterranean operations: Blackburn Botha I W5065 seen at Brough in 1938.*

Blackburn Firebrand Mk III DK373 seen here at Brough 1943. The Mk I (1942) and Mk II (1943) were fitted with the Napier Sabre III 'H' in-line engine. Carrying a torpedo of 1,850 lb and armed with four 20 mm forward-firing cannon, it had a maximum speed of 334 mph at 12,500 ft.

In 1937 came the Skua, a fighter dive-bomber which was the first monoplane to become standard naval equipment. It was a Skua from HMS *Ark Royal* that was to claim the distinction, on September 26 1939, of being the first British aircraft to shoot down an enemy aircraft, a Do 18 flying boat.

At the outbreak of war in 1939 the Botha general purpose and reconnaissance twin-engined bomber was being produced in the Brough factory, and this programme was accelerated rapidly. But it was not fast enough and a new breed of aircraft was already needed for, with the collapse of France, the war fronts were extended, thus making the Botha, with its limited range, a second line aircraft. It therefore saw very little service in any of its operational roles and was used principally as an (unpopular) trainer. Meanwhile, the airfield was taken over by Flying Training Command and Brough became the home of No 4 EFTS with Tiger Moths.

Throughout the war Blackburn's own production and test aircraft also used the airfield. After the Botha contract was complete in 1943, the works at Brough were completely re-equipped for the production of the Fairey Barracuda torpedo bomber, of which 695 were produced. As well as building aircraft Blackburn also made valuable contributions to the war effort in other fields, and the company repair organisation was sister-design firm for all United States Navy aircraft in UK service and provided modification sets for Martlets, Avengers, Corsairs and Hellcats so they could operate under British conditions. Some 400 modifications were incorporated in nearly 4,000 aircraft and a British Modifi-

cation Centre was established at Roosevelt Field in the USA.

At Brough the training of pilots continued and the Tiger Moths remained a familiar sight throughout the war years as they buzzed around doing circuits and bumps. The nearby airfield at Bellasize was used as a RLG from November 1939 until June 1945.

The end of the war brought Blackburn serious problems and in the winter of 1948/49 the company merged with General Aircraft Ltd to become Blackburn and General Aircraft Ltd. This move brought to Brough the Universal Freighter which was subsequently developed into the Beverley for the RAF. One GAL 60 Transport was built in 1950 followed by 47 Beverleys. All flight testing was done from Brough with some 'heavy' take-offs and landings from Holme-on-Spalding Moor.

In 1950 the possibility of using flying-boats on the Humber was revived and a plan was put forward for services from Hull to Glasgow, Leith, Belfast, Southampton and Falmouth. The aircraft were to be Hythe flying-boats that were capable of carrying 50 passengers and everyone was enthusiastic about the idea, but nothing came of it in the end and it died a quiet death. In May 1955, Blackburn and General Aircraft were awarded the contract for the NA39, later to become famous as the Buccaneer, and Brough was to be the company's main plant. However, the take-off and landing facilities at Brough were inadequate for the testing of this twin-jet low-level strike fighter. The company then took over the old wartime RAF airfield at Holme-on-Spalding Moor, some 12 miles north-west of Brough, so that testing could be carried out there. All aircraft were transported there by road, the early ones towed there on their own wheels, the later ones ignominiously strapped to the backs of large transporters. In September 1958 it was announced that the aircraft was to be ordered in quantity for the Navy and in 1960 it became known as the Buccaneer—a name to remember for in 1962 the Station Hotel at Brough was renamed the 'Buccaneer' as a permanent reminder of the contribution made by Brough's labour force to Britain's air power.

Blackburn joined Hawker Siddeley Aviation in 1961 and since 1965 the historic name of Blackburn has been officially obliterated, the firm being known merely as Hawker Siddeley Aviation Ltd, Brough subsequently to become part of the Kingston-Brough Division of British Aerospace.

By the early 1960s Hull still had no plans for either a national or international air hook-up and had not taken advantage of using one of the ex-RAF stations. In March 1964, a report by aeronautical experts, economists and geographers concluded that Brough was the most suitable airfield and within three years could be handling 58,000 passengers and 450 tons of freight per year. But Hawker Siddeley refused Brough because it simply was not suitable for use as a civil airport. However, they later agreed to the use of the airfield at Brough and, on October 3 1966, Autair started to operate from here. Until the early 1970s civilian aircraft operated from Brough airfield on both

Below *Aerial view of Brough circa 1930—one can see the relation to this view from the map on page 30.* **Bottom** *Aerial view of Brough factory taken May 1978. The slipway from the early seaplane days is still there to the right of the photograph.*

Top *View of the Harrier wing and fuselage join-up production photographed in 1979 but still relevant today.* **Above** *View of production of the Hawk at the Brough factory, taken in 1979 but also relevant today.*

charter flights and a daily service to Luton. However, the civilian services ceased when a tall chimney was erected at the nearby smelting works to the east of the airfield. Even before this potential hazard arose it had long become apparent that the airfield was inadequate for the aircraft in production at the factory.

The Brough factory has 1¼ million square feet of floor space. The total labour force of Brough and the satellite airfield at Holme-on-Spalding Moor is 4,900, of which some 400 are at the latter. Today Brough is the company's third largest site and is engaged upon a multiplicity of product programmes. These include production of some 500 components for each wing of the Airbus; production of wings plus assembly of centre fuselages and the join-up of complete fuselages,

together with manufacture of flight refuelling probes, pylons, etc, for the Harrier. The manufacture of wings, forward centre fuselages, fins, rudders, tailplanes and pylons for the Hawk; navigator's station and wingtip pods for the Nimrod; production of fins, flaps, flap tracks and fairings for the BAe.146; plus repairs, spares and modification sets for the Buccaneer and Phantom, and support of research and development flying at Holme-on-Spalding Moor.

The design and production departments at Brough are contributing to many of British Aerospace's major programmes, military and civil. It was in Yorkshire that Blackburn wrote the early history of aviation and Brough has had an association from those early days. The Brough runway length is 3,400 ft with a width of 100 ft, suitable only for light aircraft, but their presence makes a welcome sight when they are at the airfield, which is still used today.

Burn, Yorkshire

105/SE603284. SW of Selby on E side of the A19 near Burn village

Bounded by the Selby Canal to the north, the main LNER Doncaster to Selby railway line to the east, and to the west by the A19 road and the hamlet of Burn, after which it was named, this somewhat restricted site was turned into a bomber base for No 4 Group. Construction work started in late 1941, and it was transformed as best as possible into a standard bomber base with three concrete runways, the main being 5,700 ft long; site limitations decreed that it should be almost north/south, parallel with the railway line. The two intersecting runways were 4,620 ft and 4,290 ft in length.

The control tower was the wartime austerity square two-storey type, 12096/41, and there were two 'T2's and a 'B1' hangar. With the airfield far from complete it was occupied by 1653 Conversion Unit which arrived in June 1942 from Polebrook where it had previously formed on January 7. This unit had a very brief life and disbanded at the end of October, as the airfield neared completion.

Burn officially opened as a bomber station in No 4 Group, Bomber Command, in November 1942, by which time it was in a fit state to be used operationally. On November 11, No 431 (Iroquois) Squadron, RCAF, formed as a bomber unit with Wellington B Mk Xs, coded 'SE'. The badge was an Iroquois Indian's head and the motto 'The hatiten ronteriics' is in Iroquois and means 'Warriors of the air'. The squadron's first bombing mission was on March 5/6 1943, when three Wellingtons attacked Essen. But on July 14 the unit was transferred to No 6 (RCAF) Group and Tholthorpe when, for some unknown reason, the airfield ceased to be a front-line bomber station and for the next few months was without a resident flying unit, although used as a relief landing ground by the aircraft of 4 Group conversion units.

On December 31 1943, the Austers of No 659 AOP Squadron arrived from York and these were followed on New Year's Day by the Auster Mk IIIs of No 658

AOP Squadron: two rather unusual units for a bomber station. However, Burn was soon to return to operational status and, by February 6, the Halifaxes of the newly-formed 578 Squadron (code 'LK') began to arrive from Snaith. Still part of No 4 Group, the squadron was immediately in the breach and with the pace of operations the crashes were frequent. But not all were serious.

On March 14, Halifax *LK756*, 'J'-Johnny was returning on three engines from a raid on Le Mans railway yards. The bomber made it back to Burn but crashed near Stainer Hall as it attempted to overshoot. Luck held for Flight Sergeant Boyce and his crew who escaped without injury. Two days later, Halifax *LW495*, 'C'-Charlie crashed near Selby brickworks at 03.20 hours on return from operations over Stuttgart. Its crew, however, were unlucky, Pilot Officer F.W. Lerl and four others being killed.

On the fateful Nuremberg raid of March 30/31 1944, No 578 Squadron despatched 12 bombers. Pilot Officer Barton, captain of Halifax *LK797* 'E'-Easy, was one of the 12. About 70 miles from target he was attacked by a Ju 88. In the attack the Halifax's guns were put out of action and the intercom system made useless.

An Me 210 then joined in the attack and, unable to contact the rest of their crew, the navigator, bomb aimer and wireless operator baled-out. Despite his serious condition—the starboard inner engine badly damaged, three of his crew gone, no guns working and unable to contact his remaining crew—Barton continued his mission. On reaching the target he released the bombs himself and, as he turned out of the target area, the propeller of the damaged engine flew off. Undeterred, he headed for home using his captain's map and steering by the stars and compass.

In spite of strong headwinds and no navigational aids he eventually crossed the English coast at Sunderland about 90 miles north of Burn. Barton then turned back out to sea to avoid a balloon barrage and signalled SOS with an Aldis lamp to the ground defences. By now the aircraft was low on petrol for during the numerous attacks two of the petrol tanks had been holed. Suddenly both port engines spluttered and stopped. The crippled bomber, which was now flying on only one engine, was too low to be abandoned successfully and the three

Burn, November 1943. Halifax 'Q'-Queenie LK640 of 431 (Iroquois) Squadron.

remaining crew took up crash positions. With precious seconds ticking away Barton looked for a clear space and, as he did so, steered the crashing bomber away from some houses. It finally crash-landed at 05.50 hours near Ryhope Colliery, County Durham.

Barton was unable to avoid the end of a row of houses, which were demolished before the aircraft came to rest in the Colliery yard. Unfortunately, Barton died 30 minutes after the crash, but his three remaining crew survived. Pilot Officer Cyril Barton, RAFVR, was posthumously awarded the Victoria Cross—the only Halifax crew member to receive a VC. For the part he played in bringing back 'E'-Easy, Sergeant Maurice Trousdale, the flight engineer (who escaped with serious injuries after an accumulator burst near his head), received an immediate DFM. The two air-gunners, Sergeants Brice and Wood, who escaped with minor injuries, received their DFMs some time later.

Of the 12 Halifaxes that set out on the Nuremberg raid only one returned to Burn, and this had engine trouble. Another that had returned early, also because of engine trouble, landed at Snetterton Heath. Halifax *LW478*, 'S'-Sugar managed to make it back to Silverstone but the bomber hit some trees after overshooting, killing the pilot and five of the crew. 'N'-Nan was shot down, never to return. The other seven Burn Halifaxes landed at airfields all over England.

Towards the end of April 1944, the Austers of Nos 658 and 659 Army Co-operation Squadrons moved back to York leaving 578 Squadron to get on with the bombing offensive. The unit's Halifaxes took part in the main force targets on Germany and German-occupied Europe

and continued to have their share of accidents. At 03.15 hours on July 21 1944, Halifax *MZ696*, 'K'-King, piloted by Flight Lieutenant Day, collided with Sergeant Davidson in Halifax *LK834*, 'E'-Easy. The aircraft was returning from a raid against Bottrop when they hit at 2,000 ft over Balkholme, Yorkshire. Both crews were killed.

The squadron also took part in the campaign against oil targets, during which Bomber Command mounted some daylight raids. One such attack was on October 6 1944 when a force of 159 aircraft was despatched to bomb Sterkrade-Holten. Two previous raids on September 27 and 30 had both been unsuccessful and the synthetic plant was again the target. 578 Squadron put up 24 Halifaxes which took off from Burn between 14.13 and 14.36 hours. Over the target area the bomber force encountered heavy flak but made it back to Burn, although 17 of them were badly damaged.

The New Year saw two of the squadron's Halifaxes pass the century mark—both on the same night, March 3/4 1945, when they bombed Kamen. They were *LW587* and *MZ527*.

The last operational mission of the war came on March 13, when 14 Halifaxes were despatched to bomb Wuppertal. On April 15 the squadron disbanded. 578 Squadron had flown 2,721 sorties and dropped 9,676 tons of bombs. Halifax B III, *LW587*, completed 104 sorties and was sent for scrap in September 1946. Halifax BIII, *MZ527*, completed 105 sorties and was SOC immediately the unit disbanded—reward indeed.

With the disbandment of the resident squadron Burn closed to flying, its brief operational life over. In 1946, the airfield was taken over by the War Department and used as a disposal store. During this period the airfield housed vast numbers of surplus tanks and all other kinds of armoured vehicles. These remained many months but as soon as this phase was over the facilities were dismantled.

Today, the airfield has almost disappeared. No hangars remain and the control tower and runways have been demolished, as have many of the buildings. A few buildings, including the gym and ops blocks, were still intact as at February 1981. Also, a piece of taxi track leading to dispersed hardstands could still be found. The water tower was also standing and being used by a local farmer.

Carlton, Yorkshire

105/SE640255. W of Goole

A site that was nothing more than a grass strip which was used as a landing ground by 'B' Flight of 33 Squadron from March to October 1916 while on Home Defence Duties. The whole area is marshland and the site had very little use and was never developed with any permanent buildings.

Carnaby (Bridlington), Yorkshire

101/TA140640. 1¾ miles SW of Bridling-ton between Haisthorpe and Carnaby

This large flat site on Carnaby Moor was perfect for the construction of an emergency runway and, being almost on the coast, was ideal for bombers needing to make a landing immediately after returning from a mission; this area also gave them a long clear approach. There was a great need for an emergency airfield for badly shot-up bombers were making it back to England and landing at the nearest airfield in all sorts of conditions, which gave rise to many problems. There-fore, an ELG was an obvious solution to overcome the problem.

Construction work started in 1943 and Carnaby opened on March 26 1944 as a Bomber Command Emergency Landing Ground—one of three such sites, the other two being Manston and Wood-bridge. All three were coastal airfields specially designed to handle aircraft in any kind of situation. Carnaby became operational under No 4 Group, Bomber Command, in June 1944. It only had a single runway, which had a special bitumen surface, 9,000 ft by 750 ft with a 1,500 ft grass extension at each end. The

control tower, type 343/43, was sited in the centre and to the south of the runway and taxiway off which were Dispersal Loop hardstandings. Carnaby was equipped with FIDO (see *Action Stations 2*, page 12) so that the landings could be made in all weather conditions, and it was fully equipped with emergency services. No hangars were erected and all accom-modation was temporary. The station strength as at December 1 1944 was a total of 548 personnel made up of 18 officers, 36 SNCOs and 494 Other Ranks. No accommodation was available for visiting personnel and they were sent to Lissett which was the nearest airfield.

December 1944 proved to be a particularly busy month and, for example, on the 22nd no fewer than 92 USAAF Liberators and Fortresses landed here because of bad weather at their bases. However, the end of the war was near and Carnaby's excellent crash rescue and medical teams finally stood down in September 1945. The field had played an important role and during its brief operational life over 1,500 landings were recorded.

The station closed in March 1946 and over the next few years was left in a state of neglect. The outbreak of the Korean War caused the RAF to expand its pilot training programme and, after repairs had been carried out, Carnaby re-opened on April 1 1953. The airfield was used as a RLG for No 203 Advanced Flying School at Driffield. The school's Meteors used the long runway for practice landings but for only a short period and the airfield closed again in 1954.

After a further period of disuse the airfield was once more re-activated when selected as a Thor missile site, to open in October 1958. The three Platforms and Long Range Theodolite Buildings were constructed on the south-west side of the airfield. The blocks of 32 bases were constructed just west of the wartime control tower. No 150 Squadron reformed in 1959 as a Thor IRBM unit. However, by 1963 the Thor sites were disbanded and Carnaby closed for the last time.

In 1972 the airfield was bought jointly by Bridlington Corporation and Bridling-ton RDC for the sum of only £50,000. Today, the eastern part of the airfield has been turned into an industrial estate and the runway has become the main road through the estate. The control tower and many of the concrete dispersal loops have been removed.

Catfoss, Yorkshire

107/TA135485. NE of Beverley

This was one of the early airfields and one
of the 14 listed on the 1935 war map for
this area. Because of its close proximity to
the coast, its site was perfect as a training
station and the early Air Gunnery and
Bombing Range was sited just out to sea
in an area between Skipsea and Hornsea
(see map below). Situated on the east
side of the A165 road, the airfield was
only some five miles from the coast. The
nearest village was Brandesburton which
lay in the south-west corner. On the
eastern edge of the airfield was Catfoss
Grange from which it was probably
named.

Catfoss opened in the early 1930s and,
on September 16 1935, No 97 Squadron
reformed here from 'B' Flight of No 10
(B) Squadron with a few Handley Page

Heyfords; that same month, however,
they moved to Boscombe Down,
Wiltshire. Catfoss was not to be a bomber
airfield and since conception had been
earmarked for training, so remained as
No 1 Armament Training School until
September 1939 when, after the outbreak
of war, the unit moved out. It was then
decided to enlarge the airfield and the next
few months saw very little flying activity.
During this period it housed only a
detachment of Spitfires from 616
Squadron which arrived from Leconfield
on October 1 1939 and operated from
Catfoss until May 1940.

The station re-opened in August 1940
and, on October 1 1940, No 2 (Coastal)
Operational Training Unit formed with
five Ansons and 12 Blenheims. Being an
early airfield, Catfoss was considered
important enough to have two decoys,
both being sited to the north-east.

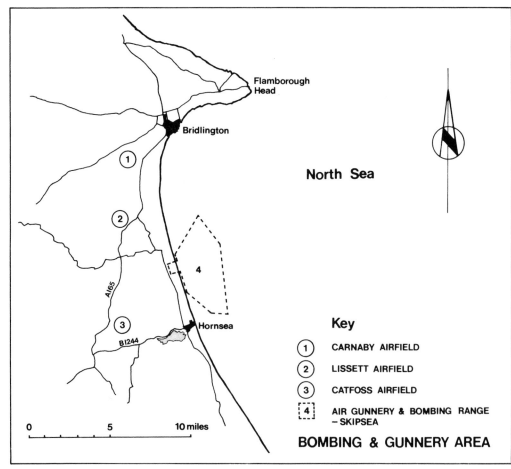

North Sea

Key

① CARNABY AIRFIELD

② LISSETT AIRFIELD

③ CATFOSS AIRFIELD

④ AIR GUNNERY & BOMBING RANGE – SKIPSEA

BOMBING & GUNNERY AREA

Flamborough Head

Bridlington

Hornsea

0   5   10 miles

Dunnington was a QX site nearest to the airfield, the other was a KQ site at Skipsea a few miles past Dunnington. The decoy at Skipsea had dummy Whitleys installed but by very early in the war both decoys had been abandoned.

While Lissett airfield was being constructed between December 1942 and February 5 1943, it was used as a Relief Landing Ground by No 2 OTU's aircraft. The OTU was responsible for training the majority of Coastal Command Beaufighter crews, which revitalised Coastal operations. For some unknown reason it was decided that Catfoss should have three concrete runways which were laid to the standard pattern and were 5,280 ft, 4,620 ft and 5,100 ft long respectively. Hangars and other buildings were also erected and there was a general expansion of the whole site.

On February 15 1944, No 2 OTU disbanded to be replaced by the Central Gunnery School which moved from Sutton Bridge during the latter part of the month. The status of the station at June 6 1944 was the Central Gunnery School flying Wellingtons, Spitfires, Beaufighters, Martinets and a few Masters as part of No 25 Group. During this period the CGS Officers' Mess was at Brandesburton Hall in the nearby village of Brandesburton.

At the Central School all gunnery subjects were lectured on very profoundly by the Royal Air Force's top tutors. The CGS covered air sighting, Boulton & Paul and Frazer Nash turrets, 0.303 and 0.5-in Browning machine-guns, Hispano 20 mm cannon, aircraft recognition, and Mark IIc gyro sights—these lectures being given by Professor Hill, ballistic advisor to the Air Ministry. Also included were tactics, navigational and radar aids to gunnery and manoeuvres. All the training was advanced and featured leadership as well as special training in the control and direction of firepower from groups of bombers on daylight raids.

The Central Gunnery School was an advanced training unit and Catfoss had a very important role to play. The Gunnery Leaders' Course at the CGS was designed to produce Section Leaders to take over the Gunnery Sections at squadrons and training units. Gunnery Leaders were commissioned and had the rank of at least Flight Lieutenant.

Fighter pilots also came to the CGS to improve their gunnery, and flew Spitfires, Mustangs and Thunderbolts. They would have lectures similar to gunners on appropriate subjects. From July 1944 until the end of the war in Europe Group Captain A.G. (Sailor) Malan was CO and he had on his staff many famous air fighters—Closterman, Skalski, Kingaby, Jack Charles, and 'Screwball' Beurling. Many American Aces also served at Catfoss.

The CGS continued to operate after the war but its role at Catfoss was almost over. On November 5 1945 the advance party moved to Leconfield and, after the main party had left on November 12, the station closed down. Catfoss lay derelict until, in the spring of 1947, two civil aviation applications were made for the re-opening of Catfoss for landing-ground facilities for charter aircraft bringing fruit to the UK from Europe. The stumbling-block was having Customs officials on call and this held up the project.

In July 1947 Lord Natham, then Minister of Civil Aviation, announced that Catfoss was one of the 43 aerodromes outside the London area which was intended to be State-controlled. Catfoss was to be developed to serve the Hull area as an airport. For some time it had been understood that Catfoss would be earmarked for civil aviation purposes. Representations had by this time been made for the temporary Customs facilities to be installed. However, nothing came of the Hull airport idea and Catfoss was left to fall into decay. The years passed with no further interest until, in 1959, Catfoss re-opened as a satellite of the Driffield Thor missile complex when three missiles were housed here along with 226 Squadron. This phase was very shortlived and in 1963 the Thor unit disbanded along with all the others and once again the airfield fell into disuse.

Today, the control tower, engine and trailer sheds are derelict but the runways are intact and used for caravan storage. An 'A' type hangar is being used by a container firm, two other hangars and buildings also remain. Also, on the technical site the MT shed and para store are intact, but their future looks bleak.

Catterick, Yorkshire

99/SE250968. S of Catterick between the main A1 road and the River Swale.

Almost 2,000 years ago the Catterick area was the site of the Roman Army Station at Cataractonium (Catterick), commanding Dere Street, an important routeway from

York to Hadrian's Wall. The Romans, during the reign of Antoninus Pius, had conquered the Brigantes, a tribe in ancient Britain who occupied the region south of the Antonine Wall extending to the Humber estuary in the east and the River Mersey to the west. Cataractonium was one of their forts. After nearly four centuries the Romans withdrew from Britain and Catterick became a prominent town under the Saxons. Later, the Normans constructed Castle Hills which was a pentagonal earthwork built beside the River Swale to defend the town. Castle Hill stands today at the eastern end of the runway and is a registered Ancient Monument. These historic associations are depicted in the Station badge of RAF Catterick. The centurion's helmet marks the links with the Roman military settlement. The five-sided green and blue background device is symbolic of the fortress of Castle Hills.

The site for the airfield was no doubt influenced by the proximity of Catterick Barracks for, despite being a restricted site, it is bounded to the west by the main A1 road, to the east by the River Swale and the small town of Catterick to the north. Catterick was opened in 1914 as a Royal Flying Corps airfield to train pilots and to assist in the defence of north-eastern England. The units were engaged in Home Defence Duties and consisted of only a few aeroplanes in the early years.

On November 27 1915, No 6 Reserve Aeroplane Squadron arrived from Montrose and took up residence at Catterick. New units began to form and Captain A. Claude-Wright formed 'A' Flight of 53 Squadron on May 15 1916. 'B' and 'C' Flights were completed by June 8. The squadron used a few Avro

504s and Armstrong Whitworth aircraft. By October, 53 Squadron was fully equipped with BE2s and by the end of 1916 it had moved to Farnborough en route to France. No 37 Reserve Squadron formed here on November 2 1916 but, on the 13th of the month, it moved to Scampton in Lincolnshire. During the latter part of 1916 a flight from 76 Squadron arrived and was to remain here for the duration of the war. This unit had the responsibility for the defence of Leeds and Sheffield.

The New Year saw a further build-up at Catterick and during January 1917, No 83 Reserve Squadron formed. This was a Canadian unit which moved to Beverley the following month. On March 15 a second Canadian unit formed here. This was 88 Reserve Squadron which, in April 1917, moved to Canada. Also during April, 68 Reserve Squadron formed on the 7th but a week later moved to Bramham Moor.

On July 23 1917, 46 Reserve Squadron arrived with their BE2s and Avro 504s from Bramham Moor. 69 Reserve Squadron also formed here on October 1, with DH4s and DH6s, but ten days later moved to Bramham Moor. Catterick then opened as a full aerodrome on December 1, and that same day No 115 Squadron, RFC, formed here as a training squadron from a flight of No 52 Training Squadron. The year was brought to a close with the arrival of 52 Reserve Squadron from Montrose.

On the formation of the Royal Air Force on April 1 1918 the airfield became Royal Air Force Catterick. It is thus one of the oldest military airfields in the world. During April, the Sopwith Pups of 115 Squadron moved to Netheravon, Wiltshire. July 1918 saw many changes

Sopwith Pup B4128 'Ickle Poop' at Catterick in 1918. Built by No 2 (Northern) Aircraft Repair Depot. Note the Bessoneaux hangars in the background, the type erected on many of the World War 1 airfields.

when Nos 46 and 52 TSs disbanded, No 49 Training Depot Station being formed from them on the 15th of the month. The TDS was equipped with 36 DH4s and DH9s plus a few Avro 504s. Catterick remained in a training role and, in 1919, No 49 TDS disbanded. During March 76 Squadron moved to Tadcaster and flying ceased at Catterick.

More for its buildings, which now included ten hangars and one repair shed, Catterick airfield was retained by the post-war RAF but very little flying took place. During the mid-1920s five aircraft sheds replaced the hangars and other more permanent buildings were added including the watch office, type 178/27. Married quarters were constructed to the north of the airfield close to Leeming Lane, now the main A1 road.

On October 11 1927 No 26 Squadron re-formed here on a single Flight basis as an Army Co-operation Squadron in Army Co-operation Command, which controlled the station until September 1939. Equipped with Atlas aircraft, 26 Squadron re-equipped with Audaxes in July 1933.

During this period it was decided to modernise Catterick airfield and, in 1935, under the mid-1930s Expansion programme, many new buildings were erected. All the new buildings were still within the north end of the airfield and included two 'C' type hangers, built just south of the other aircraft sheds. To the east of these a new watch office with tower and nearby a fire tender shelter were also built. Other buildings included barrack blocks, airmen's and officers' married quarters, MT sheds, operations building (Fighter) and main stores and workshops for three squadrons.

Following this modernisation programme, No 41 Fighter Squadron

arrived in September 1936 to join the resident unit. In August 1937, 26 Squadron re-equipped with Hawker Hectors and in spring 1939 converted to Westland Lysanders. Meanwhile, 41 Squadron had re-equipped with the Hawker Fury Mk II in October 1937, changing to the Spitfire I in early 1939.

During August a detachment from No 64 Squadron arrived and at the end of the month they were joined by the Spitfire Mk Is of 609 Squadron which arrived from Yeadon. Final preparations were made as the war clouds deepened and Catterick had an important role to play. In September 1939 Catterick became a Sector Station in No 13 Group, Fighter Command, RAF. The next few weeks were very hectic, October being a particularly busy month. No 41 Squadron, coded 'EB', quickly converted to the Spitfire and, in mid-October, moved to Wick but was back again on October 25. That same month 26 Squadron, now coded 'RM', moved to France and 609 to Acklington. 219 Squadron re-formed on October 4, with an establishment of Blenheim 1f fighters, coded 'FK', and had moved to Scorton before the end of the month.

Over the next three years Catterick was to play a vital role in the defence plans of the country, being at its peak in 1941. The station was used for fighter squadrons that were resting and re-equipping after they had been in action over southern England. The station also provided fighter cover for the north-eastern part of the country and for convoys in the North Sea.

Records show that Catterick had a decoy airfield at Low Moor, but I have not been able to find any trace of it. It was listed as a 'Q' site and did not have any buildings or dummy aircraft.

During May 1940, the Spitfires of 54 Squadron arrived from Hornchurch and the 64 Squadron detachment returned to

Avro 504K, E2959, of 49 TDS in 1918.

Church Fenton. 41 Squadron was again on the move, moving to Hornchurch on May 28, then back to Catterick on July 8, only to return to Hornchurch on July 26. Early the following month they were back *again*, but returned to Hornchurch on September 3. September also saw 64 Squadron back for the third time plus the arrival of 600 Squadron from Redhill and 504 Squadron from Castletown, but the latter moved to Hendon before the end of the month.

On November 23 1940, No 256 Squadron re-formed with Boulton Paul Defiants, coded 'JT', and in January 1941 moved to Pembrey. 1941 proved to be a very busy year for Catterick and saw many nationalities pass through the station. No 68 Squadron re-formed on January 7 as a night fighter unit with an establishment of Beaufighters carrying the code letters 'WM'. Amidst a hive of flying activity 68 Squadron began working up to operational status.

During February 1941, No 54 Squadron returned to Hornchurch in exchange with 41 Squadron and, in March, 600 Squadron moved to Drem after having converted to Beaufighters. The following month 68 Squadron moved to High Ercall.

No 313 (Czech) Squadron formed at Catterick on May 10 1941. This unit was the third Czech fighter squadron and was equipped with Spitfires, code letters 'RY'. By July they were ready for action and moved to Leconfield. The previous month had seen the arrival of 122 Squadron from Ouston, and this was followed in July by the Spitfires of 131 Squadron. On the 21st of the month, No 331 (Norwegian) Squadron formed with an establishment of Hurricanes, unit code letters 'FN', and began working up to operational status. On July 28, No 145 Squadron arrived at Catterick in a Harrow, having left their Spitfire Vbs at Tangmere. The squadron was now down to seven of the original pilots, and they took over the Spitfire Mk IIbs of 41 Squadron which had moved to Merston upon their arrival.

Like all the other fighter squadrons that arrived at Catterick, 145 found life very different to that at Tangmere. They spent much of the time on either Flight or Section readiness, usually covering convoys moving up and down the North Sea. Says Sergeant Frank Twitchett, a pilot with 145 Squadron: 'This was usually very boring and not too easy in bad weather. Also, the ships did not seem briefed on the code colours of the day and often let off a few rounds at us'.

The hectic movement of squadrons continued and, during August, 331 Squadron moved to Castletown and 131 to Tern Hill. October saw the departure of 122 Squadron, having changed their Spitfire Mk Is for the Mk IIa; during this period 145 Squadron assumed a training role and began to receive numbers of ex-OTU pilots who stayed for two or three weeks before going down to No 11 Group. The few pilots who had come up from Tangmere in late July remained for they were officially on rest. During this period

Catterick—October 1941. Pilots of No 145 Squadron. Sergeant Twitchett is in the back row at far left.

Sergeant Twitchett was promoted to Flight Sergeant, backdated to May, and drew £37.00 back pay: a fortune in those days at 12s 6d per day. He was later commissioned as a Pilot Officer just before being posted broad.

The year 1941 was brought to a close with the arrival of 134 Squadron from Vaenga, Russia, on December 7. It was only a whistle stop and, during the first week of January 1942, it moved to Eglington. On January 16 a second Norwegian fighter squadron was formed. This was No 332 with Spitfires which, at birth, was coded 'HG', but a few days later was re-coded 'AH'. February 1942 saw the departure of 145 Squadron to the Middle East.

During June 1942, No 332 Squadron moved to North Weald and was replaced by No 403 Squadron, RCAF, which arrived from Martlesham Heath on June 19. Coded 'KH', this unit was flying Spitfire Mk Vbs and immediately upon arrival at Catterick sent four aircraft to West Hartlepool. Three days previously No 63 Squadron had arrived with Mustang Mk Is but their stay was brief and they departed at the end of November 1942.

The pace was now beginning to slow and the New Year brought it to a trickle. On January 22 1943, No 403 Squadron moved to Kenley, Surrey, to be part of the Canadian Kenley Wing. The Canadians were replaced the following day by another Canadian unit, No 401 Squadron, RCAF. On January 25 the squadron sent four aircraft to Thornaby.

The Spitfires of 401 Squadron said goodbye to Catterick on May 28 1943 and moved to Redhill to join the Kenley Wing. The Canadians were replaced that same month by the Spitfire Mk Vbs of No 306 (Polish) Squadron, which remained until the following August.

September 1943 saw the Spitfires of 130 Squadron arrive from West Malling. But by now Catterick was no longer an important fighter base and, in November 1943, No 130 Squadron moved to Scorton. There was a further run-down when, on November 15 1943, No 1472 (DB) Flight disbanded. This unit had formed on June 1 1942, to give air support training to the Home Forces Battle School at Barnard Castle a few miles to the north-west of Catterick. The unit's Battles and Tomahawks, coded 'RG', had been based at Catterick during its brief life.

During mid-February 1944, the Spitfires of 222 Squadron arrived from Woodvale but moved before the end of the month to Acklington, and this was, in fact, the last wartime fighter unit to use Catterick. After their departure the airfield was used by second line units.

After the cessation of hostilities the station became an Aircrew Allocation Centre in 1945 and the following year it was decided to move the RAF Regiment Depot from Belton Park, near Grantham, to Catterick. The single short runway of 3,330 ft, bounded at one end by the River Swale and at the other by the Great North Road, could not be extended to take the

Aerial view of Catterick (circa 1970).

Above *DH Venom NF 3 ex-WX849 of No 89 Squadron seen at the RAF Fire School at Catterick where it was used for fire practice (photographed April 1963).* **Below** *Their flying days over, Javelins FAW 6 XA816 and XA830 suffered a lingering death at the hands of the RAF Fire School at Catterick where they were repeatedly set alight and extinguished by trainee firemen. Here we see XA816 that once noisily boomed over the North Yorkshire Moors (photographed April 1963).* **Bottom** *On June 9 1981, Vulcan B Mark 2 XH554 landed at RAF Catterick, its final resting place. It will be used as a training aid for RAF firemen. An undignified end after such fine service. XH554 first flew at Avro's Woodford airfield on February 21 1961 and was handed over to the RAF on April 6 1961. It served first at Finningley with Bomber Command Development Unit and its last unit was with No 230 Operational Conversion Unit at Scampton.*

higher performance aircraft then coming into service.

The Band of the RAF Regiment also arrived in 1946 with the RAF Regiment Depot. At that time the station functioned solely as a training establishment at which all ranks of the regiment gained their professional skills. Throughout this period the airfield remained in use for light communications aircraft and for gliding.

The arrival of an operational Wing Headquarters and squadrons of the RAF Regiment in 1964 once more gave the station an operational function. These units still continue to be held at readiness to be moved rapidly to the trouble spots of the world. In 1967 Her Majesty presented a new Colour to RAF Catterick when she reviewed the RAF Regiment on its 25th Anniversary.

RAF Catterick is also the training school for the RAF Fire Service which is officered by, and trained under, the auspices of the regiment. Thus, the station is organised into Operations Wing, commanding two or more RAF Regiment Squadrons at any given time; and Training Wing, commanded by the Chief Instructor and controlling the Advanced and Basic Combat Training Squadrons, the Fire and Rescue Training Squadron and the Education and Training Squadron. The Training Wing conducts over 20 different courses and trains about 1,400 students annually. To do this, it utilises both purpose-built and adapted accommodation, which includes a Training Centre with cinema, lecture theatre and model room. It also uses a Battle Training Simulator which incorporates cine and electric target ranges together with a variable light system utilising infra-red and closed circuit television which makes the James Bond world a reality. Administrative and logistic support is formed by Personnel, Station Services and Supply/Engineering Squadrons.

Today, Catterick is the home of the RAF Regiment Depot which had a fighting force of over 85,000 men during the last war. Although this large force is now much reduced in numbers, it retains several Rapier-equipped short range air defence and field squadrons and has one squadron able to operate in the parachute role. During 1981, the field squadrons were scheduled to re-role as light armoured squadrons, thus keeping the RAF

Catterick Guardroom (photographed December 1980).

Regiment an up-to-date and highly flexible force.

In 1981 Catterick, with Group Captain Marcus Spence Witherow as CO, also housed HQ No 3 Wing RAF Regiment, No 58 Squadron RAF Regiment and the band of the RAF Regiment, which in 1980 repeated its former success and was awarded the Cassell Trophy. The band has also produced four long-playing records of military and traditional music.

The RAF Regiment Museum is also located at RAF Catterick. It contains a wide cross-section of exhibits illustrating the regiment's past and present roles. The Fort-type control tower is intact and the runway remains operational for light aircraft and gliding by 645 GS. There is a good view of the airfield from the main A1 road. The presence of the large military training areas renders Catterick particularly suitable to be the RAF Regiment Depot and it will remain so for the foreseeable future.

Fort type control tower at Catterick.

Church Fenton, Yorkshire

105/SE530380. NW of Selby on S side of the B1223 road

This airfield was constructed as a fighter base under the pre-war Expansion scheme and was one of the primary stations in No 12 Group, Fighter Command. It was situated a few miles south-west of the City of York and just north-east of the village after which it was named. It was only a few miles to the north of the airfield at Sherburn in Elmet, and this gave circuit overlap. On the credit side it was within easy reach of Church Fenton railway station, which was always very busy. It was also close to the River Wharfe, which was to the north, and the whole area was criss-crossed with drains. On the west side of the airfield, just north of the village, two 'C' type (Hipped) hangars of the short seven-bay pattern were erected and a space left between them for a third. This became a casualty of the massive construction programme and a 'T2' hangar was eventually put on the site. The usual other buildings were grouped behind the hangars on both sides of Busk Lane. Construction work was not completed until 1939.

However, Church Fenton opened as a grass airfield in June 1937 and was soon occupied by two fighter squadrons: No 72 with Gloster Gladiators which arrived on June 1 from Tangmere, and No 213 with Gloster Gauntlets which arrived from Northolt on July 1. During the second week in May 1938 the Gauntlets of 213 Squadron moved out to Wittering and were replaced that same month with the Demons of 64 Squadron which immediately re-equipped with Blenheim 1fs.

The station remained a two-squadron base until the outbreak of war in September 1939 when it was transferred to No 13 Group, Fighter Command. During August, 72 Squadron had converted to Spitfire Is in readiness to defend the vital areas of Yorkshire and, on October 15 1939, it moved out to Leconfield. It was replaced from that station by a detachment from 245 Squadron, and by 242 Squadron which re-formed at Church Fenton on December 30 1939 with an establishment of Hurricanes.

For the first 12 months of the war Church Fenton deployed its aircraft in the defence of the East Coast of Yorkshire and the West Riding towns. It was an important station with two decoy airfields. One was at Kelfield a few miles to the east and close to the River Ouse; the second was a QX site a few miles to the south at Hambleton. Other records show it had a decoy airfield at Menthorpe which was a 'Q' site and had dummy Hurricanes installed, but I can find no trace of it. Therefore, the decoy airfields that were possibly used were those previously mentioned, and not Menthorpe.

January 1940 saw the return of 72 Squadron. The following May the 245 detachment moved out. No 64 Squadron also moved out in May, having converted to Spitfire Mk Is the previous month. The third unit to move out during May was No 242 which was now operational and moved to Biggin Hill on the 21st to take part in the Battle of France. Squadron Leader Douglas Bader was later placed in command of 242 Squadron at Coltishall whose main equipment was Hurricane Mk Is in addition to a few Blenheims.

Meanwhile, on May 16, No 249 re-formed with Hurricane Mk Is, code letters 'GN', but moved out two days later to Leconfield. Those incoming during May were 87 Squadron with Hurricanes and 234 Squadron with Spitfires. The latter unit flew north-east coastal patrols for a few weeks before moving out again on June 18 1940 to St Eval.

Hurricane Mk Is of No 73 Squadron flew into Church Fenton during mid-June and, on July 5, the Hurricanes of 87 Squadron left for Exeter. Two days later 249 Squadron returned from Leconfield as an operational unit. They did not have to wait very long for their first kill for, at 11.30 hours on July 8 1940, Green section of 'B' Flight shot down a Ju 88, 15 miles north of Flamborough Head.

Church Fenton was then put under the control of No 12 Group on August 10 1940 and, four days later, 249 Squadron moved to Boscombe Down in Wiltshire. They arrived at their new station during the afternoon and took up residence in a hurriedly prepared dispersal area on the south-west corner of the airfield. At about 16.00 hours the station air-raid siren sounded and three of 249's Hurricanes were soon airborne. They were circling the airfield in an anti-clockwise direction at approximately 1,000 ft and, as they turned along the western leg of their circuit, three Ju 87s dived out of the clouds directly astern of them. The Stukas dived straight down one behind each other, delivered their bombs and pulled back into the clouds. Meanwhile, the three Hurricanes sailed serenely on, completely unaware of the attack—the pilots must have thought they were still flying in Yorkshire. It was a different story for 249's dispersal which was at panic stations. On that particular day, LAC William Baguley, a fitter of the Blind Approach Training and Development Unit, had been detailed for dispersal guard and was patrolling an area adjacent to 249 Squadron's dispersal.

'My most vivid memory is of a Flight Lieutenant leaping on to the port mainplane of the nearest Hurricane, snatching his flying helmet from the control column and bellowing into the microphone, "Behind you! Behind you! For Christsake turn the bloody things round!"' The whole episode was over in seconds and the only damage was three cows killed in a nearby field. Two days later Flight Lieutenant J.B. Nicolson of 249 Squadron, flying *GN-A:P3576,* was awarded the Victoria Cross, the only Fighter Command pilot to be so honoured during the Second World War. He was later killed on May 2 1945 (then Wing Commander, VC, DFC).

It was then the turn of Yorkshire to be at the receiving end and, on August 15 1940, many of the airfields were attacked. Church Fenton hit back and 73 Squadron claimed at least two Ju 88s, one by Sergeant McNay and one by Pilot Officer Carter. On August 28, No 306 (Polish) Squadron formed here with an establishment of Hurricanes. This was the first all-Polish fighter unit.

No 73 Squadron moved out to Castle Camps on September 5 and was immediately replaced by the Hurricanes of 85 Squadron from that station. Then, on September 19 1940, No 71 Squadron formed at Church Fenton. This was the first American Eagle squadron and was made up of Americans who had slipped over into Canada and enlisted. 71 Squadron took the motto 'First from the eyries' and its badge displayed the American bald eagle bedecked with three nine-pointed stars symbolising the States from which its earliest members had come.

The first pilots for the Eagle squadron were Pilot Officer G. Tobin, Pilot Officer V.C. Keough and Pilot Officer A. Mamedoff. These three pilots had been evacuated from France where they had gone to join the French Air Force. A few days later Squadron Leader Walter M. Churchill, DSO, DFC, arrived from command of No 605 Squadron at Croydon and assumed command of the new unit. Also to arrive were Pilot Officer F.H. Tann, Adjutant, and Pilot Officer A.G. Donahue who was posted from 64 Squadron.

Over the next few weeks more men joined the new Eagle squadron—but they had no equipment. The only aircraft they had been provided with, a Miles Magister trainer, was unserviceable. They now became irritable and, on October 23 1940, at his own request, Pilot Officer Donahue was allowed to go back to an all-British squadron that was operational.

October 23 also saw the departure of No 85 Squadron to Kirton-in-Lindsey. Two days later four single-seat, single-engine Brewster F2A Buffalo American fighters arrived for No 71 Squadron. The Eagles' enthusiasm soon faded when they found the fighters were deathtraps. They were too slow, too lightly armed and they lacked self-sealing fuel tanks. These were an integral part of the wing, and a single bullet could set them afire.

After an early accident only three Buffaloes remained operational and Churchill decided the squadron had to be rid of them. To do so, he ordered Tobin, Mamedoff and Wilkinson to take-off in them and come right back to land without locking the tail wheels. Each pilot landed as ordered and in one stroke the entire Buffalo squadron was wiped out. No one was hurt, for to land in that manner meant the aircraft would ground loop, tip to one side and end up with a damaged wing.

By the end of October, No 4 Radio MU, which had been housed at Church Fenton for the past few months, had moved away. The RAF remained discreetly silent over the Buffaloes, but better equipment was on the way. November 7 1940 saw the Hurricanes of 306 Squadron move to Tern Hill and the arrival of nine Hurricanes for the Eagle squadron. They were delivered by 85 Squadron and, leading the Hurricane flight, was the commanding officer, Squadron Leader Peter Townsend, who was later to become well known as equerry to King George VI and as a frequent escort of Princess Margaret. The Eagle squadron also received eight pilots from No 5 FTS, Sealand. Two weeks later, after additional fighters had been delivered, No 71 (Eagle) Squadron was transferred to Kirton-in-Lindsey.

Throughout 1940 Church Fenton had been a busy operational fighter station. Its squadrons had moved to relieve the depleted units in the south when the Battle of Britain was fought. Battle-weary and newly formed squadrons replaced them and at all times sustained the defences of the West Riding.

Church Fenton was now tasked with training night fighter pilots for twin-engined Blenheims and Beaufighters and, on December 16 1940, No 4 Operational Training Unit was formed for this task. The unit's original equipment was 31 Blenheims, 24 Defiants, ten Masters, six Havocs, six Oxfords and four target-towing aircraft.

On December 21 1940, the OTU was redesignated No 54 OTU and, while it continued to carry out its training programme, a brief visit was paid by No 46 Squadron which arrived on February 25 1941, but departed again a few days later on March 1. There were many accidents during this period of training for it involved flying in the dark and in almost all kinds of weather. The North Yorkshire Moors claimed many aircraft and others were lost at sea. No 54 OTU remained until May 1942, when it then moved to Charterhall after re-equipping with Beaufighters the previous August, and the squadrons returned once more, many of them night fighter squadrons to provide cover from the German night bombers.

The first of these units was No 25 Squadron which arrived during mid-May 1942, equipping with Mosquito NF Mk Is on October 21. No 488 Squadron re-formed on June 25 with Beaufighter Mk IIF aircraft and in September they moved out having been replaced on the 1st of the month by the Beaufighters of 600 Squadron.

October saw 25 Squadron re-equip with the new Mosquito NF Mk II and, on November 1 1942, No 183 Squadron formed with Hurricane Mk Is. On November 14, 600 Squadron moved to Portreath.

March 1943 was a very busy month for 183 Squadron for, on the 1st, they moved to Cranfield only to return to Church Fenton 12 days later after a flying visit to Snailwell, but they were not to remain here for very long and on March 26 they moved to Colerne. After the Spitfires of No 308 (Polish) Squadron had arrived from Northolt on April 29 1943 there was a lull in the movements for the next few weeks. Then, on July 6, No 308 Squadron moved to Hutton Cranswick and on the

19th of the month the Mustangs of 26 Squadron arrived from Ballyhalbert. These were followed on August 4 by the Mosquitoes of No 96 Squadron. This latter unit remained only a month and moved to Drem on September 3 1943.

December 1943 saw a few changes with the departures of 25 Squadron to Acklington on the 19th and No 26 Squadron to Hutton Cranswick on the 28th in exchange for 234 Squadron. The Spitfires of the latter unit only remained a month and moved out to Coltishall on January 28 1944.

The pace had now slowed down with a build-up of forces in the south and the next unit to arrive was No 124 Squadron from West Malling on March 18 1944. Their stay was very brief and their Spitfires moved to Bradwell Bay on April 23 1944. Two days later the Mosquitoes of 604 Squadron arrived from Scorton, but their stay was also brief and they moved to Hurn on May 2 1944.

The status of the station on June 6 1944, was part of No 93 Group with No 307 (Polish) Squadron which had arrived from Coleby Grange the previous month. This became the resident squadron and, on November 19 1944, was joined by the Spitfires of No 288 Squadron from Collyweston.

The year was brought to an end with the arrival of 456 (RAAF) Squadron, which arrived on December 31 1944. In the New Year the squadron re-equipped with Mosquito Mark 30 aircraft and began to work up to operational status with them. This was a more powerful Mosquito which was designed for high altitude, fitted with drop tanks, an advanced type of air interception radar (AI Mk X), a tail warning device and the usual armament to enable it to be used as long-range escort for night bombers over Germany. Having converted to Mosquito NF 30s, No 307 Squadron moved to Castle Camps on January 27 1945 and left the Aussies to get on with their training.

February 1945 was cross-country and other exercises for 456 Squadron and by the end of the month the Aussies were ready for action. But bad organisation caught them with their trousers down. With victory in sight the enemy was underestimated. On March 3, the ground crew of No 456 left Church Fenton by train for Bradwell Bay which was their new posting. That night, the Luftwaffe staged its long-planned major incursion against bomber airfields in the United

Kingdom. Church Fenton had only one resident squadron, No 288, and, although officially 'stood down from operations', No 456 was called upon to get what aircraft it could into the air. Within an hour of the alert five Mosquitoes scrambled although there were no starter batteries or ground crews. Also, the aircraft had only one channel available on their radio-telephone transmitters. Nevertheless, they patrolled for three hours, albeit without success.

The next day it was controlled chaos at Church Fenton, the train party was ordered back and 50 ground crew with essential equipment were flown back by Dakotas, which should have been done in the first place rather than splitting the squadron. At panic stations a petrol bowser was procured from Bomber Command and the squadron was required to keep ten aircraft at a night readiness state each night in case the Luftwaffe returned. They did attack a few airfields on the night of March 4/5 in East Anglia and five Mosquitoes from 456 Squadron were on patrol. Flying Officer R.D. Hodgen scored hits on the engine and wing of a Ju 88 but lost his target when the vibration of his cannon firing caused his gunsight to fall apart, exposing the lamp and temporarily blinding him. This was the last fling by the Luftwaffe, having lost the element of surprise. However, 456 Squadron did not know it and continued their fruitless vigils for the next ten days. Finally, on March 16, No 456 Squadron moved to Bradwell Bay for bomber-support duties.

They had been replaced by the Mosquito NF Mk 30s of No 68 Squadron which had arrived the day previous from Coltishall, but victory was now in sight and, on April 20 1945, 68 Squadron disbanded. Church Fenton then became No 112 Personnel Centre, for refresher courses, and on April 24 No 125 Squadron arrived from Coltishall.

During August 1945, No 288 Squadron moved to Hutton Cranswick and the following month the Meteors of No 263 Squadron arrived from Acklington. The Mosquitoes of 125 Squadron remained, then, on November 20 1945, the unit was renumbered No 264 Squadron and re-formed as a Mosquito unit.

Church Fenton was retained as a permanent station in the post-war Royal Air Force and, complete with two concrete runways 06/24 and 16/34, it was one of the first stations in the RAF to have operational Meteor jet fighter aircraft which had arrived with 263 Squadron. These moved out to Boxted in June 1946 and on the 28th of the month the Spitfires of 129 Squadron arrived. On September 1 1946, 129 Squadron was re-numbered 257 and re-equipped with Meteor IIIs, coded 'A6'.

During April 1947 there were many changes with the departure of 257 Squadron on the 15th of the month, No 41 Squadron arriving from Wittering the following day to be followed by 19 Squadron, also from Wittering, on the 23rd.

On July 22 1947, the Mosquitoes of 264 Squadron moved to Linton-on-Ouse. The resident units now settled in for a few years at Church Fenton. In November 1949, they were joined by two Mosquito squadrons from Coltishall, Nos 23 and 141. The following March 72 Squadron arrived from North Weald and made Church Fenton a very busy station. The situation was eased on September 22 1950 when the Mosquitoes of Nos 23 and 141 Squadrons moved to Coltishall. On the 18th of the following month the Meteors of No 609 (West Riding of Yorkshire) Squadron, RAuxAF, took up residence; this was to be their last home before all these fine Auxiliary squadrons disbanded.

The Hornets of 41 Squadron bade the station farewell and moved to Biggin Hill on March 29 1951. By the late 1950s the facilities at Church Fenton were inadequate for the latest jet fighters. The long-reigning 609 Squadron had disbanded on March 10 1957, and No 85 Squadron had disbanded on October 31 1958, having arrived from West Malling on September 23 1957, with Meteors. Church Fenton's fighter role came to an end when the Hunters of 19 Squadron and the Javelins of No 72 departed for Leconfield on June 28 1959.

In July 1959 the station's long association with Fighter Command also came to an end. The station was transferred to Flying Training Command and over the next few years was the home of several important units, the principal ones being No 23 Group Headquarters, No 60 Maintenance Unit, No 2 Police District and Leeds University Air Squadron.

Still in Flying Training Command, No 7 Flying Training School formed here in April 1962 with Jet Provost T3s and T4s. This unit was tasked with training 100 pilots a year to fly Jet Provost aircraft and continued in this role for the next few

Left The 'real' Station Commander meets his wartime number. Group Captain K.R. Briggs, Station Commander RAF Church Fenton (left) with Group Captain Eglin (James Taylor, an actor) during the filming of Airline, a Yorkshire Television 13-part serial, sequences of which were shot at RAF Church Fenton in January 1981. Dakota in the background. Note the modern-day uniform on the left and the wartime one on the right.

Below right *Tiger Moth used in filming* Airline *at RAF Church Fenton in January 1981.*

-years. For a brief period in 1966 an advanced training Flight using Vampire T11s operated alongside No 7 FTS. In April 1966, Leeds University Air Squadron returned to Church Fenton together with No 9 Air Experience Flight and, with their Chipmunks, made it a very busy flying station. September 1966 saw the arrival of Headquarters No 6 Recruiting Region, together with associated Schools Liaison Officers. There were still further changes before the end of the year, including the disbandment of 7 FTS in November.

On January 1 1967 the station was transferred from No 23 to No 25 Group and the Primary Flying Squadron arrived from South Cerney. January 1 1968 saw the station transferred to No 22 Group and Training Command and the PFS was joined by the Aircrew Officer Training School, also from South Cerney. This latter unit moved out to Henlow in 1969 where it merged with the Officer Cadet Training Unit and, although the effective date of the merger was May 19 1969, the transfer from Church Fenton was phased over a period of three months from that date. Church Fenton continued as a flying training school and included, from September 15 1969, the Royal Navy Helicopter Specialist Pilot Squadron from Linton-on-Ouse. This unit was later renamed the Royal Navy Elementary Flying Training Squadron and in July 1973 Bulldog aircraft were introduced on the station. During this period other flying units on the station included No 9 Air Experience Flight and the Yorkshire Universities Air Squadron which is found from the Universities of Bradford, Hull, Leeds, Sheffield and York.

On November 28 1974, No 2 FTS disbanded and the following day the RN EFTS moved to Leeming. The rundown continued and in June 1975 the Yorkshire Universities Air Squadron and No 9 Air Experience Flight moved to Finningley, and Church Fenton closed as yet another economy drive. The airfield was then reduced to Care and Maintenance under the control of a small holding unit and the runways remained in limited use to provide relief landing ground facilities for the Jet Provosts of No 1 FTS at nearby Linton-on-Ouse.

In 1978, with the need for more pilots, new flying training schools were required. Thus, in September of that year it was announced that Church Fenton was to be re-opened as the base of a new Flying Training School. The station officially re-opened under the command of Group Captain John A. Bell, OBE, on April 2 1979, as No 7 Basic Flying Training School with an establishment of Jet Provost aircraft. The new station Commander led a flypast of eight Jet Provost T3s to mark the occasion. Air Vice-Marshal Peter Bairsto, CBE, AFC, AOC Training Units at Support Command, took the salute at a march past.

In February 1980, a 609 Room with mementoes and some 22 charcoal drawings by Cuthbert Orde, was opened in the Officers' Mess by the Earl of Scarborough. It is dedicated to the deeds of 609 (West Riding) Squadron, which disbanded in 1957.

Today, Church Fenton is a station in Support Command, housing No 7 Flying Training School made up of the Flying Wing, Engineering Wing and Administrative Wing. The Flying Wing is commanded by the Chief Instructor, who is a Wing Commander and is made up of two basic flying squadrons, plus a Standards Squadron, a General Service Training Organisation and Flying Wing Headquarters and Air Traffic Control. The Flying Wing is tasked with training officers as pilots up to the required standard to commence advanced training on either the Hawk, the Jetstream or the Gazelle helicopter.

The Engineering Wing consists of a Headquarters Flight, Aircraft Engineering Squadron, Support Squadron and the Electrical Engineering Squadron. The role of the Engineering Wing is to ensure the provision of sufficient serviceable aircraft throughout the flying day to meet the station task. Finally, the Administrative Wing, which consists of the Station Services Squadron, Supply Squadron and Personnel Management Squadron, is responsible for the administration, management and support of the complete station.

Church Fenton had played many roles during its chequered history and several famous fighter squadrons fought with great distinction from this Yorkshire airfield during the Second World War. Therefore, it was an excellent choice when Church Fenton was selected as the airfield to turn back the clock and be used in the filming of *Airline*, a Yorkshire Television 13-part serial which is based on the exploits of a fictional ex-RAF pilot but includes true incidents. The station was enlivened and injected with the wartime atmosphere as Bedfords, Hillman staff-cars and Jeeps in RAF Police markings were once again at the station. Much of the material shot at Church Fenton will be used to portray a typical RAF base in Germany in 1946. To convey the period atmosphere the attention to detail was across the board and the Tiger Moth and Dakota were in correct markings. It must have made a big break from routine flying training for the Station Commander, Group Captain Kenneth Briggs, who had a rival CO to contend with. Past, present and future, Church Fenton still has a vital role to play.

Clifton (York), Yorkshire
See York

Copmanthorpe, Yorkshire
105/SE575465. 3 miles S of York

Sited near the village of Copmanthorpe, adjacent to the Leeds-York railway line, this was the replacement site for Knavesmire and was developed into an aerodrome complete with hangars and other buildings.

During May 1916, 'B' Flight, 33 Squadron, moved in from Knavesmire with their BE2C aeroplanes. 'B' Flight remained until September of that year and for a few weeks 'A' Flight also used the airfield. On June 8 1916, No 57 Squadron, RFC, was formed here from a nucleus flight of No 33 Home Defence Squadron. Equipped with FE2ds, No 57 Squadron moved to France in December of the same year as a fighter-reconnaissance unit, and remained in Europe for the duration of the war.

From September 1916, 'A' Flight, 76 Squadron, RFC, operated from here with Avro 504s and 504Ks, until March 1919. The airfield closed that same month and the facilities were soon dismantled and the

land sold. Today, the only remains are some concrete foundations from the hangars and a small mound of earth which was the former firing-range.

Cottam, Yorkshire

101/SE995644. N of Great Driffield. Turn W off B1249 at Kilham Junction

This remote site on a hilltop immediately south of the hamlet of Cottam, after which the airfield was named, was considered to be suitable for use as a satellite airfield for Driffield and opened in that capacity during September 1939.

Despite so many unfavourable factors, the airfield was developed as a bomber station under No 4 Group, Bomber Command, with no thought given to its position or access to the site by road, which were very poor. Because of its close proximity to the North Yorkshire Moors the airfield was subject to unusual wind effects which gave problems for aircraft in the circuit. However, work proceeded and Cottam, with its three concrete runways, 5,280 ft, 3,960 ft and 4,050 ft in length, perimeter track and dispersed hard-standings, was completed and ready for use by September 1940. But, owing to the adverse weather conditions, it was rejected and only used on rare occasions. There is no record of any flying unit being based at Cottam.

During March 1944 a USAAF B-24 Liberator made a forced landing at Cottam after returing from ops and after

Cottam control tower (now demolished) was unusual in the fact it had pillars to support the balcony. Photographed in September 1973.

a period of near disuse the station was later used as a bomb-dump by No 91 MU who put the concrete runways and hardstandings to good use by storing on them vast quantities of bombs which were delivered by road from the rail-head at Driffield. This was the only major use made of the airfield and as soon as 91 MU moved out it was abandoned. During the late 1970s, the control tower was demolished and during the early part of 1980 the airfield was in the process of being cleared and the runways were being removed. Today very little remains.

Croft, (Neasham), Co Durham
93/NZ285068. S of Darlington

Situated on the West side of the A167 Northallerton to Darlington road, this was one of the most northerly of the airfields built during the Second World War for use by Bomber Command. Construction work started in 1940 and it was developed into a standard bomber airfield with three concrete runways. It was almost adjacent to the main LNER London to Newcastle railway line.

Known officially as Croft but frequently called Neasham by local inhabitants, the airfield opened in October 1941 as a satellite for Middleton St George, a base a few miles to the north-east. The airfields were in No 4 Group, Bomber Command, and the first squadron to arrive at Croft was No 78 which brought its Whitleys in from Middleton St George on October 20 1941.

In the spring of 1942, the resident squadron began converting to Halifax BIIs, aided by a Squadron Conversion Flight which had formed on March 23 in preparation for the changeover, and it was considered to be sufficiently proficient on these new aircraft to be able to participate in the first 'Thousand Bomber' raid at the end of May 1942. Shortly after this the squadron returned to Middleton St George and the conversion flight moved to Dalton. Croft was then made ready to be transferred to the Royal Canadian Air Force.

On October 1 1942, No 419 Squadron, RCAF, arrived from Topcliffe with their Wellington Mk IIIs but Croft was not to be their station and, on November 9, the unit moved to Middleton St George after re-equipping with Halifax BIIs. It was replaced by No 427 (Lion) Squadron, RCAF, which formed at Croft on

November 7 1942 with an establishment of Wellington Mk IIIs coded 'ZL'. This was the RCAF's eighth bomber squadron formed overseas. 427's first operational mission was on December 14 1942 when three Wellingtons were despatched to lay mines in the Frisian Islands area, two aborting owing to bad weather.

Croft was then transferred to No 6 Group, (RCAF) on January 1 1943 and, on January 15/16, the resident unit's first bombing mission got underway when six Wellingtons were despatched to bomb Lorient, France; one failed to return.

During March 1943, the station became No 64 Base Sub-station under the control of Middleton St George. By the end of March 427 Squadron had re-equipped with Wellington Xs and continued operations with these for a few weeks. Then, in early May it converted to Halifax B Mk Vs and on the 4th of the month it moved to 63 (RCAF) Base, Leeming.

The station now had a brief change of role and, on May 10, No 1664 Heavy Conversion Unit formed at Croft. Equipped with Halifaxes, code letters 'DH' and 'ZU', the unit's role was to provide conversion training on these aircraft. Training was continuous and with such a crowded circuit there were many crashes and, sadly, many fatalities.

A bad month was September. On the 9th, Halifax V *DG339* crash-landed at Croft after a fault developed in the starboard outer while on a training flight. Only one crew was injured. Six days later, Halifax V *EB198*, coded *ZU-O*, was abandoned by the crew at 12.45 hours after the pilot's escape hatch blew off, causing loss of control. Six crew baled out successfully but one remained in the aircraft and was killed when it crashed at Stillington, near York. The worst crash of the month was at 00.07 hours on the 23rd when Halifax V *EB181*, piloted by Pilot Officer R.H. Highstead, was flying too low and crashed on the Moors near Helmesley, Yorkshire, killing the five crew.

The crash crews were kept very busy and, on October 21, Halifax V *EB136* swung on take-off and hit the pyrotechnic store at 20.40 hours. The following day at 01.35 hours Halifax V *EB199* crashed at Church House Farm, South Cowton, Yorkshire, killing the crew of five. On November 22, Halifax V *EB150* had just taken off from Croft and had reached 500 ft when it suddenly dived into the ground at Blue Anchor Farm, Scotch Corner, at

19.26 hours. Six crew were killed and one injured. But the station's training days were over and, on December 7 1943, No 1664 HCU moved to Dishforth. It was replaced by two operational units from Tholthorpe. On December 10, 431 (Iroquois) Squadron arrived and the following day was joined by No 434 (Bluenose). Both Canadian units were to make Croft their last home in England, and once again they had to contend with primitive conditions and oozing mud during the winter months. A change of location did not bring a change of luck and both units were badly mauled in January and February.

During March 1944, 431 Squadron re-equipped with Halifax IIIs and the following May, No 434 followed suit. During the conversion period activities had been somewhat reduced but the Croft squadrons still managed many tactical targets, marshalling yards and airfields. As D-Day grew nearer both 'Iroquois' and 'Bluenose' attacked the enemy's coastal defences at Calais, Boulogne, Trouville, Le Clipon and Merville. Both units continued to play their part in the Battle of Normandy and then turned to targets in Germany.

In October 1944, No 431 re-equipped with the Avro Lancaster B Mk X and 434 re-equipped with Lancaster Xs in December. These aircraft saw both units through the final months of the war.

January and February 1945 were characterised by bad weather and a few very long missions which entailed eight or more hours' night flying in extreme cold conditions. Then, on the night of March 3/4 1945, when intruders ravaged the East Coast airfields, Croft was a diversion airfield for the Leeming aircraft and received many of them.

At 02.30 hours Captain Notelle announced himself in the Croft circuit, lowered his undercarriage and flaps when suddenly an intruder jumped him. The German night fighter had stalked his prey and bided his time. A burst of tracers set the bomber's port wing ablaze but the aircraft continued its landing approach. It was now difficult to control and overran the runway, crashing in a small wood. However, Notelle's luck held and miraculously the trees tore off the burning wing, leaving the fuselage intact and hardly touched by the flames. This gave the crew time to get out and save Captain Notelle who was covered in blood after hitting his head against the instrument panel. He recovered after a few weeks in hospital but carried a deep scar on his forehead as a reminder of that March night.

The last operational mission for both Croft squadrons was on April 25 1945 when each despatched 15 aircraft to bomb gun positions on the Island of Wangerooge. Two aircraft failed to return from 431 Squadron.

During its wartime career 431 Squadron logged 2,573 sorties, plus 11 airlifting 240 PoWs back to England. The squadron dropped just over 14,000 tons of bombs. It lost 72 aircraft and 490 aircrew, of whom 313 were killed, 54 missing, 104 PoW, 18 safe and one injured. 14 non-operational personnel were also killed. The squadron honours and awards were one DSO, 63 DFCs, ten DFMs, two CGMs and one Mention in Despatches.

During its tour with No 6 Group, No 434 Squadron had flown 2,597 sorties, dropped 10,358 tons of bombs and laid 225 mines and in so doing lost 74 aircraft, the casualties in personnel totalling 493 officers and men. Of these, 358 were killed or presumed dead, 117 PoWs, 14 evaded capture, two escaped and two others reported safe. The Bluenose's awards and honours included six Bars to DFCs, 108 DFCs, six DFMs, one BEM and seven Mentions in Despatches.

After VE-Day No 434 took part in Operation 'Exodus' and made 45 sorties. 431 also took part in the airlift of PoWs, but made only 11 sorties. Both units were selected as part of 'Tiger Force' for duty in the Pacific. Therefore, in mid-June, they flew their Lancasters back to Canada for reorganisation and training. The sudden end of the war resulted in both squadrons being disbanded at Dartmouth, Nova Scotia, on September 5 1945.

After the departure of the two RCAF squadrons Croft saw very little activity until being brought back into use in the autumn as a satellite for No 13 Operational Training Unit which flew Mosquitoes from Middleton St George, finally closing to flying in the summer of 1946. It was now a redundant satellite airfield and was quickly abandoned by the RAF.

Today, the hangars have been demolished and only a few buildings remain on the technical site. The water tower remains on a dispersed site to the south. The control tower is now used as a car race control and part of the runways and perimeter track serve as a racecar track.

Cullingworth (Manywells Height) Yorkshire

104/SE065355. W of Bradford between the B6144 and A629 roads

Situated just south of Cullingworth village a few miles south of Keighley, this was nothing more than a grass landing strip that was used from 1916 to 1919 by 33 and 76 Squadrons while on Home Defence duties. This primitive site, known also as Manywells Height, was soon abandoned after the First World War, and there is no trace of it today.

Dalton, Yorkshire

99/SE420760. E of the main A1 road between the villages of Topcliffe and Dalton, just S of the A168 road

Situated a few miles south of Topcliffe airfield, Dalton was an undeveloped site when it opened as a bomber airfield in November 1941, and the first to arrive were the Whitleys of 102 Squadron from nearby Topcliffe. Situated to the east of the small Cathedral town of Ripon, the new site was called Dalton after a nearby hamlet. From its conception Dalton was to remain linked with Topcliffe.

By the end of the year the squadron was ready to re-equip with the Handley-Page Halifax, so the resident unit was joined in January 1942 by 102 Squadron Conversion Flight. With an establishment of Halifax Mk Is, this unit had the task of converting the squadron from Whitleys to Halifaxes. However, these units remained only a few months and in June 1942 both returned to Topcliffe. That same month Nos 76 and 78 Squadron Conversion Flights arrived with Halifax Mark Is. On July 13, No 1652 HCU took up residence but the following month all units moved out and on August 31 the airfield closed for reconstruction.

Dalton re-opened in November 1942 and was now to Class A standard with three concrete runways, 5,280 ft, 4,290 ft and 4,185 ft in length, but it was to be some months yet before the four-engined bombers arrived. No 428 (Ghost) Squadron formed here as a bomber unit of No 4 Group on November 7 1942. The unit code letters were 'NA' and it was equipped with Vickers Wellington Mark IIIs. On January 1 1943, the airfield was one of six stations transferred to No 6 RCAF Bomber Group, becoming No 61 Base Sub-station when the group

One of the few remaining wartime buildings on the Technical Site at Dalton, photographed in July 1980.

began to re-organise under Bomber Command's Base system during March 1943. The resident squadron was also transferred to No 6 Group, RCAF, and their first operational mission was on January 26/27 1943, when six Wellingtons were despatched to bomb the U-boat base at Lorient, France.

No 424 Squadron, equipped with Wellington B Mk Xs, arrived from Leeming on May 3 but this unit was non-operational and on the 16th of the month moved to North Africa to be part of the Mediterranean Air Command. No 428 Squadron then moved to Middleton St George on June 3 and by so doing brought to an end the brief operational life of the airfield.

Dalton was now to take on a training role and, on May 15 1943, No 1666 Heavy Conversion Unit was formed here. This unit was to provide conversion training on Halifax aircraft, but it did not remain here for very long and moved to Wombleton on October 21. Meanwhile, on July 2 1943, No 1691 (Bomber) Gunnery Flight formed here with the task of training air gunners. This unit was later redesignated No 1695 Bomber Defence Training Flight on February 15 1944.

November 6 1943 saw the arrival of 420 Squadron from Hani East Landing Ground, Tunisia. On returning to the UK the RCAF squadron acquired Halifax IIIs and, on December 11 1943, moved to 62 Base, Tholthorpe.

For administrative reasons the station was transferred to No 7 Group, Bomber Command. This was an RAF Training Group and Dalton was renamed No 76 Base Sub-station. It still retained its Canadian personnel and association with No 6 RCAF Group for the duration of the war.

One of the many to pass through Dalton training camp was Sergeant Charles Whitmore. This was for a two-week escape course, most of the Lecturers and Instructors being escaped ex-POWs or Evaders. The end-of-course exercise was to take the crew out during the hours of darkness in a sealed 3-ton lorry and then drop them off in twos and threes all over the Yorkshire Moors and let them find their way back to base. They had to report to the Orderly Room at Dalton without being apprehended by any of the military or civilian police or the Home Guard who were all involved in the exercises. Many decided to walk all the way back but Charles Whitmore decided there had to be an easier way. He struck out until he came to a country pub and, after making sure there were no police about, he inquired about a bus stop. After some nourishment of the liquid variety he took a bus into Middlesbrough where he booked into a hotel for two nights until his money ran out. He then started to hitch-hike back to camp, his last lift being in an RAF garbage truck that was returning to Dalton with some new bins. He explained what he was doing to the driver who told him to climb into one of the bins for he had already passed one road check. As they neared journey's end they were stopped by an RAF Police road block but the trouble started after they had passed through. Feeling the vehicle move off again Whitmore raised the bin lid to see the cause of the halt and spotted two RAF motor cycle police. He could not resist a wave and minutes later they were on their motor cycles and he was taken into custody with only a mile to go!

Dalton expanded its training role and, on August 6 1944, No 6 Group Aircrew School was formed here as a holding unit for aircrew passing from Nos 22, 23 and 24 OTUs to heavy conversion units. The unit provided lectures on escape and evasion, administration and discipline. It also provided physical training and instruction in synthetic trainers.

At the end of the war the units began a quick run-down and on July 28 1945, No 1695 BDTF disbanded to be followed on August 3 by No 6 Group Aircrew School.

Dalton had been a faithful satellite to Topcliffe but its days were now numbered and it closed down at the end of 1945. The site was soon dismantled and over the years much of it has returned to its former use. Today, the site houses an industrial estate and only the hangars, two 'T2s' and a 'B1' plus pieces of runway and a few huts remain from the wartime days.

Dishforth (Ripon), Yorkshire

99/SE380720. E of Ripon on E side of the main A1 road

Dishforth was one of the early bomber bases to be built under the pre-war RAF Expansion schemes. Situated adjacent to the Great North Road just south of Dishforth village, after which it was named, it was provided with substantial brick-built accommodation typical of the period with an arc of five 'C' type hangars round the south-east boundary close to North Hill Farm.

Dishforth opened in September 1936 but at this time very few of the permanent buildings had been completed except for some of the airmen's married quarters. The first aircraft to arrive were the Heyfords of No 10 Squadron from Boscombe Down, Wiltshire, in January 1937. This unit began to re-equip and became the first squadron with Whitley Mk Is. It was joined the following month by 78 Squadron, which also arrived from Boscombe Down with Heyfords, and the following July it also re-equipped with Whitley Mk Is. Over the next few months both squadrons carried out day formation flying as much as possible.

At the outbreak of war in September 1939, 78 Squadron were coded 'EY' and a detachment moved to Tern Hill. By the end of September it had become No 4 Group's reserve squadron, its role being to supplement the Group pool with trained crews, and act as a back-up unit. Meanwhile, the other resident unit, now coded 'ZA', prepared for war and the first operational mission was on September 8/9, when eight Whitleys from 10 Squadron were on a 'Nickel' raid over north-west Germany.

The following month a detachment from 78 Squadron went to Linton-on-Ouse and in December the entire squadron moved there in exchange with 51 Squadron.

Meanwhile, during November and December, 10 Squadron had a detachment at Kinloss. The squadron's first bombing raid of the war was on March 19/20 1940, when eight Whitleys, each with mixed bomb loads of 1,500 lb, attacked the German seaplane base at Hörnum. All aircraft returned safely. The squadron also took part in the raid on the Fiat works at Turin during which one Whitley was struck by lightning and had to abandon the mission, and one other failed to return.

The following month 10 Squadron moved to Leeming and was immediately replaced by the return of No 78, which was still flying Whitleys. Being one of the early airfields, Dishforth was provided with two decoy airfields, a KQ site at Cold Kirby and a QX site at Boltby.

For the remainder of 1940 and early in the New Year the resident squadrons continued the bombing offensive. Then, in February 1941, both 51 and 78 Squadrons supplied Whitleys and crews for operation 'Colossus'. This was the first Allied airborne operation of the war and took place on the 10/11th of the month. During this mission British paratroops destroyed an aquaduct at Tragino in Southern Italy.

Mid-April 1941 saw 78 Squadron move to Middleton St George. This left 51 Squadron to continue alone from Dishforth, which had been earmarked for the Canadians. On September 22 1941, No 12 BAT Flight formed with an establishment of Oxfords. In November all these flights were renumbered in the 1500 Group and 12 BAT Flight became No 1512.

During February 1942, 51 Squadron again participated in a paratroop operation. This time it was operation 'Biting' which was carried out on February 27/28, a raiding party capturing a complete German Würzburg radar installation at Bruneval, near Le Havre. The paratroopers were carried in Whitleys of 51 Squadron, led by their commanding officer, Wing Commander P.C. Pickard. He was already well known, having been the pilot of Wellington 'F'-Freddie in the documentary film *Target for Tonight*, but he was later to achieve undying fame when, on February 18 1944, as Group

Dishforth—February 1942. Wing Commander P.C. Pickard looks at a German helmet brought back by the paratroopers.

Captain, he led the Mosquito attack on Amiens prison to release French patriots. He was killed when his aircraft was shot down by Fw 190s.

In May 1942, No 51 Squadron moved to Chivenor, Devon, on loan to No 19 Group, Coastal Command, and Dishforth then prepared to receive the Canadians. No 425 (Alouette) Squadron formed here on June 25 1942 as a unit of No 4 Group. It was the Royal Canadian Air Force's fifth bomber squadron formed overseas but this unit was unique for the organisation order designated it 'French-Canadian'. The first commanding officer was Wing Commander J.M.W. St Pierre who remained until September 30 1943, when he was then replaced by Wing Commander J.A.D.B. Richer, DFC.

The squadron was equipped with Wellington Mk IIIs, unit code 'KW', and their first operational mission was on the night of October 5/6 1942, when eight aircraft were despatched to bomb Aachen. The mission was not a success. One Wellington crashed in Essex en route to target, all crew killed. Two more returned early because of icing and it is thought only one bombed the primary target.

Dishforth then saw the birth of a second Canadian unit when, on October 15, No 426 (Thunderbird) Squadron, Royal Canadian Air Force, formed here as a bomber unit in No 4 Group. This was the RCAF's 7th bomber squadron, unit code 'OW', and it was also equipped with Wellington Mk IIIs. This unit was commanded by Wing Commander S.S. Blanchard.

Towards the end of October No 6 Group Communications Flight was formed and the remainder of the year continued with 425 taking the war to the enemy but, during October and the first week of November, they managed only Osnabruck, Kiel, Cologne, Krefeld, Emden and Wilhelmshaven because of difficult weather conditions. The last three missions had been daylight raids. During November and December 1942, 425 Squadron was one of the only two Canadian bomber squadrons which were operational and most of this period was on Gardening. Meanwhile, No 426 worked up to operations.

On January 1 1943, Dishforth and its resident units were transferred to the newly formed No 6 Group, RCAF, and it then became No 61 Base Sub-station. Two weeks later 426 Squadron flew its first mission on the night January 14/15 when seven Wellingtons bombed Lorient, France. The following month 426 Squadron lost its commander and on February 15, Wing Commander L. Crooks (RAF), DSO, DFC, took command.

The Battle of the Ruhr began with a raid against Essen on the night of March 5/6 1943. Essen had always been a main target for Bomber Command and had been raided many times during the preceding three years. 'Butcher' Harris was now ready. The second raid was prepared for March 7/8 but was abandoned because of bad weather and the second raid came on the night of March 12/13 when 457 aircraft were despatched; again the Dishforth squadrons participated.

Sergeant J. Gilles Lamontagne, in Wellington *BK340 T* of 425 Squadron, took part in the second raid and had successfully bombed Essen and was going all-out for Dishforth when he ran into trouble. He had just reached the one-time Dutch border when the Wellington was attacked from below and behind by an unidentified night fighter. Lamontagne had no time to take evasive action and, immediately the night fighter passed, fire broke out in the cockpit and in the bomb-aimer's position. Sergeant Lamontagne remained in control while other crew members set about extinguishing the flames but, before they had a chance to do so, the night fighter struck again and another fire started amidships. This time the extinguisher fluid ran out but the bomb-aimer, Flight Sergeant J.A.V. Gauthier, managed to beat out the flames with his hands. However, their luck did not hold for the fighter administered the coup de grace with a third attack. This left the Wellington blazing furiously and with crippled elevator controls.

Seeing they had no chance of saving their aircraft, Sergeant Lamontagne ordered his crew to bale-out while he fought to keep the doomed bomber steady. As all too often happened, the escape hatch jammed with the heat and Flight Sergeant A.W. Brown, the navigator, had to hack it open with an axe. The bomber struck the ground 20 miles north-east of Altmark near Spaabruck, Holland, and the crew landed safely on Dutch soil. However, all but Lamontagne were apprehended the next morning by the Gestapo. Once on the ground Lamontagne found himself separated from his crew for he had been the last one to leave the aircraft. He tried to hide as best he could, but after a couple of days he too was apprehended by the

Gestapo and taken to a concentration camp. What a world away Dishforth seemed now.

Lamontagne, Brown and Gauthier remained fellow prisoners for more than two years. Flight Sergeant M.J.A.J. Aumond, gunner, and Sergeant J.R.A. Goulet, wireless operator, who had both been severely wounded, were repatriated before the war's end. Sergeant Lamontagne was a PoW in Stalag Luft III and VI under Stalag Camp 357. He was liberated on May 6 1945, during the so-called 'Death March', by a British armoured division, north-east of Hamburg going towards Lubeck. When the Royal Canadian Air Force learned the details of his actions that March night, he was Mentioned in Despatches in the King's New Year's Honours List of 1945. Following the February 1980 elections in Canada, The Honourable J. Gilles Lamontagne of Quebec City was appointed the new Minister of National Defence. He could now take an active part in the freedom he so gallantly fought for.

During April both units received Wellington B Mk Xs and at the end of the month 425 Squadron became non-operational. It then moved to North Africa on May 15 1943. The Oxfords of 1512 BAT Flight then moved to Banff, Scotland, on May 25 and on June 17 426 Squadron moved to No 62 (RCAF) Base, Linton-on-Ouse, Dishforth closing so that runways could be laid and the airfield enlarged in preparation for four-engined bombers.

When Dishforth re-opened in November 1943 it had the usual three runways, the main one being 5,900 ft long and parallel to the Great North Road. The

Dishforth—425 Squadron RCAF. Wellington BK340 T of Sergeant Lamontagne.

two intersecting runways were each 4,400 ft long and linked by a perimeter track. Other buildings had also been erected on the technical site behind the original hangars.

The first unit to arrive was the headquarters of No 331 (Medium Bomber) Wing and No 425 Squadron from Hani East Landing Ground, Tunisia, on November 6. No 425 Squadron rejoined 6 Group, re-equipped with Halifax IIIs and, after a short leave break, moved to No 62 (RCAF) Base, Tholthorpe, on December 9 1943. Two days earlier No 1664 Heavy Conversion Unit had arrived from Croft and this became the resident unit. The role of the station was to be the training of bomber crews. December also saw other changes for, on the 18th of the month, No 331 (Medium Bomber) Wing disbanded, the squadrons having been redeployed within No 6 Group. The Wing had formed on May 7 1943, at West Kirby, Cheshire, with Nos 420, 424 and 425 Squadrons for the invasions of Sicily and Italy. The Wing had dropped 3,745 tons of bombs, plus 1,881 mines, with a loss of 21 aircraft.

There were two very bad crashes during December. On the 2nd, Halifax V *DG282* crashed half a mile south of No 3 runway at 21.31 hours due to steam from a nearby railway—poor visibility on circuit. It was on a training flight from Croft. Five crew were killed and one injured. The second happened just before midnight on the 23rd: Halifax V *EB191* broke up in the air after being abandoned by four crew and crashed into houses near 57 Kent Road, Harrogate, around Oakdale Golf Course and the Power Station. Three crew, Flight Sergeant M.L. John, the pilot, Sergeant C.R. Choma, air gunner, and Sergeant J. Quinn, the flight-engineer, were all killed. Along with many more, all three are buried in the regional cemetry in Harrogate, Yorkshire.

The status of the station at June 6 1944 was No 1664 HCU equipped with Halifaxes as part of No 61 Base, under 6 Group, RCAF. The resident unit was officially nicknamed 'Caribou' on June 21.

Like all the training and conversion units, 'Caribou', had its fair share of accidents. The worst month for the unit was October 1944. On the 2nd, Halifax II *JP204*, piloted by flying Officer J.M. Hamblin, was on cross-country exercise when the aircraft suffered engine fire. Four crew baled out and at 01.55 hours

the aircraft struck the ground half a mile west of Galphay, near Ripon. Three survived from the eight-man crew. On the 10th, Halifax II *HR802* went missing with all crew and was never heard of again. The 17th saw two crashes, the first being at 22.42 hours. Flying Officer R.E. Hutcheon, the pilot of Halifax II *JP197*, opened the bomb-doors instead of raising flaps after take-off for cross-country. The aircraft sank from 300 ft and landed with wheels-up in a field two miles west of Dishforth village. Five crew were killed and two injured. At 23.50 Halifax V *LL240*, piloted by Flying Officer G.J. Strickland, took off on cross-country exercise but crashed four miles west of the airfield. All seven crew were killed. At 21.00 hours on the 29th of the month, Halifax V *DK115*, piloted by Pilot Officer M.W. Rohalack, swung on landing while doing circuits and bumps. The crew were safe but the aircraft was written off. The last crash of the month was at 17.50 hours on the 30th when the starboard inner engine of Halifax V *LL151* caught fire while taxiing after an air-to-air firing and bombing exercise. All crew were safe but the aircraft was a write-off.

January 1945 saw the Halifax Mk III enter service with the HCU, and the arrival of No 1695 BDT Flight. On April 6 1945, No 1664 HCU disbanded at Dishforth and the following month No 1695 BDT Flight moved out.

After the hostilities ended in Europe Dishforth was transferred to Transport Command in August 1945 and continued in the training role. Transport Command now required many crews to cope with the movements of returning troops and it was Dishforth's duty to supply them. Forty-five ex-Bomber Command crews were always under conversion training at any one time. On completion of their nine-week course they would be posted into squadrons of the Command. During the first week of November 1945, No 1332 Transport Conversion Unit arrived from Riccall and took over the aircraft of 1659 and 1665 HTCUs. The Liberators and Yorks of 1332 Transport Conversion Unit were coded 'YY' and this unit was training crews for the long-distance transport routes.

During this early post-war period Group Captain Des Scott, DSO, OBE, DFC and Bar, Commander Order Oranje Nassau, Croix de Guerre and Palm (French), Croix de Guerre and Palm (Belgian), took command of Dishforth, having previously been commanding officer of No 123 Rocket Firing Typhoon Wing which he had led to Normandy, through France and the Low Countries and including the Ardennes counter-offensive. Group Captain Scott was mentally and physically exhausted. Having more than earned an easier seat he was looking forward to his new post. However, due to the effects of demobilisation on the station strength, commanding Dishforth was like holding a tiger by the tail. Keeping the Yorks and Liberators serviceable with ground staff that was forever changing proved a major headache. Skilled technicians and cooks were demobbed as fast as they were posted in. Also, many aircrew had little time to serve after completion of their conversion course. This was an expensive waste of time and it was reported to higher authority many times but Group Captain Scott's pleas fell on stony ground.

Says Group Captain Scott: 'At 26 I was a young product of the wartime years, a member of the RNZAF and a Group Captain, whose previous appointment had been in the 2nd Tactical Air Force. Perhaps it was this combination that made things so difficult when shaping up to the Higher Staff echelons. No command except Transport seemed to know where it was going and we still had to churn out the crews from a platform that held many fractures, and to a tempo that always required a maximum effort'.

At this time, Dishforth housed a small Prisoner of War camp in the Nissen huts in the south-east corner of the airfield on the left of Boroughbridge road. There were two or three hundred German prisoners who were employed on menial tasks such as removing blackout paint from the many windows of the station's hangars. Having completed this task Group Captain Scott put many of the prisoners on to a large vegetable production programme. The dispersal areas were ploughed up and planted with potatoes and cabbages, which was highly successful.

On Wednesday, June 5 1946, a signal was received at Dishforth that the Commander in Chief, Air Marshall Sir Ralph Cochrane, was on his way and would be spending the day at the station. It is a day Group Captain Scott will always remember for he was about to fly to Epsom for the Derby. Like so many New Zealanders he was a keen follower of the horses and the one he would have backed, the grey horse *Airborne*, won at 50 to 1. To add salt to the wound his batman later told him that he had put £2 each-way on *Airborne* with a local bookmaker.

On May 5 1948, No 1332 (T) CU was redesignated No 241 OCU and tasked with the training of crews for Nos 46, 242, 246 and 511 Squadrons. Dishforth continued in this role then, on October 17 1948, the Halifaxes of 297 Squadron arrived from Fairford. This unit converted to Hastings and moved to Schleswigland on December 13 1948 to take part in the Berlin Airlift.

In January 1950, No 241 OCU moved to Topcliffe and, in April 1951, No 240 OCU arrived from North Luffenham. This unit then combined with 241 from Topcliffe to form 242 OCU at Dishforth and remained here for the next decade. In December 1961, 242 OCU moved to Thorney Island and the airfield was

THE AIRFIELDS

Below left *1946 Derby Day at Dishforth—Cochrane giving the crews a pep talk and the CO, Des Scott, with his tongue out behind him. Cochrane was annoyed with him for not having them in Battledress. Far right Wing Commander Bennett.*

Right *Hastings aircraft on a training flight over Yorkshire with port-outer engine feathered.*

Below *Dishforth 1961. Hastings C1 TG561 in front of No 3 hangar.*

Bottom *Dishforth 1961. Avro Anson T 21, VV323. Hastings in the background.*

Three Beverleys X, Y and Z of Royal Air Force Transport Command seen at Dishforth in 1961.

reduced to Care and Maintenance.

Today, the airfield buildings are used by North Yorkshire Police for training. The airfield is used during weekdays by the Jet Provosts from Leeming. Both the pre- and post-war control towers are still used.

Doncaster, Yorkshire

111/SE590020. SW of racecourse on A638 road

Site of the first British aviation meeting in 1909, Doncaster racecourse was used as a landing ground during the First World War. In between the wars the site was used as a civil airfield and in 1939 it was designated a 'Scatter' field. During the Second World War Doncaster was host to No 7 Aircrew OTU, then the Civil Aircraft Flight of the National Air Communications Unit which became 271 Squadron in 1940. In 1941 No 613 Squadron arrived, and later in the war Wellingtons of 18 OTU from Finningley used Doncaster as a satellite. The field then became a Dakota modification centre. Post-war it was used briefly by No 9 RFS.

For further details see *Action Stations 2.*

Driffield (Eastburn), Yorkshire

106/SE995565. W of Great Driffield between the A166 and A163 roads

One of the early airfields, this site was first used by 'C' Flight of 33 Squadron, Royal Flying Corps, while on Home Defence Duties. Contrary to other material the site was never developed as a permanent aerodrome until 1918. Situated approximately two miles west of the small market town of Great Driffield on the north side of the A163 road, the site extended from Kelleythorpe in the east to

Eastburn in the west, and it was the latter after which it was originally named.

During April 1918, No 3 Fighter School took up residence, but this was only a cadre unit equipped just with an Avro 504 and a Bristol Monoplane. There were no aircraft other than these, no pupils and no instructors, only Captain (later Lord) Balfour who was the Chief Flying Instructor and Commanding Officer.

No 3 FS was the only unit at the airfield and was housed in the one and only temporary hangar. No living quarters were available and Captain Balfour was billeted in Driffield town with a Mr and Mrs Good. Towards the end of May 1918, Captain Balfour moved with No 3 FS to Bircham Newton.

Work now started on the airfield and it officially opened as Eastburn Aerodrome on July 15 1918, when No 21 Training Depot Station was formed here from No 3 Training Squadron, Shoreham, and No 27 Training Squadron, London Colney, with an establishment of 36 SE5as and 36 Avro 504Ks. Even though the airfield was open, it was far from complete and construction work was still in progress with makeshift buildings.

In February 1919, the construction work was finally completed. Eastburn now had seven 170 ft × 100 ft hangars on the southern edge of the airfield which covered an area of 240 acres. On the 24th of the following month, No 202 Squadron arrived and was followed four days later by No 217 Squadron with their DH4 aircraft. On October 19 1919, the latter disbanded followed by No 202 on January 22 1920.

The following month No 21 TDS also disbanded and the station was reduced to a Care and Maintenance basis. Eastburn was not scheduled to be retained as a permanent aerodrome and was eventually dismantled some years later.

During the early 1930s the site was surveyed and found suitable to re-activate as an airfield. Although work did not start until the end of 1935, the airfield was one of the 14 listed on the 1935 war map for the north-east. The airfield was planned to the standard pattern with five 'C' type hangars on the eastern side and substantial brick-built administrative buildings, officers' and other ranks' messes and living quarters grouped neatly behind them.

The new airfield, now known as Driffield, opened on July 30 1936, as a bomber station within No 3 Group, under the command of Group Captain Murliss-Green (who later was CO of Digby). The grass airfield was far from complete and the hangars and living quarters were not completed until early 1937.

In September 1936 the first aircraft arrived with Nos 58 and 215 Squadrons from Worthy Down. Their Vickers Virginia biplane bombers touched down on the grass runways and an extensive course of day and night flying training was begun.

Two squadrons re-formed here on March 15 1937. The first was No 51 from 'B' Flight of 58 Squadron, but this moved immediately to Boscombe Down on the 24th of the month along with 58 Squadron. The other squadron to re-form was No 75 from 'B' Flight of No 215 Squadron. 75 Squadron was initially equipped with Virginias and Ansons but later re-equipped with the Handley-Page Harrow. As the build-up continued the station was transferred to No 4 Group on June 29 1937.

There were further changes in July 1938. During the early part of the month 75 Squadron exchanged places with 102 at Honington, Suffolk. In the latter part of the month 215 Squadron also moved to Honington and the Honington-based Wellesleys of 77 Squadron moved to Driffield.

The two resident squadrons began to re-equip with the Armstrong Whitworth Whitley during October and November 1938, and it was with these aircraft they entered the Second World War. Driffield sent some of the first fully operational bomber squadrons to operate against the enemy. Their first operational mission of the war was by No 102 Squadron, coded 'DY', on the night of September 4/5 1939, when three Whitleys dropped 'Nickels' over the Ruhr. 77 Squadron, coded 'KN', repeated the operation on September 5/6 with two of their Whitleys.

Immediately after the outbreak of war Driffield was allocated Cottam as a satellite and Sealand as a scatter airfield for its two Whitley squadrons.

Crashes were numerous for both squadrons but one of the worst was on October 18 1939, when Whitley K8996 of 102 Squadron, with pilots Sergeant H.J. Gaut and Pilot Officer R.A.M. Iluckman, stalled from 100 ft on take-off due to being too heavily loaded, crashed and caught fire. The Whitley was conveying stores and men of 41 Squadron from Catterick to Drem. Seven were killed and two injured, the aircraft being a write-off.

No 77 Squadron has claim to the most unusual incident. It was on March 15/16 1940, during the operation to Warsaw— no mean feat of navigation at this period of the war—that, having dropped its 'Nickels', Whitley N1387 returned safely across Germany. Then, owing to bad weather, it put down in what Flight Lieutenant Tomlin and his crew thought was France. The crew wandered off but after a few words with the local peasants realised their mistake and dashed back to their aircraft. German troops were now approaching and the Whitley took-off under rifle fire and on their last drop of

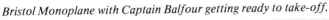

Bristol Monoplane with Captain Balfour getting ready to take-off.

petrol landed safety at Villeneuve airfield in France.

A few days later, on March 28 1940, Whitley *N1357* of 77 Squadron was shot down at 07.00 hours by Dutch aircraft while over Holland. The Air-Observer jumped out at 60 ft and was killed. The burning aircraft force-landed near Rotterdam.

During these early months both Nos 77 and 102 Squadrons had detachments at various times in France and at Kinloss on loan to Coastal Command. On May 1 1940, No 97 Squadron re-formed but disbanded on the 20th of the month. Bomber Command was feeling its way by trial and error and in reply to Italy's declaration of war on June 10 1940, 36 Whitleys of Nos 10, 51, 58 and the two Driffield squadrons made the first raid on Italy. The primary target was the Fiat aero-engine factory at Turin but, after refuelling in the Channel Islands, only ten aircraft reached the target. Owing to severe icing and thunderstorms 23 returned early, five of these from the seven despatched by 102 Squadron. On the 14th of the month No 88 (Hong Kong) Squadron arrived from France where it had been engaged in heavy fighting and had suffered drastic losses. This unit was equipped with Fairey Battles, code letters 'RH', and after a brief stay it moved to

Belfast, Northern Ireland, on the 23rd of the month.

Driffield was becoming one of the most important bomber bases and, at midday on August 15 1940, the enemy, while busily attacking airfields in the south of England, detailed a force of some 50 Ju 88s to wipe out Driffield as a bomber base. The Ju 88s were from Kampfgeschwader 30 and entered just off Flamborough Head during the latter part of the morning. Radar warning was given but the enemy force split into eight groups. The main force attacked Driffield and caused considerable damage; 169 bombs of various calibres were dropped on the airfield. Four hangars and many other buildings were either bombed or raked with cannon fire. Twelve Whitleys of Nos 77 and 102 Squadrons were destroyed and 13 Royal Air Force personnel were killed. The whole airfield was pock-marked with bomb craters causing the station to be non-operational for the remainder of the year while repairs were carried out.

What was left of 102 Squadron moved to Leeming on August 25, and three days later No 77 Squadron moved to Linton-on-Ouse. Repair work now got underway at Driffield. Records also show that Driffield used the decoy airfield at Skipsea and that dummy Whitleys were installed. This decoy was used by Catfoss and I doubt if it was ever used by Driffield for it was over ten miles away from the station. Driffield did have a decoy airfield at Skerne a few miles to the south-west but it obviously had no effect. It is a fact that dummy aircraft were installed at Driffield to cover up after the real aircraft had been withdrawn after the attack. This was the first time that dummies had been used on an airfield, having previously been rejected by all three Commands. The dummy aircraft were being used at Driffield when the Canadians arrived and Edward Curotte recalls camouflaged replicas of Whitleys which were laid on wooden stilts. Their location was varied each night at dispersal points, and from the air they looked like the real thing.

The airfield now had a change of role and when it re-opened in January 1941, No 13 Group, Fighter Command, had taken over. Hurricane Mk Is of No 213 Squadron arrived at Driffield in January

1941 from Leconfield and remained a few weeks before moving out the following month to Castletown. As 213 Squadron departed, No 1 (Fighter) Squadron, RCAF, arrived from Castletown, Scotland, where they had just spent a harsh winter. The Canadians arrived after a long train journey and on arrival found the quarters to which they were assigned had been left in a filthy condition by the outgoing unit. Ex-6106 Edward Curotte, RCAF, recalls his brief stay: 'Driffield aerodrome was "dim and dismal" and the meals matched the atmosphere of the station. They mostly consisted of jaundiced-looking kippers that stared up at you from the table'.

The Canadians were not overjoyed at this transfer and a number of pubs and hotels were posted 'out of bounds', due, they were told, to fifth columnist and spy activity. However, the Canadians were soon on the move and on March 1 1941, No 1 (Fighter) Squadron, Royal Canadian Air Force, moved to Digby, Lincolnshire, where the unit was re-numbered No 401 (Fighter) Squadron.

No 485 Squadron, Royal New Zealand Air Force, was formed here with Spitfire Mk 1s on March 1 1941, and for a few weeks during February and March the airfield was used as a RLG by the Ansons of No 5 SFTS at Tern Hill. The role as a fighter station was now over for Driffield and on April 1 the station was transferred back to No 4 Group, Bomber Command. April 1 also saw 104 Squadron re-form as a Wellington medium-bomber unit, and it was alloted 'EP' as the unit code letters. The Spitfires of 485 Squadron had remained throughout the changes but on April 21 they moved to Leconfield. Two days later No 405 (Vancouver) Squadron, RCAF, was formed, the first Canadian bomber squadron formed overseas. The unit code letters were 'LQ' and it was equipped with Wellington Mk IIs. 104 Squadron was the first to see action and on May 8/9 1941, six Wellingtons were despatched to bomb Bremen but only four bombed the primary target.

On the night of June 12/13, just ten weeks after its birth, 405 Squadron despatched four Wellingtons to bomb the marshalling yards at Schwerte, near Dortmund, Germany. It is interesting to note that the bomb load for each aircraft was one 1,000 lb and four 500 lb bombs and two 750 lb canisters of incendiaries. A far cry from what was to come. This was the RCAF's first bombing mission and all aircraft returned safely. No 405 Squadron moved to Pocklington on June 19 1941 and 104 Squadron continued with the night-bombing offensive against Fortress Europe, but changes were in the wind. In mid-October 1941, 15 Wellingtons and crews plus some ground crew were transferred to Luqa, Malta.

During this period No 2 Beam Approach Training Flight arrived in mid-April 1941, its role being to teach 4 Group operational captains the use of the Standard Beam Approach landing system (The 'Beam'). The course lasted one week, pilots assembling from their various squadrons on Sunday afternoon and returning the following Friday evening. There were four Instructors in addition to the CO. One Instructor was Pilot Officer H.H. Drummond who was posted in from Middleton St George after a tour of ops as Sergeant Pilot with 78 and 76 Squadrons. The CO was Bruce Bintley who was succeeded as CO by John Russell, who later flew one of the BAT Flight Whitleys on the first Thousand Bomber Raid on Cologne, was shot down and taken prisoner. The BAT Flight flew two details each day from Monday to Friday, one in the morning and one in the afternoon. Each period in the air was of 2–2½ hours duration, split equally between two

Driffield, June 12 1941: just ten weeks after its formation No 405 (RCAF) Squadron prepares for its first mission.

It was straight into action for the new squadron and on the night of February 14/15 1942, No 158 made its first operational mission when it dispatched seven Wellingtons to bomb Mannheim. However, this did not take place from Driffield for the runways were unserviceable and Pocklington was used to blood the squadron. All aircraft returned safely. The squadron then stood down from operations in order to convert to Halifaxes at nearby Marston Moor. Despite this they took part in Operation 'Millennium', the first Thousand-Bomber Raid on May 30/31 1942, against Cologne. 158 Squadron supplied nine crews for the main force and despite the raid being a huge success it was not so for 158 Squadron who lost two crews. These were captained by Squadron Leader Harkness and Sergeant O'Brien, RCAF. Of the remaining aircraft only three reached Cologne. A week later the squadron moved to East Moor.

Driffield now began to run down in preparation for reconstruction work. However, on October 15 1942, No 466 Squadron, Royal Australian Air Force, formed here with Wellington Mk III aircraft, code letters 'HD', as a medium-bomber unit under No 4 Group.

A few weeks later, No 196 Squadron formed on November 7 1942. That same month No 2 BAT Flight was redesignated 1502 BAT Flight. The unit later re-equipped with Oxfords. At the end of December 1942, the Wellingtons of 196 Squadron moved to Leconfield along with 466 Squadron and Driffield was again non-operational. The station now closed for the laying of three concrete runways which were 6,000 ft, 4,350 ft and 4,050 ft long with an encircling perimeter track off which were hardstandings of the frying-pan type.

As part of No 4 Group, Driffield became No 43 Base on June 6 1943, with Leconfield and Lissett as Sub-stations. Work was still in progress but during this non-operational period the station was far from idle. No 1502 BAT Flight moved out to Leconfield on July 21 1943, and that same month 1484 TT Flight also vacated the airfield. With the departure of both of these units flying at the station came to a halt. About this period No 4 Group Battle School was started at the station so that experienced pilots could pass on their experience and instruct the pupils on new bombing techniques which Bomber Command was now employing in increasingly

March 1942. Sergeant Pilot Ralph O'Brien, RCAF, poses for the last time. He went missing on the first Thousand-Bomber raid at the end of May 1942.

student pilots, each of whom received about ten hours' flying instruction during the course in addition to periods on the Link Trainer and ground lectures. All instruction was given on Whitley Vs which were still the main type in use in 4 Group at that time. The Whitleys used were *N1471, N1469, N1477, N1504, P4969, P4988* and *T4214*. The unit flew in all types of weather, the only limitations being that horizontal visibility at ground level had to be at least 1,500 ft and the cloud base no lower than 500 ft.

In October 1941, No 4 Group Target Towing Flight also took up residence with a motley collection of Whitleys, Lysanders and Battles. The following month the unit became No 1484 Target Towing Flight. Meanwhile, the home echelon of 104 Squadron continued to operate from Driffield for a while then, on February 14 1942, No 158 Squadron re-formed from the home echelon of 104 (B) Squadron. The new squadron was equipped with Wellington Mk IIs, the unit code letters being 'NP'.

heavy raids on Germany.

Also during this non-operational period, many crews were posted in from No 10 Operational Training Unit at Abingdon, Berkshire, and on reporting at Driffield were placed under the instruction of a section of the King's Own Yorkshire Light Infantry and told that for the duration of the course all rank was to be disregarded. The RAF members, who numbered approximately 60 aircrew, accepted this with a smile, but when they each received a rifle, bayonet, webbing, back-packs and other accoutrements, and were advised that one must always move at the double, it was a different story. Over the next few weeks, they climbed over high brick walls, jumped great ditches full of icy water and mud, crawled under low bridges, fixed bayonets and charged madly at straw dummies and screamed like banshees.

After charging about the Yorkshire countryside, day after day, in wind, rain and snow, Flight Sergeant Doug Bancroft and his crew were relieved (and exhausted) to be posted to the Halifax Conversion Unit at Rufforth. The reason they were given for the commando battle course at Driffield was that at some future date they might be called upon to land troops and assist in the securing of airfields from which to operate. They might also be required to hold airfields whilst landings were taking place. Also, they might become involved in glider-towing details.

During April 1944 the Heavy Conversion Units of 4 Group began to use the airfield and in early June 466 Squadron returned to Driffield and the station was again operational. This unit was now equipped with Halifax BIIIs with the more powerful engine, and remained here for the duration of the European War. The status of the station at June 6 1944, was 466 Squadron, RAAF, in No 4 Group, and D-Day saw Driffield's Halifaxes supporting operation 'Overlord' and bombing targets in Normandy.

August 1944 saw the arrival of a second RAAF squadron when Halifaxes of 614 (B) Squadron arrived from Celone, Italy, and on August 12, No 462, RAAF, re-formed here as a heavy-bomber squadron in No 4 Group.

Equipped with Halifax B III aircraft, code letters 'Z5', it operated with its sister unit, No 466, as part of the Main Force on day and night bombing operations. These included the oil targets and an attack on the German garrison at Le Havre. During the afternoon of September 10 1944, 16 Halifaxes from 462 Squadron and 14 from 466 made up the small force of 69 aircraft that attacked a coastal defence battery. This attack was immediately followed by 930 heavy-bombers with 4,700 tons of bombs. Smoke and a great dust cloud hung over Le Havre but the task was not yet done and on the final raid on September 11, the Driffield squadrons each despatched 11 Halifaxes to make up the total force of 218. Ten hours after this final attack by Bomber Command the German garrison at Le Havre capitulated to two Allied divisions. Later the squadrons took part in the bombing of the German stronghold on the flooded island of Walcheren in the Dutch Scheldt. Then, during November 1944, back again to Germany when attacks were made on Duisburg by the Driffield squadrons. Essen was also a target and during one raid a Lancaster collided with the Halifax of Flight Sergeant Grace, a bomb-aimer of 462 Squadron. On impact he lost consciousness, but as he fell through space he recovered and managed to pull his rip-cord; the remainder of his crew perished.

Towards the end of 1944, during the height of the 'Battle of the Bulge' in the Ardennes, 462 Squadron was screened from operations pending a move for Special Duties with No 100 Group, which was responsible for radio counter-measures and bomber support duties. Then, on December 27, No 462 Squadron moved to Foulsham, Norfolk, leaving 466 to continue with the 'Battle of the Bulge'. Having failed to secure either Malmedy or Bastogne, the Germans were forced to push all their main road traffic through St Vith and Bomber Command was given the task of destroying this hub of communications. 466 took part in the St Vith raid on December 26 1944. The ground was pure white with snow and the whole area was covered with vehicles. With no opposition the Master Bomber called to the bomber force to take their time and the crews reported 'It was a picnic'. St Vith was blocked and the whole area around the town deeply cratered.

During January 1945, Bomber Command dropped more than 7,000 tons of bombs on specific railway targets in nine night and seven day attacks. 466 Squadron played its part and 16 crews from Driffield on January 28/29 bombed the Kornwestheim marshalling yards at

Stuttgart the same time as a much larger attack was made on the city that night.

For 466 Squadron, the last operational mission of the war came on April 25 1945, when 18 of its Halifaxes bombed gun batteries on the island of Wangerooge. On May 7 it was transferred to Transport Command and re-equipped with 20 Halifax B VIs from Leconfield.

Many Halifaxes were now redundant and in the process of being moved to storage bases and eventually reduced to scrap. However, for Halifax B Mk III *NR169*, there was hope and it was purchased by Captain Geoffrey Wikner, ATA, and flown to Australia. The legend *Waltzing Matilda* with her 51 bombs remained on the nose of the aircraft and were supplemented by the dove of peace to represent its peaceful flight to Australia. The 466 code letters had been overpainted with the civil registration *G-AGXA* and all wartime armour was stripped out. After nine months of red tape *Waltzing Matilda* took off on May 26 1946 and. after 71 hours' flying time, arrived at Mascot, Sydney, Australia. The Australians had never seen a Handley Page Halifax bomber, but Captain Wikner could not get support for the exhibition flight and had to sell the aircraft. The RAAF did not want it so it was advertised, but with no success; and it was even offered to the Canberra War Museum as a gift, but was not accepted. Finally it was sold for trading with the Far East but after only one flight the company went into liquidation and *Waltzing Matilda* was sold by auction to a scrap dealer. I mention the fate of this aircraft to show why there are so few World War 2 aircraft left today. Such reward for

faithful service, such patriotism, such short memories.

On May 25, No 426 Squadron, RCAF, arrived from Linton-on-Ouse having just been transferred to No 47 Group, Transport Command. This unit remained only a few weeks and, on June 24 1945, moved to Tempsford, Bedfordshire, where it completed its transfer to the Consolidated Liberator after having received one or two while at Driffield. No 466 also moved out to take up transport duties and, by the end of June 1945, the station was reduced to Care and Maintenance. For over 12 months its fate hung in the balance then, in September 1946, the station re-opened with the arrival of No 10 Air Navigation School under Flying Training Command. This unit was equipped with Ansons and Wellington Mk Xs and XIIIs which had the new four-letter codes. The Commanding Officer of the unit was Wing Commander Strong who arrived in his own Magister aircraft.

During March 1948, No 10 ANS disbanded and Driffield transferred from No 21 to No 25 Group in Flying Training Command. On the 10th of the month No 204 Advanced Flying School arrived from Cottesmore with their Mosquito Mark 6s. This unit moved to Brize Norton during August 1949. That same month Gloster Meteor T7 aircraft arrived at Driffield. These were for No 203 Advanced Flying School which had arrived in mid-July to replace 204 AFS, and this unit was to be the Royal Air Force's first jet flying training school. Introduction on the twin-seater jet trainer meant that after completing 200 hours' flying in Prentices and Harvards, pupils could miss out the advanced piston-engined aircraft, like the

Consolidated Liberators C Mk VIII of No 426 (T) Squadron at Driffield. Although 426 Squadron was officially disbanded on January 1 1946, personnel volunteering for further service were assigned along with the squadron's aircraft to an RAF Liberator squadron at Tempsford.

Spitfire, and graduate straight to jets. The pupil would then go on to an Operational Conversion Unit. The station became settled in this role for the next five years and the jets screamed relentlessly over the moors. In June 1954, No 203 AFS was redesignated No 8 Flying Training School and during the early part of July 1955 it moved to Swinderby, Lincolnshire.

Driffield once again had a change of role and, on September 5 1955, it was transferred to No 13 Group, Fighter Command. That same day No 219 Squadron re-formed with Venom NF3 aircraft and became the resident unit. It was joined by a second Venom unit when No 33 Squadron re-formed on October 15 of that year. However, the life of both units was short and, on June 3 1957, No 33 disbanded, to be followed by No 219 at the end of the following month.

Driffield then housed the Fighter Weapons School which arrived from nearby Leconfield in October 1957. This unit had various fighter aircraft and remained here until March 1958 when the airfield was again reduced to Care and Maintenance. Driffield had been selected as a site headquarters for a Thor missile complex, which consisted of a main Headquarters site and four satellites, Full Sutton, Carnaby, Catfoss and Breighton, each with three missiles.

Driffield re-opened in that capacity in October 1958, and on the 16th of the month was transferred to No 1 Group, Bomber Command. On November 1, No 98 Squadron re-formed as a Thor IRBM unit. The Thor missiles were ferried in to the parent station by Douglas C-124 Globemasters. However, this was a very short role and, by 1963, the tactical situation had changed. The Thor units were disbanded and the missiles returned to the United States. Driffield closed and in December 1963 the station was again placed on Care and Maintenance, while the married quarters were used by Royal Air Force Leconfield.

From September 1967 to February 1968 Driffield was used as a flight test base by Hawker Siddeley whilst their own test airfield at Holme-on-Spalding Moor had the runways resurfaced. During this period Buccaneer aircraft were test-flown from Driffield. The production batch of *XV352* to *XV360* made their maiden flights from Driffield, having been towed there by road. After Hawker Siddeley had vacated the airfield it was once again reduced to Care and Maintenance. The

Water tower at Driffield.

airfield took on an abandoned look and remained unwanted for almost a decade.

Driffield, where it all began so many years ago, was transferred to the Army on January 1 1977, and re-named Alamein Barracks. On April 1 1977, the Army School of Mechanical Transport formed here and it now houses 32 Junior Leaders Squadron, Royal Corps of Transport, and a Support Flight, Royal Air Force.

Many wartime buildings still remain, including the Fort-type control tower, but the airfield has been converted into a cross-country driving circuit. The barracks are at present used as administrative accommodation for the resident units and will remain so for the forseeable future.

The hangars have been converted to grain stores and have been leased to the Agricultural Produce Intervention Board, and in 1980 were filled with tons of grain. Like Manby, they now form part of the 'grain mountain'. The hangars have been wind- and rain-proofed. Also, sophisticated temperature and airing techniques are used to keep the grain in peak condition. These hangars, conceived in wartime to house the bombers that sowed the seeds of death, now in peacetime house the seeds of life.

Dunkeswick, Yorkshire.

104/SE 305470. Midway between Harro-gate and Leeds.

A World War 1 site that was situated to the north of Leeds on the west side of the A61 and north of the A659 road, this was only a grass field that covered an area of 40 acres and was used as a landing ground by 'B' Flight, No 33 Squadron, Royal Flying Corps, between March and October 1916. The site was also used by 76 Squadron during their patrols in this area but it was never developed and has no further aviation connection.

Eastburn (Driffield), Yorkshire

See Driffield

East Moor, Yorkshire.

100/SE 600640. N of York. Turn E off B1363 road at Sutton-on-the-Forest

During the Second World War many sites were surveyed for possible bomber airfields. One such site was Strenstall, but it was abandonded because of nearby rivers and becks. However, a few miles to the north-west of it another site was found and the airfield was built on East Moor, after which it was named, the nearest village being Sutton-on-the-Forest on the north-west corner of the airfield. To the north and east lay Whitecarr Beck and the River Foss.

It was built to the standard pattern of the period with three concrete runways, 4,620 ft, 4,290 ft and 5,610 ft long laid out to the standard triangular pattern, and encircled by a perimeter track off which were frying-pan type hardstandings to the

north, east and south. The administrative site and sick quarters site were to the west of the airfield. Eventually there were three 'T2' hangars type 3653/42 with provision for a fourth on the western side.

East Moor opened at the beginning of June 1942, as a bomber station in No 4 Group, Bomber Command, and on June 6 No 158 Squadron arrived from Driffield. This unit had just started to re-equip with Halifax B IIs and was to remain here only a few months for East Moor had earmarked for the Canadians.

During the first few weeks the squadron was stood down in order to convert to the four-engined Halifax. This was done at Marston Moor and here at East Moor where a Squadron Conversion Flight under Squadron Leader Wilkerson had been established immediately upon their arrival. The ground crews had been working with 35 Squadron, to gain experience. During September 1942, 158 Squadron Conversion Flight moved to Rufforth. However, during their conversion period the squadron was called upon to put up 14 Halifaxes for the third Thousand-Bomber raid. They managed only 11 but this was their first mission with the Halifax and all returned safely to East Moor.

Other raids followed, to Wilhelmshaven, Duisburg, Bochum and Karlsruhe to name but a few on their list. During their brief stay at East Moor the squadron had taken part in 45 bombing raids in which they lost 16 aircraft over enemy territory from which 68 aircrew were killed. At the end of October 158 Squadron moved to Rufforth.

On November 7 1942, No 429 (Bison) Squadron formed as a bomber unit of No 4 Group. Equipped with Wellington Mk

East Moor—the derelict Nissen hut of the Officers' Mess on the WAAF site photographed September 1979.

IIIs, unit code 'AL', this was the tenth Canadian bomber squadron formed overseas. In January 1943, the unit began to re-equip with Wellington Mk Xs. That same month it was adopted by the City of Bradford, Yorkshire, and its unofficial name became 'Bradford's Own Squadron.'

The station and its units were transferred to No 6 (RCAF) Group on April 1 1943 and East Moor became No 62 (RCAF) Base. The following month, on May 20, No 1679 Heavy Conversion Unit formed at East Moor with an establishment of Lancaster B Mk II aircraft. The role of this unit was to provide conversion training on the Lancaster Mk II for 408, 426 and 432 Squadrons of No 6 Group. Of the 300 Lancaster Mark IIs that were built about 125 were used by the three Canadian squadrons. The Lancaster IIs delivered to 6 Group were in the serial blocks *DS632-852* and *LL617-725*. With these Lancaster IIs the Canadians played a major role in the Battle of Berlin.

The Canadians were now building up their Group and squadrons were moved around to find their permanent bases. 429 Squadron moved to Leeming, No 63 (RCAF) Base, on August 12 and was replaced by 432 (Leaside) Squadron which arrived from Skipton-on-Swale on September 19 1943.

No 432 Squadron became the main resident unit and, during October 1943, it converted to Lancaster Mk IIs, which were powered by Bristol Hercules engines and not the usual Rolls-Royce in-line Merlins. The 'Leaside' Squadron soon worked up to operations and on November 26/27 put up ten Lancasters for their first Berlin operation, from which all aircraft returned safely. Having completed their

task at East Moor 1679 HCU moved to Wombleton on December 13 1943.

To open the New Year the German night fighters were out in force but Lancaster *DS792* 'U'-Uncle survived an attack by a Bf 110 and in the combat that followed the two Canadian gunners had the satisfaction of seeing the German fighter go down in flames. But, the bomber had been damaged for the fighter had scored numerous hits with cannon shells and machine-gun bullets. However the pilot brought it out of its death dive and nursed the crippled bomber back to base. On landing it was found that every propeller blade had at least one bullet hole and there were five large holes in the fuselage.

During February 1944, 432 Squadron began to convert to Halifax Mk IIIs and the following July to Halifax Mk VIIs. The resident unit was joined by No 415 (Swordfish) Squadron, RCAF, from Bircham Newton on July 26 1944, and East Moor became a two-squadron base. Equipped with Halifax Mk IIIs, the unit code letters were changed to 'GU'. The squadron was previously coded 'GX' and 'NH' when with Coastal Command. Having transferred to Bomber Command, the squadron now assumed a heavy-bomber role and its first mission in that capacity was on July 28/29 1944, when 16 Halifaxes were despatched to bomb Hamburg. One aircraft crashed on take-off, crew safe, 14 bombed the primary target and one failed to return.

Over the next nine months both units attacked strategic and tactical targets. As with all squadrons, take-off was always a problem and the Canadians were no exception. On July 28 1944, Halifax *MZ686* of 415 Squadron was about to take-off at 22.18 hours when an engine caught fire as it thundered down the

East Moor's wartime control tower overgrown and derelict in September 1979.

runway. The aircraft swung and burst into flames. The crew escaped before the bombs exploded. At 01.06 hours on August 6 1944, Halifax *NA517* of 415 Squadron overshot with a full bomb load and the undercarriage collapsed. Two nights later, *LW552*, also of 415 Squadron, overshot on take-off. The pilot, Pilot Officer A.W. Tinmouth, throttled back and the bomber overshot across two fields. All seven crew were unhurt. On August 21, Halifax *MZ633* piloted by Squadron Leader B.S. Wilmot, collided at 18.20 hours with Halifax *NA609*, piloted by Wing Commander J.G. McNeill. The starboard inner propeller broke off *'609* during unauthorised close formation flying with *'633*; *'609* then swung and hit the other bomber which immediately caught fire. Both aircraft crashed between Birkin and West Haddlesey, Yorkshire. Seven were killed in each aircraft, both of which were from 415 Squadron.

On February 9 1945, Halifax *NP682* from 426 Squadron was taking off for operations but, due to engine failure, the pilot, Flying Officer J.D. Wadleigh, failed to maintain height and it crashed at 02.50 hours near Wetherby. Its bomb load exploded, killing five and injuring two.

In March 1945, No 415 received six B Mk VIIs but the war was at an end. The last mission of the war for both units was on April 25 1945. 415 Squadron despatched 18 Halifaxes and 432 Squadron 19 Halifaxes to bomb gun positions on the Island of Wangerooge.

Both Canadian units disbanded at East Moor on May 15 1945. 415 Squadron had flown 1,608 bomber sorties and lost 22 aircraft, 151 aircrew killed, missing or prisoners of war. Awards won were one DSO, one Bar to DFC, 86 DFCs, one GM and nine DFMs. 432 Squadron had flown 3,130 sorties and in so doing lost 73 aircraft, 448 aircrew, of whom 30 were killed, eight missing, 252 presumed dead, 123 PoW (five escaped) and 35 evaded capture. The 'Leasides' collected 144 decorations and several other honours, including two DSOs, one CGM, one Bar to the DFC, 119 DFCs, 20 DFMs, one Croix de Guerre and a number of Mentions in Despatches. A proud record of a job well done and our Colonial Cousins could return home in triumph.

On May 1 1945, No 54 Operational Training Unit moved in from Charterhall, flying Mosquito NF30s whose code letters were 'LX'. The role of the unit was to train night fighter crews and Croft was used as a satellite. During this period 288 Squadron arrived from Hutton Cranswick on May 24 1946. Flying Vengeance aircraft, this was to be their last station and on June 15 1946 the unit disbanded. East Moor had also outlived its usefulness and, on June 24 1946, the OTU moved out to Leeming and the airfield closed

Over the years the airfield has slowly been returned to agriculture. In 1979 the tower still stood in a derelict state and was being used by the local farmer for storage of hay. The bomb dump site is used for pheasant breeding and the technical site as a piggery. Some of the runways have been broken up and the main one reduced to 1,000 ft. The north-east runway section is now built on for poultry rearing. All hangars have gone and the few remaining buildings are rapidly becoming mere heaps of rubble.

Ecclesfield, Yorkshire
111/SK 365940. N of Sheffield

This was a small and unimportant site that was brought into use as a landing ground and was used by 'A' Flight of 33 Squadron, Royal Flying Corps, during March to October 1916. No buildings were ever erected and the site was quickly abandoned. Now part of Sheffield and completely built up, it would be difficult to land a model aircraft never mind a BE2C of the early days.

Elvington, Yorkshire
105/SE 665480. 7 miles SE of York on the B1228 road

This heathland area on Langwith Common was chosen to be the location of a bomber airfield for No 4 Group. It was constructed as a grass airfield in 1940 but by that time the concept of operating bombers from grass surfaces was already outdated, so it was obsolete on completion and was never used in its original form.

The airfield was completely rebuilt and Elvington eventually opened in October 1942 as a Sub-station to Pocklington in No 4 Group, Bomber Command. It was sited between Grimston Wood in the north and Black Plantation in the south. There were two runways, the ends of which were joined by cinder paths that ran through the woods to the dispersed hard-standings. The technical site and other main buildings lay to the east of the airfield. The hangars were two 'T2's and a 'B1'.

The first arrivals were the Whitleys of No 77 Squadron which arrived in October 1942. This unit had been on detachment to Coastal Command at Chivenor and upon arrival at Elvington it immediately began to convert to Halifax BIIs in which it carried the war into Germany from their Yorkshire base.

The squadron took part in the main force targets and was fully operational with Halifaxes to take a major role in the Battle of the Ruhr, during the early part of 1943. Towards the end of the year the unit began to receive Halifax Vs. In May 1944, No 77 Squadron moved to the new airfield at Full Sutton.

Two heavy-bomber squadrons of the French Air Force were then formed at Elvington. The first was No 346 (Guyenne) Squadron, FAF, which formed on May 16 1944, with an establishment of Halifax Vs, unit code letters 'H7'. The second was No 347 (Tunisie) Squadron, FAF, and it formed on June 20 1944, also with Halifax Vs and code letters 'L8'.

For both units the commanding officers and aircrew were French, many of whom had previously served with the French Air Force in North Africa, but the adjutant was English. Otherwise, Elvington was exclusively French even down to the fact that every man had a right to a glass of Algerian wine with each meal. The cooks were also French but the food remained British.

No 346 Squadron began operations on June 1 1944 when 11 Halifaxes bombed the radar station at Ferm d'Urville and one aborted. No 347's first mission was a few weeks later on the 27/28th of the month when 11 Halifaxes bombed a V-weapon site at Mont Candon, and again one aborted.

During July both units switched to Halifax IIIs and continued operations with these. On September 10 1944, Halifax III *NA585* of 346 Squadron was returning from a raid on Octeville with a hung-up 1,000-lb bomb. Once the bombs were released the bomb-aimer made certain that all the lamps on his indicator dials—showing the presence of bombs—did not light up. Many on the return journey over the sea opened the bomb doors and checked again. Some, when making this check, asked the pilot to shake the aircraft in order to dislodge any bomb that might have got stuck. Despite all these precautions one remained and on touch-down dropped out and exploded. Six crew were killed but the pilot was blown clear with injuries.

A brief switch in duties came a few days later and, from September 25 to October 2, No 346 Squadron made 108 sorties and ferried 80,875 gallons of petrol from Elvington to Brussels for the 2nd Army. No 347 Squadron also ferried the much-needed petrol and made 113 sorties with 84,850 gallons.

After their transport duties both units resumed the bombing offensive. Security was usually very good, an example being on October 14 1944: 15 Halifaxes from 'Guyenne' squadron took off at dawn and headed for Duisberg. They had only been left a short while before squadron commanders were again in a huddle for a second raid. As they returned they had no idea that the target for the second wave was Duisberg, and those in the second wave had no idea where the first ones had returned from. Some had found out for they made up the numbers and were also in on the second raid

At 14.10 hours on December 28 1944, a bomb fell from the rack of Halifax *NA174* during bombing up and exploded, setting off the main load plus incendiaries. 13 were killed and five injured.

On January 13 1945, Halifax *LL590* of

Elvington in May 1980 showing the post-war control tower which is still used by the RAF.

347 Squadron collided with *MZ465* at 20.10 hours. Four crew managed to bale out before the aircraft crashed. Ten days later, Halifax *LL587* of 347 Squadron was returning from ops when the port-inner engine caught fire while at 7,000 ft. The crew abandoned the aircraft which crashed at Cranford, Northants. Two of the crew were killed.

On the night of March 3/4 1945, a Luftwaffe intruder force attacked the Halifax aircraft while in the circuit at Elvington. The German radio had threatened this raid for a long time and had even mentioned the Fighting French at Elvington. The threats were soon forgotten and at this period of the war observations were relaxed. Ju 88s and 188s slipped in with the bomber stream as the No 4 Group Halifaxes returned from a raid against Kamen, a Fisher-Tropsch plant and one of the Bomber Command's original oil targets. They had met very little opposition and the Halifax crews were returning triumphantly when they were surprised over their own base.

As the airfield lights came on and the crews switched on their navigation lights the Luftwaffe pounced like vultures in for the kill. 'Bandits! Bandits!' Suddenly all airfield lights went out and the Halifax crews were warned by radio to go to their diversion airfields. One Halifax was shot down north-west of the airfield. Some just ran out of fuel and crash-landed while some preferred to wait in the air for the all clear, but most managed to land at the diversion airfield at Croft.

The Luftwaffe had a field-day and to hide its embarrassment no figures were ever published by Bomber Command. At the time it was estimated 70 bombers were brought down over England from the 210 returning from Kamen. The Luftwaffe lost only seven from an estimated force of 70. However, no-one will ever know the real figures but it is certain they were bad for Bomber Command.

During March 1945, both units began to receive Halifax VIs, but the war was nearly over and their last mission was on April 25 1945, 18 Halifaxes from No 346 and 12 from No 347 being despatched to bomb gun batteries on the island of Wangerooge. One failed to return from 347 Squadron.

After the war both units were employed in the dumping of unwanted bomb stocks. During June it was intended to re-equip both squadrons with Liberators for the transport role but this did not materialise and they came under the operational control of No 1 Group. Both units were also detached from Elvington for transport duties in France. Finally, in October 1945, the two FAF squadrons ceased to be part of the Royal Air Force and left Elvington for Bordeaux, France, taking with them many of their Halifaxes which had been presented to France by the British Government. Sadly, this peacetime transfer ended in tragedy for Halifax *RG561* was not to make it to the French Air Force. On October 29, pilot P. Roque lost control temporarily after a shudder at 800 ft. The starboard-outer engine then caught fire and this spread to the airframe. The navigator baled out but it was too low and he was killed. At 12.06 hours the aircraft force-landed at Sheep

Elvington 1979—memorial to FFA Squadrons Nos 346 and 347. It depicts a Halifax bomber in silhouette and has the French Tricolor and the Cross of Lorraine carved in the supporters.

Walk Farm, Deighton, Yorkshire. Two were killed, eight injured and two were OK.

For a short period No 4 Group Communications Flight was at the station before moving in July 1945 to a more permanent base at Full Sutton. After their departure Elvington was reduced to Care and Maintenance on November 15 1945. The station was then transferred to No 40 Group, Maintenance Command, on January 31 1946, becoming a Sub-station for No 14 MU, Carlisle.

The station remained in this role until 1952. Then, during the expansion programme of the 1950s for both the 3rd AF and 7th Air Division (SAC) bases, Elvington was earmarked for this purpose. It was announced that the US would be spending $33,653,000 (£11,018,900) on 19 US Service bases in Britain. In June 1953, the airfield was allocated to the United States Air Force and, in January 1954, American units moved into Elvington and major reconstruction work was carried out which included extending and strengthening one of the runways to take the new Douglas B-66 and RB-66 Destroyer aircraft. The other runways were removed and the hardcore used to build a vast apron to hold the United States Air Force jets. Also constructed was a modern red-brick headquarters building and control tower about halfway along the new runway. However, a change in policy caused the airfield to be completely vacated by the United States Air Force by the end of December 1958.

The extended runway, some 9,800 ft in length and on an east-west axis, was never used and the improved facilities were wasted; $2,038,000 (£724,000) had been spent for the main construction work. However, during the early 1960s the airfield was used as a Relief Landing Ground for No 7 Flying Training School at Church Fenton and remained as such until 1970. It then became a RLG for the Jet Provosts of No 1 Flying Training School at Linton-on-Ouse and is still used as such.

During a visit in 1980 the old main entrance was still well-kept and many of the wartime buildings still remained on the technical site. In the south-east corner of the airfield around Elvington Grange a few of the dispersed sites are still intact and used by farmers. The three hangars remain and one of the 'T2's has been modernised with red brick. The wartime control tower, type 4533-32/43, was also derelict but in fair condition. The airfield is still used by the Royal Air Force for surplus from Linton-on-Ouse, but they now only control the post-war control tower which is used during weekdays, the runway, a building that is used as a mess and rest room and another building for the radio section. The rest of the site has been returned to the farmers.

A reminder of those wartime days can be found about 600 ft north of the old main gate where a polished granite memorial has been erected to the Free French Air Force squadrons which served at Elvington.

Farsley, Yorkshire
104/SE210350. NW of Leeds

A primitive grass strip, Farsley was used by 'B' Flight, 33 Squadron, Royal Flying Corps, from March to October 1916 during the defence of Leeds and was one of three such sites around the city. The site was restricted and never developed but its location possibly led to the site a few miles to the north being opened as Yeadon which today is the Leeds/ Bradford airport.

Finningley, Yorkshire
111/SK665980. SE of Doncaster, to W of Finningley village

Finningley was one of the airfields planned for Eastern England during the Expansion period of the RAF in the mid-1930s. In September 1935, 433 acres of farm land were compulsorily purchased for £11,584. Crops were to be harvested with all speed and work quickly started to level and seed the site with special grass to make it into an airfield. Construction work began almost immediately and brick-built accommodation typical of the period was constructed, mainly in the north-west corner of the site behind an arc of five 'C' type, ten-bay hipped hangars. The airfield was sited between the main A638 and A614 roads, almost on the border of Yorkshire and Nottinghamshire and only a mile or so from the World War 1 site of Brancroft. Reflecting its location, the station badge was to be the white rose of York and a sprig of oak; its motto 'Usque ad coelum fines' meaning 'To the furthest reaches of the skies'.

An advance party of one officer and 40

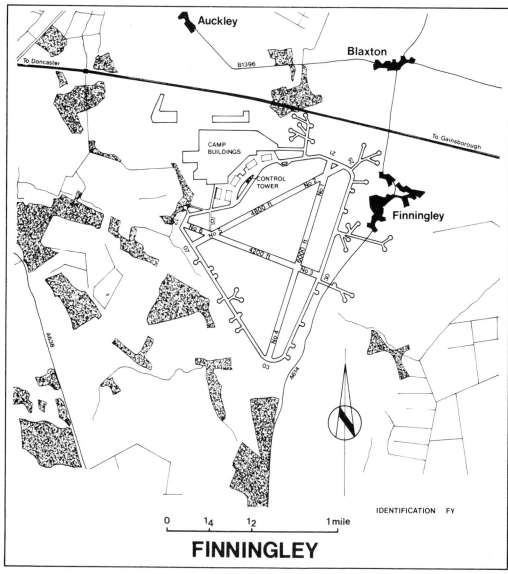

FINNINGLEY

men moved into Finningley on July 30 1936, to prepare the station and, in August, Wing Commander A.N. Gallehawk took up his post as the first Commanding Officer. The first aircraft arrived from Worthy Down on August 31, followed a few days later by the remaining Handley Page Heyfords of No 102 Squadron, which had just re-formed. That same month, No 7 Squadron also moved to Finningley from Worthy Down.

The airfield was still far from complete when it officially opened on September 3 1936, in No 3 Group, Bomber Command. The station now had a strength of 35 officers and 350 men.

In common with many other squadrons during the pre-war build-up, the two resident units were each split into two. On April 12 1937, No 76 Squadron re-formed from 'B' Flight of No 7 Squadron as a bomber unit equipped with Wellesleys. A few weeks later, on June 14, No 77 Squadron re-formed from 'B' Flight of No 102 Squadron as a bomber unit with an establishment of Hawker Audaxes.

The following month Nos 77 and 102 Squadrons moved to Honington.

In the spring of 1938, No 7 Squadron began to re-equip with the Armstrong Whitworth Whitley which was classed as a heavy night bomber. The local people had a chance to see the Finningley bombers in a mass formation flight when they were part of the Fifth Empire Air Day in May. However, by September the RAF was brought to a high state of war readiness. It was during this period that the squadron numbers on the aircraft were painted out and replaced by code letters: No 7 Squadron was coded 'LT' and No 76, 'NM'.

During April and May 1939, both the resident units began to re-equip with Mark 1 Handley Page Hampdens and Mark 1 Avro Ansons. At the end of June 1939, the Gauntlets of No 616 Squadron AAF, were detached to the station but moved out during October to their war station at Leconfield. By the outbreak of war in September the station had transferred to No 5 Group, Bomber Command, and all squadrons were allotted new code letters. Finningley's battle strength on September 3 1939 was eight Hampdens and eight Ansons of No 7 Squadron and 20 Hampdens, seven Ansons and a Magister of No 76 Squadron. Since June 1, both units were Group pool squadrons and No 7 had been training crews to operational standard from Doncaster. During mid-September it returned to Finningley and during the third and fourth weeks both Nos 7 and 76

Squadrons moved to Upper Heyford, Oxon, to form No 16 Operational Training Unit. Both squadrons eventually lost their identity.

No 106 Squadron arrived from Cottesmore on October 6, with their Hampdens and Ansons. The role of the unit was training aircrews for operational squadrons in No 5 Group. As Finningley expanded it was provided with a decoy airfield at Owston Ferry which was a few miles to the east of the airfield but, like all decoys, records do not show whether it achieved its purpose. It is listed as having had dummy Whitleys installed and was also equipped with a dummy flarepath.

In the latter part of March 1940, No 98 Squadron moved in from Scampton. This was a reserve squadron equipped with Fairey Battles and was soon on the move. The main body of the squadron marched

Right *Finningley, 1938. Wing walking over the Yorkshire countryside on Heyford K3490 which was struck off charge on May 10 1938.* **Below** *A Handley Page Heyford, which was the RAF's last biplane bomber, at Finningley.*

to Finningley railway station on April 13, bound for Cherbourg, via Southampton in SS *Viking*. Three days later the eight battles of 98 Squadron took off from Château Bougon, near Nantes. The unit's stay in France was brief and it suffered heavy losses. During the evacuation of France the SS *Lancastrian* was bombed and sunk on June 17 1940. On board were many from 98 Squadron, 75 being officially reported lost and another 15 believed to have perished.

During this period, No 7 had re-formed as a Hampden bomber squadron on April 30, but was disbanded three weeks later on May 20. Another Battle squadron that was withdrawn from France was No 12 and during mid-June the few remaining Battles arrived at Finningley from Souge. This small depleted force moved to Binbrook on July 3.

As the pace increased so did the accidents, but with primitive landing aids and pressure for operational crews this could be expected. Minor accidents were daily but major ones were all too frequent. On August 7 1940, Hampden *L4187* of No 106 Squadron dived into the ground at Owston Ferry while on a cross-country exercise. Four crew were killed and the report shows the pilot was blinded by a searchlight.

All training flights ceased on September 8 1940, and the 24 Hampdens of No 106 Squadron were made ready for operations. Minelaying was to be the squadron's main role and this was pioneered by No 5 Group. 'Gardening' was the code word for minelaying operations in general, minelaying itself being 'planting'; the mines were 'vegetables' and the designated area was the 'plot'. On October 6 1940, Hampden *L4100* of 106 Squadron was on cross-country when it was attacked by two aircraft near Stradishall. These were believed to be Spitfires and although the aircraft landed safely, one crew-member was killed. It was not unknown for Hampdens to be engaged by 'friendly' anti-aircraft gunners and fighters for the twin-engined aircraft, with its twin-fins and rudders, bore some resemblance to the German Dornier Do 17. There were other hazards also and, on December 7 1940, while in circuit training, Hampden *L4103* of No 106 Squadron struck the ground in a shallow dive 1½ miles north-west of Blaxton, Yorkshire. Two crew were killed. The cause of the accident was

established as engine failure due to lightning strike.

The squadron's Hampdens took part in the 'Battle of the Barges' during the invasion scare and laid mines off Brest, St Nazaire, Lorient, La Rochelle and in the River Elbe estuary. The squadron continued to operate on mining and bombing attacks but, during January 1941, snow and bad weather prevented flying from the airfield. On the 18th of the month No 7 Blind Approach Training Flight formed and this unit, later No 1507 BAT Flight, was initially equipped with Blenheims and Ansons. Oxfords later became the standard aircraft in the unit's role, which was to train pilots on the radio beam equipment which would facilitate flying at night and in bad weather.

The following month 106 Squadron reverted to front-line status and, on February 12, moved to Coningsby. 'C' Flight remained at Finningley to form No 25 Operational Training Unit which became official on March 1 1941, and it was as a training station that Finningley was to remain for the rest of the war.

During February the station had many visitors. On the 10th, 17 bombs were dropped but only one aircraft was damaged. On the 11th the station received its first Royal visit when HRH the Duchess of Gloucester inspected the WAAF quarters. On the 19th the Luftwaffe returned and eight bombs were dropped on the airfield but only one exploded, destroying a training hut near No 2 hangar.

The airfield was again attacked on March 1, when two landmines were dropped, and once more in early May when only three bombs were dropped but damage was caused to an Anson, a hangar and the Airmen's Married Quarters. It was during May that the first of the somewhat unsuccessful Manchesters arrived but these were soon phased out along with the Hampdens and No 25 OTU remained only with Wellingtons and Ansons. During this period the OTU had expanded and to ease the congestion Balderton and Bircotes had been taken on as satellites.

Training progressed and, during 1942, No 25 OTU took part in the Thousand-Bomber raids against Cologne, Essen and Bremen. The OTU continued to supply aircraft and crews for operations over the next few months but its main role still remained training and accidents were frequent, for most of the trainee aircrew were very inexperienced having only had limited flying before reaching Finningley. Here they found themselves on bomber type aircraft which were more advanced and granted little margin for error. One bad accident was on July 24 1942, when Wellingtons *T2701* and *DV476* collided in circuit, one mile north-west of the airfield.

By the end of 1942, Finningley was faced with urgent repairs to the airfield and dispersals and it was reduced to a Care and Maintenance basis in January 1943. Since January 26 1942 the airfield had been used by the navigation flight of No 18 OTU and, since January 29, by No 1 Group Communications Flight. During this period No 25 OTU was disbanded and replaced by No 18 OTU from Bramcote which officially 'took over' Finningley when it re-opened on March 18 1943. The unit's main equipment was the Wellington but it also had some Martinets and Lysanders and Defiants for target towing. Like its predecessor, the unit's role was training, but its aircraft did take part in 'Nickel' raids and other occasional operational sorties.

The airfield was still very crowded and, on March 13, No 1507 BAT Flight moved to Warboys only to be replaced two days later by the Oxfords of No 1521 BAT Flight which arrived from Stradishall. It is interesting to note that homing pigeons, two of which were carried on each bomber whilst on an operational mission, now totalled 184. They were housed in a new pigeon loft that had been completed the previous November.

On April 14 1943 the Proctors and Lysanders of No 1 Group Communications Flight left Finningley and on April 23 No 1521 BAT Flight also moved out. The first of the 'Nickel' sorties was flown on the night of May 4/5 1943, when a Wellington piloted by Sergeant Anglik dropped leaflets in the Rouen area. These leaflets were like a miniature four-page newspaper which was titled *Le Courrier de L'Air*. They were designed to stimulate the morale of the occupied French and undermine that of the enemy. Each week a new issue appeared and each week aircraft from Finningley and other stations distributed them throughout occupied France.

It had become obvious almost from the outset that the airfield at Bircotes was ill-suited for all-weather flying and even moderate rainfalls gave problems. With inexperienced pilots, crashes were frequent as shown in *Action Stations 2*,

and the airfield was never used more than necessary. A better satellite was needed and, on November 11 1943, Worksop opened in that capacity. Four days later Finningley closed for runway construction, though flying continued unabated from Bircotes and Worksop.

Finningley re-opened on May 23 1944, and No 18 OTU returned from Worksop, leaving 'B' Flight at the satellite airfield. In June, the Wellingtons of the OTU began using Doncaster as a satellite airfield. By the end of 1944 it was decided that No 18 OTU should disband early in the New Year. During their time at Finningley, Nos 18 and 25 OTU had trained over 10,000 crew members. To replace 18 OTU, Bomber Command Instructors' School (BCIS) was formed on December 5 1944, with an establishment of ten Lancasters, three Halifaxes, 16 Wellingtons and a few Spitfires and Hurricanes for fighter affiliation. This unit comprised the most experienced men of Bomber Command and students were taught fighter and bomber tactics, air gunnery, radio, radar, the German air defence system and the means of countering it. The first course started on January 20 1945, each course lasting six weeks for pilots and four weeks for other crew members.

One of the Lancasters used by the BCIS was 'A'-Able, *ND458*, from 100 Squadron, universally known by the inscription painted across her veteran's nose, *Able Mable*. This had 123 operations and two kills to its credit but even that distinguished war record could not save the old veteran from the scrapyard when her working days were over.

The war in Europe ended on May 8 1945, VE-Day, and the Prime Minister, Winston Churchill, announced the German surrender in the House of Commons. Finningley celebrated with a brief thanksgiving service and then with a night on the town. The first Battle of Britain Day was held on September 15 1945 and 15,000 people watched the displays at Finningley.

The station's peacetime role began with the Mosquito when, after a brief post-war disbandment No 616 (South Yorkshire) Squadron, Auxiliary Air Force, was re-formed here with Mosquito night fighters on June 6 1946.

The tide had turned against the Royal Air Force and this was shown on September 14 1946 when only 3,000 people turned up for the second Battle of

Britain Day. What payment for those grieving their loved ones, clearly showing the state of post-war apathy into which the country had fallen. On November 11 1946, No 21 OTU arrived from Moreton-in-Marsh with their Wellingtons and Spitfires. That same month Worksop ceased to be a satellite.

The New Year saw many changes and, on January 22 1947, the BCIS moved to Scampton. On March 1, No 21 OTU became No 202 Advanced Flying School, but remained with the same aircraft. Finningley was then transferred to Flying Training Command on May 1 1947.

During the first week of January 1948, No 1 Pilot's Refresher Flying Unit moved in from Moreton-in-Marsh to replace No 202 ATS. The unit was equipped with Oxfords, Harvards, Spitfires and Wellingtons, its role being to re-familiarise pilots who had returned to flying.

Refresher courses continued and in January 1949 No 1 Refresher Flying Unit became No 1 Flying Refresher School, subsequently becoming No 101 Flying Refresher School in September 1951 when the original piston-engined aircraft were supplemented by Meteor jets. In February 1952, No 215 (Jet) Advanced Flying School was formed with the role of converting pilots to the new Meteor jet. The unit continued in this role until April 21 1954, when all regular Air Force flying ceased in preparation for the closure of the station.

May saw the departure of No 215 AFS and, on June 1, the station was placed on a Care and Maintenance basis, though No 616 Squadron remained. Throughout all the changes, 616 Squadron had continued to operate during the weekends. Its Mosquito night fighters had been replaced with Meteor jet fighters in 1949 but at all times it was a most efficient squadron. In its post-war role, No 616 Squadron was manned largely by local men, who had civilian jobs during the week and gave their weekends to flying. 616 Squadron continued to operate at weekends until, in May 1955, it moved with its Meteors to Worksop.

Finningley had been selected as a V-bomber base and was transferred to No 1 Group, Bomber Command. A new runway, 8,993 ft in length and built of reinforced concrete to withstand the forces of aircraft landing and taking off at weights over 300,000 lb, was constructed. The new extended runway necessitated the closure of a minor road from West Barrier

to Finningley village, but it was a small price to pay.

Finningley re-opened in May 1957 and, on August 24, No 1 Group Communications Flight arrived with a variety of aircraft, which included Meteors, Canberras, Ansons and Chipmunks. On October 1 the first Avro Vulcan arrived and, on October 15, No 101 Squadron re-formed as part of the V-force. The squadron began familiarisation flying and exercises involving long-distance flights, also giving flying displays both here and in many parts of the world.

No 101 was then joined by a second 'V' squadron when No 18 re-formed on December 16 1958 as a specialist unit flying with Vickers Valiants. These aircraft were equipped with top secret radio and radar jamming equipment and did not carry bombs.

February 1960 saw the arrival of the Bomber Command Development Unit from Wittering. Originally formed at Boscombe Down in 1940, it was a highly specialised unit whose role was to test and develop various electronic devices and other equipment necessary for the effective operation of the bomber force. Although only equipped with a few Canberra, Valiant and Vulcan bombers, it contributed much to the effectiveness of Bomber Command. During June 1960, No 101 Squadron accompanied the Secretary of State for Air on a goodwill visit to South America, and covered 17,000 miles. In September 1960 Finningley was 'At Home' to the public and now 75,000 people attended the Battle of Britain Day.

Changes were in the wind, 101 Squadron moving to Waddington on June 17 1961, while two days later No 230 Operational Conversion Unit came to Finningley from Waddington. This unit was responsible for training the V-bomber crews, which was a role much in the Finningley tradition. However, there had been a lot of water under the bridge since the station embarked on a training role. The constant demands from the operational squadrons was gone, but they now had to deal with a vastly more complex aircraft and systems.

Before the arrival of the OCU and the departure of 101 Squadron, it had been planned that Princess Margaret would visit the station and present Standards to both Nos 18 and 101 Squadrons. However, she was not able to come until June 14 1962. No 101 Squadron returned

Above *Vulcan XA895 of Bomber Command Bombing School at Finningley.* **Below**
*Finningley, August 1979. View in the Search and Rescue Wing engineering hangar where
all SAR helicopters are given major servicing.* **Bottom** *Pilot's eye view of the approach
when coming in to land at Finningley, as seen on this training flight with pilot Squadron
Leader Dave Bridger (left) and Flight Lieutenant Jack Stone (Advanced Navigation
Training Instructor) in the co-pilot's seat.*

for the occasion and rejoined 18 Squadron at Finningley. Princess Margaret arrived in a Heron of the Queen's Flight and was received by the Lord Lieutenant of Nottinghamshire, Major-General Sir Robert Laycock, and Mr W.J. Taylor, the Under Secretary of State for Air. After inspecting the parade and presenting the squadron Standards, Princess Margaret 'scrambled' four Vulcan bombers.

The Standard, a fringed and tasselled silken banner, mounted on a pike surmounted by a golden eagle, is presented to squadrons after 25 years' service or for especially meritorious operations. It came just in time for No 18 Squadron, for by 1963 it had outlived its usefulness. The majority of aircraft in Bomber Command now carried their own electronic counter-measures and it was not needed. Therefore, on March 31 of that year, No 18 Squadron disbanded, leaving No 230 OCU as the only major flying unit, though the BCDU and No 1 Group Communications Flight each continued to operate a few aircraft. June 1963 saw the arrival of the Bomber Command Vulcan Servicing School but this was a non-flying unit. Its role was to train engineering personnel in Vulcan servicing techniques.

In July 1965, No 232 (Victor) OCU disbanded at Gaydon and 230 OCU took over its ground training responsibilities. Flying training of the Victor aircrews was undertaken at Wittering with Mk 2 Blue Steel Bombers or at Marham with Mk 1 Tankers.

Like all RAF stations, the future of Finningley was always a matter of concern and in 1965 doubt was cast when a question was tabled in the House of Commons on the possibility of using Finningley (or Lindholme) as a civil airport. Only in July 1964 had an Air Ministry spokesman reassured everyone concerned that Finningley's retention as a flying and bomber station was assured for at least another 30 years.

On November 1 1965, Finningley became the 'parent' station for the small Bomber Command detachments stationed at Goose Bay in Labrador and Offutt, near Omaha, in Nebraska, USA. These far-flung RAF units give support facilities for aircraft of Bomber (now Strike) Command in Canada and America. An essential feature of the training of V-bomber crews is long-range flights into unfamiliar areas. These outposts play an important role just as they did in the Second World War. In June 1943 a far-flung base allowed Bomber Command to bomb Friedrichshafen and fly on to Algiers where they reloaded and refuelled to bomb Spezia three nights later on their return home. The USAAF then used small bases as stepping stones and on June 2 1944 inaugurated 'shuttle' bombing between Italy and Russia. On that occasion B-17s of the XV Air Force took off from Italy, attacked Debrecen airfield in Hungary and then landed at Poltava, Russia. Times may have changed but the strategy is the same, the only difference is that the stepping stones are now the other side of the world or in space.

On April 30 1968, Bomber Command was amalgamated with Fighter Command to form the new Strike Command. No 3 Group having been absorbed into 1 Group six months earlier and Finningley having long been in 1 Group, both became part of the new formation and the occasion was marked by a station colour-hoisting parade with a flypast by a single Vulcan. During August 1968 the Vulcan element, No 1 (Bomber) Group Standardisation Unit, moved in from Waddington and the year closed with the Bomber Command Development Unit being disbanded on December 31.

Early in the New Year the Victor element for Marham arrived to join No 1 (Bomber) GSU which is responsible for checking the proficiency of Vulcan and Victor aircrews on all the squadrons and training units of the Bomber and Tanker forces. On January 27 1969 two Bassets and crews of the Strike Command Communications Squadron (later numbered 207) were attached from Northolt but remained only until the end of the year. September had seen the departure of No 1 GSU and in December 1969, No 230 OCU moved to Scampton. That same month the Strike Command Vulcan Servicing School also moved out and the station was placed under Care and Maintenance pending a major change in its role.

Finningley was then transferred from Strike Command to Training Command and, in May 1970, No 6 Flying Training School re-formed with Varsity navigational trainers. The new unit assumed the combined roles of No 1 Air Navigation School, Stradishall, and No 2 Air Navigation School, Gaydon. In October 1973 the station again expanded when the Air Electronics and Air

Engineers School was transferred to Finningley to become the Air Electronics and Air Engineers Wing of No 6 FTS. This made Finningley responsible for all non-pilot aircrew training for the RAF. At the end of the 44-week course, which involved some 810 hours' classroom instruction with 150 hours' flying, plus a period in the simulator, all students are trained to a common standard. The navigators are then posted to the appropriate Operational Conversion Unit and after a further three- to six-month period of training, will be posted to an operational squadron. Today, the station is the home of 'Air Navigation', and provides aircrew for the Royal Air Force's front-line squadrons.

In June 1975 the Yorkshire Universities Air Squadron (YUAS) and No 9 Air Experience Flight (9 AEF) joined the station from Church Fenton with their Bulldogs and Chipmunks.

During January 1976 the Whirlwind HAR Mk 10 helicopters of the Head-quarters flight of No 22 Squadron arrived at Finningley from Thorney Island, to be joined in September by the Headquarters Flight of No 202 Squadron from Coltishall. Together these formed the HQ of the UK Search and Rescue Wing (SAR Wing), a part of No 18 Group, Strike Command. The Wing administers the entire Search and Rescue operations in the United Kingdom, its aircraft from time to time returning to Finningley for any major servicing.

After nearly 25 years in the training of navigators, the faithful Varsities were retired in April 1976. All their work was now being done by the Dominie and, in December 1976, training in blind navigation at low level using radar was introduced in the Dominie. With the arrival of the Dominie force from RAF College, Cranwell, in 1977, all the Dominies in the RAF are now at No 6 FTS.

In June 1977 Finningley became part of the new RAF Support Command, due to reorganisation of the whole service. The following month the station put on an outstanding display for the Queen's Silver Jubilee review on July 29, for an audience of about 10,000 past and present RAF and WRAF personnel. It was code-named operation 'Teabag' because Group Captain John Tetley masterminded the events. This special performance was repeated the following day when over 200,000 members of the public attended.

During May 1978, the first of the new Sea King HAR Mk 3 helicopters arrived to begin the replacement of the Whirlwinds of No 202 Squadron. With the improvement in range, payload, performance and navigation equipment these will take the SAR units well through the 1980s.

The station's training role was further enlarged when, on April 23 1979, the Multi-Engined Training Squadron (METS) transferred to Finningley with its nine Jetstream aircraft. Two extra Jetstreams were added to meet the increased flying tasks, and Royal Air Force Lindholme was reactivated as a relief landing ground, so that Finningley could absorb the extra flying. The role of METS is to convert student pilots to multi-engined aircraft, to introduce them to asymmetric flying techniques and to train them in airways flying prior to advancement on to the operational multi-engined aircraft of Strike Command. On successful completion of the course students are awarded their Pilot Flying Badge.

The METS will now increase the intake of student pilots to the flying training system. Thus, the 1980s will see Finningley as one of the busiest Royal Air

BAC Jet Provost T5 XW287 of No 6 FTS at Finningley.

Above *Hawker Siddeley Dominie T1 XS736 of No 6 FTS at Finningley.* **Below** *Scottish Aviation Jetstream T1 XX497 of the Multi-Engined Training Squadron at Finningley.* **Bottom** *Scottish Aviation Bulldog T1s XX529 and XX520 of the* Bulldogs *Aerobatic Team at Finningley, 1981.*

Force stations in the country and already the training is beginning to reflect the needs of the next generation of aircraft.

Finningley Air Day has established itself as the biggest one-day air show in the UK and an addition to the 1981 show was RAF Finningley's own railway station which was built within the airfield boundary.

Firbeck, South Yorkshire

120/SK555892. Approximately 7 miles N of Worksop, S of the A634 road

A poorly sited grass field which opened in 1940 occupied by the Lysanders of No 613 Squadron, Firbeck remained an Army Co-operation airfield throughout the war with Nos 654 and 659 Squadrons and as a RLG for 25 EFTS from Hucknall.

For further details see *Action Stations 2*.

Full Sutton, Yorkshire

106/SE748540. E of York. To S of the A166 road at Stamford Bridge

Full Sutton was one of the last Second World War airfields to be opened in Yorkshire and became operational in May 1944, as a bomber station in No 4 Group, Bomber Command.

The airfield was built on three commons, Gowthorpe, Full Sutton and Fangfoss. It was a standard heavy bomber station with the usual three paved runways, the main one 5,940 ft long and the two subsidiaries 5,100 ft and 3,900 ft in length. These were linked by a perimeter track around which were dispersed hardstandings for the aircraft. There were the usual 'T2' hangars and Nissen and Maycrete huts on the various dispersed sites, for at this stage of the war building airfields was a way of life for many workers.

The first, and as it turned out, only operational unit at Full Sutton was 77 Squadron which arrived from Elvington in May 1944. The unit had just started to convert to the Halifax Mk III with which it continued to play a prominent part in the bomber offensive. The unit's first operation with the Mark IIIs was on the night of June 1/2 when the squadron took part in a raid against Ferm d'Urville, near Cherbourg. This was an important target for it was the Headquarters of the German Signals Intelligence Service in north-west France, but the target was shrouded in cloud and the mission was not a success. It was left to No 5 Group to

Full Sutton control tower, type 343/43, photographed in September 1972.

destroy it the following night.

During September/October 1944, the squadron shared in the task of flying nearly half a million gallons of desperately needed petrol to an airfield in Belgium for the Second Army. The resident squadron then returned to the bombing offensive which continued throughout the winter months when the weather permitted.

During March 1945, the squadron began to receive the Halifax B Mk VI and the last operational mission of the war came on April 25, when 19 Halifaxes bombed gun batteries on the Island of Wangerooge.

In keeping with many of 4 Group squadrons, No 77 was transferred to Transport Command which took effect as from 00.01 hours on May 8 1945, and at the same time was informed it would re-equip with Dakotas.

Full Sutton was not selected as a permanent station but for a short perioid it housed several units. On July 4, No 4 Group Communications Flight arrived and two days later a mobile transport training party arrived in order to train 77 Squadron for future transport duties. The day after their arrival four Dakotas flew in and by July 18 the station had on strength 16 of them. New crews were now being posted in to make up their complement of 48. Aircraft also continued to arrive and by the end of July the unit strength was 21 Dakotas and seven Halifaxes. July had also seen the formation of No 30 Aircrew Holding Unit.

On August 30 1945 the advance party of 77 Squadron departed by rail for Broadwell and the following day the main party moved out with their 20 Dakotas.

Towards the end of November aircrews began to arrive and 231 Squadron re-formed. This was a Lancastrian training unit which, by the end of the year, had on strength nine Lancasters and two Lancastrians. In the New Year it was joined by No 1699 Lancastrian Flight which re-formed here on January 15 1946 but saw very little activity and on April 1 disbanded. By the end of April 231 Squadron had moved out and the station continued to process redundant aircrew at the rate of 30 officers and 30 NCOs per day.

By April 1947 the airfield had outlived its usefulness, all units had moved out and at the end of the month the station was put on a Care and Maintenance basis. A few years later repair work was carried out at the airfield and Full Sutton re-opened in 1951 as a result of the emergency in Korea. It housed No 104 Refresher Flying School, later re-named 207 Advanced Flying School, and this remained until the mid-1950s.

On March 26 1954, a Bovingdon-based C-47, with its VIPs who were on a visit to Elvington, touched down at Full Sutton for it was the nearest active airfield. However, it was not to remain active and was soon afterwards vacated by the RAF. From 1955 to 1957 the airfield was designated a reserve site for the US Air Force but it was not used operationally and housed only 3930 Air Base Squadron, SAC.

The station was returned to UK control on February 5 1957 and re-occupied by the RAF. Full Sutton then became a satellite of the Driffield Thor missile complex and housed three missiles. No 102 Squadron was re-formed as a Thor unit on April 1 1959 but, along with all other Thor units, it disbanded in April 1963 and Full Sutton finally closed.

Today, the control tower is used as offices for Buccaneer Caravans Ltd who have taken over the eastern side of the airfield. Many other buildings remain but the future looks bleak for it is thought the site is to become a prison. The runways and former missile emplacements have now been almost completely removed.

Gilling, Yorkshire
100/SE615768. Between Thirsk and Malton

This was a very isolated site near the village of Gilling East, and it is believed the landing ground was in fact located in Gilling Park. The site was used as a night landing ground by 'B' Flight, 33 Squadron, Royal Flying Corps, with BE2cs during 1916, but with no buildings erected it is impossible to locate.

Goosepool, Tees-side (Middleton St George), Co Durham
See Middleton St George

Greatham (West Hartlepool), Cleveland
See West Hartlepool

Hatfield Woodhouse (Lindholme), Yorkshire
See Lindholme

Hedon (Hull), Yorkshire
See Hull

Helperby (Brafferton), Yorkshire
99/SE448712. S of Thirsk

Situated close to the villages of Helperby and Brafferton on the east side of the River Swale, this was a large grass meadow that was brought into use as a night landing ground for the BE2cs of 'B' Flight, 33 Squadron, who used the site from March to October 1916.

Unlike so many of these World War 1 sites, some buildings were erected including two substantial brick hangars with the typical bowed wooden roof of the period. During September 1916 'B' Flight of No 76 Squadron moved in with Avro 504Ks, remaining until March 1919 when they then moved to Tadcaster. With their departure the airfield closed and no further flying took place. The site reverted back to its former use.

During the Second World War the site was again brought into use but this time as an auxiliary bomb dump for local airfields of No 6 Group. A few buildings were erected and roadways and concrete hardstandings were laid in and around a

The small World War 1 hangar that still remains at Helperby.

small wood. The usual blast walls surrounded parts of the bomb dump.

The site closed soon after the Second World War but, up to the early 1980s, some of the buildings were still to be found, albeit in various stages of decay. Also, tucked away in the corner of the field, was one of the small World War 1 hangars which had been brought into use as a cinema during the Second World War. It is impossible to imagine that this site was ever used as an airfield.

Holme-on-Spalding Moor
(Spaldington), Yorkshire

106/SE 830350. NE of Goole on E side of the A614 road

The airfield was built on Holme Common between the A614 road to the west and the Market Weighton Canal which formed the eastern boundary. A short distance to the south was the River Foulness and to the north the Land of Nod road and the village of Holme-on-Spalding Moor from which it was named. Approach by road could only be made from the west. Airfield construction workers moved to the site in 1940 and started to develop it into a standard pattern airfield with the main technical and accomodation site on the northern side of the landing area, the main hangar being a 'J' type. Briefing rooms, control tower, officers' and mens' quarters were built in record time.

The airfield was officially opened in August 1941 under No 1 group, Bomber Command, although it had been used by light aircraft prior to then. The first units, which both arrived during August, were No 20 BAT Flight which formed here with Oxfords and was later to become No 1520 BAT Flight; and No 458 Squadron, RAAF, which came into existence at

Williamtown, New South Wales, on the 8th of the previous month. It was officially established in Britain on August 25 1941 at Holme-on-Spalding Moor, as a medium bomber unit in No 1 Group. The unit code letters were 'FU' and it was equipped with Wellington Mk IVs. The commanding officer, Wing Commander Mulholland (later killed in action on February 16 1942) and one of his flight commanders, Squadron Leader Johnston, were Australians and many RAAF aircrew were immediately posted in, but it was not fully RAAF.

The Aussies were quickly into their stride and began operations on the night of October 20/21 when ten Wellingtons were despatched—two to Emden and eight to Antwerp. One aircraft was unable to locate Antwerp and returned with its bombs and one failed to return. By the end of January 1942, 458 Squadron had bombed Mannheim, Aachen, Cologne and Düsseldorf in the campaign against German transport centres as well as attacking ports and other North Sea installations. The last operation was on January 28/29 1942, when two aircraft bombed Boulogne docks, and at the end of the month 458 Squadron was withdrawn from all Bomber Command duties and, after having re-equipped with Wellington 1cs, moved to the Middle East in March 1942. The airfield was then used mainly by non-operational units while further construction work was carried out.

During August the newly formed 460 Squadron Conversion Flight arrived from Breighton with Halifaxes. At this stage of the war the existing heavy conversion units were unable to accomodate all squadrons that were either forming or re-equipping with four-engined bombers, and many crews were trained by this emergency method. On these units the more experienced crews first learned to fly the new aircraft and then acted as instructors. This was the case with 460 Squadron Conversion Flight, but for some reason it was decided to discontinue Halifax training and to equip 460 Squadron with Lancasters. Therefore, on September 26 1942, the conversion flight moved back to Breighton.

Then, in September 1942, No 101 Squadron, code letters 'SR' arrived from Stradishall, Suffolk, with their Wellington Mk IIIs. The following month they began to convert to Lancasters, the newest and most up-to-date bomber, and with these began to operate almost nightly from Holme-on-Spalding Moor against targets in Germany and Italy.

On October 23, Wing Commander Bruce Bintley, of 102 Squadron, Pocklington, had been on a raid to Genoa and was diverted on his return to Holme-on-Spalding Moor, where he landed safely with a burst tyre. Before he could leave the runway another aircraft landed on top of him, killing him and his wireless operator. A tragic accident.

Accidents are always unwelcome, more so when they are caused by friendly guns. On December 17 1942, Lancaster *W4319*, piloted by Sergeant M.A. Fussell, was returning from ops when it was hit by Bofors at Grangetown, Yorkshire. The IFF was either not working or not switched on. Whatever the reason it caused the death of the seven crew members.

During the first week of January 1943, No 1503 BAT Flight, which had arrived from Mildenhall on September 5 1942, moved out to Lindholme. 1943 saw the long distance raids continue with Milan and Spezia being added the list of Italian targets. The New Year also brought many crashes for 101 Squadron. At 11.30 hours on March 20, Lancaster *ED446*, piloted by Sergeant I.H. Hazard, crashed on the beach at Atwick, Hornsea, Yorkshire, during unauthorised low flying while gun testing. Eight of the nine crew were killed. Nine days later Lancaster *ED552* crashed at 03.31 hours just south of South Cliff, Yorkshire. The pilot, Pilot Officer W.T. Hobday, failed to raise the nose properly and the aircraft sank on to trees after it had climbed to 800 ft. The bomber had just taken off for cross-country and probably the pilot raised the flaps too quickly. Six of the seven crew were killed. On April 14 Lancaster *ED807*, piloted by Sergeant T. Fee,was returning from ops when at 22.20 hours, just two miles south of the airfield, it crashed out of control

while on three-engined approach. All seven crew were killed. Another to run into trouble after returning from ops was Sergeant J.R. Browning's Lancaster, *W4863*, on May 5. Due to bad weather it was diverted to Scorton but owing to pilot error it hit some trees and crashed. Four of the crew were killed. Also on the 5th, Lancaster *ED835* struck the ground at 04.45 hours near Hotham, just east of the airfield. The bomber was on beam approach and the cause was probably due to the pilot, Flight Sergeant G. Hough, failing to concentrate after the strain of ops. Three men were killed and four injured.

After flying an impressive number of operations with Lancasters, 101 Squadron moved south to Ludford Magna in June 1943. It was immediately replaced by No 76 Squadron from Linton-on-Ouse and the station was transferred to No 4 Group and became No 44 Base Station. Within three days 76 Squadron made its first attack from its new base when, as part of the main force, it bombed an armament works at Le Creusot.

On June 22, the squadron led by Group Captain D.L. Wilson, an Australian, took part in an attack on Mulheim. One aircraft failed to return to Holme-on-Spalding Moor, the one piloted by the Group Captain. He had been attacked by enemy fighters over the target, was forced to bale out with his crew, and was a PoW in Germany until liberated by the British Army in May 1945.

Operations from here continued on a heavy scale and in February 1944 the unit began to convert to the radial-engined Halifax Mk III and continued operations with these.

Towards the end of May the Oxfords of No 1520 BAT Flight moved to Leconfield and the status of the station as at June 6 1944 was No 76 Squadron with Halifax Mk IIIs and No 1689 BDT Flight which had recently moved in and was operating with Spitfires, Hurricanes and Martinets under No 4 Group. Flown by experienced fighter pilots, the BDT Flight did invaluable work giving bomber crews experience by making dummy attacks, which forced the bombers to take evasive action as they would have to do over the hostile skies of Germany.

During March 1945, No 76 Squadron began to convert to the Halifax Mk VI and the last operational mission of the war was on April 25, when 25 Halifaxes were

Halifax of No 76 Squadron being prepared for the night's mission from Holme-on-Spalding Moor.

despatched to bomb gun batteries on the island of Wangerooge. 22 bombed the primary target, one aborted and two failed to return.

No 1689 BDT Flight moved out during April and, on May 7 1945, the station, along with 76 Squadron, was transferred to Transport Command. The resident unit converted to Dakotas and began training for their part of flying passengers, troops, mail and freight over the main air trunk routes of the world. 76 Squadron finally left Holme-on-Spalding Moor in July 1945 and by the end of the year it was in India.

Dakotas had also arrived at Holme-on-Spalding Moor when No 512 Squadron moved in from the continent in July 1945. This unit began to train new crews to fly the Dakotas but remained only a few months and, on October 8 1945, was posted to Egypt.

With the last flying unit now gone the station closed down and was placed on Care and Maintenance. It remained under these conditions until 1952 when it re-opened during the Koream War as the base for No 14 Advanced Flying Training School whose Prentice T1s and Harvard T2b trainers made a sharp contrast with the heavy bombers that had used the same runways a few years earlier. In 1954, No 14 AFTS moved out and the site was vacated by the RAF. Only a small party of RAF men under the command of Flight Lieutenant G.F. Booth remained behind to welcome the Americans.

That same year the airfield was transferred to the USAAF and was used by the Americans until nearby Elvington was refurbished. The first 200 United States Service Engineers arrived during February 1954 to prepare the station for the arrival of the United States Air Force.

Crash tender and crew of 512 Squadron at Holme-on-Spalding Moor on August 27 1945. Many aircrew members made up their numbers and the Flight Sergeant is Andy Andrews who did a tour of Ops with 460 Squadron at Binbrook, Lincolnshire.

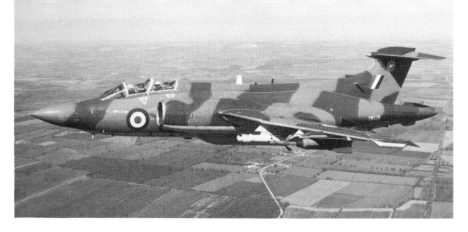

By the end of February a further 600 Americans had arrived. They soon made their presence felt in the dancehalls of Hull and York. Even in peacetime it was still the old saying from the locals: 'Over paid, over sexed—and over here'. The USAAF relinquished their tenancy in 1957 and the airfield was then taken over by Blackburn Aviation whose NA39 prototype, forerunner of the Buccaneer, first flew in 1958.

In order that the runways could be resurfaced here in preparation for the forthcoming McDonnell Douglas F-4 Phantom, permission was given for the company to use Driffield as a flight test base from September 1967 to February 1968.

Today, the current operator is British

Above Buccaneer S2B from Holme-on-Spalding Moor seen here on test. **Below** *Holme-on-Spalding Moor in May 1978. Oblique view of the airfield with main east-west runway in foreground. The control tower and signals square, wartime 'J' hangar and the two 'T2's can clearly be seen.*

Aerospace and the airfield is a satellite to Brough, being responsible for all flight test operations. The control tower, type 518/40, with the met section, hangars and technical area buildings have been kept in very good order and are still in use. The runways have been renovated but only the east-west one is used. British Aerospace are carrying out a programme of engine and equipment tests on new products and are currently operating Buccaneer and Phantom aircraft. Photography is forbidden and the airfield is under strong security guard.

Hornsea Mere, Yorkshire
107/TA198475. On W side of Hornsea

The Hornsea Mere made a perfect inland lake which could be used for military purposes and the planners of the First World War sites made full use of it. Situated to the south of the B1244 road, the Headquarters of 248 Squadron, RNAS, was established at RNAS Hornsea and two Bessoneaux hangars were built close to the Mere with two attendant slipways.

Twelve Short 184 seaplanes of 404 and 405 Flights were based here during 1917 and flew alongside those of 251 Squadron based here during that period. The site closed immediately after the First World War and the temporary facilities were soon dismantled.

Howden, Yorkshire

106/SE745328. N of Goole off the B1228 road

Howden opened in March 1916 and became one of the most important operational airship stations in the country. It was a very large site of approximately 1,000 acres just to the north of Howden. It stretched from Mount Pleasant farm in the north to Brind Lane crossroads in the south. Brindleys Wood formed the western boundary and Spaldington village the eastern.

Many buildings were erected, the first being Coastal Shed 'A', 323 ft 11 in long, 120 ft 5 in wide and 81 ft high, and Coastal Shed 'B', 320 ft long, 110 ft wide and 80 ft high, to house the proposed Coastals. The first to arrive at Howden was the Coastal *C11* from Kingsnorth on June 26 1916.

During December 1916, No 1 rigid hangar, 703 ft 10 in long, 148 ft 11 in wide and 100 ft 8½ in high, was completed to accommodate the proposed 23-Class rigid. No 2 rigid hangar, 750 ft long, 300 ft wide and 130 ft high, was not completed until 1919.

The site was divided by an airfield road laid to the north of the site. This cut across at right angles from the B1228 road until petering out just past the hangars which were on the south side. To the north of the road were the SHQ, parade ground, officers' mess, barrack huts, stores and other buildings. At the end of 1916, Howden's complement was 25 officers and 476 men, including 139 men of the Air Service Constructional Corps. At its peak in 1918, Howden was staffed with approximately 1,000 officers and ratings plus civilian employees.

The Airship Station was served with a railway branch line from the North Howden junction which led directly over the airfield with branch lines in to the two hangars, coal store and gas plant.

By the end of 1916, Howden had on strength the *C11, C4, C19, C21* and the Vickers-built Parseval *P4* which was transferred from Barrow-in-Furness and used for training by No 9 Rigid Trials Flight under Commander Masterman. Between June and December 31 1916, the Howden airships had completed a total of 521 flying hours.

The year 1917 saw an increase in the number of airships with Rigids No *9* and *25* and Parsevals No *5, 6* and *7*. *P9* made a British record flight on July 21, when it completed a 430-mile flight in 26¾ hours. Unfortunately it was later damaged while entering its shed and put out of commission for the rest of the year.

This proved a very busy year for the airships and the Coastals carried out a great deal of patrol and escort work. The old *P4* moved down to Pulham during March 1917 and *P6* was transferred on August 6 to Cranwell for training purposes. *P5* and *P7* were flown on trials during November and December. By the end of 1917 some 2,086 flying hours had been completed. To cater for this increased flying a mooring ground had been established at Gosforth Park, Newcastle but this sub-station had to close on October 1 when soldiers, utilised for landing the airship, left the district.

Early 1918 saw the newest non-rigid SSZ-Class (Zeros) start to arrive at Howden, *SSZ32, 58* and *38* all becoming operational by early April. With the formation of the Royal Air Force on April 1 1918, Howden, in line with all other RNAS airship establishments, became part RAF and part RN. The airships and their equipment were still on charge to the Royal Navy but the personnel all belonged to the RAF and thus it remained until Howden finally closed down. During April Lowthorpe opened as a mooring-out site and over the next few weeks three airships moved there and began operations.

During this period No *25* was withdrawn from operations, for over the past few months it had been plagued with 'surging' of its gasbags and was relegated to training duties at Cranwell. Its successor was the *R26* which arrived at Howden at the end of May.

Several of the older Coastals were now being replaced by the improved C-Class and Howden increased its complement of 'Zeros', *SSZ54* and '*55*. Also, several other NS-Class were hangared at Howden during early 1918 whilst en route to East Fortune and other war stations. With this increase a further mooring-out station at Kirkleatham, near Redcar, was

RAF BE2c at Howden.

commissioned and three of the recent arrivals moved there during May.

Mid-1918 saw the arrival at Howden of the first of the modified 23-Class, known as 23x-Class, and the first Womens Auxiliary Air Force personnel who were housed in their own barrack block near Station headquarters. Then, in August 1918, disaster struck Howden. The *SSZ23* had been packed for transport to America by her US Naval crew, the work having been carried out in the Rigid Shed which also contained *R27, SSZ38* and *SSZ54* plus a new un-numbered Zero. This latter had been rigged and the W/T operator was checking the W/T set when a spark from it ignited petrol in the 'car' and the resultant inferno destroyed all the airships. Only one life was lost, that being a rating who was on lookout on the shed roof. The heat bent the corrugated-iron roof and, although it subsequently leaked badly during inclement weather, the shed was still usable.

The autumn of 1918 saw a steady expansion of work at Howden and newer classes of airships began to replace the originals. Further SS Zeros were flown from here and the two mooring-out-stations which came under the direct control of Howden. Also during this period two of the North Sea Class, *NS9* and *NS16*, are known to have operated from here.

The *R31* made an unscheduled arrival at Howden on November 6 1918. Under the command of Commander Sparling it had left Cardington for its war station at East Fortune but suffered many breakages to its frames and girders and consequently landed for repairs at Howden. It was hangared in the fire-damaged rigid hangar. But the Armistice in November 1918 halted repairs and the airship programme was hit by cancellations. Howden began an immediate rundown but, being a major airship station, escaped closure. The job of clearing away the minefields from the North Sea was carried out by airships from this station. The Zeros were now being replaced by the SST-Class. However, the political and economic situation during 1919 brought more cutbacks.

As is always the case, some people are ready to make money out of war but it does not always pay off. The *R31* had throughout this period remained at Howden but the wooden airship had deteriorated beneath the leaking hangar and after all salvagable material was removed the *R31* was sold for firewood in July 1919. The dealer found out too late that all the wood had been 'treated' and fireproofed!

By October 1919 most of Britain's airship fleet was depleted and the building programme axed. Only the most modern airships were retained. Howden survived, albeit on a drastically reduced scale. After its successful transatlantic flight to Mineola, NY, the *R34* was overhauled at Howden. This had been the first transoceanic airship flight.

Early in 1920 the Americans decided to buy *R38* and delivery by air was planned. A crew was sent to Howden to train for the task of flying her across the Atlantic. They trained in the *R34* but in deteriorating weather she struck the North Yorkshire moors near Guisborough. The *R34* made it back to Howden where it had to be moored outside on the field owing to a rising wind. Next day it was found to be so badly damaged it was broken-up on the spot. The *R80* and *R32* were placed at the disposal of the Americans, the latter later being broken up in No 1 Hangar.

Finally, the *R38* was completed at Cardington and arrived at Howden in July. Trial flights began but on its fourth on August 24 1921, the *R38* broke up over Hull during high speed turning trials. The two pieces, one on fire, fell into the river

Humber, killing 44 British and US Airship officers and men. There were only five survivors, one the captain. The rigid programme came to a halt and by the end of 1920 few of the smaller non-rigids remained. Work now came to a standstill at Howden—the *R38* disaster had been the final blow. The last flight took place on September 20 1921 when the CO took-off for Pulham in the *R80*. The last of Howden's life-blood had gone and by the end of September 1921 the station had closed down.

Slowly the station became overgrown and over the years the wooden huts rotted. Then, in 1924, the Airship Guarantee Company was formed and leased the site from the Air Ministry. Howden was brought back to life and by the end of 1926 most of the broken-down buildings had been removed and replaced with nearly 20 bungalows for the wives and families of the staff.

Inside the shed work progressed on the rigid passenger-carrying airship, the *R-100*. This was built on a modified Zeppelin design with six gasoline engines and accommodation for 100 passengers. Strikes at Howden held up production but in November 1929 it was ready for trials. The completed airship was taken over by the Air Ministry on November 22, but it was not brought out of the shed until December 16. At 07.30 hours it emerged with the help of 500 troops from York to assist in the delicate manoeuvre. After ballasting, *R-100* gently lifted, circled Howden several times then left—never to return.

When, on an attempted flight to India on October 5 1930, the Government-built 'sister-ship' *R-101* crashed into a hill during a storm near Beauvais, France, and burst into flames, killing 46 persons, the Government called a halt to all airship activities. The *R-100*, which had flown to Montreal, Quebec, Canada on July 29 1930 in 78 hours and returned to England in 58 hours, arriving on August 16, was broken up in her hangar at Cardington in late 1931. Consequently the design staff at Howden, one of whom was Professor Barnes-Wallis, later to receive fame with the Dambusters and the 'bouncing bomb' in World War 2, and another his chief calculator, N.S. Norway (better known as the novelist Neville Shute), were dispersed in December 1930.

By the mid-1930s Howden's huge hangar was dismantled and sold for scrap. Over the years the buildings have been demolished but in the early 1970s many of the baseblocks and huge anchor links were still in position. The airfield road is used regularly by farm vehicles. The old water tower and a few other buildings remained *in situ*, the last remains of this historic airship station.

Huggate Wold, Yorkshire
106/SE860570. To W of Great Driffield

This bleak site close to the Yorkshire Wolds was surveyed and found suitable for development into a heavy bomber airfield. Before these plans were put into operation, they were reviewed, found to be less suitable, so abandoned in favour of an alternative site a few miles to the west at Full Sutton.

However, when the planners were preparing for the invasion of enemy occupied Europe, they realised the need for temporary airstrips on the beach-heads and Huggate Wold was one of the sites selected for the laying of experimental lengths of steel mesh runway as an exercise for the engineers. These temporary runways were tested from time to time by landing aircraft on them and, so that concentrated testing could take place, two fighter squadrons equipped

Laying the steel mesh runway at Huggate Wold.

with Mustangs were posted to Huggate Wold. On October 10 1943 No 168 Squadron arrived from Huttons Cranwick, to be joined the following day by 170 Squadron. For the next few days the aircraft took off and landed continuously. Then, on October 15, No 168 moved to Thruxton and the following day 170 moved to Leconfield. The site then closed and had no further military use after the temporary runways had been removed.

Hull (Hedon), Yorkshire

107/TA170290. To E of Kingston upon Hull

Situated close to the village of Hedon between the railway line to the north and the A1033 road to the south, this station was named Hull but referred to as Hedon airfield. Flying here goes back to before the First World War. It is ironic that local interest in flying was awakened by a young German called Gustav Hamel. The site, which had formed part of the estate of the Twyer family, was first used for horse racing and in 1888 a company was formed to establish a racecourse at Hedon but attendances dwindled and the last race took place in 1909. Gustav Hamel arrived shortly afterwards with his machine and became the first airman to fly in the City of Hull. He was also the first man in England to become an official flying postman. Designed as part of the celebrations to mark the coronation of George V in September 1911, Hamel carried over 100,000 letters and cards between Hendon and Windsor.

Hamel made a short flight from Hedon aerodrome on Saturday, July 13 1912, and a large crowd gathered on the racecourse to watch the proceedings, including the Mayor of Hedon. The first flight was only to Hull and back. Shortly afterwards he made a second flight lasting 32 minutes.

The outbreak of the First World War put paid to any further civil flying and the site became a garrison town for the East Yorkshire Regiment. The old racecourse was brought into use as a parking ground for the heavy artillery. In 1915, Mr W.R. Watkinson chose the site as the 'collecting ground' for Holderness inhabitants leaving their villages in the event of an invasion by German forces. Between March and October 1916 the site was used as a night landing ground for the BE2cs of

'C' Flight, 33 Squadron, RFC, but it saw very little flying activity. 76 Squadron is also known to have used the site, which was listed as a 2nd Class Landing Ground.

It was not until 1929 that the Hull Flying Club was founded at Hedon. The club was run by the National Flying Services and a spacious bungalow which served both as an office and a clubhouse, hangar and ambulance hut were erected on the western side of the landing area close to the minor road. The grass-covered landing area gave 4,830 ft from east to west and 2,040 ft from north to south. But it was a restricted site with telegraph wires on the west side and 850 yards from the south-west corner of the aerodrome on the north side of the Hull-Hedon road were two 83 ft-high radio masts. One mile south-west of the aerodrome was the Salt End Chemical Works. Aircraft were warned not to fly below an altitude of 1,000 ft over these works owing to the inflammable nature of the material handled. The roof of these premises was distinguished by a white cross by day and by lights at night. The aeroplanes used during that period were Gipsy Moths and, as one person wrote at the time flown with virtually no instruments, a wind indicator, rev-meter, petrol gauge and two wheels to land on.

On October 10 1929 the municipal airfield at Hedon was opened by Prince George and during the early months the airfield was visited by Air Vice-Marshal Sir Sefton Brancker, the Minister for Civil Aviation who was later killed in the *R-101* disaster. But the greatest day was on August 11 1930 when Hull gave a Civic Reception for Amy Johnson, Hull's greatest flyer. She flew into Hedon aerodrome and the airfield was thrown open to the public for the occasion.

For the National Flying Services it was all very good publicity for one of their objectives was to interest the general public in flying and to this purpose they put on several displays at the airfield. For the same reason Sir Alan Cobham visited Hedon with his flying circus. After his historic flights he toured the country giving flying displays and taking people for 'joy rides' which carried on throughout the 1930s. The 'Flying Flea' from France even paid Hedon a visit but it required perfect weather conditions and could not cope with the north-east winds so quickly disappeared from the Yorkshire scene.

The Royal Dutch Airline, KLM,

provoked serious thought about the airfield when they inaugurated a service between Liverpool, Hull and Amsterdam in May 1934. The single fare from Hull to Amsterdam was £5 0s 0d and return fare to Berlin was £18 18s 0d. In a few years time many brave young fliers would be buying a single to the German capital. Weather, which was also to be a problem during the Second World War, restricted the services. It also became apparent that Hull would have to find an airfield that was better equipped to allow for night and all-weather flying. Therefore, it was no surprise when KLM decided that they would stop flying to Hull and by the end of 1935 all services had ceased.

Club flying continued but with the outbreak of the Second World War this also ceased. The site was surveyed as a possible military airfield but was rejected for many reasons, the main one being that it was too close to the oil tanks at Salt End. Rejected by the RAF, the airfield was littered with hundreds of old cars to render a landing impossible for it constituted a danger in being a suitable place for enemy aircraft to land. In the north-west corner of the airfield an anti-aircraft battery was established for the duration of the war years.

In June 1945 Lord Swinton, the Minister for Civil Aviation, recommended that local RAF stations should be surveyed with a view to adopting them as civil airfields once the RAF left. Facilities for civil aviation at Hull were at a low ebb and towards the end of the 1940s Hedon opened as a speedway track. The clubhouse was renovated and the hangar was used as a grandstand but the team, called 'Hull's Angels', failed in their venture.

With lack of interest Hedon was discarded as a Municipal airfield on July 11 1951 and Hull Corporation Airfield Company disbanded. But there were still interested parties and in October 1964 a demonstration was given at Hedon by a Nottingham firm, using a German Dornier aircraft. Watched by the Hull Corporation Town Planning Committee, it took off from the bumpy airfield, flew around and then landed. Unfortunately it hit a pothole, damaging both the undercarriage and the slim chance of bringing aircraft back to Hedon. Today only the hangar survives in the north-west corner and only memories remain of those distant flying days.

Hutton Cranswick, Yorkshire
106/SE010516. To the S of Great Driffield

Hutton Cranswick was only a few miles to the south of the pre-war airfield of Driffield as the crow flies and, presumably, the aircraft which would obviously cause circuit overlap. However, it opened under No 12 Group, Fighter Command, in January 1942, and was used throughout its existence as a fighter station. Indeed, it might have been termed a Spitfire station for numerous squadrons were to pass through here and the vast majority were equipped with Spitfires. No 4 Group, Bomber Command, had taken over the nearby fighter station of Leconfield, and Hutton was to be the replacement fighter airfield.

Sited on the west side of the A164 Watton to Hutton Cranswick road, the airfield was laid out more as a bomber station for it had three concrete runways. The main 10/28 runway was aligned east to west and was 4,950 ft long. The two intersecting runways were 3,960 ft and 3,330 ft in length. A perimeter track linked the ends of each one.

The technical site, which was equipped with two hangars of the 'T2' type, was situated in the north-east corner of the airfield near the village of Hutton Cranswick while the dispersed sites were all around the tiny hamlet of Watton with WAAF sites 2 and 3 each side of the road. The sick quarters site was some distance away on the east side of Watton and close to the LNER railway line. The bomb dump was in Cawkeld Chalk Pit in the south-west corner of the airfield.

The first resident unit was No 610 Squadron which arrived from Leconfield in January 1942. This squadron had Spifire Vbs and remained until April 1942 when it exchanged with 19 Squadron at Ludham. This squadron, code letters 'QV', had Spitfire Vs and on May 6 1942 moved to Perranporth. It was replaced the following day by No 308 (Polish) Squadron which arrived with Spitfire Vbs from Exeter. During early July the squadron moved to Redhill but returned after only six days and at the end of July moved out in exchange with another Polish unit, No 316 Squadron from Heston. This unit, flying Spitfire IXs coded 'SZ', became the resident squadron and was joined the following November by the Typhoon Mk Ibs of No 195 Squadron.

Both units saw the winter out at Hutton

Cranswick and, on February 12 1943, No 195 Squadron moved out to Woodvale. The following month 316 Squadron moved to Northolt. That same month No 306 (Polish) Squadron arrived, to be joined in April by 302 Squadron. No 306 remained only a few weeks and at the end of May moved to Catterick.

June 1943 saw the departure of 302 Squadron with their Spitfire Vbs, code letters 'WX', and the arrival of yet another Polish fighter squadron when 315 arrived from Northolt. This unit, flying Spitfire Mk Vbs, code letters 'PK', was only on detachment and left the following month. They were replaced by 308 Squadron which returned from Church Fenton. This unit was still flying Spitfire Vbs and remained until the following September when it then moved to Heston once again.

During mid-September 1943, No 234 Squadron arrived from Rochford with Spitfire VIs. A week later Nos 168 and 170 Squadrons arrived with North American Mustangs. Both units had arrived in order to test out the steel mesh runway at Huggate Wold and after a few test flights from Hutton Cranswick both units moved into Huggate Wold on October 10 and 11.

On December 1 1943, No 291 Squadron formed here from 613, 629 and 634 Anti-Aircraft Co-operation Flights. The main task for this unit was target towing on the east coast for anti-aircraft batteries and it was to remain at Hutton Cranswick for the duration of the war. On December 19 a detachment from 278 Squadron arrived with a few Ansons and at the end of the month 234 exchanged places with 26 Squadron at Church Fenton.

The New Year saw the arrival of the Canadians into this part of Yorkshire, and Hutton Cranswick became No 16 Armament Practice Camp, absorbing in the process No 1489 Fighter Gunnery Flight which had arrived in 1943.

During early February 1944 a detachment from 91 Squadron arrived from Tangmere but returned in a matter of days. On February 12, No 26 Squadron went to Scorton but returned again at the end of the month. It then moved to Peterhead on March 30 but Hutton Cranswick had not seen the last of it yet. Meanwhile, the Spitfire Vcs of 310 Squadron had arrived from Mendlesham on February 21 but went back again after only four days. As they departed 403 Squadron, RCAF, arrived but on the last day of the month it returned to Kenley. The next Canadian unit to arrive was No

443 Squadron which arrived from Holmsley on March 27. At the end of the month the detachment from 278 Squadron moved out. April then saw the departure of 443 Squadron on the 7th and on the 21st No 26 Squadron arrived from Ayr, but this was its last visit and a week later it moved to Lee-on-Solent.

Two more Canadian units were in and out during April, 441 Squadron from the 12th to the 22nd and 442 from the 25th to May 1. The last of the Canadians arrived from Hurn on May 11. This was 439 Squadron, RCAF, which was equipped with Hawker Typhoon Mk Ibs, unit code '5V'. Like all the previous units it remained only a few days and moved back to Hurn on the 20th of the month.

Still under No 12 Group, the status of the station as at June 6 1944 was 291 Squadron which was now equipped with Hurricanes and Martinets, a detachment of 2 Tactical Exercise Unit, Balado Bridge, with Spitfires, and 'B' Flight, 309 (Polish) Squadron with Hurricane IIcs.

During July and August 1944 No 310 Squadron, flying Spitfire Vcs, was detached from Digsby and the Czechs took over during this period. After their departure the pace began to slow down and the hectic days of the transient fighter units was over. For the remaining months training continued from Hutton Cranswick, but its role was almost complete.

With the war in Europe almost over the Spitfire IXs of No 124 Squadron arrived on April 27 1945, moving out again during mid-June only to return again on July 10, but after only five days they departed for the last time. Meanwhile, the long reigning 291 Squadron had outlived its usefulness and disbanded on June 26 1945.

During the latter part of July the Spitfire F21s of No 1 Squadron moved in from Ludham and the following month they were joined by Spitfire F9s of 288 Squadron. Then, on September 24, No 1 Squadron moved out, only to return again on October 22. December 1945 saw the arrival of No 129 Squadron, the last of so many and the end of an era. Flying Spitfire F9s, this unit moved out early in the New Year but was back again on February 2 1946. It was then decided not to retain Hutton Cranswick as a permanent station and it began a rundown of units. At the end of April 1946, No 1 Squadron moved to Tangmere and on May 3, 129 Squadron moved out to Lubeck. Finally, on May 24, No 288

Squadron, which had re-equipped with Vengeances, moved to East Moor. By the summer, all units had gone and after No 16 Armament Practice Camp had closed the airfield closed to flying in mid-1946.

Today, the control tower has been preserved and is in use as a private dwelling. An industrial estate now occupies the old technical site and one 'T2' hangar remains. One piece of the 10/28 runway survives and is used by the Miller Crop Spraying Company for one of their aircraft which is based here. The rest of the runways have been removed. The rasp of the Merlin no loger rips asunder the still Yorkshire air.

Kettleness, Yorkshire

94/NZ830158. NW of Whitby

Situated on the north-east Yorkshire coast, this was an isolated site that was used as a landing ground for the Royal Naval Air Service during the First World War. Being right on the coast it also served as an inshore reconnaissance station and continued in this role for the duration of the war. Although having no further military use the site was retained and is today a Coastguard station.

Kirkleatham, Yorkshire

93/NZ590220. W of Redcar

Situated a few miles inland from Redcar, the site was of very little significance. It was commissioned as a mooring-out station for Howden and opened in May 1918, with the arrival of 'Zeros' *SSZ54, 55* and *62*. During August, September and October 1918 the *SSZ31, 33, 56* and *64* operated from here and at Lowthorpe. But, it had a very brief life and closed immediately after the Armistice in November 1918.

Knavesmire, Yorkshire

105/SE595495. S of the City of York between the River Ouse and A1036 road

York racecourse, known as Knavesmire, was first used for would-be flyers as far back as 1912. Early that year two all-steel Type E monoplanes were built by Blackburn and the second machine was brought to Knavesmire for flight testing by Norman Blackburn and R.W. Kenworthy. This was a two-seater with a 70 hp air-cooled Renault 'vee' engine, but it proved too heavy to leave the ground and in fact never did get airborne. However, it did have claim as the first

aeroplane with all-metal structure of original British design.

During the First World War, York racecourse was used as a landing ground by 'B' Flight of 33 Squadron, RFC, during April and May 1916. This unit was equipped with BE2c aeroplanes and formed part of the Home Defence Organisation whose role was to provide air defence for York against attacks by German Zeppelins.

As in many other cases, there was considerable local resistance to the use of Knavesmire as an airfield. After the Zeppelin raid on May 2/3 1916, when bombs fell on York, this airfield was closed. It was felt that the glare of the flare-path would attract further raids. Efforts were made to find an alternative site and by the end of May, 'B' Flight had moved to Copmanthorpe, about three miles further south.

During the Second World War the site was again brought into use when an AA battery was formed here. Today, it is once again used for the Sport of Kings and is the main racecourse for the north of England.

Leconfield, Yorkshire

107/TA030435. N of Beverley on E side of the A164 road at Leconfield village

Situated only about two miles north of Beverley, this rather restricted site was chosen to be developed as a bomber base during the Expansion schemes of the mid-1930s. The main Beverley to Great Driffield railway line formed the eastern boundary and the A164 road the western. An arc of 'C' type hangars was built on the western edge of the landing area, backed by substantial workshops, messes and living accommodation.

Leconfield opened on December 3 1936 in No 3 Group, Bomber Command, and No 166 Squadron, equipped with Heyford biplanes, arrived from Boscombe Down on January 7 1937. This unit was joined a few weeks later by 97 Squadron, also from Boscombe Down. Leconfield was then taken over by No 4 Group, Bomber Command, on June 29 1937.

In an attempt to speed up the flow of qualified observers into the rapidly expanding Air Force, both squadrons became components of an air observers school from June 7 1938. They both ran 12-week courses for direct entry observers during that period. In March 1939, No 97 became a Group Pool squadron followed in May by 166 Squadron. During the next two months both squadrons converted to Whitleys and in September they moved to Abingdon, Berkshire, as Group Pool squadrons, leaving Leconfield inactive for a few weeks.

The station was then reduced to Care and Maintenance until it was taken over by No 13 Group, Fighter Command, in October 1939. On the 23rd of the month the Spitfires of 616 Squadron, code letters 'QJ', arrived from Doncaster and were joined a few days later by their detachment from Finningley. On October 15, No 72 Squadron moved in from Church Fenton but on the 28th moved out to Drem. On the 30th, two squadrons re-formed with Blenheim Ifs, No 234 coded 'AZ' and No 245 coded 'DX'.

For the next two years the station was temporary home for many of the famous squadrons of Fighter Command which made short stays, usually from the front-line stations in Southern England. Throughout this period Leconfield was equipped with a decoy airfield at Routh, a few miles to the east, but records are not clear as to what purpose it served. It was listed as a 'Q' site but did not have any dummy aircraft or buildings.

January 1940 saw the Spitfires return with No 72 Squadron but within days they moved to Church Fenton. The following month 616 Squadron moved to Catfoss but returned during early March.

May 1940 was a very busy month with the departures of 616 Squadron to Rochford, 234 Squadron to Church Fenton and 245 Squadron to Drem, having just converted to Hurricanes. On the 18th of the month the Hurricanes of 249 Squadron from Church Fenton arrived at Leconfield and on May 27 eight Spitfires and two Magisters of No 74 (Tiger) Squadron, together with ground crews. For 74 Squadron, code letters 'ZP', the move was to rest after the casualties of May and to re-arm with Spitfire IIs. On June 1 1940, news was received that Flight Lieutenant (Sailor) Malan, of 74, had been awarded the DFC. With the rest spell over No 74 returned to Rochford on June 6, albeit without the Spitfire IIs. It was replaced the same day by the return of 616 Squadron.

On July 7 the Hurricanes of 249 Squadron returned to Church Fenton and on the 13th of the month No 302 (Polish) Squadron was formed at Leconfield. No 616 Squadron then moved to Kenley on August 19 and that same month a detachment of Spitfires from 64 Squadron, Church Fenton, arrived.

Having worked up to operational capacity, No 302 Squadron moved to Northolt in mid-October to relieve 303 Squadron which replaced it at Leconfield. 72 Squadron returned during October but moved out after only a few days to Coltishall. No 258 Squadron re-formed on November 20 1940 with an establishment of Hurricanes. A week later the Hurricanes of No 213 Squadron arrived from Tangmere and on November 30 the newly-formed 258 Squadron moved to Duxford.

During the first week of January 1941 No 303 Squadron returned to Northolt, being replaced by the Hurricanes of 253 Squadron which arrived from Kenley. On January 15, No 213 Squadron moved out to Driffield and on February 19, 253 Squadron moved to Skeabrae.

On April 28, No 60 Operational Training Unit was formed at Leconfield with a complement of 24 Blenheims, six Defiants and six Oxfords. It was the second such unit and was tasked with the training of night fighter pilots for the squadrons of Fighter Command. Its stay was very brief and, on June 4, the OTU moved to East Fortune.

On June 16 1941 No 129 Squadron was formed at Leconfield and a week later 16 Spitfire Mk Is arrived. The following day two more Spitfires arrived and the squadron was allotted the call sign 'Taker' and the code letters 'DV' were painted on all the aircraft. By the end of the month Pilot Officer D.O. Cunliffe and Sergeant/Pilot V.E. Tucker from Jamaica (the only West Indian pilot in the RAF) were posted in and, with the allocation of a Miles Magister, No 129 Squadron began to take recognisable shape. No 129's diarist wrote on June 30: 'The allowance of three Spitfires per pilot and a 'Maggie' for the Adjutant was felt to be reasonable'.

On July 1 the Spitfires of 313 Squadron arrived from Catterick. Two more pilots were then posted in for 129 Squadron during the first two days of the month and on the 5th, Flying Officer J. Walker arrived from Scotland, ostensibly as Medical Officer to the squadron. 129's diarist wrote at the time: 'He immediately attempted to justify his existence by declaring four pilots u/s owing to ear trouble, but was promptly packed off to

129 (Mysore) Squadron at Leconfield.

Church Fenton by the Adjutant before he could do any further damage'.

For the next ten days 129 Squadron proceeded with its training as far as the English summer would allow. Various pilots were attached to 129 for training but as fast as they reached operational standard thay were snatched up by other squadrons. On July 16 the new unit was allotted the name of 129 (Mysore) Squadron in honour of the Indian State which had subscribed to present a squadron of Spitfires.

The Lysanders of No 26 Squadron, code letters 'RM', arrived from Weston Zoyland on July 19 but after only three days they moved to Gatwick. On the 24th of the month 129 Squadron made its first operational patrol lasting for one hour and 45 minutes.

On July 26 Sergeant/Pilots A.J.L Boddy, B. Ibbotson and R.G.E. Wilson joined 129 Squadron from 53 OTU, Llandow. The following day Sergeant/Pilot W.F. Sims arrived; No 129 Squadron was now beginning to assume reasonable proportions and proceeded to Wittering for its first Wing Formation Practice.

July 29 saw the arrival of No 81 Squadron from Debden and at the end of the month Sergeant/Pilot Sherk arrived from 412 Squadron at Digby to join 129. A busy and satisfactory month came to an end with the formation of No 134 Squadron, code letters 'GQ'.

August started with a rush of pilots to join 129 Squadron, two arriving from 411 and two from 412. On August 2, No 129 Squadron took over readiness for the afternoon and at just 16.00 hours Flight Lieutenant McPherson and Pilot Officer 'Butch' Cunliffe took off on a scramble. One hour later they had found and shot down a Ju 88 off Flamborough Head. No 129 (Mysore) Squadron had brought down its first Hun and it was not yet fully operational.

During the morning of August 8, 129 made its first Formation Flight and was returning to lunch when Flight Lieutenant Thomas and Sergeant Bowman were sent up to investigate an inquisitive German off Flamborough Head. After 15 minutes an Me 110 with two extra fuel tanks under its wings outboard of the engines was sighted. The enemy aircraft swung round and headed south-east, diving at about 430 mph. Blue 2 followed in the dive but the enemy aircraft was lost in a haze which reached up to 1,000 ft, forcing Blue 2 to pull up to 3,000 ft from where he could see down through it. He saw the Me 110 flying about 50 ft above sea level.

Blue 2 dived and attacked with a two-second burst at 250 yards from the quarter astern on the port side and saw hits register but did not notice any returning fire. Blue 2 then positioned himself dead astern on same level and fired a series of two-second bursts from 100 yards. The Me 110 tried evading action by wide swinging movements which caused his starboard wingtip to touch the water on one occasion. A burst from Blue 2 hit the starboard engine and extra fuel tank of the enemy aircraft. Black smoke came from the engine and petrol tank. The next burst hit the port engine and extra fuel tank with similar result. This continuous attack finished with a final burst directed at the fuselage which exhausted the Spitfire's ammunition.

Blue 2 was satisfied the Me 110 was fatally damaged and climbed to 1,000 ft to watch results. Sergeant (Bowey) Bowman saw the Me 110 slow down and port, then starboard propellor stop. The enemy aircraft made a good touchdown during which the extra fuel tanks were ripped off and the aircraft sank after about one minute, its position plotted approximately 70 miles east of Flamborough Head. Two men were seen in the sea, but no dinghy. Throughout all this Blue 1, who had lost the enemy aircraft in the haze but heard Blue 2 on the R/T, had arrived in time to see the touchdown and the men in the sea. Both 129 Spitfires landed at Leconfield undamaged. Two victims for 129 Squadron and it was still not operational.

August 8 saw two Australian pilots, Pilot Officer Dekyvere and Pilot Officer Armstrong, join 129 Squadron from 257. Two days later 129 Squadron suffered its first bad accident. Sergeant Purdy broke away from formation and dived straight into the ground near Driffield. The cause of the tragedy was unknown and a good pilot was lost. For the next ten days 129 continued training with the squadron showing greater precision and skill with each formation practice. During this period 129's diarist wrote: 'The doctor was noticed prowling around with itching stethoscope but was prevented from doing any harm by the Adjutant's order that pilots were not allowed to speak to him'.

During this final work-up for 129, Nos 81 and 134 Squadrons moved to Russia. At 16.00 hours on August 20, No 129 Squadron was at official readiness for the first time. Scrambles came thick and fast on this and subsequent days but the enemy sheered off before being engaged. On August 25 No 129 Squadron celebrated its becoming operational by a party in the NAAFI at which roughly 150 all ranks were present. During the day Sergeants P.P. Stuivenga and H.W. Sangerhaus, both from Rhodesia, and Sergeant B.D. Waghorn arrived to join the squadron which was now representative of nearly all the Colonies.

On August 26 the Spitfires of 313 Squadron moved to Portreath and the following day it was known that 129 Squadron was going to Tangmere. The arrangements were confirmed on August 28 for 129 to leave on the following day. So, at 13.30 hours the Advance Guard consisting of the Adjutant and the Intelligence Officer said goodbye to Leconfield and set out by road for 'down south'. The main body left that evening by train and the flying personnel flew 14-strong on August 29 to arrive impressively and still 14-strong at the Tangmere satellite station of Westhampnett around mid-day. Here they found 20 Spitfire Mk

Vbs—nearly new ones too—waiting for them. The squadron was now in No 11 Group and very much on active service in the front line.

Meanwhile, back at Leconfield the Spitfires of No 610 Squadron from Westhampnett had arrived to replace the outgoing unit, but the fighter role and the hectic days of fighter squadrons were almost over for Leconfield. During October 1941, No 28 Conversion Flight was formed here, receiving its first five Halifax BIs on October 28. During December 1941, No 107 Conversion Flight formed here but by the end of the month both No 28 and No 107 Conversion Flights had moved to Marston Moor. Leconfield was then transferred to No 4 Group, Bomber Command, and closed for reconstruction to make it suitable for heavy bomber operations. 610 Squadron remained until the new fighter airfield at Hutton Cranswick was ready, moving there on January 14 1942. On March 1, No 15 (P) AFU formed at Leconfield and over the next few months operated from here with Acaster Malbis and Kirmington as satellites. It operated from the latter until early October.

In 1942, it was decided to create the Canadian Group and during the reconstruction period the headquarters unit was formed at Leconfield on October 25, although by December it had moved to Allerton Park.

Leconfield re-opened on December 2 1942 as a standard heavy bomber station with the usual three concrete runways encircled by a perimeter track and hardstandings for the bombers. With the airfield now operational again the Oxfords of No 15 (P) AFU moved out to Andover on December 15 and with their departure the first heavy bomber units arrived. These were two newly formed Wellington squadrons from nearby Driffield, Nos 196 and 466. The latter was first into action and the first bombing mission was on the night of January 15/16 1943, when three Wellingtons bombed Lorient and another aircraft aborted.

The first operational mission for 196 Squadron was on the night of February 4/5, eight Wellington Xs bombing Lorient. Another Wellington was damaged on take off, but circled the airfield while the rest of the squadron took off and then landed safely. Both units continued to play an active part and made many raids on enemy ports and industrial centres of Europe. They also undertook many minelying missions.

During July 1943, No 196 Squadron moved to Witchford, Cambridgeshire, and at the end of the month 1502 BAT Flight arrived from Driffield. This unit saw very little training and on August 9 1943 it disbanded. Throughout this period the bombing offensive continued with the resident squadron and in September 466 converted to Halifax B MK IIs which were used for training and also for some air/sea rescue searches. October 14 1943 saw the arrival of 170 Squadron from Huggate Wold but after only two days their Mustangs moved to Thruxton. That same month No 466 began to receive Halifax B IIIs and remained with these for the remainder of the European War.

The New Year saw the birth of yet another squadron when No 640 was formed at Leconfield on January 7 1944 as a heavy bomber unit from 'C' Flight of 158 Squadron. Equipped with Halifax BIIIs, code letters 'C8', it flew its first two missions from Lissett but all subsequent missions were flown from Leconfield. During February 640 Squadron lost two

aircraft through fatal crashes and three on operations.

On February 15, Halifax III *LW585* was returning from ops when it hit high ground near Cloughton, four miles north-west of Scarborough, at 01.30 hours. The pilot was Flying Officer Barkley and the bomber was either lost or out of fuel. Six crew were killed.

The second fatal crash came the following night when Halifax III *LW439*, coded *C8-V*, was returning from ops and had made it back to Yorkshire despite all navigation aids being u/s. Visibility was poor and the bomber was short of fuel, so pilot and crew baled out, during which three were injured, one seriously. The Halifax crashed near a railway line between Sessay Wood and Coxwold, Yorkshire, between 01.20 and 01.50 hours, some 50 miles north-west of the airfield. It is interesting to note that the pilot was none-other than Flight Sergeant E.T. Vicary who had also had one or two near misses while training at Riccall (see page 157).

No 640 Squadron became the main resident unit for, on June 3 1944, No 466

Below *Leconfield in August 1952: Lincoln of the Central Gunnery School.* **Bottom** *Meteor TT4 VT312 at Leconfield in 1952.*

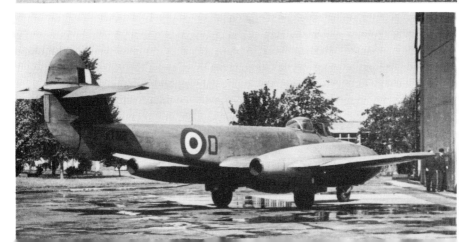

Squadron returned to Driffield. The status of the 4 Group station as at June 6 was 640 Squadron and 1520 BAT Flight which had arrived with its Oxfords the previous month from Holme-on-Spalding Moor. The BAT Flight remained here only a few months and on September 18 moved to Sturgate in Lincolnshire.

No 96 Squadron, Transport Command, re-formed here on December 30 1944 and was allotted the code letters 'ZJ'. For the next few weeks crews were posted in and one to arrive in late January 1945 was Flying Officer Doug Bancroft. His previous posting had been as an instructor to the Lichfield OTU and now he was back again in Yorkshire and reunited with some of his friends from 158 Squadron during their Lissett days, including his good friend Flying Officer 'Dumbo' Smith, still with his white elephant 'Dumbo'.

As 96 Squadron was forming the aircraft began to arrive—25 brand new Halifax VIIs. The ground crews set to work on the new aircraft, setting them up to carry troops and stretcher cases and polishing the fuselages and wings to a silver colour. The new squadron was informed that they would be flying troops and materials to India and bringing wounded personnel back to England, using Cairo as a staging post.

A few weeks later they were told that 96 Squadron would be operating from a base in southern England and were sent on two weeks' leave. After only a week they all received telegrams cancelling their leave and ordering them to return immediately to their unit at Leconfield. Arriving back they were told to prepare to fly the aircraft to Cairo where they would be based. Sadly, during flight testing, one of the aircraft, Halifax *MZ464* piloted by

Flying Officer Max Hubbard, RAAF, crashed at 15.30 hours into high ground at Brantingham, near Brough, Yorkshire, during descent in bad visibility. All the crew of six were killed.

Within days of being detailed to go to Cairo several crews from 96 Squadron began to ferry the new aircraft back to the Handley-Page works to be scrapped, much to the complete disgust of the whole squadron. During the latter part of March 1945 several of the squadron aircrews, as advance party, were then flown out to Cairo West whilst the remainder entrained for Gaurock on the Clyde and embarked on a troopship for Egypt. Thus ended 96 Squadron's formation and stay at Leconfield.

On April 20 No 51 Squadron arrived from Snaith and flew a few missions from here, but the end was in sight and both 51 and 640 Squadrons flew their last operational missions of World War 2 on April 25 1945, when each despatched 18 Halifaxes to bomb gun batteries on the Island of Wangerooge.

From January 1944 to April 1945, No 640 Squadron had dropped 8,482 tons of bombs and had won the No 4 Group Bombing Cup no less than five times—a record unequalled during any span of time by any other squadron in No 4 Group. However, its days were now at an end and on May 7 1945 it disbanded and the station was then transferred to Transport Command. No 51 remained as a transport squadron and during June converted to Stirling Mk Vs, finally moving out to Stradishall on August 21 1945.

Leconfield was retained as a permanent airfield and on November 5 1945 the advance party of the Central Gunnery School arrived from Catfoss, the main party following a week later. This unit was

Leconfield on July 30 1963. Lightning line-up of Nos 19 and 92 Squadrons. Also very good view of the 'C' type hangars.

to remain for the next decade during which time it became the Fighter Weapons School and re-equipped with Meteor F8s. The station then had a change of role and during October 1957 the Fighter Weapons School moved to Driffield. Airfield improvements were carried out and the main runway, unusually north-south, probably because of the confines of the site, was extended and then for several years it was a front-line jet fighter base as well as the home of a flight of search and rescue helicopters from 275 Squadron which moved in from Thornaby on October 9 1957, with Sycamores.

The first fighter squadrons, No 19 with Hunters and No 72 with Javelins, arrived from Church Fenton during the latter part of June 1959. The following December No 275 was re-numbered 228 Squadron and continued in a search and rescue role alongside the fighter squadrons. These were further increased when the Javelins of 41 Squadron arrived from Wattisham. The arrival of 41 Squadron was partly to do with repairs being carried out at their home base and partly in connection with the visit of six Vautour 2Ns of the 30e Escadre de Chasse Tous-Temps which were at Leconfield between July 19-28. During this period a contingent of 72's Javelins paid a return courtesy visit to their base at Tours, France. No 41 operated with 72 Squadron until returning to their own base on September 15 1960. This left 72 Squadron to soldier on with their old Javelin FAW 4s, despite many rumours that they would be re-equipped with Javelin 9s. The ground crews worked hard to keep them in service and many of the FAW 4s had red adhesive strips around the engine intake lips to prevent the cracked paint from peeling off and being sucked into the engines.

At the end of February 1961, the Javelins of 72 Squadron moved to Leeming while Leconfield's runway was re-strengthened. No 72 returned on May 2 and was greeted with the news that disbandment was scheduled for the near future. At the end of May the Hunters of 92 Squadron arrived from Middleton St George. With disbandment now imminent eight Javelins of 72 Squadron flew north to Ouston, the headquarters of 13 Group, and took part in a last flypast on June 29 1961 before disbanding the following day. Meanwhile, the two remaining fighter squadrons converted to Lightnings. On September 1 1964, 228 Squadron was re-numbered 202 Squadron, now with Whirlwind helicopters. During this period Sailor Malan's old squadron, No 74, had a detachment of Lightnings at Leconfield for a short period.

Throughout the changes the search and rescue helicopters continued to operate out of Leconfield and took part in many notable incidents such as the evacuation of 300 men and women from RAF Fylingdales in January 1963 when the station was cut off by snow.

The days were now numbered for Leconfield as a front-line jet fighter station and, on September 23 1965, No 19 Squadron moved to Gütersloh, Germany. The last fighter unit did not remain for very long and on December 29 1965, 92 Squadron moved to Gelsenkirchen, Germany.

After the fighter squadrons had moved out No 60 Maintenance Unit took over but remained only a few months before moving to Abingdon the following year when Leconfield closed, apart from a small enclave from which the helicopter flight continued to operate.

Leconfield was then handed over to the Army who took over on January 1 1977, with the arrival of the advance party of

Westland Whirlwind HAR 10 helicopter XP354 of the ASR unit at Leconfield.

Above *Aerial view of Leconfield in April 1981.* **Left** *Control tower at Leconfield in December 1980.*

and training location of the Army School of Mechanical Transport. The runways have been converted to a nursery driver training circuit with traffic lights, hill starts, manoeuvring areas etc. The hangars remain, two having been converted to instructional accommodation, one to a workshop and one to a maintenance and quick repair area, while the fifth serves the need of the RAF Search and Rescue helicopter flight.

Leeds/Bradford (Yeadon), Yorkshire
See Yeadon

Leeming, Yorkshire
99/SE305890. W of Northallerton

Situated in the Vale of York on the east side of the Great North Road to the south of Leeming Bar and junction with the A684 road, Leeming dates back to early in 1938 when parts of Clapham Lodge and Wilson's Farm were made into an airfield for use by the Yorkshire Air Services, one of the first flying clubs in England. But this site and the adjacent land of Newton House Farm were immediately acquired by the Crown in the latter half of 1938, drained, levelled and made into an airfield for the Royal Air Force. It was a standard bomber airfield with the permanent buildings to the south-east of the landing ground. The barracks were brick-built and the hangars were 'C1's, the austerity version of the 'C' type. The airfield came

the Army School of Mechanical Transport. At the time of their arrival 'B' Flight 202 (Search and Rescue) Squadron, RAF, still operated from here with a complement of 35 officers and men. This unit was subsequently redesignated as 'D' Flight 22 Squadron, with a search and rescue role. Their two yellow-painted Whirlwind Mk 10 helicopters are a familiar sight in these parts for the crews are kept very busy. On December 8 1980 the ASR unit carried out their 2,000th mission. The crews work 24-hour shifts followed by a further 24-hour period of being on call at their homes. During each shift the crews are expected to carry out training flights. During summer 1981 the Whirlwinds were replaced by the more modern Wessex.

Leconfield, renamed Normandy Barracks, is to remain as the Headquarters to the edge of Leeming village, after which it was named, and the three village pubs were destined for greater things, particularly the *Black Bull*. A decoy airfield was sited at Burneston, approximately four miles to the south of the main airfield.

Leeming opened in June 1940, the first occupants being the night fighters of 219 Squadron on detachment from nearby Catterick. In July 1940, however, the Whitley Mk V bombers of 10 Squadron arrived from Dishforth and Leeming first saw action on July 20, when nine Whitleys bombed an airfield at Wejendorf, Germany. The squadron continued the offensive from Leeming and took part in the 'Battle of the Barges' along the French and Belgian coasts. The Channel ports of Calais, Boulogne, Le Havre, Lorient and Antwerp were also high on the target list.

The build-up of units continued and No 7 re-formed as a heavy bomber squadron on August 1 1940. It became the first squadron in Bomber Command to have four-engined bombers. Equipped with the new Short Stirling Mk Is, unit code letters 'MG', it immediately began working-up for operations. The first Stirling, *N3640*, which was delivered on August 2, crashed at Hodge Branding, Kirkby Lonsdale, Lancashire, on September 29 1940. After many cross-country navigational flights 7 Squadron moved to Oakington in October of that year. That same month the Blenheim Ifs of 219 Squadron left Leeming.

Meanwhile, during the latter part of August 1940, the remaining Whitleys of 102 Squadron arrived from Driffield but the following month they moved to Linton-on-Ouse. This unit was quickly replaced by No 35 (Madras Presidency) Squadron which arrived in November from Boscombe Down where it had just re-formed on the 5th of the month. The squadron was alloted the code letters 'TL' and had reformed for the express purpose of introducing the new four-engined Handley Page Halifax into operational service. The unit remained here only a few weeks and, in early December 1940, it also moved to Linton-on-Ouse.

Throughout the changes, 10 Squadron had continued operations with the Whitleys. On August 23 1941 Whitley V *T4234* was returning from a bombing mission over Le Havre when, at 00.41 hours, it crashed on Widdale Fell in the Yorkshire Dales. Pilot Officer Liebeck

and Sergeant Fletcher were killed, the other crew member, Flight Lieutenant R. Silver, survived. The aircraft was descending through cloud in ignorance of the exact geographical position and flew into a hillside. Parts still remain today and are blown about by the wind on the fell.

September 1941 saw the Whitleys of the resident unit joined by those of No 77 Squadron which arrived from Topcliffe. This unit had, in fact, been at Chivenor for temporary duty with No 19 Group, Coastal Command. It had been on anti-submarine patrols over the Bay of Biscay and on September 3 sank the *U-705* with depth charges.

During the latter part of 1941, 10 Squadron began to convert to Halifaxes and during January 1942, No 10 Squadron Conversion Flight had formed for this purpose.

No 77 Squadron remained until May 1942, when it then returned to Chivenor on loan to Coastal Command. That same month 10 Squadron put up 22 aircraft on operation Millennium, the first Thousand-Bomber raid on Cologne. Two nights later the squadron sent 20 aircraft on the second such raid against Essen and, on June 25/26, 20 aircraft for the third against Bremen.

The following month, 16 Halifaxes and crews of No 10 were detached to No 205 Group in the Middle East. Six of the squadron's Halifaxes took part in a daylight attack on the *Gneisenau* and *Scharnhorst* at Brest, but this was not a success. Also, for the first four months of 1942, detachments had been at Lossiemouth for operations against the *Tirpitz* in the Trondheim area of Norway. This was a difficult target for a heavy bomber, which was ineffective in this role. The *Tirpitz* was sheltering along the coast and was made more difficult to hit by means of an effective smoke-screen. During one of the attacks, on April 27/28, the Commanding Officer, Wing Commander Donald Bennett (later to form the Pathfinder Force and command No 8 Group), was shot down. Wing Commander Bennett had descended from 2,000 to 200 feet but, by the time he had identified the *Tirpitz*, his Halifax had been hit and the starboard wing was ablaze. Bennett struggled back to height, ordered his crew to bale out and he then followed suit. He escaped via Sweden and was back in command of the squadron within five weeks.

In August 1942, No 10 Squadron and the Conversion Flight moved to Melbourne. That same month, Royal Canadian Air Force bomber squadrons began to concentrate at stations of No 4 Group in Yorkshire. It had been agreed to form a Canadian Bomber Group and this was now underway. On August 13, No 419 (Moose) Squadron, RCAF, arrived here from No 3 Group, Mildenhall. The squadron was equipped with Wellington Mk IIIs, unit code letters 'VR'. However, the unit was only here a few days and on the 17th of the month it moved to Topcliffe.

The next Canadian squadron to arrive was No 408 (Goose) Squadron, RCAF, which was transferred from 5 Group to No 4 Group and arrived at Leeming on September 14 1942. The squadron code letters were 'EQ' and it exchanged its Hampdens for the Halifax Mark Vs. To facilitate this, No 408 Squadron Conversion Flight was formed on September 20 1942.

Under the Empire Air Training Scheme a number of Canadian Operational Training Units were to be formed; amongst these was No 1659 Heavy Conversion Unit which formed here on October 6 1942 from No 408 (Bomber) Squadron Conversion Flight and 405 Conversion Flight which arrived from Topcliffe on October 7. The role of the HCU, whose code letters were 'FD', was to provide conversion training on Halifax aircraft. On January 1 1943 Leeming, and its resident units, were transferred to No 6 Group, RCAF, and the station became No 63 (RCAF) Base.

Further changes were still needed to make the Canadian Group an effective force and 405 Squadron, Royal Canadian Air Force, arrived from Topcliffe on March 6, in exchange with No 1659 HCU which moved out on the 14th to Topcliffe, which had now become the training centre. The movement of men and aircraft was now quite hectic throughout both No 4 and No 6 Groups, RCAF.

April was a very busy month and, on the 7th, No 424 Squadron arrived from Topcliffe with Wellingtons. On the 18th, having re-equipped with Halifax B IIs, 405 Squadron was tranferred to Gransden Lodge, Bedfordshire, to join No 8 (Pathfinder) Group: it was to be the only RCAF Pathfinder squadron. Their badge was an eagle's head erased, facing to the left and holding in the beak a sprig of maple. The motto, 'Ducimus' (we lead),

indicated that this was the first bomber, and only Pathfinder, squadron. The first pathfinder mission was on April 26 when 11 Halifaxes were despatched to mark Duisburg, at which time their Commander was Group Captain J.E. Fauquier, DSO and two Bars, DFC, who had taken over six days previously.

On May 2 1943, No 424 moved to Dalton and was replaced three days later by 427 (Lion) Squadron which moved in from Croft and began to re-equip with Halifax B Mk Vs. Leeming was to be their home for the next three years. During May 1943, the 'Lion' squadron was formally 'adopted' by Metro-Goldwyn-Mayer Studios, Hollywood, (MGM also being symbolised by a lion). This adoption meant a little more than others for all squadron members were granted special concessions at MGM cinemas. Also, several of the squadron Halifaxes bore the names of MGM stars, eg, *DK140* was named *Lana Turner*.

Units were now beginning to get settled and, on August 13 1943, No 429 (Bison) Squadron arrived from East Moor and began to re-equip with Halifaxes. Commanded by Wing Commander J.D. Pattison, DFC, who took over just prior to coming to Leeming, this was to be the second squadron for the station.

On August 26 'Goose' (No 408) moved out to Linton-on-Ouse, which left the 'Lion' and 'Bison' squadrons to get on with the task ahead. Both brought honour to their names whilst operating from Leeming. September saw Hanover as the main target with an attack on September 22/23 when a force of 716 was despatched, and again on September 27/28 when 683 heavy bombers were sent. Hanover was again the target on October 8/9 and 18/19.

Second in importance to Hanover in this area, Kassel, an industrial centre producing locomotives, aircraft engines and armoured vehicles, was attacked twice during October. The first raid was on October 3/4 when 540 were despatched and the second on October 22/23. This second raid was nearly spoiled by bad weather and severe icing. Flight Sergeant Keith Bowly was pilot of Halifax *JD384* and this was his third mission with his own crew. For the Kassel mission he and his crew had been briefed to take off and climb to 1,300 ft over base before setting course as there was a severe icing front over the North Sea. The Gee set was u/s and could not be made serviceable by

Leeming: Halifax Mk II 'Easy Does It' of No 429 Squadron on November 22 1943.

ground or aircraft crew beforehand, so eventually they were ordered to take off without it operating.

The pilot set course in a steep climbing turn over Leeming at 500 ft and was now 20 minutes late. As a consequence of this they were about 12,000 ft over the North Sea about an hour later and flying in heavy cloud. Suddenly chunks of ice started to fly off the airscrews and clang against the fuselage. Flight Sergeant Bowly says: 'I looked out to see clear ice about a foot thick on the airscrew spinners and about six inches thick on the leading edges of the wings'. At this stage the aircraft was at full power and going steadily down to the North Sea, but eventually at about 6,000 ft it ran into rain and the ice came away slowly. By the Dutch coast Bowly had made 19,000 ft and got to Kassel on time in spite of the late take-off. The return journey was uneventful and his Halifax landed back at base safely in spite of the icing.

After a trip to Dusseldorf on November 3/4, *JD384*'s next mission was to Cannes on November 11/12 when, on the return leg, the Halifax almost ran out of fuel and had to land at Marston Moor, causing a minor flap in the process.

During the late evening on December 3 1943, a new crew arrived from nearby Topcliffe having just been posted to 429 Squadron. Duly reporting to the Orderly Room for 'billets', they were informed the NCOs' aircrew billets were all filled and that they would have to bunk in the Airmen's Quarters for the night. They were then cheerfully informed that an 'Operation' was in progress that night and that there would be plenty of space for them in the morning. This shook them up, especially when they saw all the NCO

aircrew queued up to get their 'operational supper' that night at the Sergeants' Mess, all looking very serious and grim, with no horseplay or joking.

Sure enough, in the morning they found that many aircraft were missing from the Leipzig raid. A total force of 527 had been despatched and 451 had attacked the primary target. Total aircraft losses on the mission were 23 and Leeming was one of the stations that had many empty bunks. Charles Whitmore, the navigator, and the rest of the crew moved into Barrack Block No 13, promptly renumbered 12A by their little mid-upper gunner, 'Taffy' Duglan from Wales. The missing crew had left a target chart on the wall and this Leipzig operation had been their 17th.

After they had settled in they were paraded before Wing Commander Pattison, the CO of 429 'Bison' Squadron, for their 'welcome' chat, during which they were told to do their jobs while at Leeming and warned that if anyone didn't he would promptly be removed and replaced.

The new crew quickly got started doing cross-country training flights. It was on one of these high-level daylight exercises across Scotland that the pilot, Flying Officer Les Thompson, called up the flight-engineer, Flight Sergeant Stan Fisher, on the intercom and asked him if he could see the black cat walking across the wing between the two engines. The crew all woke up on hearing this and Flight Sergeant Budgen, the wireless operator, found the pilot's oxygen line was disconnected. He quickly coupled it up before he could pass out. During this period the skipper got his two 'Second Dickey' flights done—one to Berlin and one to Frankfurt. On the Berlin raid both the flight-engineer and the rear gunner filled places as 'spares' with other crews, so there were three of the new crew all on that Berlin operation, each in a different aircraft, and all returned safely.

At the end of December Flying Officer Thompson and his crew went on leave, after which they were on squadron 'Battle Orders' for the next operation which was Frankfurt. The crews attended briefing and were all ready to start up engines at dispersal when it was 'scrubbed'.

Flying Officer Thompson and his crew finally got started on their first 'op' which was to Magdeburg, on January 21/22 1944, in 'V'-Victor, when they were part of a total force of 648 heavy bombers. This raid was almost a total failure and the diversionary attack on Berlin failed to distract the enemy fighters which waited for the bomber stream near Hamburg and remained with them to the target. Visibility was good but enemy decoy markers misled the later Pathfinders, so many aircraft undoubtedly bombed decoys. Only the southern suburbs sustained any real damage at the Krupp Crusonwerke tank factory.

A total of 55 aircraft were missing from the Magdeburg raid but 'V'-Victor, after being airborne for 7 hours 15 minutes, touched down safely at Stradishall where they had been diverted because of bad weather over Yorkshire. They did have trouble in identifying Stradishall, having made a 'dead reckoning run' to it from the 'Occult' lighthouse, 21 miles ETA Stradishall, but they were dead centre of a triangle about ten miles a side containing three aerodromes, all lit up. They ended up in the same position after several dead reckoning runs, so the skipper took the Halifax down to treetop height and cut

across the circuit of each airfield, all of which were crowded with diverted aircraft, reading their call letter beacons until they came to Stradishall: a procedure not recommended for long life according to the *King's Rules and Regulations for Air*. From the Magdeburg raid no aircraft were lost by 429 Squadron although four were missing from 427 Squadron.

After an operation Wing Commander Pattison would hold a 'post-mortem' of all the squadron crews and would go over each crew's trip. From these meetings, their results, highlights, incidents and all points of interest, each officer could learn of other crews' problems and experiences and how to overcome them.

Pattison was quite a character but was well liked and highly respected by everyone on 429 Squadron. He was the driving force and the squadron owed a lot to his administration. He took over the reins of 429 Squadron on July 30 1943 from Wing Commander J.A. Piddington (Can/RAF), who had been killed in action on July 27, and remained at the helm until March 2 1944.

During his period as CO of 429 Squadron, Pattison used many 'tactics' and believed that height and speed were the things that saved the day. While he was in command, the squadron removed the mid-upper turrets from their Halifaxes as well as the balloon cable-cutters from the leading edges of the wings and varnished the leading edges and nose of the aircraft. As the mid-upper turret weighed 300 lb, its removal produced about 2,000 ft more height and 10 to 20 mph more airspeed. The displaced mid-upper gunner lay on a mattress on the floor and looked through a perspex blister for night fighters coming up from below.

Taken prior to night operation on November 3 1944. 427 Squadron Halifax Mk III.

As at all stations, there had been a rash of taxying accidents and the pilots had been told in no uncertain terms that there must be an end to that sort of thing. On the very next operation 429 Squadron were taxying to their take-off point with a crew bus following along behind when Wing Commander Pattison came taxying along very smartly and promptly ran an outer motor over the top of the bus. It was a Merlin engine with de Havilland wooden blade aircrew which went to matchwood; the groundcrew airman in the back of the bus nearly went through the roof. The aircraft was taken back to dispersal, a new airscrew put on and it carried on with the operation.

At the end of February 1944 Wing Commander Pattison was lost from the squadron after an accident. There were 32 bombed-up and fuelled-up aircraft of 427 and 429 Squadrons lined up on the perimeter track waiting to take off on a raid when a canister of 4 lb incendiaries, including a number of X-type anti-personnel mercury-fuzed bombs, somehow fell out below one of the aircraft. Pattison and the station Warrant Officer ran over and kicked the burning incendiaries out from under the bomber but in so doing both men were severely injured. Their actions probably saved many lives for both squadrons could have been wiped out.

Squadron Leader Kenny temporarily took over 429 Squadron and gave the crews the option of using the mid-upper turret or the floor blister, or alternatively a fixed mounting in the floor with a .50 calibre machine-gun.

During this period both resident units began to re-equip with the Halifax Mk III which had Hercules radial engines. It was a fact that Merlin-engined Halifax squadrons did not go on as many trips during the winter months for they did not have the power to climb over the bad weather peculiar to the European winter, and were stood down from a large number of sorties that were principally carried out by Lancasters.

On the Berlin raid of March 23/24, Halifax *LK806* 'Y'-Yorker of 429 Squadron ran into trouble in the Kiel Canal area after drifting south of track. As they cleared the danger area the aircraft was suddenly coned in an intense belt of searchlights and was hit several times by flak. A night fighter then engaged the aircraft, whose crew first became aware of its presence when the rear-gunner saw tracer coming from the port quarter. He was completely dazzled by the searchlights but opened fire in the direction of the tracer and at the same time ordered the captain to corkscrew port. As the pilot was rolling over a second burst of tracer appeared from the starboard quarter and again the rear-gunner sent in a burst in its direction and ordered the captain to corkscrew starboard. During the corkscrew manoeuvre and a 'stalled' turn back out of the defended area the wireless operator/air gunner had baled out. The Halifax cleared the Kiel defences and managed to shake off the fighter. Immediately preceding the attack the flight-engineer saw a red flare with green stars fall behind the Halifax which caused the flak to cease. As they headed for home the bomb-aimer went back and tossed the Photo Flash out the open rear fuselage door. The evasive action had been so violent it had thrown up the photo flash out of the flare chute and luckily the little propeller at the top end of the fuze had not become unscrewed to set off the flash.

The bomb load was jettisoned live and the trip back to base uneventful. However, as 'Y'-Yorker rolled down the runway back at Leeming the skipper found there was no brake pressure and the bomber rolled off the end of the runway and came to a halt in a sea of mud. Within minutes the squadron engineering officer pulled up alongside in a Jeep and wanted to know why the hell they were back so early and why they had blocked the runway. After a heated exchange of words from the skipper, 'Y'-Yorker was towed out of the mud and back into dispersal. The Halifax sustained damage to port fuselage in two places, several small holes in the starboard fuselage and to the starboard wing bomb compartment. The rear-gunner, Sergeant Fraser, fired about 500 rounds from his four guns with one No 2 stoppage in both left-hand guns.

The next night 'Y'-Yorker was patched up and back on ops to Aulnoye marshalling yards but just after take-off the flight-engineer found the cylinder head temperature of one of the engines up over the safety mark, so the skipper had to shut down the engine and for the next four hours they cruised up and down the River Ouse valley at about 800 ft altitude. The reason for this action was to use up fuel for with only three engines they could not gain height to get out to the jettison area in the North Sea just off

Flamborough Head. The skipper eventually made a perfect three-engined landing with the full bomb load on board.

Every day new crews came and went and for those who did stay the course a big attraction on the station was 429 (Bison) Squadron's Crew Centre Bistro. For such as Sergeant Charles Whitmore it was a blessing since he could never get up in time for breakfast and still get reported in to the navigator section in time for Muster at 09.30 every morning and ready for the 10.00 visit from the 'Met Man' for his weather report, so he ate at the Bistro. In fact it became so popular that very few turned up for breakfast and to force them back the rations were cut off. On the back wall of the Bistro was a large mural of a herd of bison, peacefully grazing in a field.

On March 29 1944, Pilot Officer Bowly, his navigator Sergeant Joe Myers, mid-upper gunner Sergeant Bill McMahon and wireless operator Sergeant Don Finlay arrived back at Leeming after being on leave in London—it was their last leave for a very long time. At breakfast the following morning Bowly was informed by the squadron Adjutant that a Welling-ton of Training Command had crashed nearby and that two Australian and one New Zealand members of the crew were to be buried in Harrogate Cemetery that morning. As he was the only available member of the RAAF on the squadron Bowly was to attend as a pall bearer for one of the coffins. Bowly objected strongly to this duty, pointing out that in the event of being briefed for a raid that night he would not be able to air-test his aircraft. Pilot Officer Bowly says: 'I did not really expect there to be an operation that night as it was nearly full moon and, as we thought, too bright to go into Germany'. How wrong he was. He was

transported to Harrogate Cemetery and helped to bury the RAAF and NZ aircrew; while there he saw the names of three Australians he was at OTU with on the headstones of the Services Section of the Cemetery a long way back from the graves they had just filled.

Bowly returned to the squadron about 09.00 hours and was informed that he was required at briefing at 10.00 hours. All his crew attended briefing with the exception of Sergeant Paddy Cosgrave, the engineer who came from Dublin and had been delayed a day in his return from leave. At briefing they found their target was Nuremburg and they were part of the main force. Pilot Officer Bowly had a new aircraft, Halifax Mk III *LK800* 'N'-Nan, which was fitted with a mid-upper turret which he had been accustomed to removing. Their bomb load was one 2,000 lb HE and 2,000 lb of 4 lb and 30 lb white phosphorous incendiaries plus a 600-gallon overload petrol tank in the rear bomb bay to cope with the length of the trip.

They took off on time, set course, flew down England and crossed the Channel on track at 20,000 ft. All the way to target they could see aircraft exploding and tracer streams lancing through the air on both sides. They arrived at what they thought was the target at 01.20 hours and, after bombing, went to 21,000 ft and set course for home. Just before 03.00 hours they were attacked and had to abandon 'N'-Nan. They were shot down over Luxembourg at about 03.15 hours and were soon taken PoW. Pilot Officer Bowly was in Stalag Luft 1 until it was overrun by the Red Army about the beginning of May 1945 and had about two weeks under their control before the Americans brought in 500 Fortresses on May 13 and flew their nationals to Le

Harrogate Cemetery became the last resting place for many Canadians and other Commonwealth aircrews.

Aerial view of Leeming taken on March 3 1944 from 10,000 ft. Note the bombers parked in the frying pan-type dispersals which branch from the perimeter at irregular intervals. Ground crewmen need cycles to get back from remote parts of the field.

Havre and the British to England.

Meanwhile, back at Leeming the empty bunks were quickly refilled and operations continued. At the end of April Kenney relinquished control of 429 Squadron and on May 1 1944 Wing Commander A.F. Avant, DFC, became the new CO. On July 28, Sergeant Charles Whitmore and crew completed their 36th operation with an attack on Hamburg. This was a Diversionary Target by 6 Group only; the primary target was Stuttgart and this proved very costly. They returned safely and now they were ready for their last mission. As one of the old Air Force sayings stated, 'The last operation of the tour was the one to return home safely from', and at 05.28 hours on July 30 'P'-Peter was airborne and, working a quick climbing turn to port, set course on the first leg of the route to Normandy at 05.30 hours. This was half an hour ahead of the briefed time and flight time plan, the reason for the early start being a heavy layer of fog which covered most of the countryside.

They were part of a small force to bomb in support of the United States Army in Normandy. The American Army had taken St Lô two days previously and now General Patton and his Third Army was ready to do battle with the 'sonofabitches'. Therefore, due to the importance of the army attack plan, Bomber Command would have to operate regardless of the weather conditions. So 'P'-Peter set ₁course half an hour early in good hopes of

entering clear sky in which to lose the half hour in comparative safety and thus avoid collision. At 06.21 hours, 12 minutes before they were due over Reading, the turning point on the outward-bound flight to Normandy, 'P'-Peter entered clear sky and turned off course 90° west for seven minutes out and seven minutes back. It did this twice to lose 28 minutes, almost the half hour. This 'Turn off Track' 90 degrees from the route plan was the second disobedience of orders. The reason for turning off course was the fact that the pilot liked to have a course to fly and not just fly around in a circle. Also, the crew could keep a much better and safer lookout for other aircraft.

'P'-Peter resumed course for Normandy at 06.44 hours and crossed over Selby Bill at 07.13. The crew then fuzed the bomb load of 16 500-pounders filled with RDX High Explosive. Over the English Channel the air was clear except for scattered clouds and coming up to the Normandy beach 'P'-Peter did a 30-degree snap course alteration to regain track. Over the target there was a layer of low cloud and their bombing height of 8,000 ft was changed to 2,500 ft by the Master of Ceremonies. This was to give the bomb aimers the necessary visibility required due to the nature of the operation. This order came over the R/T and 'P'-Peter now had to lose 5,500 ft of altitude in the short distance of only just over 19 miles.

Coming up to the target area they sighted visually the railroad embankment at 07.46 hours and opened bomb doors. Target marker flares were now also visible and they passed over an arrow followed by the number '3' which was laid out in a field in white canvas. This was pointing towards the target area, indicating three miles to target. 'P'-Peter now made the third disobedience of orders for it bombed at 2,200 feet at 07.48 hours. That was 300 ft lower altitude than ordered and one minute earlier than the briefed time.

'Bombs gone—bomb doors closed', and 'P'-Peter turned in a wide port turn and headed for home. They crossed the English coast at 08.38 hours only to find the English countryside still under a blanket of fog. Almost immediately there was a 'Diversion Order' signalled by W/T to all striking force aircraft still airborne. 'P'-Peter was directed to land at Brunt-ingthorpe and not Bitteswell (the normal alternate) which was fogged in, but this gave problems for it was not listed on the 'Flimsy'. The navigator then decided it would take too long to sort through the sheets to find Bruntingthorpe and suggested they select Wing aerodrome which was en route to their own base. At 08.50 they were over Wing but found it also covered in fog. Nevertheless, the pilot let 'P'-Peter down blind at 400 ft. This he should not have done during a blind approach to a strange airfield. Wing control ordered them to fly north for 1½ hours and then to return. They arrived back at 09.25 hours and at 09.27 got a recall to base order from Leeming. So, 'P'-Peter turned around again to fly north and with 135 miles to base ETA Leeming was 10.14 hours. At 10.20 hours they touched down in 'P'-Peter for the last time—their tour completed. They were

screened from operations, Sergeant Whitmore being posted from the squadron to Brackla, an unused grass aerodrome in Scotland, which was being used as an Air Crew Allocation Centre.

The squadrons continued the bombing offensive and in March 1945 both began to receive Lancaster Is and IIIs. It was with these aircraft they wound up their operations. For both the 'Lion' and the 'Bison' squadrons, the last operational mission was on April 25 1945 when ten Lancasters from each unit were despatched to bomb gun position on the Island of Wangerooge.

No 427 (Lion) Squadron logged 3,328 sorties and in so doing lost 90 aircraft and 522 aircrew, of whom 35 were killed and 477 missing, of whom ten were Prisoners of War and 11 proved safe. The squadron awards were four DSOs, 147 DFCs, six Bars to DFC, one AFC, two CGMs, 16 DFMs and eight Mentions in Despatches.

No 429 (Bison) Squadron logged 3,221 sorties, with a loss of 71 aircraft and 451 aircrew, of whom 82 were killed, 322 missing, 23 Prisoners of War and 24 proved safe. The awards were 45 DFCs, two Bars to DFC, one AFC, one CGM and seven DFMs.

After the hostilities in Europe, Nos 427 and 429 Squadrons remained in England as part of Bomber Command's strike force. On August 30 1945, Leeming and the two resident squadrons were transferred to No 1 Group under which they airlifted Allied Prisoners of War and British troops from Italy back to England. Both squadrons disbanded at Leeming on June 1 1946 and towards the end of the month No 54 OTU arrived from East Moor.

The year 1947 saw a change of role for the station when No 13 OTU arrived from

Opposite page, top to bottom *Ex-Flight Sergeant Gordon Ritchie looking at the Honours and Awards Board at RAF Leeming in 1960. He and Flight Sergeant John Mangione received the DFM. The other member of their crew, Sergeant E.J. Steere received the CGM. On the night of June 6/7 1944 their Halifax was struck by flak while on the way to attack Acheres, fatally wounding the pilot, Squadron Leader W.B. Anderson. On his orders three crew members baled out. Sergeant Steere, the flight-engineer, ignored the order and took the controls over, while Ritchie and Mangione, rear and mid-upper gunners respectively, who also disobeyed the order, dragged their helpless skipper to the rear escape hatch. Knowing that the inevitable crash would be fatal to the wounded pilot, they parachuted him out of the aircraft on a static line in a last endeavour to save his life. Anderson died before aid could reach him; crew of Halifax 'V' Victor or The Impatient Virgin at Leeming in 1944. Standing from left to right are Anderson, pilot; Steere, flight-engineer; Mangione, mid-upper gunner; O'Leary, bomb aimer; in the front row: Banning, WoP, and Ritchie, rear gunner; Leeming in April 1945. Lancasters at dispersal of 427 Squadron, RCAF.*

Middleton St George on May 1, and immediately merged with 54 OTU to form No 228 Operational Conversion Unit. This unit was equipped with Brigand T4s and Mosquito NF36s which remained the main aircraft until 1951 when it then converted to Meteor NF 11s. From January to July 1952 the unit was transferred to Coltishall.

During 1956 repairs were carried out to Leeming's runways, the main one being considerably extended at its southern end to make it suitable for the higher performance Gloster Javelin fighters which were soon to be taken on strength by the Operational Conversion Unit. During this period the Meteor NF 11s of 228 OCU were sent to North Luffenham, Rutland.

September 1957 saw the arrival of 264 Squadron from Middleton St George but this unit disbanded on October 1. That same day 33 Squadron re-formed as a Gloster Meteor NF 14 unit and operated with these until the arrival of Javelins in July 1958. That same month 33 Squadron moved to Middleton St George.

During this period 228 OCU had converted to Javelins, the first of which had arrived in June 1957. The unit was tasked with the training of crews for the ever-increasing number of Javelin squadrons and the first course began in October 1957. The training procedure started with 2½ weeks of concentrated ground training and during the 15-week course each crew logged approximately 75 flying hours by day and night. A Redifon full flight simulator was installed at Leeming in 1960 and until the introduction of the dual-controlled Javelin T3 in March 1959 all flying was done in the FAW 5.

The student pilot flew with a staff navigator before teaming up with his student navigator. For both pilots and navigators the training was very comprehensive. The navigators did a ten-week basic course on Valetta aircraft with the final few weeks carried out on Meteor NF 11s in order to acquaint them with high speed interception techniques. The Valetta C1s were used as 'targets' while Valetta T4s equipped with AI 17 radar in an extended nose played the part of the 'interceptor', However, these were phased out at the end of 1958 and replaced with Canberra T11s (fitted with the same AI 17E interception radar as the Javelin FAW 5s) and the Meteor NF 11s were replaced by Meteor NF 14s.

After the basic stage the navigators did a 15-week course and at this stage they were joined by the pilots. By the early part of 1959 the Javelin Mobile Conversion Unit had outlived its usefulness and lost its identity within 228 OCU. Its job had been to assist squadrons in converting to the Javelin and it had been continually on the move. Then, much to the bewilderment of the staff, it was decided to disband 228 OCU in the late summer of 1961. The OCU had done an excellent job and the Government thought there were enough trained Javelin crews, but it was another high-level blunder. The Javelin was to remain in service for seven more years, necessitating the re-formation of other training units from 1963 onwards.

However, during August 1961 the Javelins from 228 OCU were withdrawn from Leeming and either flown to 19 or 27 MU before being re-issued to 2 TAF units. On September 15 1961, No 228 Operational Conversion Unit disbanded, at which time its shadow number was No 137 Squadron. That same month No 3 Flying Training School re-formed here

RCAF Station Leeming on August 10 1945. Note the permanent two-storey buildings used for billets and administration. Well-planned roads and pathways characterise the permanent station.

Gloster Javelin FAW 5 XA690 seen here at Leeming in August 1960.

with the task of training pilots on Jet Provost aircraft. 3 FTS received pupils straight from No 1 Initial Training School for basic training and Leeming continued unchanged for the next decade.

During the rundown of Manby in the early 1970s the School of Refresher Flying arrived here in late 1973. The unit, with its Jet Provost T4s, became No 1 Squadron, 3 FTS, but was later renamed Refresher Flying Squadron. The role of the unit was to restore flying skills to pilots who had been away from flying for more than six months. In 1975 the unit re-equipped with the T5A. Meanwhile, in November 1974, No 3 FTS lost its basic flying training commitment but in compensation received the Royal Navy Elementary Flying Training School which arrived from Church Fenton that same month.

The RNEFTS is equipped with the SAL Bulldog T1s and run on Royal Air Force lines but commanded by a Naval officer. Most of the flying by the RNEFTS takes place at Topcliffe during the day with a mass exodus at the start of each flying day. The school is also responsible for the 'Bulldogs' aerobatic display team, consisting of two Bulldogs.

It was back to square one after the shuffles of the early 1970s, following those never-ending defence cuts, for the Central Flying School at Cranwell did not appear to have worked. Between November 21 and 25 1977 the Central Flying School Headquarters transferred from Cranwell to Leeming. The Spitfire that had been on display at Cranwell was included in the move. Three extra Jet Provosts were added to the strength of the Central Flying School, which is responsible for meeting the Royal Air Force's increased requirement for qualified Flying Instructors.

On May 4 1977, the Multi-Engined Training Squadron formed here with a complement of eight SAL Jetstream T1s. The role of the unit was to train pilots to fly multi-engined aeroplanes prior to joining an OCU for type training. Most of the circuit training took place at Dishforth and the advanced stage of the course involved a flight to Berlin, a far cry from the days when the Leeming Halifaxes had to battle their way to the German capital. The Jetstream is an ideal aircraft for it has the range to fly there direct. However, following the recent review of future aircrew requirements, fresh tasks fell to the Multi-Engined Training Squadron and

Just taking off—Vampire T11 XH304 of the Vintage Pair, based at Leeming.

*Jet Provost T5 XW326 flies over Leeming.
(Note very little change in comparison
with the aerial shot taken in 1944.)*

with the Leeming circuit overcrowded
another airfield had to be found. Thus, on
April 23 1979, it moved with its Jetstreams
to Finningley.

Leeming, which formerly was simply
No 3 Flying Training School, has a rather
complicated structure due to the presence
here of the Headquarters, Central Flying
School, as a lodger unit. Consequently,
the station (still officially No 3 FTS) has
two flying wings. No 3 FTS Wing consists
of the RNEFTS and the Refresher Flying
Squadron; the CFS Wing has two Jet
Provost squadrons and a Bulldog
squadron. Other units housed here are the
Northumberland Universities Air Squadron and No 11 Air Experience Flight, but
it is an unsatisfactory arrangement and
the NUAS would be better to be based
nearer to the squadron's catchment area.

It was here at Leeming that Prince
Andrew sailed through his basic pilot
course during the summer of 1980. During
the time Prince Andrew was here the
Queen Mother paid the station a visit.

It is a very busy station and to relieve
overcrowding in the Leeming circuit
Topcliffe and Dishforth are used as Relief
Landing Grounds. Leeming is also a
Master Diversion Airfield and its present
and future roles are flying training. With
its red brick quarters and five 'C1'
hangars it is an excellent example of a
wartime bomber airfield, and there is a
good view of it from the road to the west
as can be seen in the aerial photograph.

Lindholme, (Hatfield Woodhouse), Yorkshire

*111/SE685066. E of Doncaster on A614
road*

Only a few miles to the east of Doncaster,
an area known as Hatfield Moors was
selected to be developed into an airfield
and construction work started in May
1938. It was sited just to the south of the
small village of Hatfield Woodhouse.

The airfield was planned on the lines of
a typical bomber airfield of the Expansion
period with the technical site on the
southern boundary of the landing area,
backed by workshops and living accommodation. The war clouds over Europe
reflected in the austere finish of many of
the buildings, an example being the five
'C1' hangars.

At the outbreak of war in 1939 the
airfield was still far from complete and for
some reason construction work had been
very slow. Finally, on June 1 1940, Group
Captain E.F. Wareing, DFC, AFC,
assumed command of the station and it
officially opened under the name of
Hatfield Woodhouse as an operational
airfield in No 5 Group, Bomber
Command.

During the first week of July the twin-
engined Hampden bombers of No 50
Squadron arrived from Waddington. On
the 12th the AOC No 5 Group, Air Vice-
Marshal Arthur Harris, came to give a pep
talk to the personnel. Two nights later the
first ops were flown when 11 aircraft were
despatched to Hamburg but, owing to the
weather, it was a failure and only two
aircraft made it back to Lindholme, the
others having to land wherever they could.

The squadron flew many minelaying missions and during that fateful summer of 1940 the Hampdens bombed the barges which were being massed in European ports for the proposed invasion of England. The squadron also bombed the oil refineries at Paullac.

During this period the name of the station was changed to Lindholme on August 18 in order to avoid confusion with Hatfield in Herts where the the de Havilland factory was secretly producing the Mosquito. The operations continued both in size and distance and on August 26/27 Berlin was the target.

In October 1940, Wing Commander 'Gus' Walker took command of 50 Squadron and attacks continued under his fine leadership. Berlin was the target at the end of the month when, on the return leg, Hampden *X3000* ran out of fuel and was abandoned near Pickering, Yorkshire. In December the squadron took part in the first area-bombing attack on a German industrial centre, Mannheim.

Towards the end of February 1941, a detachment from No 11 SFTS at Shawbury arrived with their Oxfords but their stay was brief and the following month they moved out again. However, they continued to use Lindholme as a RLG for the remainder of the year.

Like all squadrons operating under extreme pressures, 50 Squadron had its share of accidents, its worst being on April 10 1941, when Hampden *AD830* struck some houses at Evington, Leicestershire. It happened while the pilot, Sergeant J.J. Campbell, was low flying over the home of a 'lady friend'. Two were killed and one injured in the aircraft, plus one killed in the house.

On June 24 1941, No 408 (Goose) Squadron, RCAF, formed at Lindholme. This was the RCAF's eighth squadron (second bomber) formed overseas. It was equipped with Hampden Mk Is, unit code 'EQ', and the first commander was Wing Commander N.W. Timmerman (Canadian/RAF) DSO, DFC.

July saw many changes, and on the 19th of the month the newly-formed 408 Squadron moved to Syerston, Nottinghamshire. That same day Group Captain Sanderson, AFC, took command of 50 Squadron which then moved to Swinderby, Lincolnshire. That same month the station was transferred to No 1 Group, Bomber Command, and into

Lindholme came two Polish bomber squadrons, Nos 304 and 305 from Syerston. Both squadrons were flying Wellingtons and continued the bombing offensive from their new base.

During September 1941 a few Blenheim IVs of 110 Squadron were on detachment at Lindholme but by the end of the month had returned to Wattisham, Suffolk.

Throughout the winter months the raids continued as often as the weather permitted. The resident squadron battled through it all and in April 1942 General Sikorski, the Polish Prime Minister and C in C, came to present some well-earned decorations. No 304 Squadron was then transferred to Coastal Command and left for Tiree in the Hebrides on May 7. No 305 continued operations and provided 13 aircraft for the first Thousand-Bomber raid on May 30/31 1942. The squadron also participated in the follow-up raids against Essen and Bremen. On the latter raid, the Polish CO, Group Captain Skarzynski, was lost after his Wellington had to ditch in the sea about 40 miles off Yarmouth. During the latter part of July 1942, 305 Squadron moved to Hemswell. Lindholme then became inactive for the construction of runways and general facelift.

Lindholme reopened in October 1942 and in preparation for the expansion of Bomber Command it now had a change of role. The first unit to arrive was the newly-formed No 1656 Heavy Conversion Unit which moved in from Breighton on the 26th of the month. The HCU was equipped with Manchesters and Lancasters, unlike so many others which had to use Halifaxes and Stirlings for the greater part of the training in the heavy conversion units, a brief course at a Lancaster Finishing School, as it was called, coming at the end of a course. This way large numbers of Lancasters could be left in the front line but these many changes could well have been the cause of so many of the training accidents as the crews worked under extreme pressures.

In the Yorkshire area only 6 Group had Lancasters and many of these only during the last few months of the war. Crews were immediately posted in and during November 1942 Sergeant Blumenauer and his crew arrived from 30 OTU Hixon, where they had trained on Wellingtons, to begin their training on four-engined bombers. Having selected their other crew members to bring their complement up to the seven that were now needed for the

Manchester L7434 of 1656 Conversion Unit at Lindholme with Pilot Officer Charlie Blumenauer, pilot; Sergeant Les Proud, navigator; Sergeant Bob Griffiths, rear gunner; Sergeant George Taylor, flight engineer; Sergeant Tom Wardle, bomb-aimer; and Pilot Officer Bill Whitehouse, mid-upper gunner.

heavy bombers, they made their first flight on December 1 1942 in Manchester *R5830* and for 1½ hours did circuits and landings. Local flying and map reading then followed, still using the Manchester.

Having familiarised themselves with this aircraft they continued training with a Lancaster for the rest of the course and their last training flight was on December 31 1942. At the end of the conversion course they had flown 11.15 hours in Manchesters and 8.50 hours in Lancasters making a grand total of 20.05 hours. They were now ready for operations and on January 1 1943 were posted to 103 Squadron at Elsham Wolds from where, on January 13, they flew their first mission to Essen.

November 3 1942 saw the arrival at Lindholme of No 1481 Target Towing Flight which moved in from Binbrook with its mixed bag of Whitleys, Wellingtons, Defiants, Lysanders, Martinets and Tiger Moths. The role of this unit was to train observers and gunners for No 1 Group.

During the first week of January 1943, No 1503 Blind Approach Training Flight arrived with their Oxfords, and it was their task to train No 1 Group pilots in blind landing techniques: a very

important part of the training programme for the bombers were in the air from dusk to dawn in all kinds of weather.

There was a further build-up of training units and on June 1 1943 No 1667 Heavy Conversion Unit formed here with an establishment of Lancasters, which carried the code letters 'LR', and Halifaxes which carried the code letters 'GG'.

Further changes were in the wind and on August 6 1943, No 1503 BAT Flight disbanded. September saw Lindholme become No 11 Base HQ with Faldingworth and Blyton as Sub-stations. On October 8, No 1667 HCU moved to Faldingworth, a new bomber station, not yet operational, but able to house the Conversion Unit.

On November 23 1943, the Lancaster Flights from the Faldingworth and Blyton HCUs moved to Lindholme and merged with their Lancaster Flight to form No 1 Lancaster Finishing School. HQ and 'A' Flight remained here until moving to Hemswell in January 1944. 'B' Flight was based at Blyton and 'C' Flight at Faldingworth.

By early 1944 the station strength had reached 2,700 and included 11 nationalities. Like all stations, Lindholme received visits from ENSA who put on shows consisting of concerts, concert parties, plays and cinema entertainment. Many artistes worked for ENSA, the object of which was the entertainment of the troops both at home and overseas.

By the spring a record 28 crews left the HCU for the squadrons but as the pace increased it was not enough and 'Butcher' Harris called for maximum effort. Lindholme's reply was a record monthly pass-out of 48 crews for which a record 2,000 flying hours were logged.

On November 3 1944, there was a command structure change and Lindholme was transferred to the newly-formed 7 Group and renumbered No 71 Base with Sub-stations Blyton and Sandtoft. November was also a bad crash month, the worst day being the 20th when 1656 HCU lost three aircraft. Halifax *BB254* started the run of bad luck when at 20.53 hours it lost height after the pilot, Flying Officer M.A. Gleason, raised the flaps instead of the undercarriage and hit a tree at Dunscroft, near Doncaster. Five were killed and two injured. Only minutes later, at 21.05 hours, Halifax *HR794*, piloted by Flying Officer G.L. Halsall, also failed to gain height on take-off and after being airborne for only a minute crashed just under a mile from the end of the west runway and burnt out. Six were injured.

The third crash came at 22.00 hours when Halifax *W7875*, piloted by Flying Officer J.D. East, crashed at Lings Farm, near Dunsville, Doncaster. When 1½ miles from the runway the bomber went into a steep turn, lost height rapidly and flew into a tree. It is thought the pilot selected flaps up instead of the under-carriage. It is possible that for a few seconds the other burning aircraft could have broken the pilot's concentration. Six were killed and one injured. That same month the station parted with its Halifax aircraft and became an all-Lancaster unit for the duration of the war.

Lindholme continued in the training role but with the war at an end No 1481 TT Flight moved out. After the VE-Day celebrations special 'Cook's Tours' were flown to enable the groundcrews, and many WAAFs also, to see the damage that Bomber Command had inflicted on German targets.

Lindholme was retained as a permanent station in the post-war RAF and involved in the peacetime reorganisation. No 1656 HCU disbanded on November 10 1945 and No 71 Base closed down. The unit was replaced by 1653 Heavy Conversion Unit which had arrived from North Luffenham on October 28. That same month No 1 Group Major Servicing Unit was transferred to Lindholme. This unit returned to Scampton in May 1946 when two newly-equipped Lincoln squadrons, Nos 57 and 100, moved to Lindholme, leaving 27 cast-off Lancasters for the incoming unit to deal with.

No 9 Squadron arrived from Binbrook in July 1946 but moved back again the following September. The next month Lindholme said goodbye to its two remaining Lincoln squadrons when No 57 moved to Waddington and No 100 to Hemswell. Towards the end of November No 1660 HCU moved in from Swinderby but it disbanded immediately.

1653 HCU continued to operate through-out the changes and in March 1947 it was redesignated No 230 Operational Conver-sion Unit. In February 1949 it moved to Scampton and the station was transferred to Technical Training Command and was occupied by the Armament Division of the RAF Technical College. In April 1949, the Central Bomber Establishment arrived from Marham, but it disbanded the following November.

March 5 1951 saw the re-establishment of No 5 Air Navigation School at Lindholme, operating Wellington 10s and Ansons. However, it was for only a short period and on November 15 1952 the unit disbanded, having been replaced by the Bomber Command Bombing School which had formed here on October 15.

The next two decades saw very little change. During 1958, Lindholme was one of the RAF bases with technical and storage units of the 7th Air Division, SAC, and housed No 3916 Air Base Squadron, a non-flying unit. In 1972, the Strike Command Bombing School, the BCBS having been re-titled, moved to Scampton and Lindholme closed to flying.

The station remained occupied by the RAF and until the late 1970s housed Northern Radar. Then, in order to cope with the increased flying resulting from the move of the Multi-Engined Training Squadron, the airfield opened in 1980 as a Relief Landing Ground for nearby Finningley. The runways are maintained in reasonable condition and the hangars are used for storage such as the de-icing equipment. However, the rest of the site is closed and is falling into disrepair with an

Wartime entertainment at Lindholme in 1943. The pantomine is Cinderella.

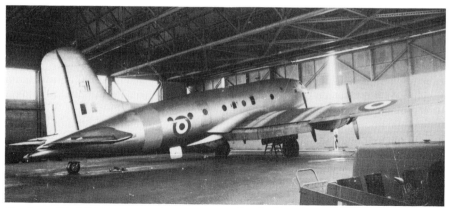

Hastings T5 TG511 at Lindholme on October 21 1962.

abandoned look about the whole site which casts doubt over its future.

Linton-on-Ouse, Yorkshire

100/SE490617. NW of York. Turn off main A19 road to W at Shipton

Situated north of Linton-on-Ouse village and the River Ouse, this is one of the earlier bomber airfields of the Expansion period, for it was constructed during the mid-1930s. The technical and living site was built in the south-east corner with an arc of five brick-built 'C' type hangars which were backed by substantial barracks and messes.

Linton-on-Ouse officially opened on May 13 1937 and was occupied by No 4 Group Headquarters on July 28. Construction work continued and was almost complete when the first aircraft arrived in April 1938. These were the Whitleys of Nos 51 and 58 Squadrons which arrived from Boscombe Down, Wiltshire.

Immediately on the outbreak of war Whitley bombers of 51 and 58 Squadrons, operating out of Leconfield, dropped propaganda leaflets over Germany. This was the first night on which Royal Air Force aircraft penetrated into Germany during the Second World War.

During September a detachment from No 58 Squadron was ordered to Rheims, France, and in October 1939 the squadron moved to Boscombe Down on loan to No 15 Group for duty with Coastal Command. A small maintenance party remained at Linton-on-Ouse.

During November 1939, No 51 ('York's

Own') Squadron had a detachment at Kinloss on loan to No 18 Group, Coastal Command, and the following month it moved to Dishforth. It was replaced by the remainder of 78 Squadron, a detachment from which had been here since October 1939, and as soon as the entire squadron became based here it began working up for operations after having re-equipped with Whitley Mk Vs.

During February 1940, No 58 Squadron returned to Yorkshire and arrived back at Linton-on-Ouse. On April 18/19 1940, 58 Squadron made its first bombing mission of the war. Two Whitleys bombed Oslo/Fornebu airfield and one aborted. From then on they were to play a prominent part in the night bombing offensive and attacked targets in Norway, Holland and Germany.

As the build-up continued it became obvious that Group headquarters needed more space so, on April 6 1940, No 4 Group HQ moved to Heslington Hall, York, leaving Linton-on-Ouse to concentrate on being an operational bomber base. The station then had a visit from Sir Archibald Sinclair, Secretary of State for Air, on June 23 1940, and by the early part of July No 78 Squadron had become fully operational. Its first mission was on July 19/20 when four Whitleys were despatched to bomb Gelsenkirchen-Buer. Only one bombed the primary target, the other three bombed alternatives. By the end of July 78 Squadron had moved to Dishforth.

A few days later the Whitley Mk Vs of No 77 arrived at Linton-on-Ouse to replace 78 Squadron and began operations just two days after their arrival. Both resident squadrons took part in attacks on German targets during these early bombing days, in which many losses

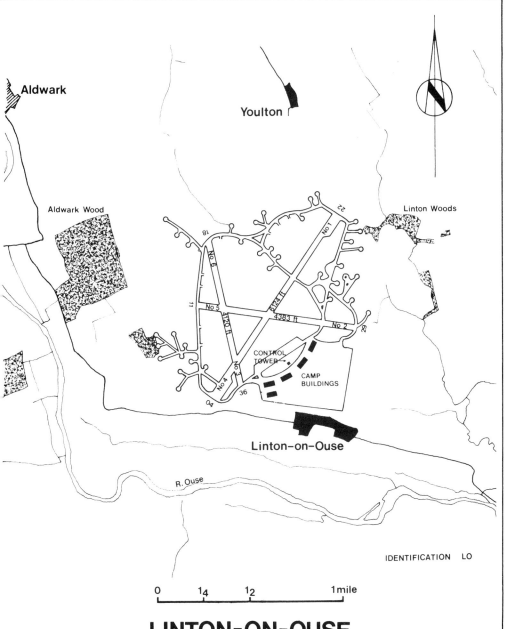

LINTON-ON-OUSE

A typical wartime bomber station with the three runways and the frying pan-type hardstandings. The airfield is still used today but runway 18/36 is no longer usable. Also, runway 11/29 is now 10/28 and the present day runway lengths and elevations have been slightly modified.

Linton-on-Ouse control tower.

were sustained, the weather being the main cause but bad navigation and lack of intelligence about the targets also playing a part.

On August 27 1940, the Lysanders of No 4 (Army Co-operation) Squadron moved to York after re-forming here following their retreat from France during the early part of June. This unit was later to become well established as a photo-reconnaissance squadron.

October 1940 saw the departure of 77 Squadron to Topcliffe and the arrival of 102 Squadron. During their brief stay at Linton-on-Ouse 102 Squadron took part in a few bombing missions, including one on the night of November 12/13, when Whitley V *P5005* 'N'-Nuts, piloted by Pilot Officer G.L. Cheshire (later Group Captain Cheshire, VC) attacked the railway marshalling yards at Cologne. While approaching the target 'N'-Nuts was shaken by a succession of violent explosions. The cockpit filled with black fumes and Cheshire lost control of the aircraft as it plunged earthwards. Fire raged in the fuselage but, remaining calm, Cheshire brought the crippled bomber under control and the fire was extinguished. With a large hole in the fuselage, Cheshire brought 'N'-Nuts safely back to base after being in the air for 8½ hours. For his action that night Cheshire gained an immediate DSO. He was later awarded the DFC for operations with No 102 Squadron. During mid-November 1940 the Whitleys of 102 Squadron moved to Topcliffe.

During this period two decoy airfields

are listed for Linton-on-Ouse, but I can find no trace of them. Bossall was a K-site and was listed as a complete decoy with dummy Whitleys installed. The other was a Q-site at Wigginton, just north of York. This would put the latter very close to the airfield at Plainville.

Throughout the changes 58 Squadron continued the bombing offensive and attacked a variety of targets from airfields to industrial centres. On December 5 1940, No 35 Squadron arrived from Leeming with their Halifaxes and began working up to operations with the four-engined bombers. During this period Halifax *L9487*, piloted by Flying Officer M.T.G. Henry, was on a measured climb and consumption test on January 13 1941 when an engine caught fire at 12,000 ft. The fire burnt off the tail control surfaces and the pilot lost control. The bomber crashed at 11.55 hours near Baldersby St James, 3½ miles north of Dishforth. The crew of six were killed.

The squadron flew its first sortie on the night of March 10/11 1941 when six Halifaxes were despatched to bomb Le Havre dockyard. Four aircraft successfully bombed the primary target whilst one which could not see either the primary or alternative target (Boulogne), bombed Dieppe. The sixth aircraft found nothing and jettisoned its bombs in the Channel. On the return journey Halifax *L9489*, piloted by Squadron Leader P.A. Gilchrist, was mistaken for a German bomber and shot down by a British fighter. The starboard-outer engine failed due to strikes by machine-gun bullets and the starboard-inner caught fire. The bomber crashed at Normandy near Aldershot. Four crew were killed, two being unable to leave the aircraft due to failure of the front escape hatch.

On April 14 1941, No 2 BAT Flight moved to Driffield having formed here during the early part of February. Two days later Halifax *L9493* of 35 Squadron, piloted by Sergeant Lashbrook, crashed into a tree in a forced-landing at Tollerton near the base after the port-inner failed. The flight-engineer cut all engines when instructed to turn on all cocks. Fortunately only two were injured.

No 76 Squadron then re-formed from 'C' Flight of No 35 (B) Squadron on May 1 1941, with an establishment of Halifaxes, unit code letters 'MP'. Their stay was also very brief and the following month 76 Squadron moved to Middleton St George.

During this period Linton-on-Ouse did not remain unscathed and on the night of May 10/11 1941 a German air raid caused considerable damage and several casualties, including the station commander who was killed.

In July 1941 No 35 Squadron made its first raid on Berlin, two Halifaxes being despatched but only one reaching and bombing the target; the pilot was none other than Flying Officer G.L. Cheshire. September saw 35 Squadron make the 1,700 mile trip to Turin in northern Italy.

The bombing offensive continued by the two resident squadrons and they attacked a variety of targets in Germany and occupied France. Despite remaining with the Whitley, No 58 Squadron played a prominent part in the night bombing offensive, its highlights being the first attack on Italy (Turin) on June 11/12 1940 and the first attack on Berlin on August 25/26 1940. But the Whitley's days with Bomber Command were numbered and, on April 7 1942, No 58 Squadron was transferred to Coastal Command. Records show that the last operational mission by the Whitleys of No 58 as a bomber squadron was an attack on Ostend docks on April 29/30 1942.

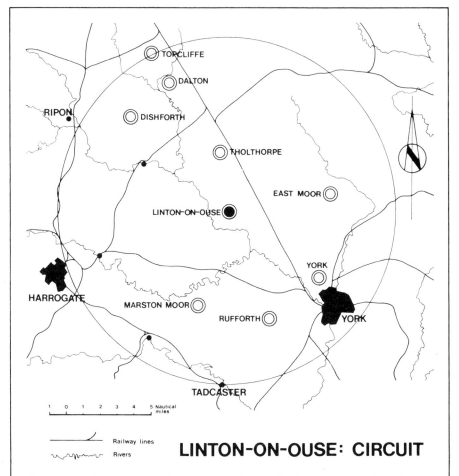

LINTON-ON-OUSE: CIRCUIT

One can see from this map that circuit overlap applied for all stations. For Linton-on-Ouse the ten nautical miles takes in eight other airfields. At all times crews had to keep a strict lookout for other aircraft. The danger of collision was further accentuated at night by the large number of aircraft taking-off on operations.

'Tea up' at Linton-on-Ouse in 1942. A typical scene at all operational stations. Crews of No 35 Squadron partake of the liquid beverage before a night flight test.

Meanwhile, during January 1942, No 35 Squadron Conversion Flight had formed here with Halifaxes and for the first few months No 158 Squadron from Driffield worked with the newly formed Conversion Flight. Then, using No 35 Squadron Halifaxes, No 158 Squadron Conversion Flight formed at Linton-on-Ouse but on June 7 moved to East Moor and took over their own aircraft.

In February 1942, 35 Squadron was one that took part in the attempt to stop the German warships *Scharnhorst* and *Gneisenau* during their escape dash from Brest to North German ports. March and April saw two unsuccessful attacks on the German battleship *Tirpitz* lying near Trondheim fjord, Norway. During one of the raids Halifax *W1048 TL-S* was hit by flak and at 01.45 hours Flying Officer MacIntyre force-landed the Halifax on the frozen Lake Hoklingen which was surrounded by hills. Sergeant V.C. Stevens, the flight-engineer, broke his foot and the others helped him over the ice but he was eventually taken prisoner. The rest of the crew made it over the border into Sweden where they were interned before returning to Britain. Soon after the crew had escaped 'S'-Sugar sank through the ice where it remained in 90 ft of water until discovered in the 1960s. It has now been recovered and appears to be the only Halifax bomber left in the world. After it has been re-assembled it will take its rightful place of honour in the RAF Museum, Hendon.

At the end of May 1942, 35 Squadron contributed 18 Halifaxes to the historic Thousand-Bomber raid on Cologne. No 35 also took part in a similar raid on Bremen on June 25/26 when 1,006 aircraft were despatched on the last of the Thousand-Bomber Raids. It was a fiasco and it was fortunate that the Cologne raid had been a huge success to prove mass bombing did work under the right conditions.

July 1942 proved a bad month for 35 Squadron. On the 14th Halifax *W7761* returned from operations with a hung-up 4,000-pounder on board. The pilot, Sergeant H.B. MacDonald, who had survived a crash in Halifax *W1159* on June 22, decided to abandon the aircraft and this was carried out successfully over Knaresborough, Yorkshire. The Halifax then flew on westwards before crashing. But the Gremlins were on board for it is interesting to note that about two seconds before the crash the aircraft released the 4,000-lb bomb of its own accord. The bomb fell a few hundred yards from a farmhouse and blew all the windows out—the crater is still there today.

That same day Halifax *W1154* crashed after engine failure in flight. The pilot, Flight Sergeant Casey and one other crew-member were killed. Then, on July 21, Halifax *R9489* had been taken up for air test and probably stalled after losing height from 1,200 ft—a suspected case of rudder overbalance. The pilot, Sergeant T.C. Murray, had taken two Army NCOs up 'Contra to Orders' and all nine occupants were killed when the aircraft crashed and burnt at Catterton, near Tadcaster, Yorkshire.

When the Pathfinder Force was formed in August 1942, No 35 was one of the five squadrons selected to form the nucleus of the new force. Thus, on August 16, No 35 Squadron moved to Graveley, Huntingdonshire, after having played a major role in the bombing offensive. Between December 5 1940 and August 15 1942 the unit lost a total of 63 aircraft, broken down thus: crashes/accidents, 22; struck off charge, one; missing on bombing operations, 33; and missing on *Tirpitz* raids, seven. Miraculously many survived. Pilot Officer Creswell, for example, in Halifax *L9526*, force-landed after returning from a raid on Turin, Italy. A month later to the day he was pilot of Halifax *L9524* and again force-landed after returning from Essen.

With the departure of No 35 Squadron, the Squadron Conversion Flight moved to Marston Moor on September 5. Eleven days later Nos 76 and 78 Squadrons returned to Linton-on-Ouse from Middleton St George. Both were flying Halifax B IIs and since the previous month No 76 had been commanded by Wing Commander G.L. Cheshire, who remained at that post until April 1943.

It was only a temporary stay for both 76 and 78 Squadrons but even so they carried out many mining operations. Returning from one such mission on November 6 1942, Halifax *DT525* piloted by Sergeant J.G. Mills of 78 Squadron made a navigational error and flew into high ground on Byland Moor, Yorkshire, at 22.30 hours. Three of the crew were killed, including the squadron gunnery officer, Flight Lieutenant G.T. Turner.

In 1942, it was decided to create the Canadian Group and the headquarters unit was formed here on October 25. HQ No 6 Group was soon looking for more spacious accommodation and on December 1 1942 it moved to a permanent base at Allerton Park. The station itself had now been earmarked for a Canadian base and in mid-June 1943 both resident squadrons moved out, No 76 to Holme-on-Spalding Moor while No 78 went to Breighton. Two days later No 426 (Thunderbird) Squadron, RCAF, arrived from Dishforth and in July 1943 the airfield was transferred to No 6 Group, RCAF, becoming No 62 (Beaver) Base Station with Sub-stations at East Moor and Tholthorpe.

Upon their arrival the 'Thunderbird' squadron began converting to the radial-engined Lancaster Mk II but, because of bad weather and general shortage of aircraft, the change-over was not completed until early August. After a series of 'Bullseye' exercises the 'Thunderbirds' were ready to show the meaning of their nickname. The thunderbird is a mythical bird, the sight of which is supposed to cause havoc and death to those who perceive it. It was the name given by some Indians to the first aeroplane they saw. The thunderbird signified disaster to those on the ground who incurred its displeasure.

The squadron carried out 6 Group's first Lancaster operation when it joined an attack on August 17/18 on the experimental scientific station at Peenemünde in the Baltic. Eight Lancasters from No 426 Squadron were included in the total force of 597 heavy bombers, and from the 40 that failed to return the 'Thunderbirds' lost two, including the one flown by the squadron CO, Wing Commander L. Crooks. At briefing, crews were urged to make a special effort and they were not informed of the true purpose of the Peenemünde raid. For security reasons they were briefed that the Germans were developing a new radar measure against night bombers and that to destroy the experimental station would save many lives.

Command of the 'Thunderbirds' passed to Wing Commander W.H. Swetman, DSO, DFC, who took up his post on August 18 1943, and it was he who led the squadron through the winter months. Berlin came on to their target list for the first time on August 23/24 and, on August 28 1943, the resident squadron was joined by No 408 (Goose) Squadron, RCAF, from Leeming. This unit was equipped with Halifax Mk IIs but in October 1943 it converted to the Avro Lancaster B Mk II, for Linton-on-Ouse was chosen as the centre of Lancaster operations. The theory was that the Canadians were already familiar with the Hercules engine, which was also used in the Wellingtons, thus the conversion could be made more quickly.

The 'Goose' squadron's first operation took place on October 7/8 when it joined 426 in a raid on Stuttgart, each squadron putting up 14 aircraft in a total force of 342 Lancasters. One of the bombers from 408 had to turn back with unserviceable guns and another, *DS724* 'X'-Xray had to be abandoned in the air over Hutton-le-Hole when the controls jammed. The crew jumped to safety but a farmer was killed when the bomber crashed at Spaunton, Yorkshire, and the bomb load blew up.

The rest flew on to target but few bombs fell on Stuttgart for the Pathfinder marking was ineffective.

Leipzig was the target for both squadrons on October 20/21 when they put up 28 Lancasters from the total force of 358 despatched. Leipzig was one of the chief commercial and manufacturing cities of Germany and the centre for Junkers aero-engines. Now it was within effective striking range of Bomber Command and suffered three attacks during the winter months.

Appalling weather conditions spoiled the first attack and only 285 reached the target. Icing caused many problems and two iced up so badly they had to turn back to Linton-on-Ouse. Incendiaries were seen burning throughout the route as many bombers were forced to jettison part of their loads in order to maintain height. Lancaster *DS686* of 426 Squadron was attacked no less than seven times by two night fighters. The pilot's windscreen shattered and the mid-upper gunner was wounded but the pilot pressed on and completed the mission. Heavy cloud was more of a problem than the night fighters and 15 aircraft were lost on the raid.

The air campaign to cripple Berlin began in earnest in mid-November and 16 major attacks were made up to March 24/25 1944. The two Linton-on-Ouse squadrons contributed to 15 of these raids. On the first raid on November 18/19, a total force of 444 heavy bombers was despatched, 14 being from 408 and ten from 426. Berlin was covered by dense cloud and the Pathfinder markers soon disappeared so the bombers were forced to bomb hurriedly. From this first raid nine aircraft failed to return but all from 408 and 426 returned safely.

On dispersal—April 9 1945, Halifax Mk VII NP790 of 408 (B) Squadron.

After the enforced lull covering the period of the full moon, both squadrons took part in the attack on Berlin on December 16/17 when a force of 492 bombers was despatched. The squadrons were airborne by 16.20 hours but adverse weather was experienced for in addition to 25 bombers shot down over enemy territory, 29 crashed in the UK with a loss of 131 lives. With fog covering many of the airfields, several bombers just ran out of fuel. Lancaster *DS837* crashed at Yearsley and *DS779* crashed between Hopperton and Hunsingore near Northlands Farm, killing five and injuring two. A 408 Lancaster crashed on Murton Common leaving two injured survivors.

The Battle of Berlin continued unabated during January 1944 and on the first raid on January 1/2 a total force of 421 bombers was despatched from which 28 failed to return, 408 losing one and 426 two, while others were damaged. For the Berlin raid on January 27/28 a long route over the North Sea was chosen in order to defeat early contact by enemy fighters, but this entailed more than four hours' flying to reach the target. It was the costliest of all the Berlin raids for the Canadians since, out of the 37 Lancaster Mk IIs they despatched, eight did not return. Bomber Command lost 33 from a total force of 530. In spite of their losses, 408 and 426 were again over Berlin the following night but this time all their aircraft returned safely.

Early in 1944 it was decided that the Lancaster Mk II should be phased-out and replaced by the Halifax B Mk III. During April 1944 No 426 Squadron began to turn in its Lancaster IIs for the Hercules-powered Halifax B Mk III. The 'Thunderbirds'' last operation with Lancaster IIs was an attack on the marshalling yards at St Ghislain on May 1/2 1944. By the time of D-Day on June 6 only two squadrons operated with the Lancaster Mk II, one being No 408 and the other being No 514 Squadron at Waterbeach, Cambridgeshire.

Both Linton-on-Ouse squadrons took part in operation 'Overlord' and at 09.30 on June 6 1944 the station commander broadcast over the Tannoy that the invasion of France had begun. That same month 426 Squadron converted to Halifax B Mk VIIs but at the end of the year brought back on strength five B Mk IIIs.

Meanwhile, 408 Squadron kept on with operations with its Lancaster IIs and from the end of March up to August 15/16 took

'Z'-Zombie of 408 Squadron being refuelled at Linton-on-Ouse on April 24 1944.

part in 30 operations flying 330 succesful sorties with a loss of only eight aircraft. In September 1944, 408 began to convert to Halifax B Mk IIIs and finally to Mk VIIs, and these aircraft remained until the end of the war.

On March 5 1945, 426 despatched 14 Halifax Mk VIIs but freezing fog in the Vale of York claimed *LW219* 'Y'-Yoke piloted by Flight Lieutenant T. Emerson. Under its full bomb and fuel load for the long trip across Germany it struggled to gain height but, as the flying surfaces iced up, the added weight was just too much and at 15.00 hours, just 21 minutes after take-off, 'Y'-Yoke fell out of the sky, partially disintegrating in the process. The fuselage fell into Nunthorpe Grove, York, and an engine plummeted into the kitchen of Nunthorpe Secondary School. The wireless operator/air gunner, Pilot Officer J. Low, baled out of the disintegrating aircraft only he was too low and his parachute failed to open properly. However, the resulting explosion from the crashing bomber blew him up into the air sufficiently to allow his parachute to deploy, decelerating his fall. He landed heavily on the shed roof, seriously injured. All other crew members were killed. Also five civilians were killed and a further 18 injured.

That same freezing fog also caused the crash of Halifax *NP793* of 426 Squadron. Sergeant H.S. Watts took off at 17.00 hours and tried to get above the freezing fog but after circling he lost control due to severe icing and at 17.45 hours crashed one mile south of Hutton-le-Hole near Kirkbymoorside, Yorkshire. The bomber burnt on impact, killing the crew of seven. Traces of this aircraft are still where they fell that March night in 1945.

The last bombing mission of the war for both squadrons was on April 25 1945, 17 Halifaxes from 408 and 20 from 426 bombing gun positions on the Island of Wangerooge. One failed to return from each squadron.

No 408 (Goose) Squadron flew 4,610 sorties with Hampdens, Lancasters and Halifaxes and dropped 11,430 tons of bombs. Its casualties were 146 aircraft and 897 aircrew of whom 877 were killed, missing or PoW, three evaded capture and 17 were wounded. On non-operational flights, 12 aircraft were lost from which 32 personnel were killed and seven injured. The squadron members won one MBE, 161 DFCs, six Bars to DFC, 32 DFMs and ten Mentions in Despatches.

After the hostilities in Europe the squadron was selected as part of 'Tiger Force'. It converted to Canadian-built Lancaster Xs and on June 13 1945 flew back to Canada to prepare for duty in the Far East. The abrupt end of the Japanese war resulted in the squadron being disbanded at Greenwood, Nova Scotia, on September 5 1945.

The 'Thunderbirds' had also done a fine job and between January 14 1943 and April 25 1945, the squadron sent out 3,233 aircraft on 242 bomb raids, 19 sea-mining operations and seven sea searches. The 'Thunderbirds' losses totalled 88 aircraft of which 70 were missing over enemy territory. Losses in personnel were 425 killed, presumed dead or missing and 133 prisoners or 'safe'; non-operational, four personnel killed. The squadron members won two DSOs, 130 DFCs, two Bars to DFC, one CGM, 25 DFMs, two BEMs, one American DFC and 13 Mentions in Despatches.

With the war over in Europe, 426

Lancaster II of 408 Squadron at Linton-on-Ouse in May 1944, showing maintenance being carried out at dispersal.

Squadron assumed a new role and on May 24 1945 it transferred to No 47 Group, Transport Command, and moved to Driffield where it was engaged on transport duties. It was replaced on May 26 by No 405 Squadron, RCAF, which arrived from Gransden Lodge, Bedfordshire, having been selected as part of 'Tiger Force'. It converted to the Canadian-built Lancaster X and on June 15 the squadron flew back to Canada where it was disbanded at Greenwood, Nova Scotia, on September 5 1945.

Linton-on-Ouse was retained by the post-war RAF, having reverted back to them in June, and was operated by No 4 Group, Transport Command. From November 7 1945 the station housed No 1665 (Transport) Conversion Unit which operated out of here with Halifax C8s. This unit disbanded on July 15 1946 and the aircraft were absorbed by 1332 HTCU at Dishforth. After this brief role the station was transferred to Fighter Command in July 1946. The first fighter unit to arrive was No 264 Squadron from Church Fenton on the 22nd of the month.

This unit, equipped with Mosquito NF 36s, moved out again the following month.

For the next decade the station housed several fighter units. During the first half of August 1946, Nos 64 and 65 Squadrons arrived from Church Fenton. Both units operated with Hornet F1s and F3s, the fastest piston-engined fighter to be built. The unit later exchanged these for Meteor F8s when the jet age finally caught up with Linton-on-Ouse. This was in October 1949 when the two resident units were joined by the Meteors of Nos 66 and 92 Squadrons from Duxford. These two squadrons were subsequently equipped with Sabres and Hunters.

For almost two years the station operated with the four fighter squadrons. Then, during August 1951, Nos 64 and 65 Squadrons moved to Duxford. At the end of August 264 Squadron returned from Coltishall. Then the station housed the Sycamore helicopters of No 275 Squadron which arrived in April 1953 but moved out to Thornaby on November 18 1954.

Over the past decade Mosquitoes, Hornets, Meteors, Canadian Sabres, Hunters and Meteor NF 14as had operated from the airfield. In addition the station had again been a headquarters, this time the peacetime home of the Yorkshire Sector Headquarters.

By 1957 it was obvious the airfield was not really suitable for conversion to accommodate the high-performance jet fighters which were now coming into service, and the squadrons began to move out. During February No 66 moved to Acklington and the following month the Hawker Hunters of 92 Squadron moved to Middleton St George, followed a few days later by 264 Squadron.

After the departure of the fighter squadrons in early 1957 the station was placed on Care and Maintenance but re-opened on September 9 as a Flying Training Command Station, with No 1 Flying Training School which moved to Linton-on-Ouse from Syerston. Initially equipped with Vampire Jet trainers, the school later received Jet Provosts. From 1960 to 1969 the school was also tasked with the training of all Fleet Air Arm pilots. In September 1969 Naval pilot training was transferred to Church Fenton, and Linton-on-Ouse reverted to training RAF students and officers from Commonwealth and foreign forces.

The station became part of Support

Top *Hornet F3 of 64 Squadron from Linton-on-Ouse.* **Above** *North American Sabre F1 XD734 of No 92 Squadron at Linton-on-Ouse in April 1956.*

Command on July 1 1977 and No 1 Flying Training School is today equipped with Jet Provost Mk 3As and the more advanced Mk 5A aircraft. The school provides basic flying training for student pilots which takes approximately nine months. At the end of basic training, those pilots selected for multi-engined aircraft or helicopters go on to other units for their specialised training. Those selected for 'fast-jet', that is Tornado, Harrier, Jaguar, etc, stay at Linton-on-Ouse for a further three months to fly the Jet Provost Mk 5A as a lead-in to their advanced flying training on Hawks at RAF Valley.

In order to prevent circuit congestion, the early stages of the course, in particular the circuit training and consolidation, are flown from RAF Elvington which is used as a Relief Landing Ground and operated on a day-to-day requirement basis by personnel from Linton-on-Ouse. At this stage there are no plans to move or disband the resident unit and I trust it will continue to operate from this wartime base for many years to come.

Lissett, Yorkshire

107/TA135580. SW of Bridlington

Lissett officially opened as a bomber airfield in No 4 Group, Bomber Command, during the latter part of February 1943, and the Halifaxes of No 158 Squadron touched down and rolled along the runways while the base was still under construction. However, the first recorded use of the airfield appears to have been in December 1942 when it was brought into use as a Relief Landing Ground for the OTU at Catfoss, a few miles to the south.

Situated on the west side of the A165 road near Lissett village, after which the airfield was named, this was a typical wartime bomber base. No frills, only the bare necessities with the usual primitive wartime hutments, but for many it was home. It was laid out with the usual three paved runways, the main one, 09/27, being 5,600 ft long and on an east-west axis. The two intersecting runways were each 4,300 ft in length, and were encircled by a perimeter track off which were 36 frying pan-type hardstandings.

The Technical Site was sited near the village on the eastern side of the airfield. In this area was the control tower, and close by were the night flying equipment store, signals and intelligence, crew briefing room, floodlight trailer shed and a Nissen hut immediately behind the control tower, which was the rest room. Then came a Standard 'T2' hangar, type 3653/42, grouped behind which were further buildings which included the station armoury, gas defence centre, MT section, flight offices, crew rest locker and drying room. The latter were two 'H' type buildings. Next to the Technical Site was the Defence Site which consisted of the sub-station and barrack huts. To the south of the airfield was the Bomb Store Site made up of 31 buildings which included six Nissen general purpose huts, fuzing point buildings, component stores, SBC stores, incendiary bomb stores, the incendiary and pyro storehouse and the two radar workshop buildings.

On March 10 1943, Wing Commander T.R. Hope became Commanding Officer and the following night ten aircraft were despatched to Stuttgart. Sadly, Sergeant H.E. Witham and crew in Halifax *NP-J:DT748* were all killed.

The squadron continued with attacks on Berlin, Essen, Duisburg and Pilsen, to name but a few. On May 12/13 the squadron put up its greatest total to date when 21 aircraft were despatched to Duisburg, a city at the junction of the Rhine and Ruhr Rivers and the largest inland port in Europe. The weather was perfect and the raid was a success with 48 acres burnt-out and many factories and chemical works severely damaged. However, it was costly and from the 572 aircraft despatched, 35 failed to return; 158 Squadron had no casualties, however.

May was brought to a close with a raid

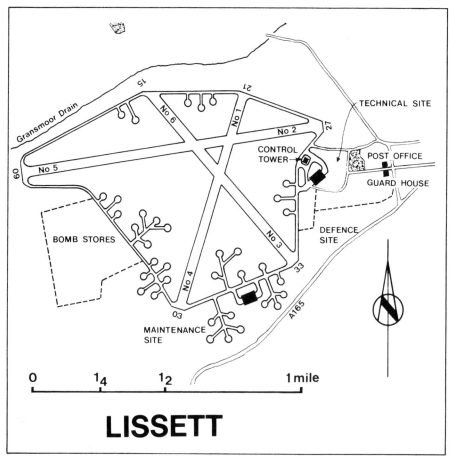

LISSETT

against Wuppertal, an important industrial centre on the fringe of the Ruhr but still within the dense network of searchlights and guns which now covered the industrial heart of Germany. The raid was carried out against very bitter opposition and two crews failed to return from the 17 despatched by the squadron. Sergeant C.K. Surgey in Halifax *NP-R: HR840* crashed at Swalmen, Holland, and only two crew, Sergeant Cottrell and Sergeant Ayton, survived to become prisoners of war. There were no survivors from the second aircraft, Halifax *HR717* piloted by Flight Sergeant J. Cooper, RCAF.

The night bombing campaign continued and in late July Bomber Command turned from the battle-scarred Ruhr to press deeper into Germany. Because H2S radar would now be needed, it was decided the first blow should be struck against Hamburg, where the coastline and river should give clear pictures on the radar screen. During late July and early August four major attacks were made within ten days.

For the first attack on July 24, 24 crews from 158 Squadron joined the main force. From the 791 despatched 12 aircraft failed to return, one being from Lissett, 'A'-Able, Halifax *HR941*, which was a brand-new aircraft on its first mission piloted by Sergeant W.H. Bolan. All crew were killed.

The success of this first Hamburg raid can be attributed to the fact that on this occasion 'Window' was first used by Bomber Command. 'Window' on the Hamburg raid was discharged at the rate of one bundle per aircraft per minute, which estimates show produced echoes similar to a force of 12,000 aircraft!

For the other three Hamburg raids, 158 Squadron again gave maximum effort and despatched 24 aircraft on each with a loss of two of their bombers.

The first mission after the Battle of Hamburg was on August 9 when the squadron despatched 15 aircraft to Mannheim. The following night 653 bombers were despatched to Nuremburg, 21 of these being from Lissett; of the 16 aircraft that failed to return, two were from No 158 Squadron. One of these was Wing Commander Hope's Halifax, *HR938*, which crashed near Wancennes, south-east of Givet, Belgium, but he; Pilot Officer Hirshbein, the mid-upper gunner; and Pilot Officer MacRae, the flight engineer, survived. From the other

Halifax—*JD249*, piloted by Flight Lieutenant I.F. McWatt—only one survived.

Having lost the commanding officer, Wing Commander C.C. Calder, DFC, was posted in and took over on the following day. The new CO led the squadron for the first time on August 17 when 24 Lissett bombers took part in an attack on Peenemünde, the experimental base on the Baltic. To ensure a successful strike on this important target, Air Chief Marshal Harris decided to bomb it in bright moonlight. For the first time during a heavy raid against Germany it was led by a 'master of ceremonies' who flew up and down the waves of bombers telling them by radio-telephone which target indicators to attack.

The raid was a success but it was a costly operation. An attempt to draw the night fighters away by staging a 'spoof' raid on Berlin did not succeed. The German fighters were called back to Peenemünde and arrived just as the main attack developed. From the force of 597 heavy bombers, 40 were lost under the bright shining moon, one being that of Flight Sergeant W.D. Caldwell, RNZAF, in Halifax *NP-S:JD260* from Lissett. Six crew were killed, one taken PoW.

Throughout the remainder of the year attacks on German targets continued whenever possible. 1943 was brought to an end with 18 aircraft being despatched to Frankfurt, from which two failed to return. During the year the squadron had lost 73 aircraft, including five which crashed in the UK.

No 158 Squadron began to re-equip with Halifax Mk IIIs in December 1943 and the New Year saw the birth of yet another bomber squadron when No 640 was formed from 'C' Flight on January 7 1944. However, after flying two operations from Lissett it moved to Leconfield before the end of the month. Meanwhile, 158 Squadron continued with conversion training and on January 20 1944, 16 of the new aircraft were despatched to do battle against Berlin. Flight Sergeant R.H. Thompson, RCAF, and crew in Halifax *LV773*, were all killed when their bomber blew up.

The next day 14 aircraft were despatched to Magdeburg. Halifax *HX335* piloted by Sergeant E.W. Brookes was shot down. Three were killed and four taken prisoner of war. Then it was a wing and a prayer for Warrant Officer van Slyke's Halifax and crew for he was very low on fuel as he crossed Flamborough Head. Fearing he would not make it back to Lissett, he ordered his crew to bale out but the flight-engineer refused to leave. Working as a team they managed to make a wheels-down forced-landing in a field some two miles east of Lissett. However, at daybreak the rescue party came across the bodies of Sergeant Evans, the navigator, and Sergeant Collingwood, the rear gunner. Sadly, both had died after striking the ground before their parachutes had fully deployed. Three other crew were unhurt.

New crews were constantly arriving to replace the heavy losses suffered by Bomber Command during those long winter nights. Among these, on February 29 1944, was Flight Sergeant Doug Bancroft and his crew who had been posted in from the HCU at Rufforth. The following night he flew as a second pilot (2nd Dickie) in Halifax III *LV792* 'E'-Easy when 14 from No 158 Squadron were despatched to Stuttgart. (It was normal practice throughout all Bomber Command squadrons that a new pilot

should fly with an experienced crew for two or three raids before taking his own aircraft and crew on an operation.)

Meanwhile, back at Lissett his crew were called out of bed at 02.00 hours to assist in the clearing of snow from the runway and the spreading of salt to prevent icing up of the surface in preparation for those returning from the operation. Bancroft was duly grateful.

During March 1944 attacks got underway to neutralise the French and German railway systems in preparation for the forthcoming invasion. One German target to come into the bomb-sight of the Lissett squadron was Berlin on the night of March 24/25. For this attack the southern part of Berlin was to be the primary target with Brunswick as an alternative should last-minute reconnaissance reveal unsuitable weather over Berlin. The crew were told which target was their objective whilst taxiing for take-off. This time, Berlin was designated following a Mosquito aircraft weather report from that area.

No 158 Squadron despatched 15 air-

Below *Air and four ground crew of 'E'-Easy.* **Bottom** *Halifax III LV792 'E'-Easy on a frying-pan type hardstanding at Lissett in April 1944.*

craft to join the second and third of five waves. Zero hour on the target was set at 22.30 hours with each wave being allocated three minutes over the target. Bancroft and his crew took part in the raid in Halifax III *NP-C:HX344* which was fitted with H2S radar. They were detailed as one of the wind-finder aircraft and were to attack in wave three over the target between 22.36 and 22.39 hours. 'C'-Charlie was airborne at 18.59 hours and the met report advised good weather with very slight and variable winds. They were detailed to fly below 1,000 ft until about 100 miles from the enemy coast and at that point climb to their bombing height of 20,000 ft and maintain to target.

On reaching the enemy coast Flight Sergeant Fripp advised the Captain they had drifted some 50-odd miles south of track, that he had calculated the wind velocity as 100 mph from the north, and that his new ETA target was about 22.52 hours (some 15 minutes late). The Captain instructed the wireless operator, Sergeant Dwan, to advise Group of this wind velocity and direction. They arrived in the target area still some ten minutes late and noted that the bomber stream was widely scattered. Anti-aircraft fire was extremely concentrated but they were still able to make a good bombing run up to the target. Coming out of the area they noticed the German night fighters were active but they were not attacked. Still using the wind velocity and direction as calculated, they were able to maintain the original flight plan track back to base without incident and landed at Lissett at 01.44 hours.

From the 810 aircraft despatched 72 failed to return, Lissett losing two. Pilot Officer Bancroft recalls: 'Whilst north of Osnabruck we could see well to the south over the Ruhr Valley and noticed that many bombers had drifted down there and were caught in the heavy defences of that area and were being shot down'. Osnabruck was in fact ready and waiting and eight bombers were shot down by flak. Essen flak claimed five and at least 20 other bombers were hit by flak in this area. (The map that Pilot Officer Bancroft used on the Berlin raid is shown below.)

Photograph of the actual captain's route map as used by Pilot Officer Doug Bancroft on the Berlin Raid on March 24/25 1944. The arrowheads on the track lines indicate the tracks to and from the target whilst ⊙ indicates an alter course point and the figures on the track lines 007°T/200 signify a course of 007° True after compass adjustments for magnetic fields, etc) and a distance of 200 nautical miles before the next change of course (in some cases only a matter of a few degrees). Different markings indicated heavily anti-aircraft gun defended areas near the route and concentrated searchlight areas. The map was designed mainly for the pilot's general information.

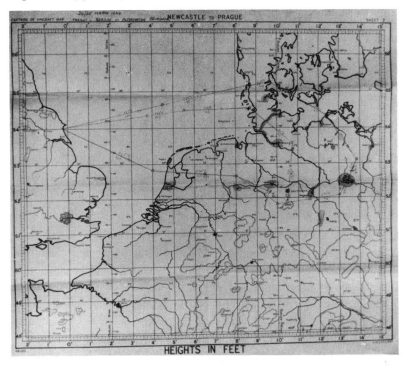

HEIGHTS IN FEET

After Berlin, Bomber Command turned its might on Essen and 705 aircraft were despatched on March 26/27. Halifax III 'E'-Easy, which had now been allocated to Doug Bancroft and crew, was over the Dutch coast on the return leg when the starboard-inner engine main drive shaft snapped but 'Easy' lived-up to its name and they successfully made it back to Lissett on three engines.

On March 30 1944, the squadron despatched 16 aircraft for Nuremburg. One making its debut on operations was Halifax III *LV907* 'F'-Freddy, or *Friday the 13th* as it was named, which was to prove a lucky aircraft from the outset. It was piloted by Flight Sergeant Joe Hitchman whose regular aircraft, *HX349* 'G'-George, in which he had completed 12 operations, had been taken over by the squadron commander, Squadron Leader Jones, leaving his crew to fly the brand-new bomber. Flying in bright moonlight, the bombers crossed the North Sea and headed south-east across Belgium. Once into Germany they were engaged by enemy night fighters, and from Aachen a running battle was fought with more and more fighters joining in. Flight Sergeant Hitchman complied with the usual procedure of logging time and position of aircraft shot down but they were so numerous that Hitchman told his crew to ignore the kites going down in flames and to keep their eyes skinned for the night fighters. From midnight on March 30 to 01.30 hours on March 31, Bomber Command was to lose 80 bombers.

Friday the 13th made it to target and, as soon as 'bombs gone' was logged, was quickly on the way home. At half way on the long homeward leg they started to have trouble with one of their engines and were also running short of fuel due to all the evasive action they had had to make on the way to target. Seven and a half hours later *Friday the 13th* touched down at Odiham, the first convenient airfield sighted in England. With the thought of their leave passes waiting for them back at Lissett the crew did not try to sleep, but instead helped the groundcrew to refill, change the plugs and do an inspection on the engine. The Nuremburg raid was a baptism by fire for *Friday the 13th*, which went on to complete 128 operations.

From the 95 aircraft that failed to return from the Nuremburg raid, Lissett lost four, one being Squadron Leader Jones, DFC, who was killed when 'G'-George, *HX349*, was shot down by flak near Westerburg. The others were Warrant Officer McLeod, RAAF, who was shot down by an Me 110 before reaching Nuremburg with six crew killed and one taken PoW; Warrant Officer Hughes, who was shot down by Metz flak on the homeward leg, with five crew taken PoW (although two escaped); and Halifax *HX322* piloted by Flight Sergeant Brice which was hit both by a night fighter and by flak. The bomber crashed between Abbeville and Hesdin in Northern France, in sight of the English Channel, killing six, the surviving member being taken PoW.

To date, no-one has yet given a reason why the tactics of Bomber Command changed to the direct approach for the Nuremburg raid, and without a deathbed confession the world will never know. Bennett claims he was overruled on this occasion and the route still puzzles students of Bomber Command tactics.

The first raid after Nuremburg was on April 9 against Villeneuve St George railway yards near Paris, when Lissett put up 19 aircraft from a total force of 225. All aircraft returned safely but over the target

The crew of 'G'-George, Halifax HX349 of 158 Squadron in 1944. Left to right: H.E. Rice (engineer), H. Harmer (navigator), R. Higgins (mid-upper gunner), J. Hitchman (pilot), L. Fisher (wireless operator), W. Tunstall (rear gunner) and A. Pearson (bomb aimer).

area close bursts of heavy predicted flak jammed the bomb-bay doors in the closed position of 'E'-Easy. After many unsuccessful attempts to discharge his bomb load, Pilot Officer Bancroft headed for home and opened the bomb-bay doors by emergency procedures over the English Channel in order to jettison. They made it back to base some considerable time after all the other aircraft.

For Pilot Officer Bancroft (commissioned on the squadron on March 28 1944) there had to be a third time, and it came on the night of June 2/3 1944 during an attack on the marshalling yards at Trappes, just south-west of Paris. Enemy fighters were waiting over the target and heavier losses than over any other rail target were suffered on this raid. In bright moonlight 16 aircraft were missing from a total force of 128 and Lissett had five that failed to return. Bancroft almost made it six. His Halifax was attacked by a Ju 88 and was extensively damaged. A fierce fired raged in the bomb bay and near the rear bulkhead, which the crew fought feverishly to control. The hydraulic system was destroyed and as a result the bomb doors and flaps fell open. The crippled bomber had a large hole, three feet long and the full width of the aircraft, in the floor of the fuselage.

With great courage Pilot Officer Alwyn Fripp, RAAF, the navigator, and the remaining crew managed to bring the fires under control while Bancroft wrestled with the shattered controls. The pilot had no communication with the crew for the aircraft's intercom system was out of action. Both turrets were also inoperative. Alone in the cockpit Bancroft steered by the North Star and by the time he reached Hurn, near Bournemouth, the crippled bomber was down to 900 ft and losing height rapidly. Bancroft recollects: 'Once the undercarriage up-locks were released on the downwind leg of the circuit and the undercarriage dropped and locked under its own weight, I was committed to the landing for it was not possible to go around again'.

His luck held and he successfully landed with two blown-out tyres. The bomber sank on to the rain-drenched concrete like a wounded eagle. Only then did Pilot Officer Bancroft discover that Sergeant Len Dwan, the wireless operator, who had been severely wounded in the attack, had either fallen or baled out through the hole in the fuselage floor. Although his body was never found, his name may be found in the Books of Remembrance at the RAF Memorial at Runnymede.

Sergeant Leonard Cottrell, flight-engineer, and Sergeant Kenneth Leheup, mid-upper gunner, were also missing. The latter was taken prisoner of war while Sergeant Cottrell was picked up by the French Resistance and eventually returned to England. Immediate DFCs were awarded to Pilot Officer Doug Bancroft, Pilot Officer Alwyn, F.C. Fripp and Flying Officer Eric Tansley, plus an immediate DFN to Sergeant David (Jock) Arundel. Not surprisingly, Halifax NP-E:LV792, which had returned only with the Grace of God, was a write-off. However, Pilot Officer Bancroft salvaged the instrument panel and head of control column and today it is displayed in the Australian War Memorial Museum at Canberra, Australia.

The survivors were not to remain non-operational for very long and a new crew was formed with Bancroft as pilot; Flying Officer Tansley, bomb-aimer; Pilot Officer Fripp, navigator; Pilot Officer Thompson, rear-gunner; Flight Sergeant Proctor, wireless operator; Sergeant W. McLean, mid-upper gunner; and Sergeant Tiltman, flight-engineer. They were allocated another H2S-equipped aircraft, Halifax III HX356, NP-G:HX356 Goofy's Gift, and the ground crew under Sergeant Fitzpatrick, fitter, proudly emblazoned the insignia of the DFC and DFM on the fuselage in their honour. Goofy's Gift had, in fact, been Pilot Officer Hitchman's aircraft for his last 22 operations, bringing him safely through his tour of 35 sorties.

June 1944 ended with a 4 Group attack on enemy troops at Villers Bocage but the initial advantage was lost because the ground attacks did not commence immediately the bombing ceased. All 24 bombers from 158 Squadron returned safely, but during the month they had lost eight aircraft from a total of 368 sorties.

July continued with attacks on French targets, and on July 28 the squadron put up a massive total of 28 aircraft for an attack on Caen from which two aircraft failed to return: that of Flying Officer B.R. Garnett and his crew of whom three were killed and four taken PoW; and that of Flight Lieutenant W.G. Davies who was killed along with his other six crew members. July 20 saw Lissett despatch eight aircraft to Bottrop and 15 to Ardouval, but over the English Channel

Left *Lissett in 1944. Air and ground crews of Halifax III HX356 'Goofy's Gift' at 60 operations.*

Below left *Bombing photograph of daylight attack on Eindhoven airfield on August 15 1944, taken by Flying Officer Bancroft of 158 Squadron in Halifax HX356:NP-G from 17,000 ft at 12.02 hours.*

Right *Lissett in June 1971. The control tower (now demolished) stands in a sea of emptiness.*

the latter force ran into severe electrical storms and the 'Master Bomber' sent out the signal 'Snapdragon', indicating the operation was cancelled. Not everyone heard the signal and six crews pressed on to target. Flight Lieutenant Platten, piloting Halifax *NP-K:NZ352*, crashed nine miles west of Neufchatel, France, killing all seven crew. July ended with three raids in the Foret de Nieppe area.

August started with a raid on the pilotless aircraft depot at Chapelle Notre Dame but with thick cloud over the target area the 'Master Bomber' abandoned the attack. 24 frustrated crews banked their bombers and headed for home. Over the

next few days Halifaxes and Lancasters bombed a variety of targets in the Bois de Casson and Forêt de Nieppe areas. On August 12, Russelsheim and Brunswick were the targets with forces of six and 16 being despatched respectively. From the Brunswick raid two very experienced crews were lost, Flight Lieutenant P.A. Cranmer (RAAF) and Flying Officer H.N. Catt, who was on his 36th sortie. The fate of Flying Officer Catt and his crew has never been determined but their names are recorded in the Books of Remembrance at Runnymede.

Three days later 21 crews made a daylight attack on the airfield at Eindhoven and entered Holland just before mid-day. Well placed target indicators fell just inside the western boundary fence and seconds later high explosives rained down on the entire area. Quickly the 'Master Bomber' ordered the backing-up force to the eastern side of the airfield and, as the raid continued unabated, the thick cloud of greyish-white smoke spiralled upwards to 8,000 ft. At 12.02 hours, Flying Officer Bancroft (newly promoted), piloting Halifax *NG-G:HX356*, released his bombs over the target area and watched in grim delight as they found their target. As they turned for home the crew could see that Gilze Rijen airfield had received similar treatment. Sadly, this did not help the British and American airborne landings planned for September.

The Lissett Halifaxes continued to support the main force and on September 1 1944, Flying Officer Bancroft and crew were screened from operations. *Goofy's Gift* had seen them safely through their tour. 1945 continued with attacks on oil and chemical works. The squadron's final wartime operation came with an attack by 27 Halifaxes on gun batteries on Wangerooge on April 25 1945. Taking part in this final raid were the squadron's two most distinguished aircraft—Halifax III *LV917 Clueless* and *LV907 Friday the 13th*, so called because its nose and fuselage was painted with superstition-defying ill omens such as a skull and cross-bones and an inverted horseshoe. On the fuselage over the door a ladder had been painted, and the navigator sat in front of a cracked mirror. Flying Officer H. Wheeler had the honour of taking *Friday the 13th* on its last mission. Both bombers had joined 158 Squadron in March 1944 and up to VE-Day flew 99 and 128 operational sorties respectively. *Friday the 13th* set up an operational record for a Halifax bomber in just (but appropriately) 13 months.

Many of the aircrew carried what they contended to be lucky charms, one of the most notable belonging to Flying Officer C.E. Smith who flew *Friday the 13th* on 29 missions between April and August 1944. He sported a real air force type moustache and carried with him on each mission a large white toy elephant some 18 inches tall which was known as 'Dumbo'. When flying, Dumbo was in the cockpit beside Smith at all times and this earned him the nickname of 'Dumbo' Smith. Other crews carried different charms or did special things before entering or when in the aircraft. Flying Officer Bancroft always insisted on having his cap hanging on the emergency hydraulic pump lever—for what reason he fails to understand even to this day.

Throughout its operational life 158 Squadron had despatched 5,366 aircraft and by coincidence 158 aircraft failed to return. Now the squadron had to adapt to its peacetime role and, on May 7 1945, it was transferred to 48 Group, Transport Command. June 1945 saw *Friday the 13th* on display in Oxford Street, London, and it was the principal attraction at 'Britain's Aircraft' Exhibition. It had helped to save the nation but, sadly, without any thought for the future it was not saved and was reduced to scrap soon afterwards—reward indeed. Fortunately, if that is the right word, the bomb log panels of *Friday the 13th* were salvaged and today are on display in the Royal Air Force Museum at Hendon.

During June, the squadron started to receive some Stirling Mk Vs and, towards

the end of August, No 158 moved to Stradishall in Suffolk. With their departure, Lissett closed down. The airfield was soon under the plough and today very few buildings remain. The control tower and hangars have long since been demolished. Only the technical site remains partly intact and is used by farmers. Also, the firing butts and a dispersed site to the north are still intact. The runways have been reduced to track only and the evening air no longer reverberates to the roar of engines. Gone are the Bancrofts and 'Dumbo' Smiths from their wartime home—having passed into history.

Lowthorpe, Yorkshire

101/TA070610. SW of Bridlington

Lowthorpe was brought into use during the First World War as an airship sub-station to Howden and opened in this capacity in April 1918. It was during this month the *SSZ23* (which had been sold to the US Navy) arrived from Howden and began to operate alongside the *SSZ32* and *38* that arrived in May. On the 19th of the month the *SSZ32* was wrecked (without casualties) near Lowthorpe and was replaced by *SSZ63* on the 25th of that month. During August, September and October 1918, the *SSZ31, 33, 56* and *64* operated from here and Kirkleatham.

During the latter period of the war, the adjoining field was used as an aerodrome by the RNAS, and 'A' Flight of 251 Squadron carried out anti-U-boat patrols with DH6 aircraft from this small grass airfield.

After the Armistice the site was quickly abandoned and was not selected for retention as a permanent RAF station.

However, the grass landing area was used by light civil aeroplanes and during the Expansion period of the RAF the site was surveyed for possible use as a bomber station, but was rejected. The Emergency Landing Ground at Carnaby was not built on this site—Lowthorpe airfield was 4½ miles SWW of Carnaby airfield.

Manywells Height (Cullingworth), Yorkshire

See Cullingworth

Marske, Yorkshire

94/NZ624225. SE of Redcar

This area was first used by Mr Robert Blackburn of Leeds for testing his monoplane on the Marske sands in 1910. Aviation at that time consisted of a short hop, a crash and then back to the drawing board and the repair shed for the machine. Marske aerodrome opened as a flying school on July 25 1910.

After the outbreak of the First World War the area was surveyed for military purposes and, on November 1 1917, No 4 Auxiliary School of Aerial Gunnery was formed at Marske with a few DH9s and Dolphins. On May 6 1918, this unit disbanded and that same day No 2 School of Aerial Fighting and Gunnery formed. The airfield had by now expanded as can be seen from the aerial photographs but most were only temporary hangars and buildings.

With the growth came further changes and on May 29 the resident unit was redesignated No 2 Fighting School. The school continued to operate from Marske and by the end of 1918 it had on strength Bristol 1cs, Camels, DH4s and 9s, but with the Armistice in November there was

an immediate rundown. In 1919, No 2 Fighting School disbanded and the airfield closed. The temporary facilities were soon dismantled and the site was not retained.

Marston Moor (Tockwith), Yorkshire

105/SE460520. W of York. Turn N off B1224 road at Long Marston

Situated between the River Nidd and the B1224 road on Marston Moor, this field lies just south-west of the village of Tockwith, the name it was referred to by the locals. The old Roman road formed the western boundary and the main aerodrome buildings were just south of Tockwith Lodge.

Marston Moor opened on November 20 1941 in No 4 Group, Bomber Command, and its role was to be as a conversion training station for heavy bombers. No 4 Group Communications Flight was already at the airfield prior to the opening but moved out the following year.

The airfield had the three standard runways, the main one being 5,610 ft in length and the two subsidiaries 4,390 ft and 4,200 ft long. The control tower was type 518/40 and there were six 'T2' hangars, four type 8254/40 and two 3653/42, plus one 'B1'.

On January 3 1942, No 1652 Conversion Unit, coded 'GV' and 'JA', formed here from No 28 and No 107 Conversion Flights, both of which had moved in from Leconfield a few days previously. During July, 1652 CU moved to Rufforth and then to Dalton before returning to Marston Moor in late August. On October 7 1942 the resident unit became No 1652 Heavy Conversion Unit,

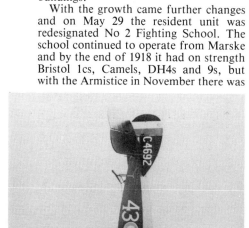

Left *Bristol F2B Fighter C4692 from No 4 Auxiliary School of Aerial Gunnery at Marske. Crashes abounded during flight training here.*

Opposite page, top to bottom *Sopwith Dolphin at No 2 FS, Marske; Sopwith Camel of 2FS with camera gun at Marske; aerial view of the landing area of No 2 Fighting School. Note the Bessoneaux hangars in line alongside the road which were soon dismantled after the war; repair shop of No 2 FS.*

absorbing No 35 Squadron Conversion Flight from Rufforth in the process. The HCU moulded crews together on the Halifax bomber and, after they had completed their conversion course, they were posted to operational squadrons where, after a few acclimatisation flights, they would be doing it for real. 1652 HCU at Marston Moor and 1658 HCU at Riccall had now taken over the responsibility of converting the whole of 4 Group to Halifaxes.

The HCU was equipped with Halifax Mk Is and throughout the life of the unit there were innumerable crashes. Unfortunately this was usual with all Conversion Units during the war. Many crashes were caused by inexperienced pilots flying new aircraft under adverse weather conditions. It was often said that conversion training was far more dangerous than actual operations. The ground crews worked very hard on aircraft that were 'clapped-out' before they started life for the HCU. All of their Halifaxes were front-line aircraft and had done many flying hours.

In April 1943 Group Captain Leonard Cheshire became station commander and passed on his wealth of experience to the new Halifax crews. During his period at Marston Moor his book *Bomber Pilot* appeared on the market. In September 1943, Group Captain Cheshire left to take command of No 617 Squadron. That some month the station became No 41 Base under No 4 Group, Bomber Command, with Rufforth and Riccall as Sub-bases.

During 1943, a few Halifax Mk IIs and Vs had become part of the HCU scene. There were also Spitfires and Hurricanes now housed on the airfield. An unexpected visitor dropped in on November 12 1943 and caused quite a flap at the station. Pilot Officer Bowly in Halifax *JD384:N* from 429 Squadron at Leeming was returning from a raid on Cannes when he ran into trouble. He had bombed the target without incident, but

on the outward trip had been flying at 15,000 ft, drifted off track and came so close to the Alps that the Monica audible warning device was working from the mountain tops: it had an effective range of 1,000 ft. On the return trip the pilot handed over the auto-pilot to Jock Dougall, the bomb aimer, who was a scrubbed pilot, while he went for a spell in the rest position. It was a very long trip, turning out to be 10 hours 20 minutes.

The bomber was off course as it crossed the English coast and by now was very low on fuel, so on seeing a flarepath on an airfield below the pilot asked for permission to land; one engine cut out from lack of fuel while in the circuit area and they made a bumpy three-engined landing. While taxying round the perimeter track the pilot opened the bomb doors and, as he did so, felt a bump. At the control tower Jock Dougall checked the bomb bay doors and found they were somewhat damaged. Walking back around the perimeter track he found a live 1,000 lb bomb lying there. The 1,000-pounders had been put on 500 lb carriers as there was a shortage of the correct ones and this bomb had bent the electrical release pin. Jock had got the engineer to check the load after bombing but he had missed the hang-up, which had subsequently affected the fuel consumption lugging it back from the Mediterranean.

It was 06.00 hours and Marston Moor was just closing down night flying when the bomb was reported to the control tower. It caused a panic because the station was not geared to handle live bombs of that size. An Aircraftsman with rifle and fixed bayonet was put on guard and he was patrolling around it as far away as he could get. Pilot Officer Bowly says: 'He might just as well have sat on it, as it had a nose and tail arming propellor device which had to spin off after it had fallen 1,000 ft or so before it was fully armed. We got refuelled, had breakfast and flew back to base. I must say we were intrigued with the Group Captain's privy

Marston Moor firing butts and machine-gun range, photographed in July 1979.

Main entrance and water tower at Marston Moor.

on the station—it had a red velvet seat'.

In December 1944 the station became No 74 Base, still controlling Riccall and Rufforth with Acaster Malbis as a relief landing ground. The airfield now came under No 7 Group, Training Command. During this period the HCU began to receive Halifax Mk IIIs and in January 1945 a few Hurricane Mk IVs arrived.

With the war over there was an immediate rundown but the crashes continued. However, one of the last was at 00.05 hours on June 13 1945 when Halifax *LW573* swung on take-off, the pilot overshot and the undercarriage collapsed. But the end was in sight and on June 25 No 1652 HCU disbanded.

During the first week of August 1945, No 1665 HCU arrived from Saltby, equipped with Stirling IVs and Halifax IIIs and IVs, plus a few Oxfords and Spitfires. Since August 1, this unit had become 1665 Heavy Transport Conversion Unit for No 4 Group, Transport Command. On November 7 1945 the unit moved to Linton-on-Ouse and the airfield closed that same month.

Today, part of the airfield is used as a Driver Training Centre and in July 1980 the control tower was still standing and being used as offices for the driving school. Around the airfield there are still many old air raid shelters and other small brick installations. The runways and perimeter track are still in reasonable condition, the NE/SW section being used by the police as skid-pan. The minor road to Tockwith village now crosses the end of runways 2 and 3. The airfield site is still occupied by the Government and the seven hangars, the two westerly ones having blast-protection earth walls, are used by the Home Office Supply and Transport for the storage of HM Prison stores, beds, chairs, etc, and for Green Goddesses which in early 1981 were being overhauled and painted. Many of the wartime buildings on the airfield site are intact, including the parachute store and both 32-bay MT sheds, but are derelict.

Melbourne, Yorkshire

106/SE765420. SE of York

This site lay between the village of Melbourne and Seaton Ross a few miles to the south of Pocklington airfield, and just south of the Pocklington Canal.

It was brought into use as a makeshift airfield during the latter part of 1940 and was utilised as a satellite by the Whitleys of 10 Squadron from Leeming. Melbourne was only a grass-surfaced landing ground, having no permanent buildings. Crew quarters and messes were either wooden or Nissen-type huts. However, even under these conditions a few operations were carried out from here, but the hard winter of 1940/41 made many grass airfields unserviceable and Melbourne was no exception. Accordingly, 10 Squadron was moved to the parent station of Leeming and Melbourne closed so that it could be rebuilt as a heavy bomber station that would be capable of operating the four-engined Halifaxes.

No 10 Squadron returned to Melbourne in August 1942, but the airfield was still under construction and the squadron's Halifaxes were obliged to fly over to Pocklington for fuelling and bombing-up. On their return from operations they had to land at Melbourne assisted by emergency lighting.

No 10 Squadron Conversion Flight had also arrived mid-August but this unit did not remain for long and on October 7 1942 it moved to Riccall to form No 1658 HCU.

After the reconstruction Melbourne had three concrete runways, the main one being 5,550 ft long and the two intersecting ones each 4,000 ft in length. These were linked with an encircling perimeter track off which were 32 frying-pan type hardstandings. The technical site and a

The crew of Halifax III 'Z'-Zebra from 10 Squadron at Melbourne in May 1944. From April 18 to August 12 1944, this crew completed 37 ops.

'T2' hangar were in the north-east corner with the bomb stores to the south of the airfield, close to Breckstreet Farm. To the east was a further 'T2' hangar and a 'B1'. This area also housed the FIDO installation, and sited on a hardstanding were sleeping quarters and stores plus two static water tanks, fire tender hut and pump house. Melbourne was the only airfield, other than the emergency one at Carnaby, to be equipped with FIDO in this area.

The squadron took part in the main force operations which included the Battle of the Ruhr during the early part of 1943. During July and August, the Battle of Hamburg, which had been given the code name 'Gomorrah', took place, these raids being the most devastating of the war. Hamburg, which stands at the confluence of the Alster River with the great Elbe just upstream from the Elbe's outflow into the North Sea, was burned by the Vikings in 845 and the rebuilt Hamburg was burned down again eight times in the following 300 years. A great fire swept the city in May 1842 and devastated one-fourth of the city centre but that did not halt the booming economy. With its 1¾ million population, Harris was again to raze it to the ground.

In the early hours of August 3 1943, Halifax *Farouk* approached the target as one of the 350 bombers on the fourth and last of the 'Gomorrah' raids. Suddenly, the bomber was attacked by a Ju 88 from the port quarter and it is ironic that Flight Sergeant Arthur Fuller, the mid-upper gunner, should have been out of his turret at this crucial time, dropping Window. It was most stupid that the mid-upper gunner should have this duty, and No 10 Squadron was the only operational unit in Bomber Command to employ its mid-upper gunner in that way.

The night fighter followed the bomber on a curve of pursuit and in the darkness red-hot circles glowed eerily for a few seconds as the attacker's bullets struck *Farouk*. Cordite fumes filled the fuselage as the rear-gunner fired back. Having survived the first attack, Flight Sergeant Fuller tried to reach his turret but before he could do so he was again thrown to the floor as Flying Officer Jenkins took evading action. Bullets again ripped through the fuselage but *Farouk* absorbed them as it hurtled earthwards. Meanwhile, Sergeant Richard Hurst, RCAF, had delivered accurate bursts of fire from his rear turret and the Ju 88 spiralled down in flames. The bomber had sustained extensive damage with both elevators being shot away, while the rudders were in ribbons and much superficial damage sustained. In spite of this the pilot displayed great courage and flew the damaged bomber back to Melbourne. For his superb airmanship he was awarded the DFC, and Sergeant Hurst received the DFM.

Flight Lieutenant Jenkins and his crew were again in trouble a few weeks later. At 18.50 hours on September 22 they rolled down the runway at Melbourne on the start of their 14th operation and climbed into the night sky over the Yorkshire countryside. Their target was Hanover and they were part of the main force of 716 bombers. Flight Lieutenant Jenkins was pilot of 'N'-Nuts, a brand-new Halifax which was fitted with H2S and had also been selected to carry a cine-camera in the flare-chute. The camera would operate automatically when the bombing run commenced. This was the

Flight Lieutenant Jenkins and crew with Farouk III. *Photograph taken at 10 Squadron, Melbourne, at the end of their tour in January 1944. Jenkins is in the centre, flanked by Fuller and Hurst.*

first instance of a raid being filmed in this manner, and in colour.

The flight to target was uneventful but, as 'N'-Nuts started its run-up, the vigilant rear-gunner sighted an Me 110, but not on the usual 'curve of pursuit' attack. A cold feeling told him something was wrong. 'Dive! Dive!' The captain acted instantly but it was seconds too late for a devastating burst of fire struck the bomber on the downward dive of its combat manoeuvre.

The crew awaited their fate but the pilot levelled the bomber out and miraculously no-one was injured nor was any fire reported in the aircraft. At that moment, the bomb-aimer, Sergeant Eric Saddington, reminded the pilot they had not bombed. The pilot ordered the instant release of all bombs while they were still in the target area but the bomb doors failed to open. Obviously, they had been damaged during the attack. A further check revealed the H2S equipment was out of action and the Perspex cover on the underside had been shot away leaving a hole about five feet long and some three feet wide. The crew surveyed for other damage and Sergeant 'Monty' Banks, the flight-engineer, found a projectile embedded in the bulletproof panel behind the pilot's head. Without that protective panel the cannon shell would have blown Jenkins' head off.

Fortunately the fighter had not returned but the crew of 'N'-Nuts were far from safe. The night fighters had now been informed of the bombers' route and began laying a lane of powerful flares as the bombers left the burning target area. 'N'-Nuts was particularly vulnerable and the two gunners. Flight Sergeants Hurst

and Fuller, were extra vigilant, but their luck held and they escaped without further sight of any enemy fighters.

Their next problem was what to do with the 'Cookie' and the flight-engineer revealed that there was a pipe in the system which, if cut, would cause the bomb doors to fall open. The pilot gave orders to locate the tube and cut it. Using a special small hacksaw-blade from his 'Pandora' box the flight-engineer did so, but nothing happened—the bomb doors remained closed.

In desperation the mid-upper gunner was selected to try and cut a hole in the plywood floor with the turret axe and eventually a hole was made. Fuller then tried to dislodge the bomb with his boot, but it would not budge. With the 4,000-pounder still on board it was impossible to belly land at either Melbourne or Carnaby and the aircraft would have to be abandoned.

Eventually 'N'-Nuts arrived over Melbourne without further mishap and the commanding officer, Wing Commander Edmunds, ordered them to bale out. The pilot confirmed the orders to flying control and turned towards the coast in the direction of Hull. Over Patrington, near the mouth of the River Humber, the bomber circled while the crew baled out, the pilot then switched on 'George', the automatic pilot, and turned the Halifax out to sea, baling out himself while 'N'-Nuts headed for a watery grave.

The local Army units had been alerted and the crew were soon collected and taken to Melbourne where they were debriefed. Some strong words were spoken when the commanding officer realised the coloured film had not been saved. It had

been a matter of saving their own lives and
the luckiest member of the crew was
Flight Sergeant Hurst, the rear-gunner.
He landed close to the edge of the cliff,
and using the best of his judgement in the
darkness, moved away from the sound of
the sea beating on the shore below him.
After walking for some minutes he
stumbled into a barbed wire fence. With
great difficulty and numerous tears he
managed to get through it. Continuing for
a reasonable distance he again ran into a
similar barrier and, following a further
struggle, succeeded in getting through the
entanglement. Proceeding once more he
came to a third such fence and once more
he crawled through the twisting circles of
barbed wire. Beyond this point he arrived
at a roadside fence which he climbed and
then found himself alongside a small
country road. Trying to get his bearings
he noticed a sign alongside the point
where he had climbed the fence: 'Danger!
Mined Land—Keep Out'. He froze when
he realised that he had just walked
through a minefield. This explained the
presence of the barbed wire barriers which
had puzzled him.

From the 716 bombers despatched for
the Hanover raid 658 attacked the target
with 2,357 tons of bombs and 25 aircraft
failed to return. Flight Lieutenant Jenkins
and his crew were among the lucky ones.

No 10 Squadron continued to play a
major part in the bomber offensive and,
during November and December 1943,
took part in the Battle of Berlin which,
during those two months alone, cost
Bomber Command 212 heavy bombers.
The Battle of Berlin continued until the
end of March 1944. Attacks were then
made on pre-invasion targets in France,
Belgium and Germany. During March the
squadron re-equipped with Halifax B IIIs.
After D-Day the squadron Halifaxes
bombed the V-1 sites at Noyelle on
Chaussee on June 24 and on the 25th at
Mont Orgueil. Both were daylight raids.

The squadron continued on a variety of

bombing raids until September when it
then took part in transporting petrol to
Belgium. After its brief transport role the
squadron resumed the bombing offensive
with attacks on German industrial targets
and oil refineries which included
Gelsenkirchen, Bohlen and Kamsen.

The last operational mission for the
resident squadron was on April 25 1945,
when 20 Halifaxes bombed gun batteries
on the Island of Wangerooge. Since D-
Day No 10 had operated on 149 nights
and days with a loss of 30 Halifaxes. The
awards earned by the squadron during the
war years totalled 523, including nine
DSOs, 333 DFCs and 173 DFMs.

On May 7 1945, No 10 Squadron was
transferred from Bomber to Transport
Command and began to convert to
Dakotas, but before the conversion was
completed it moved, in August, to
Broadwell, a transport station in Glouces-
tershire. It was replaced on August 5 by
the Dakotas of No 575 Squadron from
Broadwell, which were then joined by the
Oxfords of No 1552 Radio Aids Training
Flight which formed at Melbourne on
September 15 1945.

On November 16 1945, No 575
Squadron moved to Blakehill Farm and in
March 1946 the RAT Flight vacated the
station and Melbourne closed. The
airfield was not retained by the post-war
RAF and most of the facilities were soon
dismantled. The 'B1' hangar had survived
up to 1980 and was being used by a seed
firm. The technical site was used as a pig
farm. The control tower stood silent and
derelict.

The airfield was sold to Mr John
Rowbottom of Melrose Farm,
Melbourne, and during the summer of
1973 Sunday Markets were held on the
wartime runways. However, 'war clouds'
gathered again over Melbourne and 392
summonses of illegal trading on Sundays
were issued which brought this to a close.
It was one thing to fight for freedom and
win—but it was another matter to enjoy
it.

No 10 Squadron in flight from Melbourne.

Melbourne control tower as at June 1980.

Menthorpe Gate, Yorkshire

*106/SE690345. E of Selby on S side of the
A163 road*

A First World War site that was of little
significance, Menthorpe Gate was nothing
more than a grass area that was used as a
landing ground by 76 Squadron with their
Avro 504s. Situated on the west side of the
River Derwent, it was only used during
the autumn of 1916 and there are no
records to show that it was ever employed
again. However, during the Second World
War the site on the east side of the River
Derwent was developed into a bomber
station: Breighton *(qv)*.

Middleton, Yorkshire

104/SE310280. S of Leeds

Situated some three miles south of Leeds,
Middleton was one of three such landing
sites around the City, this one giving
facilities for the south side. Middleton was
used as a night landing ground from
March to October 1916 by 'B' Flight of 33
Squadron, Royal Flying Corps, while on
Home Defence Duties. It saw very little
activity and was quickly abandoned.
Today the site has been engulfed by the
City of Leeds.

Middleton St George (Goosepool, Tees-side), County Durham

*93/NZ375130. 6 miles E of Darlington to
S of B1273 road*

This was one of the bomber airfields
planned during the Royal Air Force
Expansion period of the mid-1930s, but
construction work did not start until just
before the outbreak of war in 1939.
Situated to the east of Middleton St
George village, after which it was named
(but known locally as Goosepool from a
nearby farm), construction work pro-

gressed at a very slow rate. Hampered by
shortages of materials only two permanent hangars, a 'C1' and a 'J', were built
on the technical site. These were later
supplemented by two 'T2's and a 'B1', all
of which were on the north-west side of
the airfield.

Middleton St George officially opened
on January 15 1941 as a bomber station in
No 4 Group, Bomber Command, Royal
Air Force. It was a standard bomber
station which followed a familiar pattern
and had a decoy airfield at Crathorne, a
few miles to the south-east.

During April 1941, No 78 Squadron
arrived from Dishforth with 16 Whitley
Mark Vs, under Wing Commander B.V.
Robinson. The squadron was immediately
in action and that same month made raids
on enemy ships and against Berlin.

In June, 76 Squadron arrived from
Linton-on-Ouse, equipped with Halifax B
Is; it was only the second squadron to fly
the new bomber. The station continued to
operate with the two squadrons and in
October of that year Croft was brought
into use as a satellite airfield. That same
month 78 Squadron moved to Croft with
the old Whitleys and began to convert to
the Halifax. It returned in June 1942 after
having re-equipped with B IIs. The
following month Wing Commander J.B.
Tait, who later commanded 617
Squadron, became CO. During this
period, 76 Squadron had detachments in
the early part of the year in Northern
Scotland for operations against the
Tirpitz, later destroyed by Nos 9 and 617
Squadrons.

Operations continued from here until
mid-September, when Nos 76 and 78
Squadrons moved to Linton-on-Ouse.
During this period one who served on
both units was Sergeant Pilot H.H.
Drummond, and targets attacked were
Bremerhaven, Rotterdam, Mannheim,

Whitley V 'F'-Freddie, Z6577, of 78 Squadron at Middleton St George in May 1941.

Brest, Bremen, Hamburg, Duisburg and Cologne. Harry Drummond had his own personal emblem, *Bulldog Drummond*, on his aircraft during operations, and it brought him luck. It adorned Whitley *Z6577*, 'F'-Freddie, on 78 Squadron and Halifax *L9534* 'T'-Tommy on 76 Squadron. The *Bulldog Drummond* was embellished on the nose of the aircraft and the black patch over the eye symbolised the practical element in night bombing, but the important feature was the boomerang around the neck—the weapon that goes out to its target and always returns. That was so with Sergeant Drummond (later Wing Commander and CO 1658 HCU at Riccall).

Nos 76 and 78 Halifax Conversion Flights, which had been at Middleton St George since their arrival from Dalton at the end of August, also moved out. Both units moved on September 16 to Riccall. Middleton St George was now prepared for the Royal Canadian Air Force and, on October 16 1942, No 420 Squadron, RCAF, arrived from Skipton-on-Swale. This unit was equipped with Wellington Mark IIIs and, on November 10, was joined by 419 Squadron from Croft. No 1516 BAT Flight had also arrived on October 17 from Llanbedr, but during the second week of December it moved to Hampstead Norris and was replaced by the Oxfords of 1535 BAT Flight (RCAF) which formed at Middleton St George on December 15 1942 and moved early in the New Year to Topcliffe.

Crews were now being posted in to make up the squadrons and at the end of December, Squadron Leader Alex Cranswick and his crew were posted in to 419 Squadron from 1659 HCU at Leeming. On January 1 1943, the station became part of No 6 (RCAF) Group. Nos 419 and 420 Squadrons were also transferred to the Canadian Group. Middleton St George now became No 64 Base Headquarters with Croft as its sub-station.

These were the two most northerly stations of the Group.

Cranswick, tired of flying a desk, had wanted to get back into the pilot's seat and with 419 Squadron he could do just that. He was a quiet man and kept himself apart. He did not go on drinking bouts with the other crews. During his stay at Middleton St George he acquired an Alsatian named Kluva of Kentwood. He gave Kluva the rank of temporary Sergeant and the dog flew with him on a few missions. He had his own flying log-book but his name never appeared in Air Ministry's records!

Cranswick had been educated at St Edward's School, Oxford, and during the Second World War over 250 boys from St Edward's served in the RAF, including Guy Gibson, Louis Strange, Douglas Bader and Adrian Warburton. Cranswick did many missions from Middleton before being posted to 35 Squadron at Graveley, Huntingdonshire, to be part of the Pathfinder Force. Sadly, he was killed while on his 107th sortie on the night of July 4/5 1944, during a raid against Villeneuve St George in Lancaster *ND846*, 'J'-Johnnie. He was one of the outstanding bomber pilots of the Second World War. He and his crew are buried in New Communal Cemetery at Clichy, on the northern boundary of Paris.

On May 15 1943, No 420 Squadron moved to North Africa to be part of the Mediterranean Air Command. This unit was replaced on June 3 by No 428 (RCAF) Squadron from Dalton. Nos 419 and 428 Squadrons were to remain here for the remainder of their period in the UK. Both converted to Halifax heavy bombers and took part in the strategic and tactical bombing operations. 428 was also engaged in minelaying and, on January 4/5 1944, six of the squadron's Halifaxes carried out Bomber Command's first high-level minelaying operation, dropping their mines by parachute from heights of

14-15,000 ft. Prior to this mines had been planted from heights below 6,000 ft.

During the early part of 1944 both squadrons converted to the Canadian-built Lancaster X and retained these for the duration of the war. During a raid on Cambrai on June 12 1944, Lancaster B Mk X *VR-A:KB726* of 419 Squadron, of which Pilot Officer Andrew C. Mynarski was the mid-upper gunner, was attacked from below by a German fighter and both port engines were put out of action. Fire immediately broke out in the port wing and between the mid-upper and rear turrets. The Captain ordered the crew to abandon the aircraft but the rear-gunner, Flying Officer Brophy, was trapped.

Without hestiation, Mynarski fought his way through the flames and made every attempt to free him but all his efforts were in vain. Eventually the rear-gunner signalled to Mynarski that he could do no more and that he should try to save his own life. Reluctantly Mynarski made his way back through the flames to the escape hatch, where he stood to attention in his flaming clothing and as a last gesture, saluted his comrade before he jumped from the doomed bomber. Mynarski died in a German hospital from his severe burns.

Miraculously, when the Lancaster crashed, the rear-gunner was thrown clear and became a prisoner of war. After the war when details of what Mynarski tried to do became known, he was posthumously awarded the Victoria Cross—the last awarded to an airman and the only one to a Canadian airman of Bomber Command.

The last mission of the war for both the Middleton St George squadrons was on April 25 1945, when 15 Lancaster Xs from 419 Squadron and 15 from 428 bombed gun batteries on the Island of Wangerooge.

No 419 Squadron had dropped 13,417 tons of bombs and made 4,002 sorties from which it lost 129 aircraft. 310 aircrew were killed, 867 missing and 187 prisoners of war. Awards were one VC, four DSOs, one MC, 150 DFCs, three Bars to DFCs, one CGM and 35 DFMs.

The awards won by 428 (Ghost) Squadron were two DSOs, 71 DFCs, two CGMs and six DFMs. 84 aircraft were lost and 463 aircrew, of whom 63 were killed, 377 missing and 13 prisoners of war.

After the hostilities in Europe, both squadrons were selected as part of 'Tiger Force' for duty in the Pacific and, in June 1945, Nos 419 and 428 Squadrons flew their Lancasters back to Canada. With the Departure of the Canadians the station was transferred from Bomber to Fighter Command and No 13 Operational Training Unit moved in from Harwell during July 1945 with Mosquito aircraft. Crashes were still all too frequent and only days after arriving a Mosquito was taking off when an engine cut and it ended up looking at its own tail. A few weeks later a Mosquito entered the circuit with an engine on fire but was unable to land and the two-man crew baled-out. The aircraft crashed near the village of Yarm.

Mosquito T3 *LR565* of 13 OTU took off from here on May 11 1946 on an exercise, but while airborne the aircraft suddenly nose-dived into a field near Bankdam Farm, Thornley, County Durham. In 1979, the North-East Aircraft Museum recovered the two engines along with other parts which are now displayed in their museum.

The year 1947 saw the arrival of No 608 (North Riding) Royal Auxiliary Air Force Squadron from Thornaby with Mosquito NF30s, Spitfire F22s and Vampires. This unit was to remain for the next decade until the disbandment of the Auxiliary Air Force in March 1957.

During early May 1947, No 13 OTU moved to Leeming and the airfield was transferred to Flying Training Command as a base for No 2 Air Navigation School that moved in from Bishops Court on October 1. This unit stayed until May 1950 when it then moved to Thorney Island. No 205 Advanced Flying School, which was later renamed No 4 Flying Training School, then took over the

Lancasters of 428 Squadron ready for take-off from Middleton St George on November 21 1944.

station, but after this unit departed Middleton St George reverted to Fighter Command in June 1956.

Operational life began again in March 1957 when 92 Squadron, flying Hawker Hunter F6s, and 264 Squadron flying Meteor NF 14s, moved in from Linton-on-Ouse. Both units stayed until the following September when 92 moved to Thornaby and 264 moved to Leeming where it was re-numbered No 33 Squadron.

The airfield then closed in October 1957 to enable the main runway to be strengthened and lengthened to 7,500 ft so that it was suitable for the supersonic fighters that were coming into service. The airfield re-opened the following year but extensive work was still being done on the buildings and runways.

Equipped with Javelin Mk 7s, No 33 Squadron arrived at Middleton St George in July 1958. The following September the Hunters of 92 Squadron returned as an air defence squadron and became Fighter Command's official aerobatic team known as 'The Blue Diamonds'. The unit remained until May 1961 when it then moved to Leconfield, No 33 Squadron subsequently remaining at Middleton St George until its eventual disbandment on November 17 1962. At the time it was disbanded the unit had been flying Javelin Mk 9s for the past two years.

On June 1 1963, No 226 Operational Conversion Unit re-formed here from the Lightning Conversion Squadron which had formed here in June 1962 with the supersonic English Electric Lightning T4. Also incorporated into 226 OCU was the Fighter Command Instrument Rating Squadron. This unit, with its three Javelin T3s, had moved to Middleton St George following the disbandment of 228 OCU in September 1961. The OCU had the task of training pilots for fighter squadrons but moved to Coltishall on April 13 1964 after it was announced that the RAF was vacating the airfield, mainly on grounds of economy. The Javelin element had moved to Leuchars in January 1964 when it became the Javelin Instrument Rating Squadron.

With the departure of 226 OCU the Royal Air Force ceased flying at Middleton St George and finally departed on April 17 of that year. Despite being classed as a Master Division Airfield, and after all the vast expenditure on reconstruction work, the airfield had become surplus to requirements. However, it was not to remain closed and was transferred to civil use with the support of Government Departments and local authorities on Tees-side.

The airport, which covers an area of 748 acres, was purchased for the bargain price of £340,000 and, to make it a first

Above *Lancasters of 419 Squadron on dispersal: KB866 went missing over Kiel on April 13 1945 and KB875 was sent to Canada in June to join 407 Squadron. The latter was scrapped in September 1960.*

Left *Middleton St George in January 1945. Ruhr Express* caught fire and was gutted after its 50th mission. Flight *Sergeants G.E. Berteau and L. Nozzolillo look over the remains of the first Canadian-built Lancaster to fly operationally.*

Hawker Tempest TT5 photographed at Middleton St George in March 1961. This aircraft is now in the RAF Museum.

class fully-equipped airport, £110,000 was spent on re-equipment plus £506,000 for the new passenger terminal which was officially opened by Princess Margaretha of Sweden on November 1 1966. It is a pleasure to note that inside the terminal building we have a reminder of the past by way of a memorial plaque to the heroic deed of Pilot Officer Mynarski, VC. £144,000 was also spent for improvement to the apron and, retaining part of the past, £250,000 was spent in turning the former Officers' Mess into the St George Airport Hotel, work being completed in 1966. £1,350,000 was a small price to pay for a first-class fully-equipped airport which, if built from scratch today, would cost tens of millions of pounds.

On October 19 1971, the Tees-side Airport Railway Station was opened by Lord Crathorne. A special electric bus shuttles passengers, free of charge, from the terminal to the railway station. What a wartime blessing it would have been, for part of every airman's wartime life was the trudge to the country station and the waiting on the cold, windy platforms.

In March 1973, the Cleveland Flying School formed and is run by professional commercial pilots with flying experience in the Royal Air Force and civil airlines. There is also the Tees-side Flying Club which offers flying tuition.

The airport has all-weather facilities and navigational aids include an Instrument Landing System, Plessey Type 424 Radar, Cossar 787 Surveillance radar, Direction Finder, Radio Beacon, approach and runway lighting with Visual Approach Slope indicators. The technical aids for the returning wartime bomber pilots were 'Lady Luck and a Prayer'.

The main airline operators are Air Anglia with their Fokker F27 Friendships, F28 Fellowships and Navajo Chieftains, British Midland Airways with DC-9s and Dan-Air with a variety of aircraft. Others operating out of Tees-side Airport are Tyne-Tees Airways, an air charter firm with nine-seat Piper Navajo Chieftains.

An oblique photograph of Tees-side (ex-Middleton St George) showing the terminal and apron. Behind the car park is the hotel.

Bristow Helicopters operate two Puma 330 J helicopters for use in the North Sea at the giant Ekofisk oil Field. The company runs two or three flights per day. Also, several tour operators offer package holidays from Tees-side, the main ones being Airway Holidays and Thompson Holidays.

The airport, which is owned and operated by the Tees-side Airport Committee, provides an essential air link. In 1964, passenger throughput was 14,258. By 1978 it had reached 321,246. Before the mid-1980s it should have reached half a million passengers a year. There are many links with its military past, one being the Airport Director, C.K. Cole, DFC, and others the familiar runway pattern and the wartime hangars. There are also many other military buildings that are still intact, the red brick quarters on the opposite side of the road, the red brick guardroom and some on the technical site.

Murton, Yorkshire

105/SE655528. E of York

Murton was nothing more than a grass landing area which was used by 76 Squadron with their Avro 504s while employed in the defence of York during the autumn of 1916. The site was never developed but during the Second World War another site a few miles to the south became Elvington airfield.

Neasham (Croft), Co Durham

See Croft

Netherthorpe, South Yorkshire

111/SK538804. W of Worksop between Shireoaks and Thorpe Salvin

Of very minor significance, Netherthorpe was used briefly in 1940 and 1945 by 613 Squadron and No 24 Gliding School.

For further details see *Action Stations 2.*

Above *April 1979 at Tees-side Airport. Dan-Air Viscount with, behind it, the tail of DC-9 just visible and in the background an HS 748.*

Left *Control tower at Tees-side Airport.*

Owthorne, Yorkshire

107/TA335285. Immediately NW of Withernsea

This was another of the First World War airfields sited along the Yorkshire coast, but this was the most southerly. Records are very much lacking as to the role of the airfield, which was just an open grass field which came into being during 1917. It was used during 1918 by the DH6s of 506 Flight who operated out of Owthorne on anti-U-boat patrols. Immediately after the Armistice in November 1918 the site returned to its former use and had no further military connection.

Plainville, Yorkshire

105/SE570600. N of York

Situated a few miles to the north of York between the A19 and B1363 roads, close to the First World War landing ground of Shipton, Plainville was just a large grass meadow that was used as an advance landing ground and 'scatter' field during the early months of the Second World War. The Whitley Mk Vs of No 58 Squadron from Linton-on-Ouse used the site until the latter part of 1941.

On May 31 1941, Whitley *Z6660*, piloted by Pilot Officer G. Lambert, overshot on landing after returning from ops. Fortunately, only one of the crew was injured. Then, on October 11 1941, *Z9204*, a Plainville-based Whitley of 58 Squadron piloted by Sergeant E.E. Jones, ditched in the sea 11 miles ESE of Skegness, Lincolnshire, at 09.15 hours, five crew being injured. After the departure of the Whitleys there is no further record of any flying and the meadow returned to its former use.

Pocklington (Barmby), Yorkshire

106/SE790485. E of York between the A1079 and B1246 roads

Pocklington was one of the bomber airfields included in the mid-1930s Expansion plans for the Royal Air Force, but for some unknown reason work did not fully begin until after the outbreak of war in September 1939. It was close to the site used during the First World War and called Barmby, but this was nothing more than a grass strip that was used as a landing ground by 'C' Flight of 33 Squadron, Royal Flying Corps, from April to October 1916 during their anti-Zeppelin patrols. 76 Squadron are also reported to have used the field during September 1916. No permanent buildings were erected and the site was soon abandoned. However, it was obviously one of the First World War sites surveyed during the Expansion period, but was an unusual site for a bomber airfield and this probably caused the delay.

The aerodrome conformed to the standard design, but was unusual in the fact that the hangars, the main ones a 'J' type and two 'T2's, were grouped together on the technical site which extended in the centre of the airfield almost up to the main runway. The other buildings were close by and bordering the old Roman Road, the A1079.

Pocklington opened in June 1941 as a bomber station in No 4 Group, Bomber Command, and had a decoy airfield at Burnby, a few miles to the south-east. No 405 Squadron, RCAF, moved in from Driffield with their Wellingtons on June 20 and continued flying night operations with these until the following spring.

On February 14 1942 the Wellingtons of the newly-formed 158 Squadron moved to Pocklington to fuel- and bomb-up for

Wellington Mk II W5537 of 405 Squadron, RCAF in summer 1941 after having just moved to Pocklington.

their first mission because their own runways at Driffield were unserviceable. At 18.11 hours the first Wellington, piloted by Pilot Officer McMillan, took off. The last away was Pilot Officer Warnock, Royal New Zealand Air Force, at 18.42 hours, who climbed slowly into the cold night sky. Severe icing prevented one aircraft from climbing above 6,000 ft and it abandoned the mission and returned to base. The remainder of 158 Squadron returned safely.

In April 1942, No 405 Squadron Conversion Flight formed with Halifaxes and during that month the squadron converted to Halifax B Mk IIs, becoming operational with the four-engined heavy bombers in time to take part in the first Thousand-Bomber raid against Cologne on May 30/31 1942; by so doing it was the first RCAF squadron to fly the four-engined bomber into action.

Over the next few weeks the missions increased and accidents were kept to a minimum. Not all accidents were operational aircraft for on April 4 1942, Magister *L8162* of 405 Squadron failed to complete a slow roll and dived into the ground near the airfield. The two Canadian crew, Squadron Leader J. McCormack and Flight Lieutenant W.H. Fetherstone, were both killed.

One tragic crash was on July 24 1942, when Halifax *W7769* with Flight Sergeant R.B. Albright as 1st pilot and Pilot Officer G.M. Strong as 2nd pilot, crashed in flames against the school in Pocklington village at 04.53 hours. It had returned from a mission against Duisburg when it suddenly caught fire. All eight crew were killed.

On August 6 1942, No 405 Squadron and the Conversion Flight, moved to Topcliffe in exchange for 102 Squadron. The incoming unit also had a conversion flight but on October 7 1942 it moved to Riccall to be part of No 1658 HCU.

No 102 Squadron now became the resident unit and went straight into action with attacks on Italian targets. Returning from a raid on Genoa on October 23 1942, the CO's aircraft was diverted to Holme-on-Spalding-Moor where he was killed in most tragic circumstances.

The year 1943 saw a great increase in operational sorties and by the summer months 20-plus aircraft were being despatched for each mission. The squadron bombed targets throughout Germany and took part in the battles of the Ruhr, Hamburg and Berlin. For two of the Berlin raids made during November 1943 the squadron managed to despatch 23 aircraft each time. Throughout the winter months attacks were also made on other German targets, and 102 Squadron played a major role. Berlin was again the target on January 28 1944 when Halifax II *JD165* 'S'-Sugar was hit by flak coming out of the target area and received serious damage. During the return leg the flight-engineer worked to repair the damage and keep the bomber aloft. But it was a losing battle and by the time they reached the Danish coast the Halifax was down to 2,000 ft and dropping rapidly. The captain told the crew to prepare for ditching and the wireless operator gave their fix as between 60 and 90 miles east of Dundee. The IFF was put on 'Distress' and an SOS was transmitted and acknowledged.

Minutes later the damaged bomber flopped on to the waves and the crew were immediately up to their necks in water. Fortunately no-one was injured and the crew inflated their Mae Wests and the dinghy. Once in the dinghy they paddled away from the Halifax which remained afloat for almost an hour. The cold sea soon took its toll and before long their fingers were numb, making it impossible to rig the transmitter mast or even eat their sealed emergency rations. Suddenly a 20 ft wave hit the dinghy and overturned it, throwing the crew into the cold January sea in the process. Only the pilot, navigator, mid-upper gunner and wireless operator managed to get back in again. The others hung on to the dinghy life-lines. The four in the dinghy tried to pull them aboard but the wet clothes and numb fingers made it impossible. Eventually all three let go of the lines and drifted away, making no cry for help as they did so.

After a day and a half the four survivors were spotted by an ASR Warwick which dropped two sets of Lindholme gear but the rough sea made rescue impossible. On their third day another ASR aircraft found them and again called up an ASR launch which located and rescued the four crew who were by this time in a very bad state. On the way to hospital the navigator died. The other three survived their terrible ordeal.

With the coming of better weather 102 Squadron was also active on the pre-invasion targets and in May 1944 the unit exchanged its Halifax B IIs for B IIIs with

Hercules engines. With these aircraft 102 Squadron bombed targets in support of 'Overlord' and on the eve of D-Day despatched 26 aircraft—the largest number it had ever done—to bomb an enemy gun battery on the Normandy coast. 102 then bombed targets in close support of the Allied Armies in the Caen and Falaise areas.

After the invasion of France the squadron then ferried much needed petrol to Belgium for the Second Army. Between September 25 and October 2 1944 the squadron carried 134,250 gallons in 179 return trips without mishap. 102 Squadron then took part in the day and night Thousand-Bomber raids on Duisberg during October of that year, without loss.

During 1944 the squadron flew a record number of sorties, the high water mark being in August when 308 were flown from the total of 2,280. The total tonnage of bombs was 6,452 which included 1,371 mines.

Bad weather caused many problems early in the New Year and on January 1 1945, Halifax *LW158* undershot on landing after returning from ops and hit a house, killing one in the process. The very next day Halifax *NR186* was returning from ops when it overshot during landing and crashed in a ditch on the edge of the airfield. Because of the very bad weather only 11 missions were flown during January.

During February the squadron converted to Halifax B VIs which were an improvement over the Mark III, and throughout the changeover managed to complete some 16 operations.

The last mission of the war for the squadron came, as for so many others, on April 25 1945, when 18 of their Halifaxes bombed gun batteries on the Island of Wangerooge and one aircraft aborted. During the Second World War No 102 Squadron had dropped a total of 14,118 tons of bombs and laid 1,865 mines. The awards gained by the squadron included five DSOs, 115 DFCs, two Bars to DFC and 34 DFMs.

On May 7 1945, No 102 Squadron transferred from Bomber Command to Transport Command and converted on to Liberators before leaving Pocklington the following September. During the period immediately after the war the airfield was retained as an emergency aerodrome, but it had no facilities and its main function was as No 17 Aircrew Holding Unit which

moved here from Full Sutton in November 1945. This was a brief role and the airfield closed in September 1946.

Over the years the facilities have been dismantled and the land returned to agriculture. Today, the control tower stands derelict, the technical and communal sites are now used as a trading estate and a section of the runway is used for caravan storage. Three hangars remain and one is used by a garage. Part of one runway is used by gliders but little else remains.

Pollington (Snaith), Yorkshire

See Snaith

Pontefract, Yorkshire

105/SE230440. Between Castleford and Pontefract

Like so many racecourses, Pontefract Park was a ready-made airfield and BE2cs of 'B' Flight, 33 Squadron, operated from here during the summer of 1916. After their departure in October of that year it was used by 76 Squadron but· by November 1918 arrangements were being made to relinquish the ground and by early 1919 it had reverted to its former use.

Rawcliffe (York), Yorkshire

See York

Redcar, Yorkshire

94/NZ605240. On the outskirts of Redcar adjacent to the B1269 road

During the early part of the First World War the racecourse was pressed into use by the Royal Naval Air Service as a Flying Training airfield. The main aircraft were Avro 504Bs and a few Maurice Farman Longhorns. Other units that operated from Redcar were No 273 Squadron which operated DH4s, BE2cs and Bristol Scouts on anti-U-boat patrols. No 7 (Naval) Squadron was based here from September 5 to November 2 1917. The airfield was also used by a flight of four Handley Page HP O/100s that operated out of here against the U-boats.

During 1918, 'C' Flight of 252 Squadron was housed at Redcar and operated with DH6 aircraft on convoy duties. That same year the North-Eastern Flying Instructors School formed at Redcar, this later disbanding into the

Left *Avro 504B comes in to land at Redcar.*

Below *Maurice Farman S7 Longhorn N5750 seen here at Redcar.*

Bottom *Handley Page 0/100 3127 fitted with Davis Gun. This was one that operated from Redcar.*

North-Western Flying Instructors School. October 5 1918 saw the arrival of No 63 Training Squadron from Joyce Green with a few Pups, 504s and Camels. But the war was almost at an end and after the Armistice in November 1918 there was a rundown of men and units. In 1919 both the FIS and No 63 Training Squadron disbanded. The airfield closed that same year and returned to its former use. The one-time technical area on the south-west side of the landing area is now a council housing estate.

Riccall, Yorkshire

105/SE636365. N of Selby and E of the A19 road

The airfield was laid out on Riccall and Barlby Commons and had the usual three concrete runways, the main one being 5,940 ft long and the two subsidiaries 4,290 ft and 4,620 ft in length. A perimeter encircled the runways. The technical site was in the south of the airfield and the bomb dump was located in Danes Hills woods in the north-east.

The first recorded residents were Nos 76 and 78 Squadron Conversion Flights which arrived at the incomplete airfield during the middle of September 1942. On October 7, the two Conversion Flights disbanded to form No 1658 Heavy Conversion Unit which was allotted the code letters 'ZB'. That same day No 10 Conversion Flight arrived from Melbourne and 102 Conversion Flight from Pocklington. Both units were absorbed into 1658 HCU and Riccall officially opened in No 4 Group, Bomber Command. It was destined to house only that one conversion unit.

On November 1 1942, 158 Conversion Flight arrived from Rufforth and became 'C' Flight of 1658 HCU. From its birth until November 9 1944, originally as Flight Commander and finally as OC 1658 HCU and Deputy Station Commander, was Wing Commander H.H. Drummond, AFC, DFM.

The purpose of the Heavy Conversion course at Riccall was to mould crews on to four-engined Halifaxes. The HCU was divided into four flights, 'A', 'B', 'C' and 'D', each commanded by a Squadron Leader who had a Flight Lieutenant as his deputy. Each Flight had an establishment of eight aircraft. The full establishment of the HCU was therefore 32 Halifaxes but the actual strength was invariably less,

allowing for aircraft damaged in training flights and the need to keep up the strength of the operational squadrons, from whom the HCU received aircraft as and when they could be spared.

The course was similar for all crew converting from twin-engined Wellingtons to four-engined Halifaxes at all HCUs in No 4 Group. Each crew picked up the flight-engineer at the HCU, which had not been necessary on the Wellingtons. With four engines, the Halifax was a more complex aircraft and so too was the fuel system with its numerous wing tanks, which had to be used in a sequence, this being the flight-engineer's duty.

The course was mainly for pilots who had to be instructed on flying the Halifax. At all times the emphasis was on the crew and they were treated and acted as one. All categories of the crews attended lectures in their own field between flying exercises which formed the bulk of the course.

The flying course would start with familiarisation and instrument flying exercises, then circuits and landings, fighter affiliation, bombing and air-to-sea firing, demonstration of evasive action and cross-country. Each course would last between two and three weeks and would end with a night cross-country 'Bullseye' exercise. This was designed to give crews as close an idea of what a raid was like. The Halifaxes would take off on a three-legged flight covering the greater part of Northern England and Scotland. The bomber would take evasive action when the fighters attacked. When they got within minimum AI (Air Intercept) range and in position for attack, the fighter pilots would so signal by flashing the navigation lights while the bomber gunners flashed a light if they had the fighter in their sights before his lights went on. Everyone agreed that the 'Bullseye' night exercises were the best kind of practice, but in keeping with all conversion units there were many accidents at Riccall.

In September 1943, Riccall became No 41 Base Sub-Station of No 41 Base, Marston Moor, and this was the worst month of the war for crashes, with ten serious ones during the month. At 14.10 hours on the 4th, Flight Sergeant E.T. Vicary, the Australian pilot of Halifax *V9989*, tried to correct a swing on take-off during a training flight but the under-carriage collapsed. One crew was injured. At 12.00 hours on the 7th, Halifax

Halifax of 1658 HCU flying on one engine. The number '19' was temporary coding only, because the establishment was 32 aircraft and there are only 26 letters in the alphabet. As aircraft were damaged or written off, a numbered aircraft was given a letter which thereby became available. Here we see Squadron Leader P. Dobson testing a Halifax II flying on one engine from Riccall to discover the rate of loss of height so that pilots could make a decision as to their chances of making a landing, depending on the altitude they had when only one fan was turning. It was safer to bale out than try to land on one engine.

DT524, piloted by Pilot Officer M.M. Caplan and Flying Officer L.G. Dunlop (Canadian), was on a training flight when suddenly it went into a steep bank to starboard with smoke coming from the starboard outer engine. The pilot recovered at 9,000 ft but it spun-in and exploded two miles south of the airfield. Ten were killed. That same day at 17.05 hours, Halifax *L9620*, piloted by Sergeant A. Berry, had just landed when the undercarriage collapsed. The aircraft was written off as irreparable.

The 18th of the month kept the crash crews very busy. At 11.00 hours, pilots Squadron Leader P.R. Gaskell and Flying Officer J.G. Rees (Australian) brought Halifax *JD153* in for a heavy landing and the tail wheel sheared off. A few hours later at 14.34 hours Flight Sergeant E.T. Vicary was again in trouble and force-landed in a field near Lissett after the starboard inner caught fire. Six crew were injured. To round off the day, Halifax *JB905* crashed at 23.55 hours near Finningley after both starboard engines caught fire at 17,000 ft. The pilot, Flight Sergeant R.W. Frawkish (Australian) and two other crew were killed, two others were injured. Also at 23.55 hours, Halifax *BB245*, piloted by Sergeant E.G. Wilson, crashed into a row of houses at Chapel Hill, Darrington, Yorkshire. The aircraft had been airborne for 4 hours 5 minutes and there was no evidence to show the cause. There could have been partial loss of control with the breakaway of the

propeller blade from the port-outer engine, possibly displacing it. The Ministry of Defence accident card states six crew and four civilians were killed. However, an eye-witness to the crash, when interviewed by Nicholas Roberts, who has compiled many crash-log books, recalls that there were definitely *eight* airmen killed. Very strange, for I believe the eye-witness and the sad part was that she owned the house on which the bomber crashed; fortunately she and her very young baby were staying with her mother 50 yards away when the aircraft crashed. However, her baby suffered the effects of all the fumes from the wreckage and died later aged five months.

Three days later, at 21.42 hours, Halifax *W7868*, piloted by Sergeant E. Render, burst a tyre on take-off; the aircraft subsequently swung on landing and the undercarriage collapsed. On the 26th at 10.45 hours, just six minutes after take-off, Halifax *BB190* with pilots Pilot Officer W.E. Welder (New Zealand) as instructor and Flight Sergeant T.A. Wickham Jones as pupil, crash-landed half a mile north of Riccall after a three-engines overshoot. The last crash of the month was at 20.00 hours on the 27th when Halifax *DT585*, piloted by Flight Lieutenant J.A. Harrison (New Zealand) and Sergeant R.E. Crockett, collided with a tree after take-off; the Halifax landed safely and the crew were all right.

The HCU's programme continued throughout 1944 and on September 14 of

The Gym at Riccall photographed on December 26 1980 and even in peacetime the mud is still plentiful.

that year Riccall received its first Halifax B Mk III from among those which were now beginning to filter through to the Conversion Units. During November 1944 all Conversion Units were transferred to No 7 Group and Riccall became No 74 Base Sub-Station to Marston Moor.

With the end of the war in Europe imminent, the role of the unit was complete and 1658 HCU disbanded on April 13 1945. The airfield was then transferred to Transport Command and the following month No 1332 Transport Conversion Unit arrived from Nutts Corner. This unit was flying Avro Yorks and a few Stirling IVs but it remained only until November 1945 when it then moved to Dishforth and Riccall closed for flying.

The site was retained by the RAF and for a short period the station was used for storage purposes by No 91 MU. The RAF then vacated the site and the facilities were dismantled. The land soon returned to agriculture and many of the surviving buildings were adapted into farm use. Today, the control tower has been demolished. The hangars have also gone, but their bases remain. Much of the runway has also been demolished. However, the dispersed site to the south of the road is mainly intact and there are many types of Maycrete buildings, including the gym, ops block and guardroom which have weathered the passage of time.

Ripon (Dishforth), Yorkshire
See Dishforth

Ripon, Yorkshire
99/SE330695. SE of Ripon to W of the main A1 road

During the First World War several Home Defence squadrons were formed to protect industrial areas against German air attacks and the unit charged with the defence of Yorkshire was No 76 Squadron, Royal Flying Corps. The racecourse at Ripon was pressed into use as its airfield.

No 76 Squadron formed at Ripon on September 15 1916; headquarters were established at Ripon and Flights were stationed at Copmanthorpe, Catterick and Helperby. There were also a number of landing grounds at which their aeroplanes could land in an emergency. The squadron operated with a variety of obsolete aeroplanes, BE12s, RE7s, DH6s, Avro 504s, RE8s, and Bristol Fighters, but was equipped mainly with BE2c biplanes.

On December 20 1917, No 189 Training Squadron formed at Ripon as a night training unit, but its stay was very brief and on April 1 1918 it moved to Suttons Farm. After the Armistice in November 1918 there was an immediate run-down of units and, in March 1919, No 76 Squadron moved to Tadcaster. With its departure the flying era was brought to an end at Ripon and the site was released for its original purpose. Once again the horsepower had four legs.

During the Second World War the Dishforth airfield a few miles to the east was often referred to as Ripon, from the nearest large town to the airfield.

Rufforth, Yorkshire
105/SE535505. W of York to S of Rufforth village on B1224 road

The airfield was situated on the south side of the B1224 road which formed the northern boundary, the Rufforth-Askham Richard road the western and Foss Dike the eastern boundary. The main buildings and the dispersed sites were to the north of the airfield, while to the south lay Rufforth Grange which obviously decided the runway layout.

Rufforth was a standard pattern heavy bomber airfield and had the three usual runways, the main one being 5,940 ft long and the two intersecting ones each 4,020 ft. These were encircled by a perimeter off which were the usual hardstandings. The bomb dump was in the south-east corner alongside Foss Dike. During the construction period the airfield was frequented by aircraft of several training units, one being 1652 Conversion Unit during July. During the latter part of September the airfield housed Nos 35 and 158 Squadron Conversion Flights. On October 7, No 35 Conversion Flight moved to Marston Moor and became part of 1652 HCU but 158 continued to operate from Rufforth. Then, towards the end of October, 158 Conversion Unit was wound up as a separate unit and on November 1 1942 it moved to Riccall and became 'C' Flight of 1658 HCU.

The airfield was formally opened in November 1942, in No 4 Group, Bomber Command, and the first operational unit to move in was No 158 Squadron from East Moor on the 6th of the month. The weather was still holding very cold, wet and foggy, which did not help for the squadron was having a lot of problems with the Halifax B Mk IIs. However, they were straight into action and the following day two aircraft and crews were sent to Linton-on-Ouse for a mining operation. That same day eight aircraft were despatched for Genoa, their last target from their former base and their first from their new one. All aircraft bombed the target but on the return nearly all ran out of petrol. Only Sergeant Bartlett, flying a brand new Halifax, made it back direct to Rufforth. The others dropped in where they could, four landing at Manston, one at Boscombe Down and one at Ossington, while Pilot Officer Beveridge ditched in the River Humber after being airborne for over 11 hours. Three of his crew were killed.

On November 9 the squadron sent four aircraft to Hamburg which all returned safely. Then, on the 15th of the month it was the turn of Genoa again and six aircraft were despatched. These long distance flights over the Alps gave many problems both for the crews and the aircraft. Lack of fuel was again the main problem and only two made it back to Rufforth. Two landed at other airfields, but Pilot Officer Herbert and his crew abandoned their Halifax, *DT558*, at 03.00 hours on the morning of the 16th. They parachuted to safety leaving their Halifax to crash near Frome, Somerset. Pilot Officer Beveridge force-landed at Great Bently Farm, Sussex, whilst attempting to land at Gatwick. Fortunately, he and his crew were not seriously injured.

The last raid of the year for the Rufforth squadron came on December 20, when they provided seven aircraft in a force of 232 for an attack on Duisburg. It was a cloudless moonlit night and, although night fighters took advantage of the conditions, so did the crews, and they bombed with confidence. All six returned safely to Rufforth. During December the squadron had detachments at Beaulieu and Manston.

The New Year did not start very well for the squadron. During January 1943, 158 was engaged on mining operations in Danish waters and four visits to the submarine pens at Lorient. The first operation, which was mining, did not commence until January 9, and got off to a very bad start. Flight Lieutenant Woolnough in Halifax *DT622* 'P'-Peter lost power on take-off and crash-landed on the main York to Tadcaster road just north of Copmanthorpe. Fortunately the crew were unhurt. Flight Sergeant Owen in Halifax *W7751* 'F'-Freddie did not return from his mission and the only survivor was Sergeant Skinner, the rear-gunner. It is thought they were hit by flak and crashed near the town of Esbjerg.

On the second Lorient raid Flight Lieutenant Ayscough was returning with the main force when, while over Somerset, he collided with a Wellington of 166 Squadron whose nose was ripped off on impact, killing the Wellington's air-gunner. The damaged Halifax spiralled to the ground, shedding wreckage and bodies in the process. Meanwhile, the Wellington piloted by Flight Sergeant Ashplant remained airborne, and he shouted to his crew to bale out. The bomb-aimer reported his parachute was damaged in the collision and without any hesitation the pilot gave him his and yelled 'jump'. Remaining at the battered controls the pilot succeeded in crash-landing in a field near Langport. For his outstanding bravery he was awarded the CGM. In the cold grey February morning airmen from Weston Zoyland recovered the bodies of Flight Lieutenant Ayscough and the bodies of Sergeant Smalley and his crew from the Wellington.

In February it was back again to Germany with an attack on Hamburg. Then, on February 26, six crews made the squadron's last mission from Rufforth. All six aircraft returned safely from Cologne. At the end of the month 158 Squadron moved to Lissett, yet another new base. During their stay at Rufforth the squadron had lost nine crews of whom 61 were killed over enemy territory, as

1663 HCU at Rufforth—'R'-Robert becomes airborne.

well as others in England, and they were hoping for a change of luck.

Rufforth now had a change of role. On March 1 1943, No 1663 Heavy Conversion Unit formed with an establishemnt of 32 Halifax Mk IIs. These were mainly ex-operational Halifaxes fitted with Rolls-Royce Merlin XX engines, many having done a considerable number of flying hours, and the ground crews had to work around the clock in order to keep a degree of serviceability under the prevailing difficult weather conditions. The unit was alloted the code letters 'OO' and 'SV'. As usual there were several crashes and the Yorkshire Moors became a last resting place for many brave airmen.

In September 1943, Rufforth became No 41 Sub-Station of No 41 Base, Marston Moor, which controlled it. At the end of November 1943 Flight Sergeant Douglas (Doug) Bancroft and his crew were posted in from Driffield. Here they joined up with Sergeant Kenneth Leheup, mid-upper gunner, and Sergeant Robert Stacey, the flight-engineer. They were now a complete crew but the bad weather

made flying impossible. Although morale was good, frustration grew as the weather continued to stop flying operations for long periods and personnel moped about in the rain, mud and snow day after day.

Doug Bancroft and crew did get a break when a lone rabbit was sighted near their Nissen hut. There followed a long chase across the muddy fields, over ditches and through hedges until the rabbit was eventually caught and triumphantly brought back to the hut where it was beheaded with a fire-axe, skinned and nicely baked in front of the coke fire. After a tasty meal came a lengthy process of drying out and cleaning clothes and boots.

On January 21 1944, Flight Sergeant Bancroft had progressed a little further and was sent across to Melbourne where he flew with a 10 Squadron crew as 'Second Dickie' on a raid against Magdeburg. His luck, which stayed with him for the rest of the war, held. Their Halifax was attacked by three night fighters and they ran into very heavy anti-aircraft fire over Wilhelmshaven but they made it

After the rabbit chase through mud and water at Rufforth. Left to right: Sergeant Len Dwan, wireless operator; Sergeant Bob Stacey, flight engineer; Flight Sergeant Alwyn Fripp, navigator; Sergeant Ken Leheup, mid-upper gunner; Sergeant David Arundel, rear-gunner; and Pilot Officer Eric Tansley, bomb-aimer.

back to Melbourne. The raid was nearly a total failure and from the 648 despatched, 55 bombers failed to return. The diversionary attack on Berlin failed to attract the German night fighters who waited for the bomber stream near Hamburg and remained with them to target.

After his operational experience Flight Sergeant Bancroft was back again training and on February 7 1944 he and his crew were detailed for three-engined daylight exercises, using Lissett as the airfield with Halifax II *EB195* from their unit at Rufforth. Following several successful three-engine landings they were again in the circuit at about 600 ft with the starboard outer engine shut down, the undercarriage down and on final approach when suddenly the starboard-inner engine exploded, sending pieces of engine cowling and carburettor air intake flying into the air. With now only two port engines, the aircraft swung to starboard in a diving turn and with insufficient power in the port engines all that could be done was to fight the controls down to the ground.

The bomber hit the ground in a landing attitude, wiped off the undercarriage in a ditch, cut through several hedges, knocked down several circuit light poles and came to rest about 30 yards from the back door of a farmhouse at Harpham Farm, near Lissett, at 12.06 hours. The farmer rushed from the house and called out, 'Is anybody hurt?' On being told the crew were shaken-up but unharmed he replied, 'What about my bloody turnips?—seven of you buggers in the last week!' Doug Bancroft recalls: 'Sure enough, when I looked over his fields there were six or more aircraft scattered about, either with their tails in the air or on their bellies with broken backs'. Doug hadn't made a friend and later, when they were posted to Lissett, their sleeping quarters were just outside this farmer's gateway. The farmer passed them many times on his way to the mess for the pig scraps but he always left them to walk the mile or so—rain, snow or sunshine. Not all their enemies were in Germany!

The station continued in the conversion role, and its status at June 6 1944 was 1663 HCU with Halifax Mk IIs and Vs. During the autumn of 1944 a few Spitfires and Hurricanes joined the Halifaxes on strength.

At 22.45 hours on August 9 1944 a Mark V Halifax, *LK700,* had engine failure just after take-off and crashed at Askham Richard. The practice bombs exploded but only one crewman was injured.

On November 1 1944, Rufforth was transferred from No 4 Group to No 7 Group, Training Command. During this period the HCU obtained a few Halifax Mark IIIs. One of the new additions, Halifax *MZ648,* overshot and crashed at Askham Bryan, Yorkshire, at 11.44 hours on November 15, which was again cold, wet and foggy. The following day, the station had one of its worst accidents. Halifax *JP128* had made several attempts to land but rolling mist obscured the approach. At 22.18 hours the Halifax made another approach but hit Grasslands farmhouse. It then careered across the airfield, crashing into Halifaxes *LK910* and *LL133.* Finally it hit the airfield fire-engine and burst into flames. Six crew plus two occupants of the farmhouse were killed.

The following month the station became No 74 Base Sub-station, still controlled by Marston Moor. The New Year brought further crashes but the end was in sight and, on may 28 1945, No 1663 HCU disbanded. After the disbandment of the resident unit the airfield was used by No 23 Gliding School and No 64 Group Communications Flight, flying a variety of aircraft which included Ansons, Oxfords, Dominies, Proctors and even Austers.

In February 1953, the Austers of 1964 Flight, No 664 Squadron, arrived from Yeadon and operated from here until returning in 1954. The airfield was used for a period for gliding and as a car racing circuit but since it was sold to a farmer both have ceased.

In 1978 the 'T2' hangar in the west of the airfield was demolished along with the Nissen huts. By 1980 only one 'T2' at the side of the York-Wetherby road remained. The runways were still intact but the perimeter was being broken up. The few buildings that remain have been vandalised. The control tower, which was painted in camouflage for a TV series, is still standing but the western access to the airfield has been sealed off by the farmer and it looks as if this little piece of wartime history will soon be gone for an application has been put in to remove the runways and hardstandings.

In July 1981, on instruction from the Secretary of State for Defence, a hangar along with 4.5 acres of land was sold at

Rufforth control tower (December 1979).

auction for £152,000. At the same auction some 63 acres of other land on the airfield consisting of runways and agricultural land was sold for £95,000.

Sandtoft, Lincolnshire

112/SK755082. W of Scunthorpe

Sandtoft was a very poor choice for a bomber airfield and should never have been built in these surroundings, near the Isle of Axholme. This somewhat desolate site was selected and, being just inside the western boundaries of the county, was an exception as it was constructed to house a training unit. The airfield was situated to the south of the A18 road with the River Torne and the South Engine Drain as the eastern boundary and the North Idle Drain and minor road as the western.

Sandtoft, after which the airfield was named, was a small hamlet on the western edge of the airfield and it was this area which housed the technical buildings. The airfield conformed to the standard late-war design in having three paved runways, the main one being 5,940 ft long and the two subsidiaries 4,950 ft and 4,290 ft. These were encircled with a perimeter track.

Sandtoft opened in February 1944 in No 1 Group, Bomber Command, as a satellite for No 11 Base, Lindholme. The first arrivals were the Halifax bombers of 1667 Heavy Conversion Unit which moved in from Faldingworth on February 20, and this proved to be the only resident unit at Sandtoft. The HCU was straight into action but their first few weeks proved to be their worst for they had six major crashes.

The first was on March 7 when Halifax *EB184* piloted by Sergeant C.A. Street collided with *HR657* (of 1662 HCU) while on bombing practice; *EB184* went out of control and crashed just north of Gainsborough at Craiselound, near Haxey, Lincolnshire. The aircraft burst into flames and the crew of eight were killed. *HR657*, which was on a cross-country exercise, broke up in the air after the collision and burnt; all seven crew were killed.

Two days later Halifax *DJ998* with Pilot Officer S. Burton as 1st pilot and Pilot Officer E.J. Patterson (NZ) as pupil 2nd pilot, was on circuit and landings when suddenly the aircraft yawed to port then entered a spin. This was probably due to engine failure and the crew had no chance to escape, all eight being killed. The third major crash of the month came on the 19th. Pilot Officer J. Hetherington in Halifax *EB149* had just completed a cross-country exercise and was on a three-engined approach when the aircraft undershot and struck a pylon. Four crew were killed and three injured.

On the 25th of the month Sergeant Pilot R.J.B. Cann was landing Halifax *DG293* after port-outer engine failure when he undershot on landing and, as he swung to avoid a hangar, hit dispersed aircraft *EB144*. Fortunately the crew of seven were safe. Sergeant D.R. Harkin, pilot of *DG305*, failed to correct his Halifax as it swung on take-off and the undercarriage collapsed. He was again the pilot when, on the last day of March, *DG307* swung to port on landing and the undercarriage collapsed. Only one was injured in each crash.

With March out of the way the HCU settled down to its training programme and April and May passed with very few problems. June heralded another bad month when, at 02.00 hours on the first of the month, *LL414* crashed out of control in a spiral dive at Glenisla, Angus, killing the eight crew. The aircraft, piloted by Pilot Officer L.L. Williams, was on night flying practice and the accident was probably caused by engine failure and poor weather conditions.

Halifax *DG345* was on night flying training with instructor pilot Flying Officer F.H. Tritton and pupil Flying Officer C.D. Thieme when, at 01.01 hours on June 6, the aircraft swung on landing, hit *EB194* and the undercarriage collapsed. Two days later Halifax *LL459* dived out of control, hit the ground and

Halifax of 1667 HCU at Sandtoft.

disintegrated south of Howden Dyke Island, Yorkshire. The crew of six were killed. The pilot, Pilot Officer R.L. Francis (Australia), had failed to gain control after stall while on cross-country. On June 26, *DG395* crashed just after take-off, two miles east of Thorne, Yorkshire, and burnt, possibly after striking high tension cables. The pilot, Flying Officer G.N.L. Smyth and his five crew, were all killled. On June 30 the port tyre of Halifax *DG338* burst on take-off, the aircraft swung and the starboard undercarriage collapsed.

July continued with a spate of accidents and an unsolved mystery, even to this day. Halifax *LL497*, piloted by Flying Officer G.F. Hutchinson and with a crew of seven, went missing on July 2 while on night cross-country exercise and was never heard of again. A bad crash occurred three days later while Halifax *DG414*, with instructor pilot Flight Lieutenant B.E. McLaughlin and pupil Pilot Officer E. Barley, was low flying on three engines. The pilot lost control from 200 ft and the wingtip hit the top of some trees. The aircraft crashed and burst into flames, killing eight and injuring one. Six more were killed and two injured on July 25 when Halifax *EB190* climbed to 400 ft

then dived into the ground on Hatfield Moor, Yorkshire.

It was said it was a good landing if one could walk away from it so, for instructor pilot Flying Officer G.G. Smith and his pupil, Pilot Officer C.R. Applewhite, it might have been just that when Halifax *LK642* overshot on a bad landing, hit a cottage and crashed one mile north-east of the airfield. The crew of eight were injured but managed to walk away, albeit some were a little bent.

At 23.30 hours on October 10, Halifax *LL501*, piloted by Sergeant R.D. Christie, crashed into the side of the River Trent whilst descending to ascertain his position after a cross-country exercise. The aircraft hit the mudbank at the mouth of the river, fell into the water and sank. Five crew were missing and two injured.

Another to run into trouble whilst on cross-country exercise was Halifax *DK116* piloted by Pilot Officer G. Haddrell. At 22.00 hours on October 15 the port-inner engine caught fire at 12,000 ft; the pilot was unable to stop or control the fire and three crew baled out. The aircraft crashed in flames on Caplestone Fell, Kielder, Northumberland. Three of the six crew were killed, including the pilot who probably remained at the controls because the rear-gunner had difficulty in getting out. Time has not eroded the crash and

Sandtoft control tower type 12779/41—now made into a dwelling (1979).

the remains can still be found amidst the trees on the Fell.

As 1944 progressed it became obvious that the demand for Halifax crews was decreasing so several of the conversion units converted on to Lancasters, 1667 HCU being one such unit. It began to receive a few Lancasters during November and December 1944. During this period control of the station passed to the newly formed 7 Group, Bomber Command, on November 3 and Lindholme became No 71 Base.

The New Year saw more Lancasters arrive and there was a steady spate of accidents as the new crews mastered their new charges. Sadly, two of the worst crashes were in April 1945 when the war was almost at an end. On April 5, Lancaster *ND639*, piloted by Pilot Officer J.E. Grayson, crashed into the ground at Crowle, Lincolnshire, at 02.58 hours while on exercise. The crew of seven were all killed. The other crash was on April 15 when Lancaster *PB565* broke up and crashed out of control at Ouston Ferry. From the eight-man crew five were killed and three missing.

With the war in Europe at an end the training at Sandtoft also came to an end and there was a run-down in the conversion programme. 1667 HCU remained here until November 10 1945 when it then disbanded and the station closed down. It never did justify its existence for the HCU could have been housed elsewhere, and with its departure the airfield was quickly abandoned by the Royal Air Force and most of the facilities were dismantled.

Today, the two-storey control tower has been altered into a private dwelling without destroying its original fabric or shape, and it stands at the side of the minor road which now crosses the airfield. The adjacent fire tender shed and airfield landing light shed are in use as garages while the concrete hardstandings serve as tennis courts and driveways.

A few other buildings remain on the technical site and the old operations block still stands in the yard of an adjacent farm. A few domestic buildings and the overhead water tank remain on a site in the village. The runways have been removed, possibly to serve as hardcore for the M180 motorway that cuts across the northern tip of the airfield.

Scalby Mills, Yorkshire

101/TA036907. N of Scarborough

During early 1914 Blackburn became one of several sub-contractors for the BE2c biplane, adopted as the main equipment for the RFC and RNAS. In June 1914 the Blackburn Aeroplane and Motor Company was formed in Leeds to produce the Type L seaplane. This was powered by a 130 hp Canton-Unné 9-cylinder water-cooled radial engine and was built for the *Daily Mail* Circuit of Britain seaplane race. However, the war clouds rolled over Europe and the seaplane was commandeered by the Admiralty.

The Type L was taken to a section of beach known as Scalby Mills, where Blackburn had erected a large hangar, thereby forging a link between the company and the Royal Navy. The seaplane was employed on offshore reconnaissance patrols but early in 1915 the Type L was flown into the cliffs at Speeton and wrecked. This brought to an end the flying at Scalby Mills and there is no record of the site ever being used again. The hangar still remained up to the late 1970s.

Blackburn Type 'L' at Scalby Mills.

Scorton, Yorkshire

93/NZ240003. 9 miles SSW of Darlington, between Scorton village on the B1263 road and the main A1 road

This was another of the many airfields sited close to the Great North Road and was just to the west of Scorton village after which it was named. It was only a few miles to the north of Catterick. Scorton opened under No 13 Group, Fighter Command, in October 1939, as a satellite to Catterick. The first unit to occupy the airfield was a detachment from 219 Squadron at Catterick with their Blenheim Mk IF aircraft. This was the squadron's first section to become operational, on February 21 1940.

Scorton was brought into full use during the Battle of Britain period when the airfield was used by many units which were stationed at the parent airfield. In October 1940 the Blenheims of No 219 moved out to Redhill.

During 1941 the airfield was enlarged to full station status and improvements were made which included three tarmac runways, the main one 4,800 ft in length and the two intersecting ones each 3,600 ft. The control tower was the standard design, type 12096/41, but all accommodation buildings were temporary. The airfield eventually had 12 Blister hangars. Scorton also had a decoy airfield at Birkby, a few miles to the east, but again records are vague as to what purpose it served.

October 1941 saw 122 Squadron arrive from the parent station with their Spitfire Mk IIbs. The following month they converted to Spitfire Mk Vs and were engaged on coastal patrol duties for the duration of their stay.

The year 1942 saw the arrival of the Canadians when four Bristol Beaufighters were detached from 406 Squadron, Royal Canadian Air Force, which was based at Ayr, Scotland; they arrived on February 2. This was a night fighter unit, code letters 'HU', whose motto was 'We Kill By Night', and it had been sent to cover the area because of increased German night-raider activity.

With the Canadians settled in at Scorton, 122 Squadron moved out to Hornchurch in April of that year. That same month 167 Squadron re-formed here on the 6th with an establishment of Spitfires, code letters 'VL'. This unit remained only a few weeks and moved to Castletown in June. On the 16th of the

month the rest of No 406 moved to Scorton and the squadron was reunited once more. It remained until September 3 of that year when it was then transferred to No 10 Group and moved to Predannack, Cornwall.

Meanwhile, No 410 (Cougar) Squadron, RCAF, had arrived from Ayr on September 1 to replace the outgoing Canadian night fighter unit. No 410, unit code letters 'RA', was also a night fighter squadron operating with Beaufighters and its role was the defence of the British coast, although intruders were rarely seen. The pace did increase with the move to Scorton and during September there were 19 sorties, a total equal to that of the past five months. But the German night fighter was equally as skilled as shown on the first night at Scorton when Wing Commander Hillock and Flight Lieutenant Sharpe were scrambled and secured contacts but the raiders escaped.

On September 6 Pilot Officer R. Ferguson with Pilot Officer D. Creed as observer were on GCI exercise when bandits entered the area at the mouth of the Tees. Guided by vectors from ground control a visual contact of a Ju 88 was obtained and closing to 150 yards dead astern, Ferguson fired two bursts from his four cannons and six Brownings. Cannon strikes were seen on the mainplane and fuselage but the Ju 88 did not go down and, as it turned out to sea, contact was lost.

This was the unit's first victory after more than a year of watching and waiting. However, the 'Cougars' went on to be the top-scoring night fighter unit in the Second Tactical Air Force in the period between D-Day and VE-Day, 60 of their 85 victories being won during that 11-month period.

On September 19 six crews were scrambled. Pilot Officers S.J. Fulton and R.N. Rivers attacked a Dornier Do 217 but missed. They did not get a second chance for the German gunner quickly returned the fire and damaged the night fighter's undercarriage and starboard wing so badly that Fulton had to make a crash-landing.

For the remainder of the month training continued and there were no further operations. During one exercise Squadron Leader Bertie Miller and Sergeant E.H. Collis (RAF) were 18 miles out over the sea when one engine of their Beaufighter caught fire and they had to bale out. They were quickly picked up by

A Black Widow night fighter from Scorton, seen in action over France.

a rescue launch and were soon back at Scorton, wet, but ready to carry on the fight.

No 410 Squadron moved to Acklington on October 20 1942 in exchange with 219 Squadron. Back once again, No 219 began to re-equip with the more up-to-date Mark VIF aircraft and in April 1943 moved back to Catterick. That same month 604 Squadron arrived from Ford. This unit, code letters 'NG', was equipped with Beaufighter Mk VIF aircraft and continued the night patrols.

November 1943 saw the arrival of 130 Squadron with their Spitfire Mk Vbs but the following month they moved to Ayr, only to return again in January 1944. Then, on February 13, the unit disbanded, having virtually lived out of a kitbag for the past three months. From February 12-28 No 26 Squadron paid the station a very brief visit.

Another squadron in a similar position to No 130 was No 56. During February 1944 it arrived from Martlesham Heath with Typhoon Mk Ibs, coded 'US', but that same month moved to Acklington. March saw them back at Scorton but by the end of the month the unit had moved to Ayr. Back again in April, the unit re-equipped with Spitfire IXs and departed that same month to Newchurch. April also saw the departure of 604 Squadron which moved to Church Fenton after converting to Mosquitoes.

During the first week of May 1944, No 422 Squadron of the American IXth Air Force arrived at Scorton from their base at Charmy Down. At the time this unit was not engaged in night operations and the Yanks were here for training with their new night fighters. On the 23rd the first Black Widow arrived at Scorton and the 422nd became the third AAF night fighter squadron to be equipped with this aircraft, which made a most unusual sight

around the Yorkshire skies. The rest of May and early June was spent getting to know the Black Widow. Then, on June 16, another American unit arrived at Scorton. This was the 425th Night Fighter Squadron which had also been based at Charmy Down. The unit immediately began checking out its new charges. To aid both American units in becoming operational there was a motley collection of aircraft at their disposal which included A-20s, P-47s, a few worn-out Wellingtons and a solitary Hurricane. The RAF also loaned experienced night fighter personnel to assist the Yanks in their duties.

The training increased for both the 422nd and 425th Squadrons and, on June 27 1944, Colonel Winston W. Kratz of the 481st Night Fighter Operational Training Group and a Colonel Viccellio from the Operations Commitments and Requirements Section of the War Department arrived at Scorton. The purpose of their visit was to determine the suitability of the 'Black Lady' for offensive combat operations in the European Theatre and, more immediately, the readiness of both units. A detachment of six P-61s (Black Widows), comprising three crews from the 422nd and two from the 425th plus Colonel Kratz flying the sixth aircraft, were sent to Hurn airfield. This site was chosen due to its close proximity to the Normandy beachhead.

As June phased into July rumour abounded that the Black Widow was to be replaced by the British Mosquito but this was not so and in order to make 422 combat-ready, Colonel Johnson made arrangements with the Canadian bomber units at Croft to engage with the 422nd in night 'Bullseye' and day 'Eric' exercises. By the end of the month the Yanks had gone and Scorton drifted into the back-waters of the air war.

Scorton remained as a satellite airfield until the end of the European War when it then closed to flying. Today there are no hangars and the control tower has gone. The runways, apart from one small piece, have been broken up and removed. However, the eastern part of the taxiway is still intact. The site has now returned to agriculture with gravel works to the west. A few small buildings remain on the technical site and to the south-east. These few wartime remains are used by the farmer.

Seacroft, Yorkshire

104/SE355365. E of Leeds

Just on the outskirts of Leeds, this was the third site for the City and gave cover on the eastern section. It was only a night landing ground with no facilities and was used by 'B' Flight, 33 Squadron, Royal Flying Corps, for Home Defence duties during March to October 1916. It was not used after that period and the site today is completely built over with houses.

Seaton Carew, Yorkshire

93/NZ523283; 93/NZ533268 (Seaton Carew II). S of Hartlepool

These First World War sites were in fact two separate stations and listed as Seaton Carew Flight Station 6th Brigade and Seaton Carew (II) Marine Operations (Seaplane) Station. Neither was on the list of permanent stations.

Seaton Carew airfield was sited just south of Hartlepool between what are today the A178 and B1277 roads. It was an L-shaped ground with Hunter House at the north end and occupied an area of 72 acres, of which five acres were occupied by the station buildings. One Aeroplane Shed, 139 × 137 ft, and two canvas Bessoneaux hangars, were erected in the north-east corner. The technical buildings included technical store, wireless hut, offices, flight commander's office, power house, guard house, armoury, bomb stores above and below ground, wireless telegraphy hut and meteorological hut. The personnel were in Armstrong Huts or billeted.

Seaton Carew came within the north-east area, No 24 Group, 46th Wing, and was the Flight Station of 6th Brigade. Their function was as a Home Defence station for 'C' Flight of No 36 Squadron

(6th Brigade). This squadron also performed the duties of aerial co-operation for coastal defence. The headquarters of the squadron was at Hylton.

Seaton Carew had been earmarked as a landing ground as early as 1914 but it was not until after the formation of the Home Defence squadrons in 1916 that any real movement towards using the site took place and temporary buildings were erected as and when needed. 'C' Flight of 36 Squadron, then flying BE2cs, moved in during the spring of 1916.

On the night of August 8 1916, *L30* was part of a force of nine German airships which attacked the area, but no damage was done. On November 27, *L34* came inland over Blackhall Rocks, just north-east of Hartlepool, at about 23.30. The airship was picked up by the Hutton Henry searchlight, which it tried to extinguish by bombing, but was unsuccessful. Meanwhile, 2nd Lieutenant L.V. Pyott of 36 Squadron took off from Seaton Carew and soon sighted the *L34* which was moving south towards him in the beam of the searchlight. He flew towards the airship, approaching midships and fired as he passed underneath, but without result. Turning he followed the airship for some five miles, firing at every possible opportunity. After 71 rounds Pyott noticed a small patch in the body of the airship and at first thought it was machine-gun fire directed at him. However, the bright patch rapidly spread and the whole airship was soon engulfed in flames. The *L34* fell burning into the sea off West Hartlepool just before midnight. It all happened very quickly and although Pyott dived to avoid burning wreckage, his face was burned by the heat of the flaming mass which he estimated to be some 300 yards away from him. The burning airship was seen from the ground for miles around; from the air it was even seen by Captain G.H. Birley of No 38 Squadron at Buckminster, some 140 miles to the south. Just before catching fire the *L34* had dropped 16 bombs as it passed over West Hartlepool. Four people were killed and 34 injured with damage done to 40 dwellings.

An FE2d, crewed by 2nd Lieutenant H.J. Thornton (pilot) and 2nd Lieutenant C.A. Moore (observer), also took off from Seaton Carew to intercept enemy raiders but failed to return. This area continued to be an entry point and, on March 13 1918, West Hartlepool was again under attack. Just before 21.00

Blackburn Kangaroo B9982 at Seaton Carew.

hours 2nd Lieutenant E.C. Morris of 36 Squadron took off in his FE2d to intercept the raider; his observer was 2nd Lieutenant R.D. Linford. About half an hour later they sighted a Zeppelin over West Hartlepool at about 20,000 ft. Morris climbed to his extreme limit but was still some 3,000 ft below the airship. Both pilot and observer fired but without results. The airship turned out to sea and they pursued for 40 miles until they lost it in the mist.

The establishment for the 6th Brigade Flight as at October 1918 was seven officers, three NCOs, two Corporals and 43 rank and file. Equipment was four Bristol Fighters and four Sopwith Pups.

In addition to the seaplanes operated by 402, 403, 451 and 452 Flights, 246 Squadron also had 495 Flight that operated from the airfield at Seaton Carew with the Blackburn Kangaroo, of which they had ten out of the 11 issued to the RAF in 1918. Between May 1 1918 and the Armistice in November of that year these machines flew more than 600 hours on anti-submarine patrols over the North Sea. During that time they were credited with 12 sightings and 11 attacks. Kangaroo *B9983*, flown by Lieutenant E.F. Waring, was instrumental in bringing about the destruction of submarine *UC 70* on August 28 1918. Waring dropped a 500 lb bomb which exploded 30 ft from the bows of the submarine and the destroyer HMS *Ouse* then dropped depth charges, the last of which exploded on top of the U-boat's hull.

Seaton Carew (II) Marine Operations (Seaplane) Station was a mile to the southeast of the other airfield. The seaplane station occupied about seven acres on the northern foreshore of the Tees estuary. The few records that are available state that the station faced east and had good

mooring facilities and a sufficient stretch of smooth water for taking off, although the water was shallow and a large area of sand and mud was exposed at low water.

Technical buildings consisted of one seaplane shed 120 × 60 ft, two canvas hangars and a slipway. There were a few other temporary buildings which served as workshops and stores. The officers were accommodated in 'The Gables' and other ranks in the 'Marine Hotel', which were taken over for that purpose.

Seaton Carew (II) came under the north-east area; No 18 (Operations) Group, 68th Wing, and was home for No 246 Squadron and Headquarters 68th Wing. The function of No 246 Squadron, Headquarters and Nos 402 and 403 (Float Seaplane) Flights was for anti-submarine patrol duties. This squadron came under the control of the Senior Naval Officer, Tyne, for operations.

The seaplane station had an establishment of 141 which included 28 officers. Equipment was 24 float seaplanes as at October 1918. The completion date for the whole station was December 31 1918 but with the Armistice in November work stopped.

Both sites were quickly abandoned and the temporary buildings were dismantled soon after the war. During the Expansion period of the mid-1930s the sites were not re-activated but the area was obviously surveyed for only a few miles to the north an airfield was built near the village of Greatham, becoming West Hartlepool.

Sherburn in Elmet, Yorkshire
105/SE520330. 12 miles E of Leeds

During the First World War a field to the east of Sherburn in Elmet was used as an RFC/RAF Aircraft Acceptance Park. By 1918 it covered some 177 acres and there were eight hangars and 21 storage sheds. It was from here that Blackburn's Cuckoo production was centred, 132 being built at Sherburn in Elmet. The Cuckoo was a big, single-seat, folding-wing, torpedo-carrying biplane and in October 1918 a squadron of Cuckoos was embarked in Britain's first aircraft carrier, HMS *Argus*. However, the Cuckoo never got the chance to prove itself in action for the Armistice came in November 1918.

After the Great War there was an immediate run-down and the airfield was not retained. In 1924, interest in flying revived the Yorkshire Aeroplane Club, which was re-opened here in January 1926 by Air Vice-Marshal Sir Sefton Brackner. The club became well established and in 1931 it moved to Yeadon. The airfield continued to be used by light aircraft but with the outbreak of the Second World War it was requisitioned and opened under Fighter Command, although it was also used as a 'scatter' field for Bomber Command's aircraft.

From June to September 1940 the Hurricanes of 73 Squadron from Church Fenton were detached here. Hurricane Mk Is were again here the following year when 46 Squadron arrived during March from Church Fenton. This was the last of the fighter units and moved out in May 1941.

The airfield was not developed into an operational station for its location with excellent roads and rail access made it a perfect choice for aircraft production. Situated on the east side of the main A1 road, close to Sherburn in Elmet, after which it was named, the northern boundary was the B1222 road. The southern boundary was Gascoigne Wood junction and marshalling yard of the Leeds-Selby railway line. The western boundary was the Sherburn branch line and Sherburn junction.

With heavy losses in the early months of the war it was soon found that aircraft repair facilities were inadequate and obstructed the output of the main factories. To overcome this, civil repair organisations were developed, one being the Blackburn Repair Organisation that was centred here with factories at Leeds and Abbotsinch.

Early in 1940, Blackburn Aircraft Ltd were asked by the Ministry of Aircraft Production if they could undertake the construction of the Fairey Swordfish torpedo biplane. A new factory was built at Sherburn in Elmet and the company now had three sites on the western end with rail sidings plus one to the north near the B1222 road.

Within 11 months of the first sod being turned, the first Swordfish rolled off the

Aerial view of Sherburn in Elmet, circa 1943. Top of the photograph can be seen the B1222 road and the factory building. The railway junction is on the left-hand side with the other three sites. The other main buildings are the World War 1 hangars. The large aircraft are identified as being Stirlings and Dakotas. The small ones are impossible to identify.

production line on December 29 1940. Over the next four years the factory completed some 1,700 Swordfish with a complement of spares equal to a further 1,000. The Swordfish was unique as a biplane for it remained an operational aircraft throughout the war.

There was only one main runway, 07/25, which was 6,300 ft long, the two subsidiaries being grass and just over 1,200 ft in length. A perimeter was laid around the landing area and there were 19 frying-pan type hardstandings.

In July 1942 the Airborne Forces Experimental Establishment moved in. This unit had many weird contraptions that got no further than Sherburn in Elmet. These included a flying Jeep and a half-scale version of the Baynes Carrier Wing that was flown from here during 1943. Most of the airborne equipment was tested here with various tugs and gliders. Six Hadrians were extensively tested at AFEE Sherburn in Elmet with a variety of tugs. The first Hadrian to arrive in Britain did so spectacularly—by air. It was towed across the North Atlantic by a Dakota which brought it to Prestwick. Thereafter all deliveries were made by sea. The Hadrian had a very low towing speed for fear of structural failure so only the relatively slow Dakota tug could cope with it. They made an uncommon sight around the bomber airfields.

The status of the station at June 6 1944 was the Airborne Forces Experimental Establishment under No 21 Group. This unit remained until the beginning of 1945 when it then moved its weird and wonderful collection to Beaulieu in Hampshire, to take advantage of the southern climate now the German forces were pulling back to Germany.

The airfield continued to be used by No 7 Ferry Pool who were based here throughout the war and it was in this unit that many women pilots played a vital role. A large contribution to the war effort was also made by the Blackburn Repair Depot which handled many naval types and some American types at the Sherburn in Elmet factories.

Immediately after the war the airfield returned to the flying clubs and civil flying once more became part of the daily scene. Today, a World War 1 hangar still remains to the south-west of the airfield and is used for storage. The factory is now occupied by Avery Scales and the main runway is used by Mintex as a test track. The grass airfield is still used by light aircraft. Most of the taxiway is still intact, but the northern section has started to crumble.

Shipton, Yorkshire
105/SE550590. N of York

Situated to the east of the A19 road near the village of Shipton, this was nothing more than a large grass field which was available to No 76 Squadron, Royal Flying Corps, as a landing ground for their BE2c aircraft. The site was brought into service from September 1916 and the facilities were minimal. It closed in 1918 and, being void of all facilities, was not retained by the post-war Royal Air Force.

The site was re-activated during the Second World War and Shipton-by-Beningbrough housed 60 MU whose role was to provide spares and collect crashed aircraft from the surrounding area. No 60 MU had many working sections, all of which contained experts in the various trades to deal with airframes, engines, armament, electrical gear and instruments. The unit had to recover all items that could be recycled and they were kept very busy, sometimes many miles from base; an extract from Shipton Station Records reads:

'13th December 1943; Halifax Aircraft D.T.578. Category 'E2' at Whernside. Main site of crash 2,600 ft high, aircraft scattered over considerable area; salvage operations handicapped by extremely bad weather and extreme cold, visibility often only 20 yards. The climb each day from billets to scene of crash approximately took 1½ hours. To date, salvage is almost complete and it is estimated salvage party will return to unit by 6th January 1944.'

No 60 MU remained until 1946 and after they had moved out the site closed.

Skipton-on-Swale, Yorkshire
99/SE370813. W of Thirsk

Situated between the River Swale in the west and the A167 road to the east, construction work started here in 1941 and the site was earmarked for the Royal Canadian Air Force. It was in fact the 7th Canadian Station. The A61 road, and the village of Skipton-on-Swale, from which it was named, formed the southern boundary.

The airfield opened in the autumn of 1942, under No 4 Group, Bomber Command, as a satellite of Leeming. It was a standard bomber station with three concrete runways, 5,610 ft, 4,500 ft and 4,020 ft in length, laid out almost like a triangle. The runways were the standard 150 ft width and encircled by a perimeter. The station was far from complete when the first squadron, No 420, RCAF, arrived from Waddington on August 7 1942 with their Wellington B Mk IIIs. This unit remained only a few weeks and on October 15 moved to Middleton St George.

On January 1 1943, the Canadians officially took over their stations and Skipton-on-Swale was transferred to No 6 (RCAF) Group. They were soon to become well known, and liked, in the Yorkshire countryside. A favourite with the Canadians was the 'Busby Stoop' public house on the junction of the A61 and A167 roads just south-east of the airfield.

As the build-up continued No 432 (Leaside) Squadron, RCAF, formed on May 1 1943 with an establishment of Wellington B Mk Xs. The unit code letters were 'QO' and it was the RCAF's 12th bomber squadron (and the first to be formed under No 6 (RCAF) Group) formed overseas. The airfield finally became operational that same month.

Commanded by Wing Commander H.W. Kerby, 432's first mission was on the night of May 23/24 1943 when 15 Wellingtons were despatched to bomb Dortmund, Germany. Sadly, Wing Commander Kerby was killed in action on July 29. He was replaced the following day by Wing Commander W.A. McKay.

Over the next few weeks the operations increased. Then, on September 18 1943, the 'Leaside' Squadron moved to East Moor.

The outgoing unit was replaced by No 433 (Porcupine) Squadron, RCAF, which formed here on September 25. This unit was equipped with Halifax B Mk IIIs, unit code 'BM', and was the 14th and last Canadian bomber squadron formed overseas.

On November 6 1943 the resident unit was joined by the 'Tiger' Squadron when No 424 arrived from Hani East Landing Ground, Tunisia. This unit re-equipped with Halifax B Mk IIIs and, on December 18 1943, Wing Commander A.N. Martin took command.

Both units were to remain at Skipton-on-Swale for the duration of the war. The first operational mission for 433 Squadron came on the night of January 2/3 1944, when three Halifaxes laid mines on the 'Nectarines' (Frisian Islands) area. The first bombing mission was on the 18/19th of the month when eight Halifaxes were despatched to bomb Berlin. On the 21st of the month the Commanding Officer of 424 Squadron, Wing Commander Martin, was killed in action. He was replaced on January 27 by Wing Commander J.D. Blane.

On May 1 1944 Skipton-on-Swale became No 63 Base Sub-station of No 63 Base, Leeming. The two Canadian squadrons settled in to their Yorkshire home and hardly any major raid on Germany or occupied Europe from then

Below left *RCAF Station, Skipton-on-Swale: aerial photograph taken on March 3 1944 from 10,000 ft. River Swale in top left-hand corner. The Nissen huts of various sizes are widely separated and scattered by muddy footpaths and often sodden fields which characterised the new wartime airfields. Note how the bombers are parked on the spectacle-type hardstandings.* **Above** *Skipton-on-Swale, November 13 1944—Halifax Mk II 'O'-Oscar of 424 Squadron ready to go.* **Below** *Motorcycle Corporal of 424 Squadron photo section at Skipton-on-Swale, 1944. Note the essentials of life—leaning on the wall to the left and right and inside on the window ledge.* **Bottom** *May 1945, and Harold Hamnett sits astride a 'Tiger' Squadron's Lancaster engine at Skipton-on-Swale.*

Above Beer is Best *of 433 Squadron at Skipton-on-Swale, November 1944.*

Below *433 Squadron bombing-up—August 1944 at Skipton-on-Swale.*

until the end of the war took place without the Skipton-on-Swale bombers taking part.

During July tragedy again hit 424 Squadron when, on the 28th of the month, their second Commanding Officer was killed in action. The new commander was Wing Commander G.A. Roy, DFC, who took over on August 15. On October 9 he was missing and taken Prisoner of War. Ten days later Wing Commander C.C.W. Marshall, DFC, took over 424 Squadron.

On the night of October 30, 'Q'-Queen took off from Skipton-on-Swale. It was the second mission for Flight Lieutenant MacLean and his crew. Cologne was their target and they were part of a total force of 905 bombers. The run to target was uneventful and they bombed without any problems. However, on the return leg strong headwinds forced a diversion for the main bomber stream. Along with many others, Flight Lieutenant MacLean chose Woodbridge at which to land. The crew were still a little green and forgot the detail of opening the bomb-bay doors after taxying to a stop. The following morning, October 31, MacLean was summoned by Tannoy to report to his aircraft to supervise the opening of his bomb bay. Unknown to all concerned a 500-pounder had hung up and was resting on the bomb doors. With an Erk unwinding the doors by hand, MacLean stood under the nose slightly to the port side. Says Pilot Officer Richard Joseph, his navigator:

'The bomb dropped to the tarmac right at MacLean's feet with an ominous clank. It was at this moment MacLean set the long distance dash record—I believe he was the first human to reach Mach 2 from a standing start'. Fortunately, the bomb failed to explode for it was not a case of just 'Q'-Queen but also 80 or more other aircraft that had dropped in and were sitting nose to tail waiting to return to their own airfields. Luck had held for everyone for not one aircraft was lost on the Cologne raid.

A few nights later on November 6, Flight Lieutenant MacLean was again in trouble, but this was now his fifth mission and he handled 'G'-George as if he had done it all his life. On the return trip from Gelsenkirchen, which had been attacked by 693 bombers from a total force of 738, they were hit by flak. The mid-upper gunner, Sergeant Jerry Porter, was hit in the leg and a big piece of shinbone was ripped out. The controls were badly damaged and the aircraft was difficult to handle. Despite this MacLean managed to land 'G'-George at Manston where it was immediately declared a total write-off. The crew felt that if anyone deserved the DFC it was their skipper, but it was not to be.

During January 1945, both squadrons began to re-equip with Lancaster B Mk Is and IIIs and it was with these that they wound up their operations against the enemy. The main targets attacked during the last two months of combat included Mannheim, Cologne, Essen, Dortmund, Hagen, Bottrop, Hanover, Hamburg (twice), Leipzig and Kiel. The last mission of the war for both units was on April 25 1945, when ten Lancasters from each squadron were despatched to bomb gun positions on the Island of Wangerooge.

No 424 Squadron had flown a total of 3,257 sorties (including 668 from North Africa and 39 with operation 'Dodge') since its birth at Topcliffe in October 1942. The squadron lost 52 aircraft, 313 aircrew of whom 37 were killed, 252

Right The local—April 4 1944. The Guardian Angels were with Flight Lieutenant Doug McGrath's crew for after many 'shaky do's' they successfully completed their 30th and final mission on January 2 1945 and were screened from operations. **Below** *VE-Day Parade at Skipton-on-Swale. Note water tower in the distance. The Maycrete huts already look forsaken as the WAAFs march past for the last time.*

missing (16 were safe), 14 PoW and ten injured. The 'Tigers' Honours and Awards were one DSO, 49 DFCs, one Bar to DFC, one CGM, 11 DFMs and one Mention in Despatches.

The 'Porcupines' flew 2,316 operational sorties of which 54 were mining and the total weight of bombs and mines delivered to the enemy was 7,486 tons. 38 aircraft were lost, 31 over enemy territory. Operational casualties totalled 241 officers and NCOs (191 RCAF, 49 RAF and 1 USAAF); of this number, 152 were killed or presumed dead, 56 were prisoners of war, seven were evaders, two

Skipton-on-Swale on August 10 1945. The water tower familiar to every wayfarer in England on high ground dominates this group of buildings. The round-roofed Nissen huts are where men slept; the other huts are the ablutions. It was a cold dash to the ablutions in the middle of winter. Note part of the village in the background of this widely dispersed station.

were escapers and 24 were RAF personnel on whom no definite information was available. Non-operational casualties totalled 13 aircrew and two ground crew. The 'Porcupines' won 160 decorations and honours. These consisted of 132 DFCs, two bars to DFC, nine DFMs, one BEM, one Purple Heart (US), one Air Medal (US) and 14 Mentions in Despatches.

After hostilities in Europe had ceased both units remained at Skipton-on-Swale as part of Bomber Command's strike force and, on August 30 1945, were transferred to No 1 Group. Both units were engaged in bringing back British and Canadian troops from Italy to the UK. Finally, both squadrons disbanded here on October 15 1945—the 'Tiger' and the

'Porcupine' gone for ever from Skipton-on-Swale but not forgotten. Wing Commander Clive B. Sinton, DFC, the 'Porcupine' Squadron's first Commanding Officer, wrote in the squadron scrapbook: 'The spirit of Porky will live wherever there is freedom, and Porky will fight when, at anytime or place, that freedom is challenged'. After disbandment of the two Canadian squadrons, flying at the airfield ceased and the station closed down.

Today, the control tower is derelict and the hangars have been demolished. The runways now house Ross Foods poultry huts. The fire and trailer sheds and a few other huts are still standing and used for farm storage, the last link with those wartime days and the spirit that goes with those rusty skeletons.

The control tower at Skipton-on-Swale that pulsed life through a network of veins is now derelict and forlorn (photographed September 1980).

Snaith (Pollington), Yorkshire

105/SE605210. Midway between Goole and Pontefract S of the A645 road

Snaith was one of the South Yorkshire sites that was selected as a bomber base during the late 1930s, but it was 1940 before construction work finally got under way. The airfield followed the standard design with the technical site and other buildings grouped together on the edge of the landing area on the south side. The main hangar was a 'J' type which absorbed fewer of the scarce conventional building materials than the older types. The two other hangars were 'T2's. The bomb dump was sited in a quarry to the west.

The airfield was wedged between the A645 road to the north, the Knottingley and Goole Canal (now the Aire and Calder Navigation) to the south and the main London North Eastern Railway to

the west. The small hamlet of Pollington lay in the south-east corner and, because of its close proximity to the airfield, it was known to many by that name. It was officially named Snaith after the larger town to the north-east. The airfield had three standard runways, the main one being 5,600 ft long and the two subsidiaries 4,200 ft and 4,600 ft.

Snaith opened in July 1941, in No 1 Group, Bomber Command, with a decoy airfield at Drax, a few miles to the north-east. The station became operational that same month with the arrival of No 150 Squadron from Newton. This unit operated from Snaith with Wellington Mk IIIs until October 1942, when it moved to Kirmington. It was immediately replaced by 51 Squadron which had returned to Bomber Command after being on loan to No 19 Group, Coastal Command. The squadron now traded in its Whitleys for Halifax BIIs, and it was to remain with

Below *Halifax crew of 'C' Flight, 51 Squadron, at Snaith in 1944.* **Bottom** *Snaith, June 1944. Flying control staff outside the control tower.*

the Halifax for the remainder of the European War.

With the arrival of 51 Squadron the station was transferred to No 4 Group, Bomber Command. The squadron was to play an active part and the Snaith bombers were on all main missions. Returning from a minelaying mission on January 21 1943, Halifax *DT581* flew into a hill near Hebden Bridge, Yorkshire, at 22.25 hours, two of the crew being killed in the ensuing crash.

The resident unit continued to play a

Below *Operations are on and Snaith control tower gets the bombers airborne. Recognition searchlight in the background. Alongside the control tower are the crews of the crash tender and blood wagon.* **Bottom** *Briefing Group at Snaith, 1944.*

prominent part in the bombing offensive and, at the end of 1943, began to convert to Halifax Mk IIIs. Then, on January 14 1944, there was the birth of yet another bomber squadron when No 578 was formed at Snaith from 'C' Flight of 51 Squadron. It had formed as a heavy bomber squadron equipped with Halifax Mk IIIs carrying the unit code letters 'LK'. It did not have to wait long to be blooded as its first operational mission was on the 20/21st of the month when five Halifaxes, one borrowed from No 51, bombed Berlin. The following month 578 Squadron moved to Burn and a new 'C' Flight was formed for No 51 with the code letters 'C6'.

During April 1944, 266 Squadron arrived from Tangmere with Typhoon Ib fighters which made an unusual sight on a bomber station. This unit had come to Snaith to practice Army Support Control, otherwise known as 'Cab Rank'. These duties involved working in close support with an advancing army unit under the control of a Front-Line Visual Control Post which would call up the aircraft on to a specific target. The aircraft would circle the post until given its target, hence the term 'Cab Rank'. But 266's stay was only a matter of weeks and in May, the squadron moved to Needs Oar Point to await the invasion.

No 51 Squadron continued operations, having its fair share of accidents and crashes in the process. The most unusual was on the night of January 13/14 1945, during a raid on the marshalling yards at Saarbrucken, which received three main-force raids within 24 hours. Shortly after bombing the target, Halifax III *MZ465* 'Y'-Yorker collided with another bomber, slicing off about ten feet of 'Yorker's nose with its tail. At the moment of impact the bomb-aimer and navigator were flung out of the aircraft and lost for neither were wearing parachutes. The four engines continued to function, although the propellers were dented by flying wreckage, and the pilot struggled to gain control. He managed to do so and brought the crippled bomber back up to 11,000 ft, at which height it stalled. At 7,000 ft the engines again burst into life and at this height the pilot nursed it back to England and landed on an emergency airfield. For a few minutes after the collision the radio remained working and in the short period before it had to be switched off because of the fire risk, as it was shorting and blue sparks were dancing

Aerial view of the small pocket of resistance at Snaith. The three hangars, the 'J' on the right and the two 'T2's plus a few buildings (photographed April 1981).

around the aircraft, the operator was able to send out an SOS.

The pilot made a good landing. An incredible feat of airmanship by the captain, Flying Officer A.L. Wilson, of Leicester. With only three of 'Y'-Yorker's flying instruments working, and despite the intense cold, he had managed to fly the crippled bomber back to England.

The last operational mission of the war came on April 25 1945, when 18 Halifaxes bombed the gun batteries on the Island of Wangerooge. Before the end of the month the squadron had moved to Leconfield and the station became No 17 Aircrew Holding Unit, in which role it remained until the latter part of the year.

Since the departure of No 51 Squadron the station had closed to flying, but it was brought back into service on September 1 1945 to house the Oxfords of No 1516 BAT Flight which arrived from Odiham. This unit became a RAT Flight on September 15 1945 and remained here until disbanding on April 11 1946 when the airfield finally closed.

For several years after the war many of the buildings survived in reasonable condition but in the 1970s the M62 motorway was built across the northern part of the airfield and most of the runways were removed for motorway material. The control tower has been demolished but the three hangars remain and are in use. Also, nearly all the technical site remains intact as does the WAAF site which is about a mile to the east of the airfield and is used by a farmer. Most of the other dispersed sites have long since disappeared, but odd buildings have survived.

South Cave, Yorkshire
106/SE925315. W of Kingston upon Hull

A site that was merely a grass field and as far as records show was only used during 1916, South Cave was brought into use as a night landing ground during March of that year, when the responsibilities of No 33 Squadron, RFC, were extended to include the defence of the Humber. The BE2cs of 'C' Flight used the primitive airfield until October 1916. Also during this period the Avro 504s of 76 Squadron also used the site for a few weeks during September. With their departure there are no records to show that it was ever used again and there is no trace of it today.

South Otterington, Yorkshire
99/SE375875. NW of Thirsk

A First World War grass landing strip that was used by the Avro 504s and BE2c aircraft of 76 Squadron, RFC, this was a field close to the village after which it was named and only used during September 1916. There are no records of any further use.

Spaldington (Holme-on-Spalding Moor), Yorkshire
See Holme-on-Spalding Moor

Tadcaster (Bramham Moor), Yorkshire
105/SE445413. SW of York

Situated west of Tadcaster on the east side of the main A1 road near Bramham

Crossroads and close to the field of a 15th century battle, the airfield was actually built on Bramham Moor and was in the first instance referred to by that name during its period as an RFC landing ground. After the amalgamation it became Tadcaster.

The airfield opened in the spring of 1916 with the arrival of the 'B' Flight, 33 Squadron, RFC. This unit was equipped with BE2c aeroplanes and was part of the air defence for Leeds and Sheffield. By mid-1916 the responsibilities for the unit had increased and 'B' Flight moved out. During December of that year No 46 Reserve Squadron arrived from Doncaster.

During April 1917, No 68 Reserve Squadron arrived from Catterick and in July of that year No 46 RS moved out to Catterick. No 69 RS arrived here in the second week of October 1917 and remained until the following year. A brief visit was paid by 74 TS which arrived on June 27 and departed on July 15 1918. During this period the site expanded and hangars and other buildings were erected to the north of the flying field just to the east of Headley Hall.

Tadcaster, as it was now known, became No 38 Training Depot Station which formed here on July 15 1918 from No 14 and No 16 Training Squadrons with an establishment of 36 SE5as and 36 Avro 504s. November 1918 saw the arrival of No 94 Squadron from Senlis, France, and the following March No 76 Squadron arrived from Ripon with Bristol Fighters but in June 1919 both squadrons

disbanded. No 38 TDS then disbanded and the airfield closed.

For the next few months the aerodrome was used for the storage of standard-type machines, but the site was not to be retained by the RAF and it was handed over to the Disposal Board for sale, after questions had been raised in Parliament regarding its future. Many of the buildings were quickly dismantled. However, one hangar still remains today on the south side of the road leading from Headley Hall to Headley Bar on the A64 road.

Thirsk, Yorkshire

99/SE420820. On W side of Thirsk

During the First World War a ready-made source of aerodromes for the Home Defence Units were the racecourses. These provided 'instant aerodromes' with very little adaption. Situated on the north side of the A61 road, the racecourse at Thirsk was pressed into such use and, during 1916, No 76 Squadron, Royal Flying Corps, flew a few Avro 504s from here. There is no record of any further flying and the site quickly reverted to its original use.

During the Second World War a different breed of aircraft were in use whose needs were much too great for the local racecourse. However, both Topcliffe and Skipton-on-Swale were sited only a few miles from Thirsk. Also, the railway station became a well-known place for many of the Canadians who were stationed at those airfields.

Tholthorpe, Yorkshire

100/SE485678. Turn off main A19 road to W at Cross Lanes

Situated between Tholthorpe village and the main railway line to the west, a grass airfield was laid out on Tholthorpe Moor in the late 1930s. The field opened in August 1940 as a satellite for Linton-on-Ouse, in No 4 Group, Bomber Command. At that time it was little more than a large meadow, and housed only the Whitley Mk Vs of No 77 Squadron which were detached here from August to December 1940. With their departure Tholthorpe closed to enable the site to be developed

Thirsk railway station became well known to the many Canadians stationed at nearby Topcliffe and Skipton-on-Swale (photographed 1944).

On dispersal at Tholthorpe on November 23 1944—425 (B) Squadron. On left Halifax Mk III MZ454 with tractor and bomb trailer to forefront.

into a heavy bomber station. This work took a long time to complete and followed the standard pattern of the period to produce an airfield with three paved runways, the main one being 5,700 ft in length and the two subsidiaries 4,200 ft and 4,050 ft.

Tholthorpe had been allocated to the Canadians and when it reopened in June 1943 it was part of No 6 Group, RCAF, as No 62 Base Sub-Station under the control of Linton-on-Ouse. The first occupants were No 434 (Bluenose) Squadron, RCAF, which formed here on June 13 as the RCAF's 13th bomber squadron formed overseas.

The squadron was equipped with Halifax B Mk V aircraft, unit code 'WL', and it began bombing operations on August 12/13 when ten aircraft were despatched to bomb Milan. Meanwhile, No 431 Squadron had arrived from Burn on July 15 and, having just re-equipped with the Halifax B Mk V, began to work-up to operations.

Both units took part in the bombing offensive but Tholthorpe was not to be the home from which they would fight it as, on December 9 1943, No 431 Squadron moved to No 64 (RCAF) Base, Croft, followed the day after by 434 Squadron.

They were replaced that same month by No 425 Squadron which moved in from Dishforth and by No 420 Squadron from Dalton. Having just returned from North Africa both units had to work up to operations and increase the squadrons' strength to operational size. Before regaining operational readiness they both had to do considerable conversion training on their new aircraft, the Halifax Mk III.

By mid-February 1944 both units announced themselves ready and operations began against German targets that were high on the list of priority targets. After only a few missions the airfield had turned into a sea of mud and during take-off for a raid against Leipzig three aircraft from 420 Squadron became bogged down in the mud in such a way that access to the runway was blocked. This prevented eight of 425 Squadron's aircraft from taking part for, by the time the obstruction was cleared, it was long past time of 'last possible take-off'. Eight frustrated crews returned eventually to their beds.

The raids continued throughout March with attacks made on Stuttgart, Schweinfurt, Augsburg, Frankfurt and the month was brought to a close with the fateful Nuremburg raid, Bomber Command's most grievous setback of all the raids.

The two resident squadrons now took part in attacking pre-Invasion targets which included railway centres in north-west France and Belgium. The squadrons also took part in operation 'Overlord' with attacks on radio and radar stations and heavy gun batteries. Between mid-June and the end of August 1944, attacks were also made on the flying-bomb sites and both squadrons gave support in the Battle of Normandy.

During the first week in September 'A'-Able from 425 Squadron had just returned from the bombing of Forêt D'Eawy when it crashed into bombed-up 'U'-Uncle, parked in dispersal. Both aircraft immediately burst into flames. One of the first on the scene was Air Commodore Ross, the Station Commander, followed by Flight Sergeant St Germain—a bomb-aimer whose aircraft had just landed—and Corporal Marquet of 425's groundcrew. The aircraft were burning fiercely but despite the heat and other dangers Air Commodore Ross and Corporal Marquet managed to pull clear the seriously injured pilot. Seconds later, everyone was thrown to the ground as the 500-pounders exploded in the bomb-bay.

The flames now licked along the fuselage towards the trapped rear-gunner, Sergeant G.C. Rochon, whose cries for help drove all thoughts of fear from the minds of the heroic rescue party. Using an axe, Flight Sergeant St Germain and Corporal Marquet finally smashed a hole big enough to allow them to haul the gunner out. He was barely clear of his turret when another explosion ripped the aircraft apart and everyone was again blown to the ground in the blast. Air Commodore Ross was hit in the right arm by flying debris and his wrist was almost severed. He was rushed to hospital where an emergency amputation was performed.

For their prompt action Air Commodore A.D. Ross was awarded the George Cross and Flight Sergeants St Germain and Marquet the George Medal; St Germain also won the DFC five months later.

During September the squadrons took part in the oil campaign when attacks on oil targets were stepped up. Well over half were daylight raids under cover of Spitfires and Mustangs. Targets that came within their bomb-sights included the flak-infested valley of the Rhur, Cologne, Essen, Dortmund, Duisburg, Bochum and Wilhelmshaven. Other targets were Homburg, Oberhausen, Hagan, Castrop, Rauxel, Wanne, Eickel and the sprawling industrial centre of Gelsenkirchen which further damaged the German industries.

The two Tholthorpe squadrons were part of the 992 Lancasters and Halifaxes that attacked Dusseldorf on November 2/3. Only a few minutes after take-off 'B'-Baker sprang an oil leak. The captain, Flight Lieutenant R.D.K. Hemphill, decided to press on with the mission. The journey was uneventful until over the target area when the port-inner suddenly exploded and burst into flames. The flight-engineer, Sergeant E.A. McAbendroth (RAF), now had a fight on his hands for he had to stop the fire from spreading. Meanwhile, the pilot held an accurate course on three engines and successfully bombed the primary target from 13,500 ft, which was 6,000 ft below briefed height. The pilot then headed 'B'-Baker for home with a second engine now giving trouble. Fuel shortage was also a problem. However, pulling out all the stops the flight-engineer applied all the tricks to keep the life-giving fuel at its maximum economy. With a prayer or two and Lady Luck on their pilot's shoulders, the 'Alouettes' made it back to the emergency landing ground at Manston. For their action Flight Lieutenant Hemphill received a DFC and Sergeant McAbendroth a DFM. A few weeks later the latter was to add a Bar to his DFM.

Targets up to the end of 1944 included the U-boat base at Bergen, Norway, a few German marshalling yards, and knocking a nail in the coffin of the small German fortified town called Julich. The object was to destroy the buildings and strong-points, blocking all roads and inter-sections. 1,946 tons of bombs rained down and devastated this little German town. A cratered area extended beyond

Halifax B Mk III MZ620 of 420 Squadron taking off at Tholthorpe on January 6 1945.

Tholthorpe: another Halifax safely returns.

the town on all sides. Two other fortified towns to receive similar treatment were Duren and Heinsberg.

For the two Tholthorpe squadrons the New Year started with a few semi-tactical targets such as marshalling yards in towns on the approaches to the battle area. February saw a return to many of their old targets. They also attacked targets in support of operation 'Plunder', the crossing of the Rhine.

March started with very bad weather and severe icing produced several problems on some of the operations. Returning from Hagen on March 15/16, 'G'-George of 425 Squadron was jumped by a night fighter and had its nose blasted off. The starboard inner engine was also hit by tracer and set on fire. As Sergeant Arcand, the flight-engineer, set about his task, fire broke out near his position. As the skipper, Flight Lieutenant J.R. Laporte, fought the bucking controls the night fighter struck again. This time the starboard outer was set on fire and Laporte was struck by a bullet that pierced both elbows. Miraculously, he maintained control of 'G'-George and feathered the two engines. Meanwhile, Sergeant Arcand and the other crew were trying to extinguish the fuselage fire.

However, they fought a losing battle and in spite of his wounds the pilot held the Halifax steady while the crew baled out. When it came to his turn he realised that his harness was caught in the windscreen de-icer pump handle. Painfully he disentangled it and moved to the escape hatch. Before he reached it he was thrown to the floor and his left foot jammed between the 'Window' chute and the wireless panel. He freed himself and struggled to the hatch. Mother nature then gave a helping hand. He was sucked out of the doomed Halifax—and out of his boots, which remained in the aircraft. Laporte landed safely in Belgium as did all his other crew except Sergeant Arcand who went down with the aircraft.

For the 'Snowy Owls', their parting fling at the enemy was a let-down. On April 22 1945, 17 Halifaxes from 420 Squadron were despatched to bomb Bremen but on arriving over the target the Master Bomber ordered them not to bomb; records do not state why.

The awards gained by 420 Squadron were 38 DFCs, one Bar to DFC and nine DFMs. They lost 65 aircraft and 324 aircrew, of whom 84 were killed or presumed dead, 228 missing, six PoW, four injured and two proved safe. Non-operational losses were three aircraft, 12 personnel killed and six injured, of whom one later died.

No 425 Squadron's last mission was on April 25 1945, 18 Halifaxes bombing gun positions on the Island of Wangerooge. The squadron logged 3,665 operational sorties on 287 bombing missions in which it dropped 9,152 tons of bombs. In so doing it lost 55 aircraft, 338 aircrew (292 RCAF, 44 RAF, one USAAF and one RAAF), of whom 190 were either killed or presumed dead. Of the survivors who failed to return from operations, 91 were taken PoW (of whom one escaped), seven were interned, 54 evaded capture or proved safe and four (all RAF) were listed under 'fate unknown'. Non-operational losses were 11 aircraft and 73 personnel of whom 64 were killed, eight injured and one died of natural causes.

The awards won by members of No 425 (Alouette) Squadron, RCAF, were two MBEs, 163 DFCs, four Bars to DFC, two GMs, 18 DFMs, one American DFC and four Mentions in Despatches.

After hostilities in Europe had ceased both units were selected, as part of 'Tiger Force', for duties in the Pacific. After converting to the Canadian-built Lancaster B Mk X, on June 11 and 12 1945 both squadrons flew their Lancasters home to Debert, Nova Scotia, for reorganisation and training. However, the atomic dust over Hiroshima and Nagasaki blotted out the Rising Sun and the sudden end to the war in the Far East made them

Control tower at Tholthorpe photographed in September 1980.

redundant; both disbanded on September 5 1945.

The airfield closed after the departure of the Canadians and was not retained by the post-war RAF. Most of the facilities were dismantled, much of the concrete was dug up from the runways and a minor road running almost north-south across the site was reopened. Today, a few buildings remain but are now overgrown with bushes and trees. Tholthorpe had two control towers, an early box-type 343 and the standard austerity type; both are derelict. The south-east corner is used by a poultry firm with battery huts. What remains of the runways and perimeter tracks are used by the local farmer. Nearly all signs of those wartime years have been erased.

Thornaby, Yorkshire

93/NZ455163. W of Middlesbrough, adjacent to the A1045 road

Constructed during the late 1920s, Thornaby-on-Tees was one of the first airfields to be opened after the First World War but had very few facilities. It was situated to the west of Thornaby village with the Stainsby Beck forming its eastern boundary. In the south-east corner lay Stainsby Wood and in the south-west corner Thornaby Wood. The technical area and all other buildings were grouped together in the north-west corner of the landing area. The site, which was then only 34 acres, was used as a 2nd Class

Landing Ground by 36 Squadron during the First World War.

On March 17 1930, No 608 (North Riding) Squadron formed at Thornaby-on-Tees as an Auxiliary Air Force light bomber squadron. Its first operational aircraft, Westland Wapitis, were received in June 1930. In January 1937 it converted to a fighter role and re-equipped with Hawker Demons. A few months before the outbreak of war it was again redesignated and became a general reconnaissance squadron. For almost the next two years its role was to be convoy escort with Anson, Botha and Blenheim aircraft. Meanwhile, in March 1936 No 9 FTS had been formed at Thornaby but after only a few months moved to Hullavington where it exchanged its Harts for Ansons. The dreaded Botha also entered service here.

No 224 Squadron arrived from Boscombe Down and No 233 from Tangmere early July 1937 and operated alongside 608 Squadron for the rest of the year. Mid-January 1938, 224 moved to Eastleigh only to return to Thornaby on March 25. It then remained here for the summer months but, on September 1 1938, the Ansons of 224 and 233 Squadrons finally said farewell and moved to Leuchars.

They were replaced the following month by the Fairey Battles of Nos 106 and 185 Squadrons from Abingdon but, before the end of the month, both units had moved to Grantham, although they were back again in October.

During May 1939, 106 Squadron began to re-equip with Hampdens plus one or two Ansons. The unit then moved to Evanton on detachment in August and the following month to Cottesmore, Rutland. Meantime, 185 Squadron had re-equipped with Hampdens during June and in August it also moved to Cottesmore.

In September 1939 the airfield was transferred to Coastal Command and came under the control of 18 Group. That same month 220 Squadron arrived with their Ansons but almost immediately began to re-equip with Hudsons. This was a general reconnaissance unit engaged on coastal patrols. During one such patrol in February 1940 three Hudsons from 220 Squadron located the German prison ship *Altmark*, just off Norway, and the Navy was able to intercept and release 299 British Prisoners of War. In April 1941, 220 Squadron moved to Wick. That same month 608 Squadron re-equipped with Hudsons and the unit was allotted more offensive missions, which included targets on the Norwegian and Danish coasts.

Thornaby was one of the early stations to have decoy airfields, with a KQ site at Grangetown and a QX site at Middleton. The decoy at Grangetown had its usual complement to operate it and was equipped with dummy buildings and dummy Blenheims. Like the Middleton decoy, it was also equipped with a dummy flarepath. However, it is not possible to derive from the records if they served any great purpose and they were abandoned during the early part of the war.

Even though Thornaby was not the best location for an airfield, it was decided to enlarge it where possible and it was fitted with three concrete runways, the main one, 05/23, being 3,750 ft long and the two subsidiaries 2,400 ft and 3,330 ft in length.

Adjacent to the airfield was a balloon barrage that was designed to protect the heavy industries of Stockton-on-Tees and Middlesbrough, the latter being the main port on the River Tees with large iron and steel works. But it brought many problems for the Thornaby pilots and one balloon had to be pulled down before the longest runway could be used. Still, the balloons had their good points and gave gunnery practice when they escaped the clutches of the WAAFs and drifted out over the North Sea.

At this period of the war many specialised units were formed to train pilots and crews and in January 1941 No 9 Beam Approach Training Flight formed here. The following November it was renumbered 1509 BAT Flight. Due to heavy losses in the Battle of the Atlantic during the early part of 1941, a few Bomber Command squadrons were detached to Coastal Command. One such unit was No 114 (Hong Kong) Squadron

which arrived at Thornaby during March of that year. This unit was equipped with Bristol Blenheims and was engaged on convoy escorts. No 114 also took part in anti-submarine and anti-shipping patrols. After its brief role at Thornaby the squadron moved to Leuchars in May 1941.

The station next had a visit from a Coastal Command Strike squadron when Beaufighter F Mk Ic aircraft of 143 Squadron arrived from Aldergrove in July 1941, but the unit was soon on the move and departed the following October.

The station was now to take on a new role and, on July 19 1941, No 6 (C) OTU was formed here from No 2 School of Army Co-operation. This unit was equipped with 36 Lockheed Hudsons, mostly Mark IIIs but including a few Mark Is and one or two Mark Vs. The satellite airfield for the OTU was West Hartlepool which was used for 'circuits and bumps'.

Training included navigation exercises, circuits and landings, night and day bombing and gunnery, in an area 20 miles out to sea from Redcar. It also included 'Local Sodium', which was a system for practising night flying in daylight. The runway flarepath consisted of sodium lights, aircraft instruments were illuminated with a sodium light and the pilot wore special goggles. All the student pilot could see was the runway lights and aircraft instruments—of course, an instructor or look-out pilot monitored the operation.

During January 1942, Spitfires of 332 (Norwegian) Squadron arrived at Thornaby on detachment from Catterick. Durng this period the OTU was well underway and, on April 6 1942, No 1509 BAT Flight moved to Church Lawford. April 21 saw another intake arrive at the

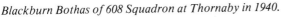

Blackburn Bothas of 608 Squadron at Thornaby in 1940.

No 6 OTU. Photograph taken in front of the Officers' Mess, RAF Station Thornaby, Yorkshire, June 1942.

railway station. On the return journey the Royal Air Force bus stopped at a florist, to collect wreaths for a late Hudson crew; on arrival at Thornaby, Pilot Officer Stratford remarked that he hoped they would not depart with wreaths on their chests. Ironically, from this course, he captained the only crew missing while on exercise on May 29 1942.

For the third Thousand-Bomber raid, which took place on the night of June 25/26 1942 against Bremen, it was once again a case of every available aircraft and, from the 1,006 despatched, 102 aircraft were from Coastal Command. 12 old Hudsons from 6 OTU took part in the raid together with 12 from the other Hudson OTU at Silloth which were deployed to Thornaby for the big event.

Each Hudson managed to get airborne with a 1,000-lb bomb load, and it is frightening to think of how they set out. Manned by instructors and a few wireless operators/air gunners from the course, most of the Hudsons had no radios—not even a serviceable intercom. In one instance during the mission, the rear-gunner spotted a German fighter and ran forward to tell the pilot. He arrived at the same time as a shower of tracer bullets. Five Coastal Command aircraft failed to return but, amazingly, all the Thornaby aircraft returned safely although one had to make a wheels-up landing. One Silloth aircraft was missing.

Under the watchful eye of the Chief Flying Instructor, Group Captain Kelly,

the training continued. On June 10, Pilot Officer Peden, pilot of Hudson *T9351*, had cause to be thankful for the thorough training. He had just completed a five-hour navigation exercise over the North Sea when he encountered a wall of fog near Whitby. At tree-top height he put into practice 'Bad Weather' approach and made it back to the airfield in one piece.

Every pilot made his own bad weather approach to Thornaby and with the balloon barrage this was no easy matter. The procedure for Pilot Officer Peden was to get out over the North Sea then coast-crawl until he located the small pier at Saltburn-by-the-Sea. At this point he turned inland and followed the A174 road; at the first 'pub' past the third crossroads he made a half turn to the right for 180° and prayed he could see the runways before ploughing into the balloon barrage cables.

During March 1943, No 6 OTU exchanged places with No 1 (C) OTU at Silloth. This was also a Hudson unit which remained at Thornaby until October 19 1943, when it disbanded. During this period Thornaby had been covered by two fighter detachments from Catterick for patrol duties. On January 25 to May 27 1943, Spitfire Mk Vbs from 401 Squadron, RCAF, gave the cover, until they were replaced by the Spitfires of 306 (Polish) Squadron which remained for patrol duties until August of that year.

Thornaby now became engaged in air-sea rescue and in October 1943 the ASR

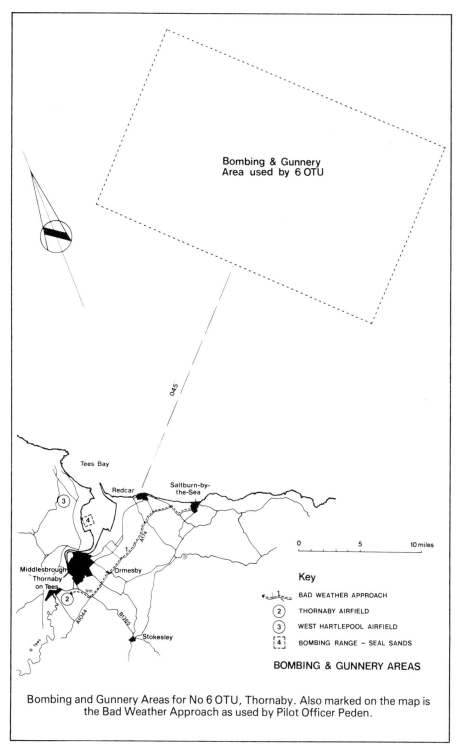

Bombing & Gunnery
Area used by 6 OTU

Tees Bay

Redcar

Saltburn-by-
the-Sea

Middlesbrough
Thornaby
on Tees

Ormesby

Inn

Stokesley

0   5   10 miles

Key

⟵1 ⟶ BAD WEATHER APPROACH

② THORNABY AIRFIELD

③ WEST HARTLEPOOL AIRFIELD

④ BOMBING RANGE – SEAL SANDS

BOMBING & GUNNERY AREAS

Bombing and Gunnery Areas for No 6 OTU, Thornaby. Also marked on the map is
the Bad Weather Approach as used by Pilot Officer Peden.

Pilot Officer R.M. Peden in front of his aircraft, a Hudson Mk V with Pratt and Whitney twin Wasp engines; No 6 (C) OTU Thornaby, Yorkshire. Posted at the end of his course to No 48 Squadron in July 1942.

Training Unit arrived. It received its Warwicks here and that same month was joined by 280 Squadron which arrived from Thorney Island with Ansons. Their role was to give ASR coverage over the North Sea and they immediately re-equipped with Warwicks.

On November 21, the Warwick Training Unit arrived from Bircham Newton and the following day No 281 Squadron re-formed with an establishment of Warwicks as an ASR unit. The following month the Air-Sea Rescue Training Unit moved to Thorney Island. At the end of February 1944, No 281 Squadron moved to Tiree to give cover over the north-west approaches. March 1944 saw the return of the Air-Sea Rescue Training Unit with their Warwicks, plus a Walrus and Lysander.

During early May 1944, the Air-Sea Rescue Training Unit moved to Turnbury and was absorbed into No 5 (C) OTU on May 15. May also saw the departure of 280 Squadron to Strubby and the following month the Warwick Training Unit moved out and became part of No 5 OTU. The status of the station as at June 6 1944 was only a detachment of 280 Squadron with Warwicks as part of No 16 Group.

Over the next few months Thornaby saw very little flying activity. Then, during October 1944, No 279 Squadron arrived from Bircham Newton with old Hudsons, but converted to Warwicks the following month. This was also an ASR unit and gave coverage over the North Sea. It remained here for the duration of the war and on September 3 1945 moved to Beccles so that it could re-equip with Lancasters.

During this period aircraft and crews, including ground staff of 455 Squadron, RAAF, moved to Thornaby. The Beaufighters of the Dallachy Wing arrived on May 3 1945 and went out in force the same day to patrol Kiel Bay and the Great Belt. The mission was successful and the Australians left two minesweepers blazing from stem to stern, but this proved to be their last action for, on May 7, Coastal Command issued an order to discontinue attacks against enemy shipping. The Beaufighters then moved out of Thornaby and 455 Squadron disbanded at Dallachy, Scotland, before the end of the month.

After the war, the airfield continued to be used by the RAF in a small ASR role and, on November 3 1945, No 280 Squadron moved back to Thornaby where it remained until it disbanded on June 21 1946.

The following month No 608 re-formed as an Auxiliary Air Force Mosquito light bomber squadron but it did not receive any Mosquito bombers. By 1947 the unit had received Mosquito NF 30s and had assumed a night fighter role. The unit then assumed a day fighter role and in 1948 converted to Spitfires, followed in 1950 by Vampire jets.

In 1954, Thornaby revived its wartime air-sea rescue role when No 275 Squadron arrived in November from Linton-on-Ouse. Equipped with Sycamore helicopters, the unit was engaged on search and rescue duties along the north-east coast.

The year 1957 saw many changes at Thornaby and, in March, No 608 Squadron disbanded for the last time along with all other Royal Auxiliary Air Force units. In September, 92 Squadron arrived from Middleton St George and the following month 275 Squadron moved out to Leconfield. The Hunters remained at Thornaby for another year but, after they had returned to Middleton St George in October 1958, the airfield closed to flying and was vacated by the RAF.

Today, the tiny village of Thornaby has

engulfed the site and there is very little trace of the former wartime airfield. Such are the changes that from the wartime map and today's OS map, the only remaining features are the woods and Stainsby Grange Farm.

Thorne, Yorkshire

111/SE698130. SW of Goole

Another of the many grass fields that was brought into use as a night landing ground, Thorne was used during 1916 by 'A' Flight, of No 33 Squadron, RFC. The site was never developed and during the Second World War it was passed by in preference for Lindholme to the south and Snaith to the north.

Tockwith (Marston Moor), Yorkshire

See Marston Moor

Topcliffe, Yorkshire

99/SE405790. SW of Thirsk between the A167 and A168 roads

Topcliffe was planned as a bomber station but by the time work started in 1939 it was victim to the austerity cuts which reflected in the buildings, and permanent hangars were completed as 'C1' types. These were sited in the north-west corner near Fox Covert and the A167 road. The airfield was built in an area known as Topcliffe Parks just north of the village of Topcliffe after which it was named. This later caused some confusion when another airfield was built almost alongside the village and had to be named Dalton after a nearby hamlet.

No 102 Conversion Flight at Topcliffe, 1942.

Topcliffe opened as a grass airfield in September 1940 in No 4 Group, Bomber Command. The first squadron to arrive was No 77 which moved in with Whitleys from Linton-on-Ouse during the early part of October. The following month it was joined by 102 Squadron, also with Whitleys from Linton-on-Ouse.

Despite being declared operational and having a decoy airfield at Raskelf a few miles to the south-east, Topcliffe was lacking in many facilities. However, both squadrons carried out bombing raids on Germany which included Berlin and the Ruhr. Attacks were also made on Fortress Europe until it became obvious that the airfield must have concrete runways in preparation for the arrival of the Halifax bomber.

In September 1941, No 77 Squadron moved to Leeming and the following November, 102 Squadron moved to the newly-opened Dalton. Topcliffe then closed for rebuilding and the construction of concrete runways. These were the standard pattern, the main one being 5,925 ft in length and the two intersecting ones 3,460 ft and 4,140 ft. A perimeter linked the runways and there were the usual hardstandings.

The airfield reopened in mid-1942 and resumed its former role as an operational bomber station with the return in June of 102 Squadron who were now flying Halifax BIIs. The Squadron Conversion Flight also arrived but neither were to remain for very long and, on August 7 1942, No 102 Squadron and the Conversion Flight exchanged places with 405 Squadron, RCAF, and 405 Conversion Flight at Pocklington.

On August 18, another Canadian squadron, No 419, arrived from Leeming. This unit was flying Wellington Mk IIIs and was still on the merry-go-round to find a permanent base. Topcliffe was not

the answer and, on September 30, No 419 moved to Croft.

No 405 Conversion Flight moved out to Leeming on October 7 and on the 24th of the month 405 Squadron was transferred to No 18 Group, Coastal Command, and moved to Beaulieu, Hampshire, where it flew anti-submarine patrols over the Bay of Biscay. It was replaced a few days later when No 424 (Tiger) Squadron, RCAF, formed here on October 15, as a bomber squadron with an establishment of Wellington B Mk IIIs. The unit code letters were 'QB' and it was the sixth Canadian bomber squadron formed overseas.

Topcliffe had been earmarked for a Canadian base and on January 1 1943 the station and its units were transferred to No 6 (RCAF) Group. The first operational mission for 424 Squadron was on the night of January 15/16 1943, when five Wellingtons bombed Lorient, France.

March 1 1943 saw the return of 405 Squadron to Bomber Command, and it arrived at Topcliffe with its Halifax B Mk IIs. However, its stay was very brief and five days later it moved to Leeming.

Changes were also in the wind for the station itself and, on March 1, it formed as Topcliffe Operational Base with headquarters here controlling RCAF stations Topcliffe, Dalton and Dishforth. On the 14th of the month, No 1659 HCU arrived from Leeming and the station now prepared for its training role. The Wellingtons of 424 Squadron moved to Leeming on April 7 and on the 30th Topcliffe was redesignated No 6 (RCAF) Group Training Base, then becoming No 61 (Training) Base on September 16, and at the same time acquired Wombleton. Throughout these further changes No 1535 BAT Flight (RCAF), which had arrived early in the year, had disbanded on August 6.

The demand for trained crews continued and at such a pace that Sergeant Charles E. Whitmore, a navigator with Flight Sergeant Thompson, had only 18 hours flying time on the Halifax entered in his Log Book when his crew got their posting to No 429 (Bison) Squadron at Leeming. They had just started a cross-country exercise when they were recalled to base for posting to Leeming that night. Their conversion course was over and they would soon know if they were a good team. With their kitbags, the seven crew were soon in the back of a lorry and on their way up the Great North Road to Leeming.

The extensive training programme continued unabated and crashes were all too frequent under the pressures. Yorkshire became the last resting place for many of the Canadians. The worst accident month for 1659 HCU was January 1944. The month was not a day old when, at 12.40 hours, Halifax II *W1095* undershot on three-engined practice, due to gusts. 1st pilot Warrant Officer S.J. Pearce and 2nd pilot Flight Sergeant E.A. Vigor were on circuits and landings practice when the pilot aimed to land short in order to avoid a contractor's working party. Fortunately the crew of eight were uninjured.

On January 15, Halifax B III *LK878* crashed at 20.58 hours at Catecliffe Wood, near Felixkirk, Yorkshire, shortly after take-off, killing all nine on board. Three days later the gear wheel on the impeller shaft of the port-outer engine on Halifax B II *R9386* disintegrated in flight; power was lost and the pilot, Flying Officer F.H. Baker, feathered the engine. In the process he overshot and at 10.12 hours hit some trees ¾-mile south-east of the airfield. Of the eight-man crew, two were killed and three injured. That same day, a few minutes later at 10.30 hours, Halifax B II *LW334*, piloted by Flying Officer P. Lavellee, crashed into a hillside at Black Hambleton, near Osmotherley, at 1,100 ft in fog. All six crew were killed. The aircraft was on cross-country and crews were instructed to remain at 3,000 ft if ground was not visible. Parts of this aircraft can still be found, such as the propeller blade from *LW334* which was found in the heather a few years ago.

On November 9 1944 the station transferred to No 7 (Training) Group and was renumbered No 76 (RCAF) Training Base. Ten days later the HCU converted to Lancaster B Mk Xs. Topcliffe remained a training station for the remainder of the war. On September 1 1945 No 76 Base disbanded and on the 10th of the month No 1659 HCU also disbanded.

Topcliffe was handed back to the RAF in September 1945, at which date it reverted to No 4 (Transport) Group. The station was selected for retention by the post-war RAF and was then used by Air Navigation Schools for several years. No 5 Air Navigation School moved in from Jurby, Isle of Man, on September 17 1946 and was redesignated No 1 Air Navigation School. The last of No 5 ANS arrived in October, one signaller being 3040138

Above Thor *visiting Topcliffe from Manby in October 1947.* **Below** *Ansons at Topcliffe in July 1947: No 1 Air Navigation School.*

Geoff Lenthall: 'We arrived at Topcliffe to find it just as the Canadians had left it with chewing gum stuck under every table and chair in the dining hall, the only reminder of those hectic wartime days'. The school was equipped with Ansons and Wellington Xs and they quickly settled into their Yorkshire home in their peace-time role.

During October 1947 the station had a visit from *Thor*. This was a Lancaster from the Empire Air Armament School at Manby and was equipped with the latest armament for Empire tours. The Empire Air Navigational School also had a Lancaster equipped with the latest navigational equipment. *Thor*, so named in place of its undignified call sign 'White Pants Nan', toured Australia, New Zealand, India and south-east Asia, covering over 25,000 miles in under 50 days.

The severe winter of 1947 grounded all aircraft and everyone was sent home on indefinite leave. During this period the Mountain Rescue Team was based at Topcliffe and they assisted in getting supplies through to villages that were snowed-in.

At 15.00 hours on January 13 1948, Wellington T 10 *RP555* of No 1 ANS dived into the ground and burst into flames after elevator control was lost just after take-off. The 2nd pilot abandoned the aircraft before the starboard wing dropped and the aircraft crashed. It was on pilot training and the pilots were W.T. Barber and Frederick Bosomworth, the latter being the only survivor, the other three crew being killed.

Even under peacetime circumstances, many crashes still occurred during training. On March 17 1948, aircraft of No 1 ANS were taking part in a navigation exercise when, at 09.47 hours, Wellington T10 *RP499*, piloted by C. Bass, was struck by Wellington T 10 *RP565*, piloted by Flight Lieutenant F. Kula (Polish), which flew into it from behind while joining a left-hand circuit. The aircraft disintegrated and the Sergeants' Mess was wrecked. Four

bodies were recovered from aircraft wreckage which had been flung against the wall of the mess. All eight airmen forming the two crews lost their lives.

There were other minor crashes but one unsolved mystery was a Wellington that failed to return from a navigation exercise and was presumed lost over the North Sea. No SOS or wreckage was ever found.

The school had several Polish pilots, Flight Lieutenant Jeziorowski, 'Ted' Poludniak and Warrant officer Zawodny, to name but three. The latter took great delight in stalling his Anson over a nearby Polish resettlement camp at the end of each flight. On July 7 1949, No 1 ANS moved to Hullavington where it disbanded on April 30 1954.

The airfield was then transferred to Transport Command and over the next few years housed some Hasting units. No 53 Squadron re-formed here with Hastings on August 1 1949 and, on August 22, No 47 Squadron arrived. 53 Squadron then moved to Wunsdorf during early October and was replaced at the end of the year by 297 Squadron. In January 1950, No 241 OCU arrived from Dishforth in order to re-equip with Hastings and after having done so it moved back to Dishforth where it combined with 240 to form 242 OCU.

On November 15 1950, No 297 Squadron disbanded only to be replaced by the Hastings of 24 Squadron which arrived from Lyneham on February 9 1951. Conditions remained stable for the next two years, then further changes were in the wind and during the early part of May 1953 both Nos 24 and 47 Squadrons moved to Abingdon.

The airfield was then taken over by Coastal Command and No 210 Squadron, flying Lancasters, moved from St Eval to Topcliffe during October 1952, where it re-equipped with Neptunes. The unit was joined the following year by 203 Squadron which arrived from St Eval in March 1953, and by No 36 which re-formed at Topcliffe on July 1 1953 with Neptunes in a maritime recce role.

This phase finished in 1957, No 203 Squadron having disbanded here on September 1 1956, No 210 on January 31 and No 36 on February 28 1957. During this period four specially-equipped Neptunes were used from November 1952 to June 1956 to provide airborne early warning for Fighter Command. For these duties No 1453 Flight, originally known as the Vanguard Flight, used *WX499, WX500, WX501* and *WX542*.

When navigator training recommenced in England in 1957, No 1 Air Navigation School re-formed at Topcliffe on March 15. No 1 ANS was organised into Flying, Technical, Administration and Training Wings. The Flying Wing comprised two squadrons, No 1 with Miles Marathons and responsible for basic training and No 2 with Valettas and Vampires for primary and advanced training.

Training at Topcliffe began in the spring of 1957, the first courses being of 20 weeks' duration for radio observers who passed out as Senior NCOs before completing their training at either 238 OCU at North Luffenham or 228 OCU at Leeming. In November 1957 the 20-week courses were terminated and replaced by 49-week straight-through courses where cadets passed out as fully trained navigators with the rank of Pilot Officer.

Varsity aircraft began to replace the Marathon during February 1958, the last one leaving the unit on June 12. After the departure of the last Marathon, the unit had on strength 23 aircraft: eight Varsitys, four Vallettas, nine Vampire NF 10s and two Vampire T11s.

Heavy snow again hit the Topcliffe area during the winter of 1958/9 and No 1 ANS was temporarily based at Dishforth.

Pilot Ted Poludniak warming up his Wellington at Topcliffe, July 1947.

Top *Lockheed Neptune MR1 WX501 seen at Topcliffe and one of the 52 supplied under MDAP.* **Above** *The control tower at Topcliffe as seen in March 1981.*

On January 15 1962, No 1 ANS moved to Stradishall.

The flying role at Topcliffe was now coming to an end. In June 1965, No 26 (Northern Command Communications) Squadron accepted its first two Bassetts at Topcliffe and formed the Bassett Conversion Flight in July 1965. This unit became Training Command Communication Squadron on January 1 1967 and moved to Wyton on January 13 1969. The station was then transferred to the Army in 1972 and 24 Brigade took over on November 1 1973. They moved from Barnard Castle to Topcliffe on November 3.

Topcliffe has now become Alanbrooke Barracks and the general camp-site and buildings are still in perfect condition. The runways are still intact for occasional use by certain flying units. The five 'C1' hangars also remain and are used as garages or stores, and one as the gymnasium. The wartime control tower is still standing but has, however, had a cupola added on the top and various electrical modifications made inside, for it is used as the present air traffic control tower.

The present-day units are: 1st Regiment, Royal Horse Artillery; No 3 Flight of 7 Regiment, Army Air Corps; The Royal Navy Elementary Flying Training Squadron and a Royal Air Force Air Traffic Control Detachment. Topcliffe's present and future role is as Army barracks but its wartime link can still be found around the perimeter of the airfield with the decaying remains of wartime huts and buildings.

Welburn Hall (Wombleton), Yorkshire

See Wombleton

West Ayton, Yorkshire

101/SE985850. W of Scarborough

During the First World War, West Ayton was one of the only two military sites in the area around Scarborough and in the Second World War this area was devoid of all airfields. The site was, in fact, Scarborough racecourse and the landing ground was first used in 1916 by the Royal Naval Air Service who flew BE2c biplanes on anti-Zeppelin patrols. The area was never developed and it saw little use until near the end of the First World War.

During the latter part of October 1918, 510 Flight of No 251 Squadron operated from here with DH6s. This unit was used for convoy duties and inshore reconnaissance. It is interesting to note from the log-book of one of those early pilots that the operational height was only 1,000 feet. 510 Flight moved out during January 1919.

The site was not retained by the post-war Royal Air Force but it was used for a number of years by civil light aircraft and, in 1928, The Prince of Wales, later Edward VIII, departed from West Ayton after attending a conference in Scarborough.

A page from the flying log book of a pilot from 510 Flight, 251 Squadron, while at West Ayton.

West Hartlepool (Greatham), Cleveland

93/NZ503283. Just S of Hartlepool

One of the 14 airfields listed on the 1935 war map, West Hartlepool was never developed owing to its position and by 1944 was not even listed on the July 1944 Royal Air Force war map of the airfields. It was situated between the A689 road to the north and the railway line to the south, near the village of Greatham after which it was better known and referred to by those who had cause to use the airfield. The main use was as a satellite for Thornaby and by fighters, mostly from Catterick, which were on convoy duty. Should the convoy be one of no great importance they would land at West Hartlepool where they would remain in a state of readiness while any convoy was moving in the area. This replaced the continuous patrols and the fighters would be at the airfield from half-an-hour to several hours. If the fighters were scrambled they had to return to their own base for refuelling. The only squadron on record to use West Hartlepool was No 403 with a detachment of four Spitfires from June 19 1942 until January 22 1943.

The airfield was nothing more than a grass strip with a limited run, aligned north-east/south-west. To the west side of the strip was a wooden flying control hut which doubled as a crew room with a couple of beds and filthy blankets. This was the only building for there were no aircraft servicing facilities or permanent personnel. The fire and crash services were provided by Royal Air Force Thornaby, the nearest main airfield. On many occasions aircraft were caught by the weather at West Hartlepool and the crews had to leave their aircraft behind while they were taken to Thornaby for meals and overnight billets.

From April 17 1942, 'N' Flight of No 1 Anti-Aircraft Co-operation Unit, redesignated No 1613 Flight on October 1 1942, flew a few Tiger Moths and Henleys from West Hartlepool.

The landing strip was camouflaged with hedges painted across the clear area and a hedge of dead shrubs and tree branches marked the usable section of the field on the south-east side. Pilot Officer Peden from No 6 OTU can well remember West Hartlepool, and the hedge, for on July 10 1942, while pilot of a Hudson Mark III, *V9050*, he had cause to use the landing strip. Since he was not used to the heavier Hudson and the slower control response, he undershot badly. Pilot Officer Peden says: 'I avoided the hedge by bouncing over it for a 'so-so' landing. My navigator, who was having his first ride with me, was so impressed that I believe he left his fingerprints etched in the arm-rests of the co-pilot's seat'.

During March 1943 the airfield ceased to be a satellite for Thornaby and was used less and less. On December 1 1943, No 1613 Flight moved to Hutton Cranswick and was absorbed into 291 Squadron. After the war this primitive airfield was not retained by the Royal Air Force, and today the site is under the British Steel Factory and all wartime traces have long since vanished.

Wombleton (Welburn Hall), Yorkshire

100/SE670825. W of Pickering on S side of the A170 road

Situated just south of the village of Wombleton, this airfield was the highest and nearest to the Moors, which claimed many of the bombers. Prior to the Second World War there was a small aerodrome here which was known as Welburn Hall and, in common with so many other sites, it was surveyed to assess its suitability for development into a bomber airfield. Despite its close proximity to the North Yorkshire Moors it was selected for this purpose.

Wombleton was constructed as a standard bomber airfield with three concrete runways, the main 10/28 being on an east-west axis and 5,850 ft long. The two intersecting runways were each 4,050 ft long. The works necessitated the closure of a small road from Nunnington to Wombleton village and this became part of runway 17/35.

The airfield No 1 site and the Administrative site No 2 were on the west side of the airfield near Wombleton Grange. Further to the west towards the A170 road were the dispersed sites with WAAF site No 12 and Sick Quarters site No 13 being located to the south of Syke Wood. The sewage works and bomb stores were in the south-west corner of the airfield, close to Riccal Moor Lane.

Wombleton opened in October 1943 as a Sub-station of No 61 Base Topcliffe in No 6 Group, RCAF. Its wartime role was destined to be a Canadian training station and, on October 21 1943, No 1666 Heavy Conversion Unit, with Halifax Mk IIs, arrived from Dalton. Wombleton was to be their home for the duration of the war. As had been predicted in some quarters, the altitude caused problems and some difficulty was encountered in getting fully-loaded bombers airborne, in particular Halifaxes. Possibly for this reason Wombleton remained a training airfield.

A brief visitor was 1679 HCU which arrived from East Moor on December 13 1943 with their Lancaster B Mk IIs but, on January 27 1944, the unit disbanded and the aircraft were taken on strength by the resident unit.

During 1944, second-line units started to receive the relegated Mark II Lancasters and Halifaxes. These increased the accident rate and, during the last quarter of 1944, No 1666 HCU, nicknamed 'Mohawk' since June 21, had its fair share of major crashes, minor ones being almost daily. At just after midnight on October 5 1944, Halifax Mk II *JN886*, piloted by Flying Officer M.H. Cook (Canadian), had been airborne for five hours five minutes on a cross-country exercise and bombing practice when his starboard-inner caught fire at 18,000 ft. The pilot was unable to feather the prop and, as he tried, three crew baled out. The bomber crashed at Blackley, Manchester, killing three and injuring four.

A few nights later, on the 20th of the month, Halifax Mk II *LW235*, piloted by

Flying Officer J.H. MacLean, crashed on third overshoot at 02.55 hours near the village of Nunnington. The bomber was on a night flying training and bombing exercise and was flying too low in bad visibility. Two crew were killed and five injured.

A week later, on the 27th of the month, it was trouble for Flight Lieutenant H.A. O'Neill, the pilot of Halifax Mk II *HR723* which was proving difficult to handle due to icing at 15,000 ft and was not maintaining height. All the crew baled out but the wireless operator fell out of his parachute harness and was killed. The Halifax, which had been airborne for just over four hours, crashed at 23.30 hours at Pydew, Llandudno Junction, North Wales, killing one.

During another cross-country exercise on November 15, Halifax Mk II *JP201* collided at 18,000 ft with Halifax Mk V *LL137* of 1664 HCU, Dishforth, while over Devon. Visibility was poor due to frost on the windscreen. Pilot Officer H.K. Pugh (Australian) managed to bale out from *LL137* and was safe but five of his crew were killed and one injured. From the Dishforth bomber, the pilot, Flight Lieutenant R.L. Garvie (Canadian), and his seven crew were all killed.

Four days later, Halifax Mk II *DT735* disappeared during a training exercise. The pilots were Pilot Officer T.R. Bailey (Canadian), the instructor, and Flying Officer J.N. O'Connell (Canadian), his pupil. The aircraft had six other crew members on board and it has not been traced even to this day.

During the latter part of November 1944 the HCU converted to Lancaster Mk Xs but to bring November to an end,

Wombleton control tower photographed on September 5 1979.

Halifax Mk V *LL131* landed on the grass in poor visibility and the starboard under-carriage collapsed. The pilot, Pilot Officer R.J. Grisdale, and his crew were safe.

On December 11 1944, Halifax Mk V *LL285* struggled to gain height after take-off but at 18.25 hours hit a telegraph pole a mile south of Nunnington. Fortunately only two were injured. The following night at 23.35 hours Halifax *JN969*, its windscreen covered in ice, made a heavy landing and the undercarriage collapsed.

Despite the many accidents, morale was good and the unit kept pace with the heavy demands made on it. On August 3 1945, No 1666 HCU disbanded and the almost nightly noise of the powerful engines fell silent. After the Canadians had left, the station reverted to the Royal Air Force and was taken over by the Royal Air Force Regiment and used as a Battle School for several years before it was vacated and most of the facilities dismantled. Eventually it re-opened for flying by light aircraft and gliders on a site restricted by the re-opening of the minor road across the former airfield.

In 1980 a 'B1' hangar was still intact, plus the control tower, which was derelict; when visited early in 1981, however, it was about to be renovated by the owner of Windsports who has bought the tower and plans to turn it into an office and club-room. He would also like to restore the upstairs control room to its original style. The runways to the west of the road are intact but overgrown. There are also a few buildings intact around Wombleton Grange, but the friendly, gum-chewing Canadians have gone forever.

Wombwell (Broomhill), Yorkshire
111/SE410030

Another Home Defence site which was only a grass strip used as a night landing

ground by 'A' Flight of No 33 Squadron, Royal Flying Corps, from March to October 1916 while on Home Defence duties.

Yeadon (Leeds/Bradford), Yorkshire

104/SE225410. NE of Yeadon on the A658 road

Yeadon officially opened on October 17 1931 as the Leeds/Bradford Municipal Aerodrome and was operated by the Yorkshire Aeroplane Club on behalf of the joint airport committee, although passenger services did not begin until an extension was completed in 1935.

The airfield site consisted of 60 acres of grassland but by 1935 a further 35 acres had been added. Yeadon was provided with four steel and asbestos hangars in the north-west corner of the site and was used mainly by club aeroplanes. The chief flying instructor was Captain H.V. Worral and the club aircraft were Cirrus and Gipsy Moths; later, Puss and Leopard Moths were introduced.

During April 1935, North Eastern Airways began to operate a short service from Yeadon with seven-seater Airspeed Envoy aircraft. The following June saw DH84 Dragon and DH89A Rapide aircraft being operated by Blackpool and West Coast Air Services. This company was later succeeded by Isle of Man Air Services who operated seasonal holiday schedules.

With the unrest in Europe, an RAF presence was established at Yeadon with the formation of No 609 (West Riding) Squadron of the Auxiliary Air Force on February 10 1936. It had formed as a light bomber squadron equipped with Hawker Harts which were later replaced by Hawker Hinds. To accommodate the squadron, temporary hangars were constructed in the north-west corner of

Yeadon in the early 1930s. As can be seen, Gipsy Moths were the main aircraft used at that period.

the airfield. A further sign of the troubled times came in 1938 when a Civil Air Guard unit was formed within the Yorkshire Aeroplane Club, and flying training increased dramatically. In December 1938, No 609 was redesignated a fighter squadron and, having re-equipped with Spitfires, moved to their war station at Catterick on August 27 1939.

With the outbreak of war, all civil flying was suspended and the airfield was requisitioned by the Royal Air Force under No 13 Group, Fighter Command, being transferred to No 12 Group, Fighter Command, on September 1 1940. However, very little use was made of the airfield by fighter squadrons. During the first few months of the war Yeadon was also designated a 'scatter' airfield for the Whitleys of Nos 51 and 58 Squadrons and, still part of 12 Group, the site was also used by No 4 Bomber Group Central Maintenance Organisation which was formed at Yeadon on October 6 1940 to carry out major repairs and overhauls on the Whitleys of No 4 Group. Also, since October 6, No 4 Group Communications Flight had been established here.

On March 17 1941 the airfield was transferred to No 51 Group, Flying Training Command, and No 20 Elementary Flying Training School was formed with 50 DH82a Tiger Moths. The next to take up residence was 51 Group Communications Flight which remained at Yeadon until the Group, together with 20 EFTS, disbanded in January 1942. The airfield was then transferred to the Ministry of Aircraft Production and the nearby shadow factory was taken over by Avro. The factory was built at the north end of the airfield and some of the buildings were underground. This factory, when completed, had a total floor space of 1,514,190 sq ft and was probably the largest factory in Europe under one roof. This was a single unit laid out in squares around which, inside the factory, was a motor road making it possible to drive around all four sides. It was a reinforced concrete and brick construction and in the hands of the MAP experts was fully camouflaged. The flat roof was laid to merge with the countryside and the illusion of a farm was obtained with buildings, walled fields (complete with dummy cattle) and a duck pond.

Labour was drawn into the factory from near and far in a rapidly growing stream, until a total of over 11,000, 53 per cent women, were employed at the peak period in April 1944. To augment the limited accommodation available in the neighbourhood the Ministry of Aircraft Production constructed three housing estates of temporary buildings and on these estates 300 houses were allocated to Avro workers. There was also a hostel at Horsforth which provided accommodation for 700 people. The factory billeting officer also managed to find lodgings for between 4,000 and 5,000 others. A fleet of 160 buses were needed to transport the workers to and from their homes, which involved daily journeys up to 60 miles.

A 30 ft built-up metalled causeway was built from the factory so that completed aircraft could be towed straight to the adjoining airfield where they were flown by ATA pilots direct to RAF stations or to Maintenance Units for dispersal. As the output grew, the buildings and hangars around the aerodrome were enlarged to cope with the flight testing and maintenance work involved. The two runways that had been laid were extended to the maximum length of 3,750 ft at the expense of the local golf course.

The first production job was to be the Albermarle, a reconnaissance bomber, but before production had started the project was withdrawn. In October 1940 work was started on the 'Tornado', a single-seater fighter, and up to the autumn of 1941 the factory produced 100 sets of details and five aircraft in various stages of assembly, one of which was flown and handed over to the experimental staff at Manchester.

Then followed the Anson, a twin-engined low-wing monoplane which was made in many different forms. The Anson was originally designed and produced as a reconnaissance aircraft and light bomber but was subsequently modified, some being fitted with 'Bristol' power-operated gun turrets while others were adapted for communication/ambulance work. The total Anson production was 3,881 of which 2,368 were flown away and 1,513 crated. The breakdown of the 3,881 Ansons was 1,026 with Bristol turrets, 2,770 without Bristol turrets and 85 communication/ambulance aircraft. In addition, however, a prodigious number of spares was produced, representing in detail approximately a further 900 complete aircraft.

Anson production slowed down when the famous Lancaster got into production in January 1942. Many of those built at Yeadon were for the Pathfinders, which involved the task of fitting electrical and electronic gear in great secrecy. The first complete Lancaster emerged in April 1942. At this time Their Majesties the King and Queen visited the factory and His Majesty autographed the first 'Lancaster' to leave the production line. By the end of the European war production had reached 40 a month and a total of 688 were made at Yeadon.

The war with Japan demanded the production of the Lincoln and the York transport aircraft—some of the latter going to the Argentine—and it is in this role as a factory that Yeadon will best be

Opposite page, top to bottom *Taken in 1956 and showing the airfield as it was during the war since nothing had changed up to then. Aerial view looking west to Yeadon Moor and the village of Yeadon. The A658 road cuts across the top part and below it, centre right is the roadway from the shadow factory; aerial view of Yeadon looking north with the apron and terminal building to the bottom, the A658 top left corner and alongside it in the centre is the wartime Avro shadow factory. From the large hangar in the foreground one can grasp the huge area it covered. The roadway was where the aircraft were wheeled down to the airfield; aerial view of Yeadon (now Leeds-Bradford airport). The two dark runways are the wartime ones, the light one being the new 15/33 runway. One can see it comes right to the A658 road. Part of the shadow factory is in the picture in the centre on the left-hand side. Photographed in April 1973.*

remembered: a great British wartime achievement.

After hostilities ceased No 609 reformed as an Auxiliary Squadron on July 31 1946, equipped with Mosquito NF 30s. On January 1 1947 Yeadon was handed over to the Ministry of Civil Aviation and club flying was restarted by Lancashire Aircraft Corporation, who also reintroduced airline services with scheduled flights to the Isle of Man using Rapide and Consul aircraft. In April 1948 the Mosquitoes of 609 Squadron gave way to Spitfire 16s and on September 1 1949 they were joined by the Austers of No 1964 AOP Flight, 664 Squadron, which had just formed at Yeadon. The following year 609 Squadron moved to Church Fenton. Then, in February 1953, the Ministry of Civil Aviation withdrew its services, civil flying ceased and the Austers moved to Rufforth. After the MCA withdrew there was a lull in the activities at Yeadon, but not for long, for that same year Yeadon Aviation assumed control and flying recommenced. During 1954, 1964 Flight, 664 Squadron, returned to Yeadon with their Austers and the unit stayed until disbanding on March 10 1957, bringing to a close the RAF's association with the airfield.

By the mid-1950s BKS Air Transport began to operate out of the airport with scheduled services to Belfast, Jersey, Ostend and Dusseldorf. HM Custom facilities became available in 1956 and BKS began a Dakota DC3 service to London and Glasgow, but this only lasted a few months.

During 1958, the main 10/28 runway was resurfaced and another change in the airport administration came on January 8 1959, when the Leeds and Bradford Airport Committee took over full responsibility, appointing Mr G.P. Seller, the present Airport Director, as manager. Improvements quickly followed and permanent airfield lighting, including runway and approach lighting on 10/28, was installed. There were also extensions to passenger accommodation and the aircraft parking apron.

The airport continued to expand and the Yorkshire Aeroplane Club was again established here. The club is situated on the south-west side with access via the 'Southern Entrance', off the main Harrogate road.

During January 1959, Yorkshire Light Aircraft was formed to handle the overhaul and maintenance of aircraft.

The following year BKS began a daily service to London and that same year Aer Lingus joined them on the Dublin route, introducing turbo-prop airliners in 1962. Starways of Liverpool became the first company to operate a Viscount scheduled service. Many of the destinations served by these earlier carriers are covered by the present-day operators.

In October 1963, work started on a 5,400 ft runway, 15/33, which was completed in April 1965. In July of that year, Yorkshire Light Aircraft extended their activities and moved into their new maintenance hangar on the south side of the airport, the two former RAF hangars having been demolished. This expanding company are main distributors for the Rolls-Royce/continental light aero engines and are also factory-appointed Service Centre for American Piper aircraft.

In 1964, another to establish itself at Yeadon was the Northair Aviation Group which operates a fleet of six twin-engined aircraft on the air taxis side of their operation. The Group's headquarters are on the south side of the airport and they have their own terminal and cater well for the flying businessmen. Northair Aviation Ltd is the main company and they are Cessna agents for the area.

On February 20 1968, a new passenger terminal was brought into use, a most modern complex in which the airport restaurant is a popular meeting place. For aircraft spotting there is a viewing deck and, as a reminder of the airfield's history, a memorial to No 609 Squadron. In October 1970, Mr Peter Walker, the Minister with the final say, refused permission for a 2,000 ft extension to runway 15/33. An airport with a future, but held back on its vital expansion needs.

By this time, Aer Lingus were operating Boeing 737 and BAC 1-11 aircraft, while Dan Air were using NORD 262s and later the HS 748. In February 1976 Air Anglia took over the British Airways route to Amsterdam and in May 1978 the company's F27s were flying to Paris (Orly).

November 1976 saw the start of inclusive tour holiday flights from the airport by Britannia Airways Boeing 737/200 ADV aircraft, on behalf of Thompson Holidays. The airport continues to expand and, as a new regional airport is extremely unlikely, the main runway must be extended and other facilities improved. Since the new air

Yeadon—Viscount of Northeast Airways on the rain-soaked apron (photographed 1973).

terminal opened in 1968, over two million passengers have used it. In 1978, passenger throughput was 331,474 and each year sees a steady increase; terminal passengers for 1980 were 362,396. Plans are currently in hand for still further expansion involving the re-routing of the A658 and access road.

The 'Shadow factory' remains intact and is now partly occupied by a container truck operator and two light engineering firms. There is room for further occupants if the need arises but the spirit that conceived it has long since passed. Apart from the butts and machine-gun range to the south, all other wartime buildings appear to have been demolished.

York (Clifton, Rawcliffe), Yorkshire

105/SE590550. N of York City between the A19 and B1363 roads

York aerodrome officially opened as a civil field on July 4 1936 and was controlled by the Yorkshire Aviation Services Ltd on behalf of the City Corporation of York. The airfield was located just outside the northern boundary of the City and consisted of a club house, one hangar 150 × 105 ft with a door height of 10 ft and width of 102 ft, and the landing area. This was a large grass circle that gave a landing length of 1,800 ft from any direction. The club soon became a centre for flying enthusiasts and in 1938 had a fleet of seven aircraft which included Avro Cadets, Hornets and Leopard Moths.

At the outbreak of war in September 1939 the club's aircraft were requisitioned by the RAF and the civil airfield at York was taken over by the RAF as a relief landing ground and dispersal site for Linton-on-Ouse. This was a very brief role and the airfield saw little use by Bomber Command; by the end of 1939 control had been transferred to the Army Co-operation Command. A decoy airfield was established at Bugthorpe but it served very little purpose.

During the latter part of August 1940, No 4 Army Co-operation Squadron moved into York and their Lysanders soon became a familiar sight around the City.

Over the next few months the airfield began to expand and in 1941 No 48 Maintenance Unit was established here. Its function was to carry out repairs to Halifax bombers. In order to accommodate the heavier aircraft, three paved runways, the main being 4,800 ft long and the two intersecting ones each 4,200 ft, were constructed during 1941-42. Part of the runways were laid on Clifton Moor resulting in the airfield becoming better known as Clifton once it became established, and many official documents refer to it by that name. Eventually the runways were linked by a perimeter track and further temporary buildings and hangars were erected. The airfield now had 14 hangars made up of one 'T1', 12 Blisters and one civil.

On April 28/29 1942, the City of York was attacked and the airfield suffered severe damage. The guardroom received a direct hit and the Officers' Mess, hangars and many other buildings had blast damage. Bomb craters were in evidence all around the airfield. This was the so called 'Baedeker raid' and it is a mystery why the German bombers were allowed to bomb for 90 minutes before a lone night fighter appeared on the scene. Why, with an airfield so close, was the City of York undefended? British Intelligence knew of the attack for it had at this time the Enigma coding machine.

On November 15 1942 No 169 Squadron arrived. This Army Co-operation unit was equipped with Mustangs but remained only a few weeks before moving out on December 20 1942 to Duxford. A few days earlier No 809 Squadron, Fleet Air Arm, had arrived with Seafires and on March 21 1943, No 231 Squadron replaced the long-reigning No 4. The following month No 809 moved out.

No 613 Squadron arrived on May 28 with Mustang Mk Is but this unit remained only a few weeks and moved out the following month. On June 15 1943 the airfield was transferred to Fighter Command and 231 Squadron moved out the following month.

Clifton then housed a number of Air Observation Post squadrons, all equipped with Auster aircraft. The first was 657 Squadron from June 26 until August when it was relieved by 658 Squadron. This unit was joined on August 17 by No 659. Both units then moved out to Burn on December 31 1943 only to return here at the end of April 1944. Then, in June 1944, both units were transferred to France.

Meanwhile, during the early part of 1944, the Canadians with their North American Mustangs paid the station a brief visit. From February 9 to 25 Clifton housed 430 Squadron, RCAF, while on Exercise 'Eagle'.

The status of the station as at June 6 1944 was No 4 Aircraft Delivery Flight with Oxfords and Dominies, under No 12 Group. The depot was now in full swing and was largely self-supporting. It was able to carry out complete overhauls, usually taking about eight weeks per bomber as against 25 weeks if carried out at the operational stations. The station strength as at December 1 1944 was 503 personnel of whom 119 were WAAFs.

After the end of hostilities 48 MU extended its activities to include the scrapping of aircraft and hundreds of Halifaxes were brought and stored at the airfield until their fate was decided upon. Sadly, they were doomed—their reward was the scrap-heap, no-one bothered to preserve any of them. Over half of the Halifaxes that survived the war eventually went to York for final disposal. As soon as disposal programmes had been completed No 48 MU disbanded and the RAF vacated the station.

Post-war the airfield was again used by a flying club and Yorkshire Aviation Services County Club took up residence with a few light aircraft. They continued to use the airfield until the early 1950s when the site was sold to York Corporation for housing purposes. Today, houses now occupy some of the sites where during the war years the battle scars were once removed from our front-line bombers.

Allerton Park Castle, Yorkshire

105/SE416581. E of Knaresborough

Situated on the east side of the A1 road near the A59 junction, the rambling old 75-room Victorian castle at Allerton Park was requisitioned from Lord Mowbray by the Air Ministry and transformed into offices for administration and operation for the Canadian bomber group. Their new permanent quarters became known as 'Castle Dismal'.

On December 6 1942, the headquarters unit moved here from its temporary home at Linton-on-Ouse and No 6 (RCAF) Bomber Group officially assumed operational status at 00.01 hours on January 1 1943. From then on the Canadian squadrons ceased to take orders from 4 Group HQ and were transferred to 6 Group HQ which reported directly to Bomber Command Headquarters.

What should be made clear is that the full financial responsibility for the maintenance and administration of No 6 Group, with the single exception of the pay and allowances of attached RAF and other non-RCAF personnel, was voluntarily assumed by Canada and defrayed from Canadian taxes and domestic loans.

In No 6 Group, which was theoretically entirely Canadian, there was actually a small percentage non-Canadian. These were aircrew who were caught up during crewing difficulties and flight-engineers who were always RAF for the RCAF did not train any Canadians in this trade.

At the time it assumed operational status, No 6 Group consisted of six RCAF bomber squadrons located at four stations: Croft (No 427), Dalton (No 428), Dishforth (Nos 425 and 426) and Middleton St George (Nos 419 and 420). Leeming with No 408 joined the group on January 2 and Topcliffe with No 424 on the 3rd. Skipton-on-Swale was under

Above *Allerton Park Castle.* **Below** *Lancaster KB772 'R'-Ropey of 419 Squadron seen here at Middleton St George.* **Bottom** *Nose art that was painted on the interior hardboard on the inside of a Nissen hut and after the war was covered with emulsion paint. Over the years the damp has peeled away the emulsion to reveal the paintings that were done by the Canadian crews at East Moor. These were found in the main stores and Institute building in January 1981. They should be preserved in Canada.*

KB999 M—Malton Mike. The 300th built Lancaster (last production line aircraft from Victory Aircraft Corporation) which saw service at Middleton St George and returned to Canada in June 1945 only to crash on October 22 the same year.

construction as the group's seventh station.

At the war's end the RCAF had 11 bomber stations in England, of which seven were operational bases controlled by No 6 Group and four were training units. They were sited in—or just beyond—the Vale of York. Being the most northerly Group in Bomber Command, the Canadians always had that little bit further to fly with the exception of sorties to Norway and, when coming home on a cupful of petrol, those few extra miles were the most gruelling. Moreover, the topographical features of the Vale of York meant the airfields had to be constructed close to each other and this caused serious circuit overlap. Added to this problem was the prevailing mists and smog from the industrial areas, which increased the hazards of take-off and landing.

The group headquarters was responsible for ensuring that its squadrons complied with Bomber Command's instructions as to the number of aircraft to be despatched, their bomb loads, departure times, route, bombing height, etc. The stations provided the squadrons with housing and messing facilities and aerodrome security. The squadrons themselves were independent units and were responsible for their own administration and aircraft maintenance.

On March 25 1943, the Group began to reorganise under Bomber Command's newly-devised Base system. This consisted of a parent station (all of which were 'permanent' stations built for the RAF before the Second World War) and either one or two sub-stations, which were all of wartime construction.

On September 16 1943 Bomber Command issued a directive stating that bases were to be known by number and not the geographical name. The number was to be a two-figure combination, the first figure identifying the parent group and the second the base itself. The Training (or Conversion) Base was to be number one in each group. Thus, Topcliffe Training Base became No 61 (Training) Base and Linton-on-Ouse Operational Base became No 62 (Operational) Base. On May 1 1944 the Canadian Group had added enough new stations and squadrons to complete its full complement for wartime organisation and Nos 63 and 64 (Operational) Bases were formed.

The largest was No 62 (Beaver) Base with HQ at Linton-on-Ouse, home of Nos 408 (Goose) and 426 (Thunderbird) Squadrons. The two sub-stations were East Moor, home of Nos 415 (Swordfish) and 432 (Leaside) Squadrons, and Tholthorpe with Nos 420 (Snowy Owl) and 425 (Alouette) Squadrons.

In the centre of the region was No 63 Base with HQ at Leeming, home of Nos 427 (Lion) and 429 (Bison) Squadrons. The Sub-station was Skipton-on-Swale, home of Nos 424 (Tiger) and 433 (Porcupine) Squadrons. The most northerly stations were No 64 Base with HQ at Middleton St George, home of Nos 419 (Moose) and 428 (Ghost) Squadrons, and its Sub-station, Croft, which housed Nos 431 (Iroquois) and 434 (Bluenose) Squadrons.

Until the autumn of 1944 No 6 Group remained in control of No 61 (Training) Base comprising Topcliffe (HQ) with Sub-stations Dalton, Dishforth and Wombleton. The latter was situated in the North Riding of Yorkshire and was the most isolated of the Canadian bomber stations. For administrative reasons these were transferred to No 7 (Training) Group and renumbered No 76 (RCAF) Training Base on November 9 1944. It retained its Canadian personnel and close association with No 6 (RCAF) Group to the end of the war.

No 6 Group flew its first mission on the night of January 3/4 1943, when 427 Squadron sent six Wellingtons to lay mines off the Frisian Isles. The first bombing mission was on January 13/14 1943 when 14 Wellingtons were despatched to bomb Lorient, France, 11 bombing the primary target, two returning early and one failing to return. From then on the Canadians played a vital part in the heavy bombardment programme and minelaying. The development of new mines was pioneered by the 64 Base squadrons.

The Group's heaviest attack of the war was against Dortmund on the night of October 6/7 1944 when 293 Lancasters and Halifaxes were despatched, 273 bombed the primary target, three bombed the alternative, two failed to return and 15 dropped no bombs for various reasons.

Life was very hectic and, as the squadrons converted from Wellingtons through Halifax IIs and Vs and Lancaster IIs to Halifax IIIs and VIIs and Lancaster Is, IIIs and Xs, many transfers occurred from station to station. Only one squadron, No 419, remained at the one station, Middleton St George, from the formation of the Group until the end of the war. It was this squadron which received the first Canadian-built Lancaster X, *KB700*, the famous *Ruhr Express*. It was probably the most photographed aircraft ever flown by the Canadians and after three operational sorties with 405 Squadron in No 8 (PFF) Group as *LQ-Q* it flew with No 419 for a

Below *The air and ground crews assembled at their bomber,* Ruhr Express. *No 405 Squadron was the first unit to receive a Canadian-built Lancaster B Mk X, KB700. Christened in Canada* Ruhr Express, *it served with 405 Squadron from October 30 to December 20 1943 and flew two sorties before being transferred to No 419 Squadron at Middleton St George when it was then coded VR-Z. It overshot and crashed at Middleton St George on January 2 1945. (See page 150.)* **Bottom** The Queen of Spades—*Lancaster II DS708:OW-Q of No 426 Squadron at Linton-on-Ouse on November 8 1943, being serviced by LAC A.H. Nickerson (on the ladder) and D.G. Lait (on the engine nacelle). This aircraft survived the war and ended its days dumped on Foulness Island, Essex.*

Above *Flight Sergeant E.J. Wilkie (left) and Pilot Officer J.M. Hollingsworth pose in front of a Lancaster II at Linton-on-Ouse on February 21 1944, with Victory loan posters and slogans painted on 8,000 lb bomb (composed of two 4,000 lb sections and tail unit). On the bomber the four cable cutters on the starboard wing inboard section are clearly visible.* **Below** *No 6 Group RCAF. The ground crews who keep them flying pose for a brief moment in front of The Queen.* **Bottom** *Work at a No 6 Group MU.*

further 46 sorties before being destroyed in a crash at Middleton St George on returning from its 49th op on the night of January 2/3 1945.

The Group's last mission of the war was on April 25 1945, when 102 Lancasters and 92 Halifaxes, plus 160 aircraft from 4 Group, bombed gun positions on the Island of Wangerooge, one Lancaster and two Halifaxes failing to return.

After VE-Day, 6 Group took part in ferrying ex-PoWs back to Britain; in all, 4,329 men were transported during a period of three days.

With the war in the Pacific still going strong, eight squadrons—Nos 405, 408, 419, 420, 425, 428, 431 and 434—were earmarked as part of Tiger Force and returned to Canada. Main Headquarters was transferred to RCAF's Eastern Air Command at Halifax, Nova Scotia, on July 14 1945. Meanwhile, four other squadrons—Nos 424, 427, 429 and 433—remained in Bomber Command to back up the Occupation Armies. No 426 was transferred to Transport Command and made trooping flights to India.

At the end of August 1945 the Canadian Bomber Group's career came to a close, No 6 Group Rear Headquarters disbanded on September 1 1945 and the RCAF moved out of 'Castle Dismal' for the last time.

In all, 16 Canadian bomber squadrons served overseas in World War 2. The squadrons of No 6 Group flew 40,822 sorties, dropped 126,122 tons of bombs (including mines) and destroying 116 enemy aircraft and 24 probables. Operational flying hours totalled 271,981 and it had lost 814 aircraft with 3,500-plus aircrew killed or presumed dead. By VE-Day the Group's members had received 2,230 awards for gallantry including the late Pilot Officer Andrew Mynarski's Victoria Cross.

Boys became men overnight and there were many unrewarded incidents which happened in the heat of the moment. Many unbelievable—but true. One such incident occured when a Halifax of 434 Squadron had been attacked and the pilot had ordered the crew to bale out. Sergeant J.L.N. Warren, the rear-gunner, had not heard the order for his intercom had been shot away. Thinking the Halifax was on the way home he remained at his post but became uneasy and climbed back into the fuselage only to find all the crew had gone. The altimeter read only 950 ft and he hurried back to get his parachute. Before he had a chance to clip it on, the Halifax struck the ground and burst into flames. Despite injuries Sergeant Warren managed to get out of the burning bomber. He was then taken prisoner but

---

No 6 Group (RCAF) Bomber Command Order of Battle as at 18.00 hours on April 19 1945

Squadrons	Location	Aircraft	Strength
415	East Moor	Halifax III	16
		Halifax VII	5
		Lancaster III	1
420	Tholthorpe	Halifax III	19
		Lancaster X	2
		Lancaster I	1
425	Tholthorpe	Halifax III	19
408	Linton-on-Ouse	Halifax VII	20
426	Linton-on-Ouse	Halifax VII	20
432	East Moor	Halifax VII	22
424	Skipton-on-Swale	Lancaster I, III	23
427	Leeming	Lancaster I, III	21
		Halifax III	1
429	Leeming	Lancaster I, III	23
		Halifax III	3
433	Skipton-on-Swale	Lancaster I, III	21
		Halifax III	1
419	Middleton St George	Lancaster X	27
428	Middleton St George	Lancaster X	25
431	Croft	Lancaster X	25
434	Croft	Lancaster X	22

escaped and reached Holland where he made contact with the Underground movement. After six months' freedom he was recaptured and ill-treated by the Gestapo. He was put on a train for Germany but escaped on route. He was sheltered by the Dutch and finally liberated in April 1945. For Sergeant Warren it began with a miraculous escape from death and ended with the award of the British Empire Medal.

The Canadians earned a permanent place among the formations of Bomber Command and an RAF order has reserved the designation '6 Group' for Canada, should there ever be a need for another bomber force.

The commanders of 6 Group were Air Vice-Marshal G.E. Brookes, OBE, from October 25 1942 to February 28 1944; Air Vice-Marshal C.M. 'Black Mike' McEwen, CB, MC, DFC, from February 29 1944 to July 13 1945; and Air Commodore J.L. Hurley from July 14 1945 to September 1 1945.

Above The Hairy Chop—*434 Lancasters return to their birth place at Tholthorpe while on route to Canada—June 1945.* **Below left** *Sergeant Pilot J. Gilles Lamontagne, who today is Minister of National Defense, Canada (see story on page 60).*

Heslington Hall, Yorkshire

105/SE623503. SE of the City of York

Situated on the south-east side of York between the A1079 and A19 roads, Heslington Hall was taken over by Bomber Command and in April 1940 No 4 (Bomber) Group Headquarters moved in from Linton-on-Ouse. Most of the Group's airfields were in south Yorkshire and FIDO-equipped emergency airfield at Carnaby was attached to this Group and under its supervision. The Group's squadrons flew Whitleys and Wellingtons which were replaced by various types of Halifax, and it became the only all-Halifax Group in Bomber Command.

No 4 (Bomber) Group was formed on April 1 1937 with headquarters at Mildenhall, Suffolk, and its first Air Officer Commanding was Air Commodore A.T. Harris (later to become AOC No 5 Group and then, from 1942-1945, AOC-in-C Bomber Command.) The Group moved into Yorkshire when headquarters were relocated at Linton-on-Ouse on June 29 1937 and on the same date took over from No 3 (Bomber) Group the following stations and squadrons: Dishforth, Nos 10 and 78; Driffield, Nos 75 and 215; Finningley, Nos 7 and 76; Leconfield, Nos 96 and 166; and Linton-on-Ouse, Nos 51 and 58 squadrons. Actually 51 and 58 were then located at Boscombe Down.

At the outbreak of war the Group had

Above *Heslington Hall.* **Below** *Planning an operation at Heslington Hall. Ops room scene at No 4 Group HQ. Centre: Air Vice Marshal C.R. Carr, the AOC. On his left, Air Commodore W.A.D. Brooke and a Naval liaison officer who superintends mining operations.*

eight squadrons whose main equipment was Whitleys. The Group's first operation was on the night of September 3/4 (the first night of the war) when ten Whitley Mk IIIs of Nos 51 and 58 Squadrons dropped leaflets over Germany. After some early changes the Order of Battle for No 4 Group as at September 26 1939 became Nos 10, 51, 58, 77 and 102 Squadrons as operational and No 78 a Reserve Squadron.

As further changes took place, 4 Group lost all its pre-war stations except Driffield and Leconfield, the latter being, however, borrowed by Flying Training Command between February and December 1942. During the early part of 1943, Leeming, Linton-on-Ouse, Middleton St George and Topcliffe with their satellite airfields were handed over to No 6 (RCAF) Bomber Group. The Group then lost No 41 Base Marston Moor and its three base-stations, Rufforth, Acaster Malbis and Riccall when they were taken over by No 7

(Training) Group of Bomber Command in November 1944. On the credit side it opened up Snaith, Burn, Breighton, Holme-on-Spalding Moor, Melbourne, Lissett and Full Sutton.

The Royal Australian Air Force had five heavy-bomber squadrons, of which Nos 462 and 466 served in No 4 Group. The Group also had the only two French heavy bomber squadrons to join Bomber Command—Nos 346 and 347 which operated out of Elvington.

In March 1941 the battlecruisers *Scharnhorst* and *Gneisenau* arrived in Brest after a successful hunt in the Atlantic where they had sunk 22 ships. It was still early days for Bomber Command and the ships' arrival weakened its strategic force by the fact that many precious bombers were deployed against the two battlecruisers when they could have been used to attack Germany. On July 24 1941, No 4 Group dropped 2,000-lb bombs on the *Scharnhorst* and *Gneisenau* but, since

Above *The air and ground crew of a Holme-on-Spalding Moor-based Halifax of No 4 Group pose for a photograph in front of their aircraft. The aircrew are ready for a raid and the one fourth from left, standing, reading the map, is Stanley Mortensen, the famous footballer. He was later badly injured when his bomber crashed, but he fought his way back and played for England and Blackpool in the late 1940s.* **Below** *Dishforth on September 3 1940. At 21.10 hours Whitley V P5011: MH-K of 51 Squadron overshot on take-off and ran over the A1 road before coming to rest between the trees. The aircraft was a write-off. Note the armed guard.* **Bottom** *Halifax B II W1048:TL-S of No 35 Squadron during recovery from the depths of Lake Hoklingen, Norway, in 1973. It was one of 11 Halifaxes which attacked the* Tirpitz *on April 27 1942. W1048 remained submerged on the lake bed for 31 years until recovered by an RAF sub-aqua team from Strike Command.*

they lay in shallow water they could not be sunk and it was very difficult in air photographs to detect any damage. 4 Group helped to keep the two battlecruisers locked in Brest until February 12 1942, when they were patched up to make them seaworthy and rushed through the Channel back to Kiel.

For operation 'Millennium', the first Thousand-Bomber raid on May 30/31 1942, No 4 Group detailed 154 aircraft which was an incredible effort at that period of the war. For the second such raid on June 1/2 against Essen No 4 Group detailed 142 aircraft out of the 956 despatched. The raid was a failure and it was not until the following spring that the offensive got fully into its stride. 4 Group made a substantial contribution in all phases of the air war and can take pride in the fact that, in 1944, 73 enemy fighters fell to its Halifax gunners. During 1939 the Group flew 246 operational sorties. To give some idea of the rapid growth, in August 1943, on bombing and mining duties, No 466 (RAAF) Squadron alone flew 168 sorties, a record for any two flight squadrons in No 4 Group. In 1943, 4 Group flew 11,607 operational sorties with a loss of 485 aircraft.

In addition to the bombing campaign, the Group ferried 432,840 gallons of petrol to Brussels which was urgently needed by the British Second Army during the slaughter of Arnhem. After its brief transport role, there was a return to strategic bombing and 4 Group reached its peak in 1944 with 25,464 operational sorties for which it lost 402 aircraft. During the war years it flew 61,577 operational sorties and lost a total of 1,441 aircraft.

On May 7 1945, No 4 Group was transferred to Transport Command and, in April 1947, Group HQ moved to Abingdon where it remained until it disbanded in February 1948. Today, the wartime HQ forms part of York University.

The commanders of No 4 Group (Bomber Command) were: Air Commodore A.T. Harris from June 12 1937 to May 24 1938; Air Commodore C.H.B. Blount from May 25 1938 to July 2 1939; Air Vice-Marshal A. Coningham from July 3 1939 to July 25 1941; Air Vice-Marshal C.R. Carr from July 26 1941 to February 11 1945; Air Vice-Marshal J.R. Whitley from February 12 1945.

Below left One who fought with No 4 Group: Wing Commander Harry Drummond AFC, DFM, photographed August 1945. After a tour of ops on Whitleys and Halifaxes at Middleton St George, he was instructor on 1502 BAT Flight at Driffield then went to Marston Moor as Pilot Officer Instructor on Halifaxes, then went to 102 Conversion Unit, becoming Flight Lieutenant Commanding 158 Conversion Flight then Wing Commander 1658 HCU at Riccall and finally Wing Commander OC 1652 HCU and Deputy Station Commander at Marston Moor. *Below right* An interesting photograph taken April 1981 in the office in the MT shed at Snaith which shows the vehicle types used there during the war. This blackboard had been covered up until recently and still has the chalk marks as shown. From October 1942 to April 1945 Snaith was the home of 51 Squadron.

No 4 Group Bomber Command Order of Battle as at 18.00 hours on April 19 1945

Squadrons	Location	Aircraft	Strength
10	Melbourne	Halifax III	30
51	Leconfield	Halifax III	32
76	Holme-on-Spalding Moor	Halifax VI	29
		Halifax III	13
78	Breighton	Halifax III	34
		Halifax VI	11
158	Lissett	Halifax III	31
		Halifax VI	10
346 (FAF)	Elvington	Halifax VI	19
		Halifax III	12
347 (FAF)	Elvington	Halifax III	15
		Halifax VI	18
466 (RAAF)	Driffield	Halifax III	23
640	Leconfield	Halifax VI	19
		Halifax III	6
77	Full Sutton	Halifax VI	24
		Halifax III	1
102	Pocklington	Halifax VI	21
		Halifax III	1

Fylingdales, Yorkshire

101/TA865975. SW of Whitby

Fylingdales must have a mention for it is one of three tracking stations in the Ballistic Missile Early Warning System (BMEWS). The others are at Thule in Greenland and Clear in Alaska.

Situated on the windswept North Yorkshire Moors, RAF Fylingdales opened under Fighter Command in 1963 and its three giant 'golfball' 140 ft-diameter, duck-egg blue radar domes (radomes) became a distinctive landmark. With the formation of Strike Command and the consequent absorption of Fighter Command, the unit has been under the Administrative control of No 11 Group since 1968, although it is part of the US early warning organisation.

The primary task of RAF Fylingdales is to give warning within less than a handful of minutes of possible nuclear attack from the east. The three huge radar scanners are capable of detecting Soviet inter-continental missiles immediately they have been launched and the system is so sophisticated it can accurately identify the take-off and target areas. So sensitive and range-effective is the system that it can detect an object as small as a foot-square metal biscuit tin floating hundreds of miles over Moscow's Red Square.

Naturally, Fylingdales has a direct communications link with the North American Air Defense Centre at Colorado Springs where the alarm would be flashed immediately. Simultaneously, of course, the information would be flashed to MoD, No 11 Group and Strike Command.

The complex which houses the tracking equipment and its space-age computer system is the podium on which the three giant radomes sit. These are the operational buildings and are linked by and approached through a tunnel built above ground. The heart is the Tactical Operations Room which is on a higher level. It is here the RAF keeps a lonely vigil, 24 hours a day, every day of the year. Because of the great strain and the need for minds to be alert the watch is maintained by rotation of five operation shifts. Each shift is made up with a Squadron Leader as senior duty officer, one Flight Lieutenant, one Flight Sergeant and six Sergeants. There are many safeguards and any plot that appears on the radar screens is subject to a thorough check by men and not left to machines.

It is strange that all operation and maintenance engineering is carried out by Radio Corporation of America, the civilian contractors who also control transport.

To help break the monotony, Fylingdales has a secondary role of space surveillance, and this keeps everyone

A familiar Yorkshire landmark: the three giant radomes at Fylingdales.

active. This in no way prejudices its primary role. It has a military function for military experts readily accept the possibility of using nuclear weapons from space with a nuclear warhead in a satellite. For example, one could be placed in orbit and left there until required. Even more lethal weapons are also under development, as revealed in David Baker's frightening book *The Shape of Wars To Come*, also published by Patrick Stephens.

Satellites can be classed as either payloads or debris. The payload is the operational hardware placed in orbit to perform a specific function such as photographic reconnaissance, whereas debris is any other piece of hardware such as spent rocket bodies. At the beginning of October 1980 a total of 4,466 satellites were in orbit, of which only 1,068 were payloads. The life of a satellite varies from about 14 days for satellites orbiting the earth at a height of 200 km to an estimated million years for satellites at a height of 36,000 km.

With so much space traffic and its continual build-up it became necessary to devise a system to track and detect any which might constitute a threat. The Space Detection and Tracking System— SPADATS—was set up to achieve this task. The nerve centre of SPADATS is the NORAD Space Computational Centre (SCC) which is located in the Cheyenne Mountain Complex near Colorado Springs. RAF Fylingdales is just one sensor of SPADATS and on average the station tracks 1,200 satellite passes each week. The role of orbital espionage continues and this secondary role is very important, for a decaying satellite looks similar to a re-entering warhead. Whenever a satellite is predicted coming down over Soviet territory, the Centre tells the National Military Command Centre in Washington which has direct links with Moscow. Fylingdales has brought a new meaning to the old RAF saying 'If it moves, salute it', in 'If it moves, track it.' If the Soviets are setting up a permanent patrol in orbit around the Earth then the eyes of RAF Fylingdales are ever with them and new computers are planned to take the BMEWS system at least into the late 1980s.

Index of units referred to in the text

Phantom at Holme-on-Spalding Moor.